To my wife Toni who inspires me and makes me laugh

Contents

Foreword

Over the past decade, public health leadership institutes designed to enhance competency and build networks of leaders committed to continued learning and growth have proliferated across the nation. Along the way a journal *Leadership in Public Health* (another major contribution by Louis Rowitz) and a book of case studies by public health leaders have also appeared. A Public Health Leadership Society was born, from alumni of the national Public Health Leadership Institute, and a National Public Health Leadership Development Network was created to facilitate exchange between those leading leadership development programs in public health; both groups meet annually and sponsor activities through the year. To add to the mix, a Management Academy for Public Health was initiated in 1999 to provide a complementary focus to the leadership development effort. Finally, at CDC, we have recently inaugurated a CDC Leadership and Management Institute, modeled after these experiences.

Why has all of this activity occurred? There are no simple answers, but I wish to share a few reflections, based upon the experiences that many participants and supporters of this movement have shared with me. First, as pointed out very clearly in Chapters 1 and 5 of this book—and elsewhere—public health is at a crossroads, seeking to redefine its mission and role in society, to restore vitality to some of its institutions and to reenergize its professional workforce. Leadership is vital to this process of defining and revitalization. Second, current public health leaders feel the need to develop a new set of core skills in communications (Chapter 9), planning and decision-making (Chapters 10, 11), and team building (Chapter 3). Finally, public health leaders are committed to their mission and to each other. They are typically wonderful people to be admired, and when they get together, their collective energy and creativity make things happen.

In this very useful book, Dr. Rowitz has, for the first time, pulled together in one place the essential content needed to provide a systematic learning experience in public health leadership. This labor of love is based not only on his thorough review of the relevant leadership literature but, more importantly, on his own personal experiences directing an outstanding regional Public Health Leadership Institute (the first state/regional public health leadership institute in the nation) and on systematic interviews with public health leaders in the United States and abroad. Out of all of this emerges a work of substance and practical value. I imagine this book will be one of those that disappears regularly from the book shelf because of its usefulness and readability. I commend it to your reading.

Edward L. Baker, MD, PhD
Assistant Surgeon General
Director
Public Health Practice Program Office
Centers for Disease Control and Prevention

An Author's Vision

During my career as a governmental mental health agency professional, as a researcher in a state-based research institute oriented to improving the quality of life of people with disabilities, as an Associate Dean in a School of Public Health, as a Professor of Public Health, and as the Director of the Mid-America Regional Public Health Leadership Institute for eight years, I have found that each set of experiences has added to my knowledge of leadership in public health. Two important facts have come to the forefront of my professional beliefs. First, public health affects us all. It is not a field that can go away in the future. There will always be a need for professionals to monitor the health of the public and create programs to enhance our health. Second, public health leaders are needed to make the whole public health process work.

It is possible to train the public health leaders who will strengthen the infrastructure of public health in our society. Leadership knowledge and tools can be taught. However, public health professionals need to put the knowledge and tools into action. It is through action that skills become developed. In addition, leadership needs to occur within the context of public health and the paradigms that guide the public health field. Public health leaders need to synthesize the comprehensive approaches to leadership by the business community with the special needs of the public health field. The outcome will be training and educational approaches unique to public health. Leaders exist at all levels of the public health system. Leadership is more than a place on the top of the organization chart. It is a strong belief that public health leaders will influence the public health landscape. Public health leaders gain tools and skills from strong public health mentoring. Our experienced colleagues offer much knowledge and practice experiences. Mentoring puts leadership development into the real world and allows for the continuity of leadership over time.

Public health leaders not only function within the traditional public health organization, they also function across organizations. Transorganizational skills are critical. In addition, public health leaders practice their leadership within community settings. It is often to public health leaders that the validation of our community values and our beliefs in social justice occurs. Leadership development is also a way to link academic public health with the practice of public health since information integrates research knowledge with the realities of public health practice.

During the 1990s, there was increasing evidence that leadership needs to come to public health. Through the support of the Public Health Practice Program Office at the Centers for Disease Control and Prevention, a national public health leadership institute and a number of state-based or regional leadership institutes have been developed. Public health professionals in 40 states have access to a state or regional leadership institute. Almost 4,000 public health professionals have been in a leadership development program.

Public health professionals at the top of their organization are eligible for training in the national institute. Public health leaders have taught us about practice and about the multilayered realities of leadership. Public health leadership programs needs to be available to professionals in all 50 states and territories. The first decade of the 21st century will require the increasing need for leadership to guide the public health agenda in an ever-changing health care system.

My vision is to orient public health leaders to a better understanding of who they are, and how to use their public health leadership tools and skills. Leaders are committed to lifelong learning. If public health leaders will take the leadership risk, they will greatly strengthen the public health system. Common paradigms of action will be blended with a flexibility required when change is a constant factor. Not only must the leader know what leadership is all about, but the leader must learn techniques that can be transferred into reality. It is important to look to the future and always be responsive to the world around us. This book was written because I believe in the public health profession and I also believe in our ability to lead. Public health has always been oriented to solving the health problems of the present with a view to potential problems of the future.

In Part I, information is presented related to the knowledge associated with the theories and principles of leadership, leadership styles and practices, the public health system, and the five levels of public health leadership. The core functions model is presented and applied to public health leadership in Part II. Part III explores the leadership tools needed for the 21st century leader. Public health leaders continually develop their skills and put their skills to work on improving the health of the public. Part IV presents information on the personal evaluation of leadership and secondly, the evaluation of leadership programs. Part V looks to the future and presents some emerging public health trends.

Throughout the book, case study examples written by public health leaders are presented. Public health leadership exercises can be found throughout the book. There are also discussion questions in each of the chapters of the book.

This is your chance to have a key role in defining the future of public health. Carpe Diem! Seize the day!

Acknowledgments

I would first like to thank the 400 Fellows who have graduated from the Mid-America Regional Public Health Leadership Institute. Each one of these leaders has taught me much about the challenges facing public health. I have also learned much from my colleagues who over the years have struggled with the complex issues involved in leadership development. I especially want to thank Ann Anderson, Judy Munson, Beth Quill, Mike Reid, Barney Turnock, Carol Woltring, and Kate Wright for our many discussions about leadership. I also wish to thank all the case study writers for their willingness to write the cases that help strengthen the public health leadership model presented in this book.

My colleagues and friends at CDC who believed in public health leadership development must be thanked. Ed Baker, Tom Balderson, Donna Carmichael, Steve Frederick, and Bud Nicola have battled to maintain a national focus on public health leadership development. During my study of public health leaders in 1996, CDC supported my sabbatical.

I want to personally thank John Lumpkin, Gary Robinson, and Gina Swehla of the Illinois Department of Public Health for supporting leadership development. Steve Saunders and Ralph Schubert of the Illinois Department of Human Services encouraged me to stretch my approach to public health leadership by applying the leadership development model in this book to the maternal and child health professional workforce. My colleagues in Indiana (Kathy Weaver and Elise Papke) and Wisconsin (Margaret Schmelzer and Larry Gilbertson) helped me move a leadership program in Illinois to a partnership with several other states.

Part I

Leadership Theories and Principles

Chapter 1

The Basics of Leadership

In a society capable of renewal, [leaders] not only welcome the future and the changes it brings but believe they can have a hand in shaping that future.

J.W. Gardner, *Self-Renewal*

The approach of the 21st century has unsurprisingly increased the amount of attention paid to the concept of change. Yet change has always been and always will be a fact of life. For instance, the lack of substantive federal health care reform during the 1990s is no indication that the health care system has remained static during the past decade, nor that change will be unnecessary in the future. To cite two examples where change is demanded, large segments of the U.S. population remain under- or uninsured and certain minority groups have less access to health care than the general populace.

Public health agencies and professionals are experiencing an identity crisis because of the recent reconfiguring of their roles and responsibilities. Adding to the crisis is the public's lack of awareness of the nature of public health and the accomplishments of the public health system. Parents and friends still ask public health professionals what they do for a living. Of course, confusion about professional identity exists elsewhere in health care. Physicians who work for managed care organizations resist the restrictions placed on their ability to provide the tests and services they feel their patients require, not to mention the limitations on their salaries. The traditional caregiving roles of nurses are also changing as hospital bed utilization declines and many hospitals close their doors.

In order to manage the changes that are occurring, health care and public health professionals need to become involved at the political and policy development level. They need to create their own vision of what health care should be and to act in concert to realize that vision; and for these tasks to be accomplished, some of these professionals must acquire the full range of leadership skills. In 1988, *The Future of Public Health* argued that the creation of effective leaders must not be left to chance.[1] In line with this view, the report also stated a concern that schools of public health were not teaching the necessary leadership courses.

The training of future leaders is critical. Public health leaders will need training not only in the specialties of public health but also in the latest management

3

techniques and tools. To support public health activities at the local, state, and federal level, they will require good communication, decision-making, and policy development skills, among others. Leaders must learn how their organizations function, how to work across organizations, and how to integrate their organizations' activities into the communities they serve.

There is a major difference between managing change and leading change.[2] To lead change, leaders must be visionary—must be able to develop a vision to partially define the future. They must then get others to share their vision and help realize it. Of course, managing change is also important, for it keeps the system running smoothly.

Selling a vision to others can be especially difficult for minorities, people with disabilities, and women, for the vision they are trying to sell might well involve cultural, ethnic, community, and gender issues, and they will probably have to peddle it to people who have a different background than they do.[3] Developing a vision that can be shared is critical in a society where diversity is the rule rather than the exception. Any vision will remain just a vision if it falls outside the belief system of the managers.

In 1996, the Institute of Medicine released a report on the first year of its committee on public health. The report, entitled *Healthy Communities: New Partnerships for the Future of Public Health,*[4] reviewed the 1988 *Future of Public Health* report and concluded that progress had occurred in leadership development in the 1990s. Among other signs of progress was the creation of a national public health leadership program and a number of state and regional leadership development programs. The training of public health leaders needs to continue. Stress must be placed on the multidimensional aspects of leadership as well as the multidisciplinary approaches of the public health field as a whole. Building and strengthening the infrastructure of public health requires strong and effective leaders.

Note, however, that until now leadership development has been based on an industrial or agency-based paradigm of leadership.[5] Leaders of the 21st century must possess different skills. They will also need to recognize that leading is a process in which they must pursue their vision through influencing others and the places they work. Leaders will find that advancing the skills of their work force will increase the chance that their vision will become a reality. In addition, they will have to break down the barriers between organization and community to create an environment in which a shared value system and a shared vision for the future can come into being.

The remainder of the chapter comprises a short section containing a definition of leadership and a long section that discusses 16 important principles of public health leadership. As part of their effort to understand the nature of leadership, students should do Exercise 1–1, which provides an opportunity for students to express what they believe about leadership in general and public health leadership in particular.

DEFINITION OF LEADERSHIP

Leadership is creativity in action. It is the ability to see the present in terms of the future while maintaining respect for the past. Leadership is based on respect for history and the knowledge that true growth builds on existing strengths. Leading is in part a visionary endeavor, but it requires the fortitude and flexibility necessary to put vision into action and the ability to work with others and to follow when someone else is the better leader.

Public health leadership includes a commitment to the community and the values for which it stands. It also includes a commitment to social justice, but public health leaders must not let this commitment undermine their ability to pursue a well-designed public health agenda. In addition, public health leaders need to act within the governing paradigms of public health, but this does not mean that they cannot alter the paradigms. Leaders propose new paradigms when old ones lose their effectiveness. The major governing paradigm today relates to the core functions and essential services of public health. This paradigm is introduced in Chapter 5 and discussed in more detail in Chapters 6–8.

PUBLIC HEALTH LEADERSHIP PRINCIPLES

One way of filling out the definition of public health leadership in particular is to consider some of the principles that public health leaders should use to guide their actions. Below is a list of 16 such principles. In the discussion of these principles (and elsewhere in this book), mention is made of a study of 130 public health leaders in the United States, England, Scotland, and Ireland (see Case Study 2–A). The author conducted an hour-long conversation with each of these leaders to find out their view of the future role of public health agencies.

The public health leaders interviewed generally thought that they and business leaders have much in common. Good leadership is essential for the effectiveness of companies engaged in business and can increase the effectiveness of public health agencies as well. But although the leadership practices of business and public health leaders are similar, there are also important differences, which this book explores. For example, the social justice perspective that characterizes public health is more or less absent from the business world. One of the leaders interviewed argued strongly that the social justice perspective is critical for public health but that public health leaders must be careful not to let this value interfere with the work that public health needs to do. One way of putting this is that social justice is only part of the leadership value system. Gardner[6] integrates that value with the values of freedom, social and ethnic equality, the worth and dignity of each individual, and the brotherhood of all human beings.

Principle 1

The public health infrastructure must be strengthened by utilizing the core functions of public health and its essential services as a guide to the changes that should occur. The future of public health will be determined by the way in which core functions are carried out and essential services are provided. Public health leaders must evaluate the health status of the population, evaluate the capacity of the community to address its health priorities, and implement preventive measures to reduce the impact of or even avoid public health crises. Leaders must not rely on the current assurance models (service interventions) but must implement new assurance models built on integrated systems of service and program delivery. Leaders must also help to restructure the policies that govern health and public health. Leaders must be policy makers who have a view of the future grounded in the present and built on the past.

Principle 2

The goal of public health is to improve the health of each person in the community. Public health leaders believe deeply that health promotion and disease prevention are possible. In fact, a focus on prevention is intrinsic to public health. In this regard, public health contrasts with the medical care system, which places an emphasis on treatment and rehabilitation. Every citizen needs to learn about the benefits of public health and how quality of life can be greatly improved if certain rules are followed.

A public health leader who truly believes in this principle will become a teacher and mentor for the community. Education will be the prevailing program model rather than medical care. The leader will reach out to schools, churches and synagogues, businesses, households, and health care providers and promote the vision of good health for all throughout life. The leader will also be concerned with the quality of care. If someone becomes ill, access to the best possible care is a community requirement. A visionary leader sees the total health system existing in the community and helps to ensure that the system is integrated, provides the services that are necessary, and does not contain duplicate services and programs, which are a waste of valuable resources.

A public health leader can play an important role in promoting a sense of community among community members. The leader might help define the values of the community and clarify the cultural aspects of the community life. Not all geographic areas have a cohesive cultural infrastructure. In an area that lacks such an infrastructure, the public health leader can help the community to define itself. (These issues will be addressed more completely in Chapter 4.)

Principle 3

Community coalitions need to be built to address the community's public health needs. Public health is both a community responsibility and a population-based activity. This means that the mission of public health is to work with all groups in a community to improve the health of all members of the public.

All communities have assets. Unfortunately, communities, like people in general, tend to be careless with their assets.[7] Consequently, each community needs to learn how to manage its assets if it doesn't know how to do that already. In short, it needs to take responsibility for its future. It may be too dependent on those who work in human services. Promoting good health is every citizen's responsibility. Public health leaders can play a critical role in helping the community move from a value system based on dependency to one based on shared responsibility. Public health leaders and their cousins in the human services field are thus the true servant leaders.[8]

Coalition building requires knowledge and creativity. First, coalitions made up only of managers are doomed to failure.[9] Coalitions need *leaders* to guide the process. Second, coalitions require trust among their members. If there is no trust, change will not occur. Third, there must be positions of power in a coalition. Key players must not be excluded or the process will fail. Expertise is also necessary so that informed decision making will occur. Fourth, the coalition must have credibility so that it will be taken seriously by others (both inside and outside the community) who can affect the implementation of the change agenda.

Principle 4

Local and state public health leaders must work together to protect the health of all citizens regardless of gender, race, ethnicity, or socioeconomic status. Public health leaders firmly believe in the principle that all people are created equal. Several U.S. public health leaders interviewed by the author argued that the U.S. public health system must be understood within the context of the American political tradition and that it is impossible to be an effective public health leader without knowing about that tradition.

Access to service is sometimes affected by who you are. Women have found that the health care system does not always respond to their special medical needs. Public health leaders see that they have a responsibility to press for improvements in health care for women. They also have a responsibility to develop health promotion programs for women as well as men. For example, local health departments can take a leadership role in the development of breast examination programs for cancer prevention. Minorities often have difficulty in accessing health programs because of color, language, or socioeconomic status. Diabetes-screening programs are often the first programs to go when funding cuts occur, despite the critical need for these programs in our communities. Public health leaders have important tasks to perform in protecting the rights of the unserved and underserved.

We live in a culturally diverse society. Our diversity is a strength as well as a weakness. Public health leaders must deal with their personal prejudices each day and consciously move beyond them to create a public health system that respects the needs of every citizen. State public health leaders must monitor the needs of all citizens as well as create the policies of inclusion that will lead to an improvement in the public's level of health. In addition, these leaders must make state legislators partners in this enterprise. The other critical partner is the *local* public health leader, who, in conjunction with the local board of health or county board of commissioners, is the gatekeeper for the community. What the state proclaims, the local leaders must adapt for local implementation. Local public health leaders must be extremely creative in the adaptation process. They must also speak loudly for the unique needs of their local community and take the local public health agenda to places where the state leaders do not tread.

Principle 5

Rational community health planning requires collaboration between public health agency leaders, the local board of health (if such a boards exists), and other local and county boards. The relationship between the administrator of the local health department and the chair of the board of health needs to be a close one and based on a philosophy of equality. The chair and the other members of the board of health do more than approve the health department budget and select the health administrator. The board members are residents of the community. They are the protectors of the community's interests and, with the administrator, serve an important gatekeeper function. Shared leadership and a shared vision are critical here. The health department and the board of health must be partners, not adversaries, which means they must work collaboratively to achieve agreed outcomes. The exchange of information is an important part of the relationship, since relevant information is essential for the making of good public health decisions.

Principle 6

Novice public health leaders must learn leadership techniques and practices from experienced public health leaders. Mentoring is a critical part of leadership. A mentor is a person who helps another person learn about the world and how it works.[10] Mentors tend to be well-known individuals who help their protégés meet their major goals.[11]

Murray[12] discusses what she calls "facilitated mentoring," which is a process designed to develop effective mentoring relationships. It is also designed to guide the teaching of the person being mentored. If the mentoring experience is successful, there will be an impact on the mentor, the person mentored, and the agency promoting the mentoring experience.

Mentors are not threatened by the professional progress of their protégés. They personally feel good about the mentoring experience. All of the leaders interviewed by the author said that they had been mentored at various times in their public health careers. They thought that mentoring was important and that the need for mentoring does not stop with the attainment of a leadership position. Mentoring is beneficial to leaders throughout their careers. Furthermore, leaders who have been mentored have a responsibility to pass on the gift of learning that they received.

Principle 7

One issue of import is whether leaders are born or made. If leadership is innate, leaders wouldn't need to develop their skills, but if leaders are made, anyone can become a leader. The most defensible position is that leaders are both born and made—that some people are natural leaders but nonetheless need to develop their leadership abilities.[13] That is the position taken in this book.

In fact, public health leaders must continuously work to develop their leadership skills. Leaders never stop learning. They are like detectives who pick up clue after clue in order to find the solution to a mystery. Leaders seek solutions to challenges rather than to mysteries, but the attainment of new knowledge is just as important for finding these types of solutions. Not only that, but each solution leads to new challenges and the need for additional learning.

Support for programs for lifelong learning is critical. There has been a tendency in recent years not to allocate funds for learning activities, partly based on the argument that the public does not want to pay for training programs. When the funds are available, they tend to be classified as discretionary and used for purposes other than training. Yet allowing leaders to improve their skills can lead to substantial benefits.[14] Very few public health practitioners have ever received major job-related training, to the detriment of the agencies they work for.

Over the past several years, a unique experiment has been underway, funded by the Centers for Disease Control and Prevention and state health departments.

A national public health leadership institute and a number of state and regional leadership programs have been created to help state and local health department professionals, board of health members, local and state legislators, faculty members, and community leaders develop their leadership potential. The programs, which teach public health theory and practice, promote the education of public health professionals and, through them, the education of all citizens in a community. Public health leadership development, at its best, can create a partnership between public health leaders, the public health academic community, and the public health professional community in the public and private sectors. The main lesson learned from this experiment is that public health leadership development must build on the mission of public health. A second lesson is that these programs need to be experientially based and need to focus on projects that strengthen the infrastructure of public health.

Principle 8

Leaders must be committed not only to lifelong learning but to their own personal growth. Self-esteem is a key factor in personal growth and is essential to the personal competence necessary to cope with life's challenges.[15] Further, the higher a leader's self-esteem, the more able the leader is to inspire others. Research on children has shown that children with high self-esteem are more willing to take risks and to assume leadership roles than children with low self-esteem.[16] Sethi has described the seven R's of self-esteem:[17]

1. *Respect.* It is necessary to respect and trust your employees.
2. *Responsibility and Resources.* Encouraging creativity among employees and delegating responsibility for tasks are essential.
3. *Risk Taking.* Only through risk taking can innovation occur.
4. *Rewards and Recognition.* People need to be recognized for their accomplishments.
5. *Relationships.* The quality and quantity of personal relationships have an impact on self-esteem.
6. *Role-modeling.* The work practices of an organization should be consistent with its values.
7. *Renewal.* It is critical to maintain a strong belief in lifelong learning.

Self-esteem is tied to each of the seven R's. Each factor affects the self-esteem of the leaders and their associates inside the agency and in the community. Building the self-esteem of leaders and associates is a prerequisite for the building of strong organizations.[18]

Principle 9

The infrastructure of public health must be built on a foundation of health protection for all, democratic ideals and values, and respect for the social fabric of American society. The assumption underlying this principle is that physical, psychological, emotional, economic, and social health are all elements of the health of a community. By acting as role models for the community, public health leaders strengthen the infrastructure of public health in the community.

This infrastructure is not just a physical building or an official agency called the department of public health; it comprises the entire community.

Principle 10

Public health leaders should think globally but act locally. Although public health professionals practice their craft primarily at the community level, they should not ignore the rest of the world. Emerging viruses know no boundaries. Disease is carried not only on the wind but even in airplanes. Public health leaders need to be vigilant in looking for potential health problems. The Centers for Disease Control and Prevention has a national center for infectious disease that monitors emerging diseases globally, and public health professionals located throughout the world are investigating potential worldwide health problems. Some multi-region crises have been documented in recent books, such as R. Preston's *The Hot Zone*,[19] L. Garrett's *The Coming Plague*,[20] and J.B. McCormick and S. Fisher-Hoch's *Level 4: Virus Hunters of the CDC*.[21] When a crisis hits, the international public health community must work together on the problem. Public health leaders thus have several overlapping communities to which they owe allegiance, and they must understand how to coordinate their multiple allegiances.

Principle 11

Public health leaders need to be good managers. In the above mentioned interview study of public health leaders, the leaders pointed out that they, as heads of agencies, not only define their agencies' practice activities but also help to implement those activities. Managers do not have to be leaders, but tomorrow's leaders will need to possess both management and leadership skills (see Table 1–1). Reconciling these two sets of skills will not be easy, since they are based on two different ideological perspectives. Managers are oriented toward ensuring that current systems are functioning smoothly. Leaders are change agents who are concerned with moving their agencies forward. Since change is unavoidable, today's managers will become obsolete if they cannot keep up with the ever-increasing pace of change. Leaders will have to steer their organizations in new directions, and they will have to utilize cutting-edge leadership skills and managerial tools to do this.

Principle 12

Public health leaders need to walk the walk. They must not only define a vision but sell the vision and inspire others to accept it and try to realize it.[22,23] In his book on visionary leadership, Nanus[24] pointed out that there are four major types of leadership activity. First, a leader has to relate to the managers and other workers in the organization. The leader should be the guide to and motivator of action within the organization. Second, the leader has to relate to the environment or community outside the organization. A public health leader, for example, must carry the agency's vision and message into the community. Third, the leader has to influence all phases of the operation of the organization. Finally, the leader has to anticipate future events and move the organization forward in a manner that takes these events into account. If it is clear that managed care organizations

Table 1-1 A Comparison of the Characteristics and Responsibilities of Practitioners, Managers, and Leaders

Practitioners	Managers	Leaders
The practitioner implements.	The manager administers.	The leader innovates.
The practitioner follows.	The manager is a copy.	The leader is an original.
The practitioner synthesizes.	The manager maintains.	The leader develops.
The practitioner focuses on programs and services.	The manager focuses on systems and structures.	The leader focuses on people.
The practitioner relies on compliance and behavior change.	The manager relies on control.	The leader inspires trust.
The practitioner has a narrow view.	The manager has a short-range view.	The leader has a long-range view.
The practitioner asks who and where.	The manager asks how and when.	The leader asks what and why.
The practitioner's eye is on the client and the community.	The manager's eye is always on the bottom line.	The leader's eye is on the horizon.
The practitioner separates programs from services.	The manager imitates.	The leader originates.
The practitioner protects the status quo.	The manager accepts the status quo.	The leader challenges the status quo.
The practitioner is in the infantry.	The manager is the classic good soldier.	The leader is his or her own person.
The practitioner is a conflicted pessimist.	The manager is a pessimist.	The leader is an optimist.
The practitioner is a reflective thinker.	The manager is a linear thinker.	The leader is a systems thinker.
The practitioner follows the agency agenda.	The manager does things right.	The leader does the right things.

will provide medical care for all members of a community, then the public health leaders of that community need to get the public health department out of the direct service business and into population-based health promotion and disease prevention.

Principle 13

Public health leaders need to be proactive and not reactive. Up to the present, they have mostly tended to respond to public health crises as they occurred rather than focus on preventing crises. A reactive stance will probably always be part of the strategy of any state or local health department. However, reactivity tends to tarnish a health department's image. Public health agencies and professionals need to develop action plans to address the health needs of the citizens in their service area. Assessment activities will help to evaluate the health status of the community and give guidance for action. Action planning is more than planning for a crisis, which is an anticipatory activity that assumes a problem is on the horizon. Action planning is essentially preventive. Its goal is to create programs to prevent the occurrence of problems rather than create programs to deal with problems just prior to their arrival.

Principle 14

Each level of the public health system has a need for leaders.[25] In fact, a leader does not need to have an official position to be a leader, and nonpositional power is likely to become more and more important. Change will come from many different sources, and leaders will step forward to make sure the required tasks are accomplished. For example, if an environmental crisis occurs in a community, the environmental director from the health department, a community resident who is an engineer, a firefighter, a police officer, and others may form a leadership team to deal with the crisis. When the crisis has passed, the members of this ad hoc leadership team will then step back into their normal roles.

Each level of an organization also has a need for leaders.[26] And like members of a community, members of an organization often share leadership tasks by forming a team to tackle issues. These critical shared leadership experiences are often ignored in the leadership literature.

Principle 15

Public health leaders practice their craft in a community setting and must understand what a community is. A recent book argues that Americans are searching for a revitalized sense of community.[27] A community is more than a place; it consists of people living together who "participate in common practices; depend upon each other; make decisions together; identify themselves as part of something larger than the sum of their individual relationships; and commit themselves for the long term to their own, one another's and the group's well-being."[28(p.10)]

Human beings have a desire to be free and independent, but those who take independence as an absolute value risk becoming profoundly lonely by not including other people in their lives.[29] Being part of the community involves inclusivity, commitment, and consensus. It also can lead to a sense of realism, for communities, through the actions of individual members, contemplate and evaluate themselves. Finally, communities tend to be safe places, which is one reason Americans, with their increasingly well-founded fear of violence, have a renewed interest in the sense of community.

In the now classic book *Habits of the Heart,*[30] Bellah and his collaborators argue that we Americans have become committed to the lexicon of individualism and have consequently lost our way morally. We are losing our sense of community and our commitment to improve society at large. Everyone from our politicians to our educators is pushing for a return to our moral roots, by which is meant a return to community.

Public health leaders have traditionally had a strong belief in community. Their focus, after all, is on improving the health of the communities they live and work in. Public health leaders also believe that they can strengthen their communities by working with community leaders to bring about change. If they are to be effective in bringing about change, they need to study and learn how their communities function. In particular, they need to know how to empower the members of their communities and get them to take their share of the responsibility for improving their own health.

Principle 16

Public health leaders must practice what they preach. If they are promoting family values, then they must live lives that are consistent with these values. If they are promoting good health and developing programs to get people to stop smoking, they should not smoke themselves.

This principle is not always easy to abide by. Some of our most successful leaders have personal lives that are in shambles. O'Neill called this the paradox of success.[31] Leaders often become prisoners of their official position and are unable to find a workable balance between their professional commitments and their private lives. Indeed, achieving a balance between work and home is becoming more difficult, as individuals are required to work harder due to such factors as downsizing. Decisions regarding the balance between work and home must be built into the culture of the places where we are employed,[32] especially as nowadays both spouses in a marriage usually work. The costs of not achieving a proper balance are high. Conflicting pressures and stresses can have serious health consequences.

I was running a leadership program and was planning for a six-month follow-up meeting to an initial program. All trainees from the first meeting were expected to come to the second meeting. One day before the second meeting was to occur, I received a telephone call from one of the trainees. She told me that her son was ill and that she was trying to find someone to take care of him. She was worried about missing the meeting. I asked her what she thought she needed to do. She said she felt she needed to stay with her son. I told her she had made the right choice. Balancing is making the right choice.

SUMMARY

The one thing that a review of the leadership literature makes clear is that leadership is a complex series of processes affected by many factors. These factors, for public leaders in particular, include the principles described above, which apply to leadership style, leadership practices, the public health system, the core functions and essential services of public health, and leadership tools (Figure 1–1).

Leading is a multidimensional activity. Every leader uses leadership skills in his or her own way, which is to say that every leader has his or her own leadership style. Every leader engages in a unique set of practices and uses a unique set of tools. All these elements determine whether a leader is successful.

This chapter, besides offering an introduction to leadership, reviewed some of the main principles that public health leaders should be guided by. The next chapter presents various analyses of leadership styles and discusses essential leadership characteristics. Later chapters cover the three core functions of public

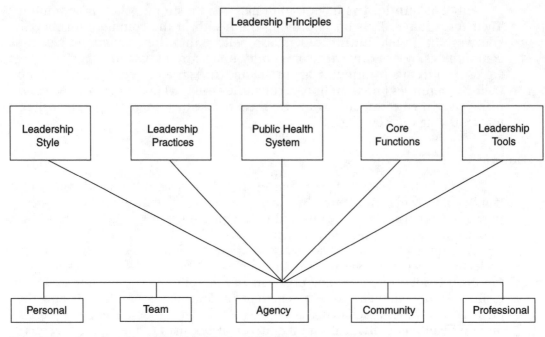

Figure 1–1 Conceptual model of public health leadership.

health, associated public health practices, and important leadership tools and skills, among other topics.

Discussion Questions

1. What is your personal definition of leadership?
2. Who is a living person whom you define as a leader and why?
3. What, in your view, are the differences between business leaders and public health leaders?
4. How does creativity play a role in leadership activities?
5. How is collaboration related to leadership?
6. What role does social justice play in public health?
7. What are the main goals of public health?
8. What does it mean to say that public health leaders should think globally but act locally?
9. Is leadership different from management?

Exercise 1–1

COURSE EXPECTATIONS

Purpose: to explore the expectations that students have at the beginning of a leadership course

Key concepts: expectations, leadership development, preconceptions

Procedure: Each student writes down initial thoughts or preconceptions about leadership and also writes down expectations for the course and for leadership training in general. The class then divides into groups of 5–10 members, and each group discusses the preconceptions and expectations. The students need to keep the lists they have created, for they will re-examine at the end of the course (in Exercise 15–1) what they thought at the start of the course.

REFERENCES

1. Institute of Medicine, *The Future of Public Health* (Washington, DC: National Academy Press, 1988).
2. J.P. Kotter, *Leading Change* (Boston: Harvard Business School Press, 1996).
3. S.E. Melendez, "An 'Outsider's View of Leadership," in *The Leader of the Future*, ed. F. Hesselbein et al. (San Francisco: Jossey-Bass, 1996).
4. Institute of Medicine, *Healthy Communities: New Partnerships for the Future of Public Health* (Washington, DC: National Academy Press, 1996).
5. S.M. Bornstein and A.F. Smith, "The Puzzles of Leadership," in *The Leader of the Future*, ed. F. Hesselbein et al. (San Francisco: Jossey-Bass, 1996).
6. J.W. Gardner, *Self-renewal* (New York: W.W. Norton, 1981).
7. J. McKnight, *The Careless Society* (New York: Basic Books, 1995).
8. R.K. Greenleaf, *The Servant as Leader* (Indianapolis, IN: Greenleaf Center for Servant Leadership, 1970).
9. Kotter, *Leading Change*.
10. F. Wickman and T. Sjodin, *Mentoring* (Chicago: Irwin Professional Publishing, 1996).
11. L. Phillips-Jones, *Mentors and Proteges* (New York: Arbor House, 1982).
12. M. Murray, *Beyond the Myths and Magic of Mentoring* (San Francisco: Jossey-Bass, 1991).
13. P. Hersey et al., *Management of Organizational Behavior*, 7th ed. (Upper Saddle River, NJ: Prentice Hall, 1996).
14. P.M. Senge et al., *The Fifth Discipline Handbook* (New York: Dell, 1994).
15. N. Brandon, "Self-esteem in the Information Age," in *The Organization of the Future*, ed. F. Hesselbein et al. (San Francisco: Jossey-Bass, 1997).
16. D. Baumrind, "An Exploratory Study of Socialization Effects on Black Children: Some Black-White Comparisons," *Child Development* 43 (1972): 261–267.
17. D. Sethi, "The Seven R's of Self-esteem," in *The Organization of the Future*, ed. F. Hesselbein et al. (San Francisco: Jossey-Bass, 1997).
18. K. Blanchard and N.V. Peale, *The Power of Ethical Management* (New York: Fawcett Columbine, 1988).
19. R. Preston, *The Hot Zone* (New York: Random House, 1994).
20. L. Garrett, *The Coming Plague* (New York: Farrar, Straus & Giroux, 1994).
21. J.B. McCormick and S. Fisher-Hoch, *Level 4: Virus Hunters of the CDC* (Atlanta: Turner Publishing Co., 1996).
22. J.M. Kouzes and B.Z. Posner, *The Leadership Challenge*, 2d ed. (San Francisco: Jossey-Bass, 1995).
23. P.M. Senge, *The Fifth Discipline: The Art and Practice of the Learning Organization* (New York: Dell, 1990).
24. B. Nanus, *Visionary Leadership* (San Francisco: Jossey-Bass, 1992).
25. S. Helgesen, "Leading from the Grass Roots," in *The Leader of the Future*, ed. F. Hesselbein et al. (San Francisco: Jossey-Bass, 1996).
26. J.W. Gardner, *On Leadership* (New York: The Free Press, 1990).
27. C.R. Shaffer and K. Anundsen, *Creating Community Anywhere* (New York: Jeremy P. Tarcher and Perigee, 1993).
28. Shaffer and Anundsen, *Creating Community Anywhere*.
29. M.S. Peck, "The Fallacy of Rugged Individualism," in *In the Company of Others*, ed. C. Whitmyer (New York: Jeremy P. Tarcher and Perigree, 1993).
30. R.N. Bellah et al., *Habits of the Heart* (Berkeley, CA: University of California Press, 1985).
31. J.R. O'Neil, *The Paradox of Success* (New York: Jeremy P. Tarcher and Putnam, 1994).
32. J. Kofomidos, *The Balancing Act* (San Francisco: Jossey-Bass, 1993).

Chapter 2

Leadership Styles and Practices

But leadership in public health involves more than individual leaders or individuals in leadership positions. Public health is intimately involved in leadership as an agent of social change by identifying health problems and risks and stimulating actions toward their elimination.

B.J. Turnock, *Public Health*

This chapter begins by examining several styles of leadership. It first describes McGregor's distinction between two main leadership styles, referred to as Theory X and Theory Y. It then discusses another way of categorizing leadership styles, based on the Leadership Grid, and explores the view that a leader needs to use different styles in different situations. The second half of the chapter is devoted to an account of the characteristics that a leader must possess in order to lead effectively.

LEADERSHIP STYLES

Theory X and Theory Y

In a classic study, McGregor discussed two leadership styles, Theory X and Theory Y, that are appropriate for different types of organizations.[1] Theory X is the more suitable for an organization in which the employees do not like their work situation and will avoid work whenever possible. In this case, the employees will have to be forced, controlled, or reprimanded in order for the organization to meet its goals and objectives. The employees are looking for control since they are not willing to guide the work process themselves. The thing they are most interested in is security.

McGregor noted that a situation in which employees are unhappy and need to be controlled will push leaders toward an autocratic style of leadership. Theory X represents a mainly negative approach to leadership. The author of this book had dinner with a local public health administrator at an American Public Health Association annual meeting several years ago. During the discussion, the question why this administrator did not send any of his staff to a leadership program was

16

raised. His answer—that he was the leader and his staff did not need leadership development—exemplifies the Theory X style of leadership.

Theory Y is appropriate for an organization in which the employees like their jobs and feel that their work is natural and restful. Further, because they accept the goals and objectives of the organization, they tend to be self-directed and even to seek higher levels of responsibility. Finally, decision making occurs at all levels of the organization. Theory Y is essentially a democratic form of leadership. A public health administrator who had completed a state public health leadership program decided that he had benefited greatly from the training. Over the following five years, he sent most of his executive staff to the program in order to develop their leadership skills. His action exemplifies the Theory Y style of leadership. Exercise 2–1 is intended to help elucidate the difference between Theory X and Theory Y.

The Managerial Grid

Blake and Mouton adapted the Managerial Grid, a tool devised by Blake and his colleagues, to form the Leadership Grid (Figure 2–1).[2] There are 81 positions on the grid and five different leadership styles. The vertical axis represents concern for people and the horizontal axis represents concern for production (task-oriented behaviors). The location of each style on the grid is determined by where the style falls with respect to the two dimensions. For example, the *country club management* approach is characterized by a high level of concern for people and a low level of concern for production and is thus placed in the upper left-hand corner of the grid. This managerial approach creates a relaxed atmosphere and makes people happy to come to work in the morning.

If a leader is not seriously concerned about the well-being of the employees or about production, the result is *impoverished management.* In this style of leadership, the leader engages in the least amount of work necessary to solve a production problem.

The third approach is *team management,* in which the level of concern for employees and production is high. Strong trusting relationships develop, and all or most employees feel a commitment to accomplish the tasks at hand.

In the *authority-obedience approach,* the primary concern of the leader is to control the production process and increase productivity. The leader's concern for the employees' well-being is minimal.

Organization man management tries to balance the needs of the employees and the needs of production.

Situational Leadership

Instead of using just one leadership style, leaders should use different styles for different situations, according to some authors.[3-6] The series of one-minute manager books, by Blanchard and others, tries to integrate the needs of organizations with the needs of both employees and customers. Blanchard and his coauthors designated their approach Situational Leadership II.[7,8] As with the Managerial Grid, leadership behavior is evaluated along two dimensions: directiveness and supportiveness (Figure 2–2). The type of leadership that is relatively nonsupportive and nondirective is termed a "delegating" style of leadership. The type that is supportive but nondirective is termed a "supporting" style of leadership. Leadership

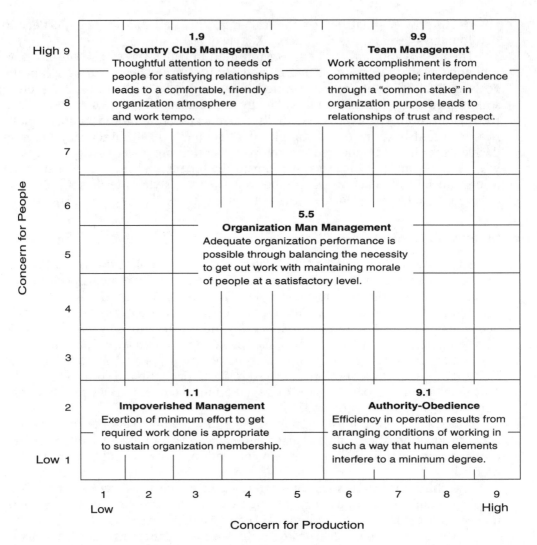

Figure 2–1 The Leadership Grid®.

behavior that is highly supportive and highly directive constitutes "coaching," and leadership behavior that is highly supportive and highly directive is called "directing."

The model is intentionally flexible. A leader will need to relate to an employee in a given situation using a specific leadership style, a style partly determined by the task and the employee's years in the organization.

There are clear overlaps between McGregor's analysis of leadership styles and Blanchard's. Theory X involves directing and some coaching. Theory Y involves some coaching, supporting, and delegating. However, the Situational Leadership II model is the more adaptive of the two. Hersey, Blanchard, and Johnson noted an overlap between McGregor's model and the Situational Leadership II model, but

Figure 2–2 Situational Leadership II.

they thought that Theory X and Theory Y represented leaders' and managers' assumptions about leadership and that these assumptions often did not get translated into action.[9]

It is clear that leaders must use different strategies for different employees. Leadership occurs in a social context in which values and norms cannot help but influence the process of leading. One leadership approach will not work for every individual in an agency. Unfortunately, some public health leaders are inflexible and use one style predominantly. For instance, one local public health administrator believed it was necessary for him to use an authoritarian approach for managing his staff. Years later, he moved to a new public health agency that he discovered to be more democratic in form. He changed his leadership style but did not seem to learn that leadership style needs to be tied to the situation at hand and not to the agency.

Other Analyses of Leadership Style

In a classic paper, Tannenbaum and Schmidt explored how a leader-manager might be democratic in some situations and autocratic in others.[10] As can be seen in Figure 2–3, both leadership styles are used to carry out the activities of the organization. In fact, most leadership practices fall between the two extremes. For example, the action of presenting ideas to subordinates and inviting questions from them involves the use of authority by the manager but also gives to the subordinates a degree of freedom or power. Tannenbaum and Schmidt's analysis is similar to the work of Lewin and his colleagues at the University of Iowa.[11,12] The Lewin group distinguished three leadership styles—autocratic, democratic, and laissez-faire. Their research showed that the democratic style seemed to be especially suitable for group process–oriented activities.

Bass and Stogdill found that leaders differ in the approach they take to leading their organizations, in part because of the variation in the issues they have to deal with.[13] Furthermore, they discovered that leadership behaviors generally fall on a continuum between task-oriented and relationship-oriented behaviors.

Fiedler explored the relationship between three factors that affect leadership effectiveness: personal relationships with work associates, the structure of the task to be performed by the work group, and the power associated with the leader's position in the organization.[14] These three factors can be combined in eight ways. According to Fiedler, leaders who are task oriented tend to be more effective in very favorable or very unfavorable situations than those who are relationship oriented. Leaders who are relationship oriented, on the other hand, perform better in situations that fall between the two extremes. Note that public health leaders must be both task and relationship oriented, since public health programs demand

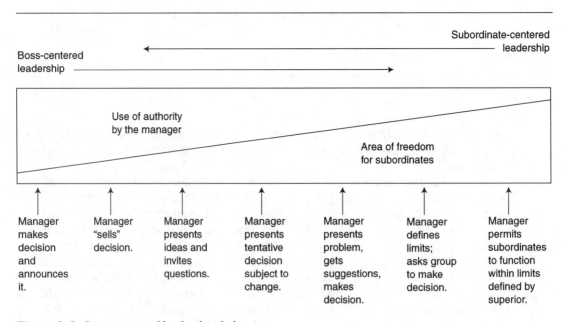

Figure 2–3 Continuum of leadership behavior.

good communication between public health leaders and their constituents (see Chapter 9).

Hersey, Blanchard, and Johnson developed a typology of task- and relationship-oriented behavior: high-task and low-relationship behavior, high-task and high-relationship behavior, high-relationship and low-task behavior, and low-task and low-relationship behavior.[15] The authors added effectiveness-ineffectiveness as a third dimension (Table 2–1). As noted above, public health leaders need to exhibit high-task and high-relationship behavior.

In the 1940s, a series of studies was done by the Bureau of Business Research at Ohio State University.[16] The researchers defined leadership as the direction of group activities for the purpose of attaining a goal. Leadership, in their view, involved two types of behavior: initiating structure (task-oriented behavior) and showing consideration for the needs of employees (relationship-oriented behavior). The researchers hypothesized, on the basis of their data, that both types of leadership behavior are necessary, but they found little relationship between the two types of behavior.

Utilizing the Ohio State model elements, House formulated a path-goal model.[17] According to this model, a leader's task was to help followers attain their goals through appropriate direction and support. In other words, the leader points the way to the right path to enhance the ability of followers to reach their goals. In addition, House characterized leadership behaviors as either directive, supportive, participative, or achievement oriented.

Researchers at the University of Michigan followed the Ohio State model by dividing leadership behaviors into those that were employee oriented (roughly

Table 2–1 How the Basic Leadership Styles May Be Seen by Others

Basic Style	Effective	Ineffective
High task and low relationship behavior	Seen as having well-defined methods for accomplishing goals that are helpful to the followers	Seen as imposing methods on others; sometimes seen as unpleasant and interested only in short-run output
High task and high relationship behavior	Seen as satisfying the needs of the group for setting goals and organizing work but also providing high levels of socioemotional support	Seen as initiating more structure than is needed by the group and often appears not to be genuine interpersonal relationships
High relationship and low task behavior	Seen as having implicit trust in people and as being primarily concerned with facilitating their goal accomplishment	Seen as primarily interested in harmony; sometimes seen as unwilling to accomplish a task if it risks disrupting a relationship or losing "good person" image
Low relationship and low task behavior	Seen as appropriately delegating to followers decisions about how the work should be done and providing little socioemotional support where little is needed by the group	Seen as providing little structure or socioemotional support when needed by members of the group

equivalent to showing consideration for employees) and those that were production oriented (roughly equivalent to structure initiation activities).[18]

LEADERSHIP TRAITS

Bass and Stogdill reviewed studies of leadership traits and abilities done between 1948 and 1970.[19] Table 2–2 contains a list of all the traits and abilities reported in three or more of the studies. Leading the list are technical skills, social nearness and friendliness, task motivation and application, supportiveness toward group activities, social and interpersonal skills, emotional balance and control, and leadership effectiveness and achievement.

Kouzes and Posner compared the traits identified in 1987 and again in 1995 as the chief characteristics of admired leaders (Table 2–3).[20] The five most frequently mentioned leadership traits of the most admired leaders in 1987 were honesty, forward-lookingness, the ability to inspire, competence, and intelligence. In 1995, honesty still topped the list, but the order of the next three traits was altered, and intelligence had dropped out of the first five, replaced by fair-mindedness.

Table 2–2 Factors Appearing in Three or More Studies of the 52 Surveyed

Factor	Number of Studies Found
Technical skills	18
Social nearness, friendliness	18
Task motivation and application	17
Supportive of the group task	17
Social and interpersonal skills	16
Emotional balance and control	15
Leadership effectiveness and achievement	15
Administrative skills	12
General impression (halo)	12
Intellectual skills	11
Ascendence, dominance, decisiveness	11
Willingness to assume responsibility	10
Ethical conduct, personal integrity	10
Maintaining a cohesive work group	9
Maintaining coordination and teamwork	7
Ability to communicate; articulativeness	6
Physical energy	6
Maintaining standards of performance	5
Creative, independent	5
Conforming	5
Courageous, daring	4
Experience and activity	4
Nurturant behavior	4
Maintaining informal control of the group	4
Mature, cultured	3
Aloof, distant	3

Table 2–3 Characteristics of Admired Leaders

Characteristics	1995 Respondents (Percentage of People Selecting)	1987 Respondents (Percentage of People Selecting)
Honest	88	83
Forward-looking	75	62
Inspiring	68	38
Competent	63	67
Fair-minded	49	40
Supportive	41	32
Broad-minded	40	37
Intelligent	40	43
Straightforward	33	34
Dependable	32	32
Courageous	29	27
Cooperative	28	25
Imaginative	28	34
Caring	23	26
Determined	17	20
Mature	13	23
Ambitious	13	21
Loyal	11	11
Self-controlled	5	13
Independent	5	10

Note: These percentages represent respondents from four continents: America, Asia, Europe, and Australia. The majority, however, are from the United States.

Leadership is dynamic, and there is no universal list of leadership traits that apply to all situations.[21] Nonetheless, whereas all the traits and abilities presented in Tables 2–2 and 2–3 are capable of enhancing the effectiveness of a leader, at least in certain circumstances, the 10 leadership abilities and practices described below have been singled out as especially important for successful leadership in the 21st century.

Leadership Practices

First, leaders must be *knowledge synthesizers*. They must bring intelligence to the leadership enterprise. They need to know about past events, understand the realities of the present, and have a vision of the future. They must not only be experts in their chosen field but be familiar with many other areas as well. Good leaders know how to use their knowledge to carve out a perspective and move their organization forward. Intelligence alone is not enough.[22] Self-awareness, self-control, self-confidence, commitment, integrity, the ability to foster change, and the ability to communicate with and influence others are all necessary.

Second, leaders need to be *creative*. They must not only manage large amounts of information but use it creatively to guide action. To do this successfully, they must ignore information that is not pertinent. It is hard to teach people to be creative, and creativity may be largely inherited. Nonetheless, it is possible for individuals to expand their creative abilities through practice, including through interacting with others in a social context.[23] Exercise 2–2 is designed to explore the creativity of the team members engaged in devising a solution to a public health problem.

Third, leaders need to be able to *create a vision* and get others to *share the vision* and demonstrate a *commitment to the vision* and the mission it represents. Creating a vision is not an easy thing to do, for it requires careful consideration of different scenarios that might occur if certain factors are present. Furthermore, creating a vision is next to pointless unless others can be convinced to share the vision. Leaders also need to be flexible enough to modify the vision to better satisfy their partners in the visioning process. Finally, leaders need to fit the vision to a mission and devise an action plan to realize the vision.

Fourth, leaders need to foster and facilitate *collaboration*. No one in an organization exists in a vacuum, nor does anything get done in a vacuum. Turning a vision into reality requires the development of partnerships and, in fact, the sharing of leadership. In shared leadership, each partner must respect the needs and wants of each of the other partners.

Fifth, leaders need to possess *entrepreneurial ability*. Traditional approaches to running companies and agencies no longer seem to be working. Leaders will increasingly need to explore alternate funding sources for their programs as well as learn how to use their resources in new ways.[24] This change in perspective will not only increase program efficiency but also program effectiveness. Perhaps surprisingly, leaders in the governmental public health sector need to learn these skills.

Sixth, successful leaders are *systems thinkers*. Acting as a change agent for an organization requires mastering the techniques of systems thinking as well as looking at the organization systemically.[25] System thinkers are consciously aware that everything is connected to everything else. The obvious problems plaguing an organization may be symptoms rather than root causes. A systems approach to change allows leaders to logically analyze the dimensions of the problems.

One way to put systems thinking into practice is to turn the organization into a learning organization—"an organization that is continually expanding its capacity to create its future."[26(p.14)] In a learning organization, the system becomes the guiding mechanism for change. This allows the organization to keep pace with the rapid rate of change in today's world, to function in a more interdependent manner, and to respond to the changing needs of society.[27] In a system, all the parts are interrelated, and activities that occur in one part affect all the others. The traditional linear approach to decision making is not appropriate for a true system. Systems thinkers see the big picture and are interested in the way organizations and individuals interrelate. They are students of change and the transformational patterns that affect change. Systems thinkers also think strategically. They try to determine strategies for facilitating change as they address the challenges of the system.

Seventh, leaders must *set priorities*. They have to determine what issues will be addressed within the organization. Because of the current focus on team development and community coalition building, leaders often set priorities in concert with team or community partners. Public health places a strong emphasis on the community assessment of health and disease, which helps in setting health priorities for a community. Since the health priorities are determined in concert with partners, subjective as well as objective factors tend to influence the priority-setting process. Decisions about priorities are often determined by political issues as well as community concerns.

Eighth, leaders need to *form coalitions and build teams*. They no longer practice the leader's craft in a vacuum, and they must be aware that their success depends on their being able to work with others. Since different individuals bring different expertise to the decision-making environment, teams are created to solve problems and make decisions. In teams, leadership is shared and different members move into the leadership position at different phases of the problem-solving process. Because of public health's strong community perspective, building coalitions to support the local public health agenda becomes critical. A community coalition is a team in which many community groups are represented, and it is a means of empowering the community to address its own problems.

Ninth, leaders, as pointed out above, must not only bring a creative spark to the organization but also help put innovative ideas into practice. Therefore, they must become masters of the latest *management techniques*. This does not mean that they should adopt all the latest management fads. Rather, they should explore new techniques and integrate into their repertoire those techniques that will likely make the organization stronger, more productive, and more customer oriented. The overall objective of managing is to guide the organization toward achievement of its vision. (Note that new management techniques will occasionally have to be adapted to the systems perspective, since even now many new techniques are linear in nature.)

Tenth, a successful leader acts as a *colleague, a friend, and a humanitarian* toward everyone in the organization. Leaders must be effective communicators and be able to empathize with colleagues, peers, and customers. They should protect the values of their organizations as well as the communities in which they live. In fact, they will occasionally need to help define organizational and community values when necessary.

Most leaders of the 21st century, to be fully effective, will need to possess the 10 leadership abilities and characteristics described above. These abilities and characteristics provide a solid foundation for the activity of leading—for the process of developing a vision (and a mission) and bringing that vision to fruition. Each ability or characteristic will be revisited at appropriate places throughout this book.

SUMMARY

Traditional theories of leadership have tended to ignore situational factors that can influence which leadership style is best for a given set of circumstances.[28] In addition, most of the leadership literature concerns leadership in the business sector, yet public agencies seem to work differently than for-profit companies. William Foege, a former director of the Centers for Disease Control and Prevention, has said on numerous occasions that social justice is the value that most motivates leaders in public health. Another way of saying this is that concern for people's well-being is primary. Case Study 2–A reviews some of the concerns and motivations of public health leaders.

Given this fact, the most balanced type of leadership in public health should probably be called, not organization man management (as it is designated in the

Leadership Grid), but something like community collaboration leadership. A public health leader's concern for people encompasses many other constituencies than his or her work associates. Furthermore, production, in a public health setting, includes all sorts of programs and activities, from community assessment to the development of effective community interventions.

Discussion Questions

1. What are the differences between the Theory X and Theory Y leadership styles?
2. What are the five leadership styles defined in the Leadership Grid?
3. What is an example of high-task, low-relationship leadership behavior?
4. How would you describe your dominant leadership style?
5. How flexible are you in modifying your dominant leadership style in situations that require a different style?
6. What are two examples of how you practice leadership?
7. What are five of the most cited traits of admired leaders?
8. What do you think are the most important traits a leader needs to possess?
9. Why do leaders of public organizations need entrepreneurial ability?

Exercise 2–1

AUTHORITARIAN AND DEMOCRATIC LEADERSHIP STYLES

Purpose: to explore alternative approaches to decision making and to investigate how alternative leadership styles can influence program outcomes

Key concepts: authoritarian leadership style, democratic leadership style, decision making

Procedure: The class should divide into two or more groups. Each group has the assignment to create a plan for developing a community's public health infrastructure using a given set of resources. The plan should address core infrastructure elements, including the local public health work force, public health facilities and services, public health surveillance and information systems, and relationships with medical, social, community, government, and business organizations. To develop this plan, each team chooses a leader, who is given an envelope containing a note designating the leader as a supporter of the Theory X or the Theory Y leadership style. The leader guides the group through a planning process according to the characteristics of the leadership style assigned but does not inform the other team members which leadership style he or she is using. After half an hour, each team reports back to the class as a whole, describing the exercise process, evaluating the leader, and describing the infrastructure plan chosen by the team and what its ramifications are.

Exercise 2–2

AN EXERCISE IN CREATIVITY

Purpose: to generate solutions to a public health problem from several leadership perspectives and to learn how to use creativity to discover the best solution for a problem

Key concepts: community coalition, creativity, problem solving, team

Procedure: The class or training group should divide into small teams of 5–8 people. Each member of each team should select a public health problem that concerns the particular member. The team then chooses one of the problems and tries to solve it from a personal perspective, a public health agency perspective, and a community coalition perspective. The exercise is repeated using the supposition that the mayor of the town or the governor of the state does not want public funds expended on the problem. The entire team should explore the advantages and limitations of the alternative solutions and the role that creativity plays in developing the solutions.

Case Study 2–A

Inner World to the Future: Leaders' Perspective on the Future

Louis Rowitz

We are at a crossroads. Public health agencies appear to be under attack from multiple sources, including government entities, government superagencies, managed care organizations, the mass media, community groups, and disgruntled citizens. There is confusion about what the thing called "public health" is. There is concern about the involvement of public health agencies in direct medical service activities. Perhaps, some say, it is time for government to get out of the public health service business and spin off public health agency activities to the private sector.

To these concerns must be added a strong belief that leaders make a difference. Leaders bring hope and vision and have an ability to find solutions for the challenges that face the field of public health. It is to the training of public health professionals that the public health community looks as a possible way to strengthen the infrastructure of public health in this country and to clarify the vision of public health for the 21st century. There is a strong belief in the public health community that leadership skills can be taught. There is also a strong belief that a commitment to lifelong learning is critical. For the last several years, national, regional, and state public health leadership programs have been developed. These programs have helped public health leaders increase their leadership skills and learn the latest techniques for improving and strengthening organizations. These programs have also trained public health leaders to work with communities to help define the role of public health at the community level. These programs have also stressed the importance of promoting the public health paradigm of core functions and essential public health services and of urging leaders to use their skills to build the public health system. These programs have developed unique approaches to training that promote an experiential application of all training materials back to the workplace and the community. The greatest challenge for these programs, other than the obvious one of financial sustainability, is the measurement of their long-term effect on the infrastructure of public health.

The combination of public health's challenges and the present-tense quality of our public health leadership programs, even when we talk about the future, raises an important series of issues related to where public health needs to go over the next several decades. The perspective is partly one of vision, but it is also one that goes to the very soul of the beliefs of public health leaders around the world. The experience of public health work changes us as professionals. Our inner world processes all our experiences and creates what the experimental psychologist Tolman called a cognitive map. Each experience changes the topography of our lives. This includes our personal experiences and our community living experiences as well as our professional experiences.

INTERVIEWS WITH PUBLIC HEALTH LEADERS

During 1996, I began a personal odyssey to find out what public health leaders think about public health today and what they perceive will be public health's future. I traveled throughout the United States, England, Scotland, and Ireland conversing with public health leaders about the future of public health. I talked to over 130 leaders in conversations that lasted about an hour. These conversations changed my cognitive map and my inner world by showing me the field of public health in ways that I had never perceived it. I talked to governmental leaders at all levels of government. I talked to public health professionals at the federal, state, and local level in the United States as well as to academics. I talked to foundation professionals as well as professional trainers. I also talked to public health leaders who moved to the private sector. These leaders have given me insights about ways to strengthen our training programs in the future so that we can make public health more responsive to the needs of the public. They have also taught me what we do wrong and the importance of blending our strengths in solutions of our problems.

LESSONS LEARNED

Public health leaders live the reality of their chosen profession on a daily basis. They struggle with the crises of the day as well as with the concerns that public health faces as it progresses into the 21st century. Leaders in the United States face concerns with the impact of managed care on the public health field. Leaders in England, Ireland, Scotland, and the Republic of Ireland (Southern Ireland) see public health within the context of a nationalized health service where managed care is a reality rather than a specter on the horizon. As I talked to the United States leaders at the federal, state, and local level as well as in both the public and private sector, I found that all the leaders struggle with what that elusive field called public health is. The confusion extends to the issue of whether public health as a profession is different from public health as an organizational entity. U.S. public health is multidisciplinary as well as multisectorial in perspective. This means that we speak with many voices and do not always convey a unified message. Despite this multidisciplinary orientation, public health has a strong medical perspective and an increasingly economic one as well. One result is that the primary prevention goal of public health is sometimes lost as we pursue treatment and rehabilitation programs for underserved or unserved populations. Many leaders argue that the local public health agency must be a provider of last resort when there are limited medical services available for the people in local communities. As local public health agencies continue to act as direct service providers, leaders argue that managed care organizations' move into the local area of service is a threat to local health agencies that rely heavily on the service dollars received for direct service. However, public health needs to be seen as a partner in a total integrated health program in the community. Some leaders see public health agencies as playing the leading role in a comprehensive community-based health care system.

There is increasing acceptance of the core functions paradigm of assessment, policy development, and assurance, along with a lesser degree of acceptance of the essential public health services perspective. There is a concern that the core functions terminology is too abstract and confusing to people outside the public health field. U.S. leaders feel that we perform assessment activities fairly well, although we tend not to be conversant with the latest technology advances in informatics. Leaders at all government levels feel that they have a critical role in policy development but do not always exercise the policy opportunities that they have. Several leaders pointed out that public health leaders need to be students of the democratic process and understand how our political process works. The leaders are concerned that politicians and local board of health members or county board members have most of the control of the budget that drives the public health machine. They also believe that the relationship between the local health agency and its boards is often adversarial. Leaders argue that boards could become more of a voice for public health in the community than they presently are. In addition, these issues point to the question of how public health leaders can affect the decision-making process.

Most questions were raised about the assurance function and the difficulties in specifying completely our assurance role, since this is the role that has undergone the most change during the last decade of the 20th century. There is agreement that public health needs to support a lifelong learning perspective and encourage and support continued educational and training opportunities for the public health work force. However, training dollars are presently scarce.

Many leaders express concern about the future of public health in the United States and the increasing split between national public health concerns and state and local concerns. The agenda of each level of government is different and often not integrated with the issues of concern at other levels. In addition, we have not explored the possibilities of regional collaboration as a viable way to share programs across counties and other local entities and across states in different geographic areas. An added challenge concerns the absorption of public health into state human services umbrella agencies. However, some leaders feel that the umbrella agency model may increase the importance of public health agencies and leadership at the local level. Public health practice is really a local concern and needs to be protected. It must not become too parochial, since public health has a global perspective. State and local public health leaders need to think globally but act locally.

Other issues of concern to public health leaders are several. First, our assessment activities tend to ignore the important perspective of epidemiology, which provides methods for interpretation of data. Leaders often do not know how to use data for effective decision making. Second, public health needs to reclaim its primary prevention perspective and its key role in health promotion. Educational models should predominate in health promotion activities. Third, public health is developing academic and practice linkages, but not too many successful ones. Next, public health needs to do a better job in the areas of social marketing and health communications, since the public still does not know what public health is. Finally, public health needs to do a better job building community coalitions to address community public health needs. However, there is much to learn about the development of coalitions and how to keep up the interest of these coalitions over time.

In England, Scotland, and the Republic of Ireland, I saw national health systems in which public health often played a secondary role. In all three countries, public health is dominated by physicians. All other public health–related groups are in secondary support roles. Only physicians can head a public health program in a district. If other professionals want to move into a leadership role, they are often limited to roles in academic teaching settings. However, all public health physicians have received training in public health and have passed national credential examinations.

Purchasing of services becomes the primary role of the health service public health physicians. Primary prevention programs may exist in some areas, like immunization, but these programs are contracted out to local physicians or hospitals and clinics. A common complaint of the district physicians was their inability to use their public health knowledge in the health districts. They felt that a large amount of their professional energies were expended on conflicts with local managers, who are often not health trained. In England, public health physicians felt that public health is losing its foothold and becoming less visible. In the Republic of Ireland, public health offices were abolished for 20 years under the mistaken belief that all of the public health concerns of Irish society had been solved. Only in the past few years has public health been re-established in the districts. However, it is taking time for these offices to re-create public health programs. Scotland is an interesting case, in that community-based programs are being developed and supported within the Scottish office of the national health service.

The major lesson to be learned is that public health often has trouble surviving in a system in which all the citizens have access to services. However, primary prevention programs do not flourish in this environment without a vigorous struggle. Time pressure resulting from calendar overload becomes a problem.

Bureaucracy and an overabundance of meetings at the local and national levels are the rule rather than the exception. In addition, each public health profession has its own organization, the agendas of these organizations conflict, and there is a consequent lack of agreement between these groups as to how to pursue a common public health agenda. However, these European countries are small, and most public health people know each other. This does offer opportunities for collaboration that are not often pursued.

THE FUTURE

Public health concerns never go away. Although it is possible to see variations in the ways public health is practiced, there will continue to be crises and issues of concern to the public health profession. There is growing anxiety about emerging infections and increasing resistance to the effects of antibiotics. Money available for health services is shrinking. Managed care organizations do not seem to hold all the answers for the health care needs of the American public.

The changing demographics of our population require public health interventions. The need for primary prevention activities and the development of health promotion and disease prevention initiatives remain critical. Ebbs and flows in the support for government-based public health programs will continue.

Public health leaders remain hopeful. They see growing support for leadership programs for the public health work force. They project a growing influence of public health activities undertaken by local health departments. They are ambivalent about the movement to create superagencies at the state level, although they recognize that public health agencies need to work closely with other human services agencies. Our technology knowledge will increase significantly over the next several decades. The Centers for Disease Control and Prevention will continue to be a major public health voice in this country. Public health will work more closely with its health care partners to develop more integrated systems of care. Some leaders see this collaboration as occurring from within an integrated health care system. Other leaders believe that public health agencies will remain part of the government system, since their oversight function must not be compromised. Closer linkages will evolve between academic institutions and public health agencies. Finally, public health's emphasis on core functions and essential services will lead to increased infrastructure strength in the future.

In summary, public health leaders bring a message of hope for the future. Public health will survive.

REFERENCES

1. D. McGregor, *The Human Side of Enterprise* (New York: McGraw-Hill, 1985).
2. R.R. Blake et al., *The Leadership Grid* (Houston: Gulf Publishing Co., 1991).
3. K. Blanchard and S. Johnson, *The One Minute Manager* (New York: Morrow, 1982).
4. K. Blanchard and R. Lorber, *Putting the One Minute Manager To Work* (New York: Morrow, 1984).
5. K. Blanchard et al., *Leadership and the One Minute Manager* (New York: Morrow, 1985).
6. K. Blanchard et al., *The One Minute Manager Builds High Performing Teams* (New York: Morrow, 1990).
7. Blanchard et al., *Leadership and the One Minute Manager.*

8. Blanchard et al., *The One Minute Manager Builds High Performing Teams.*
9. P. Hersey et al., *Management of Organizational Behavior,* 7th ed. (Upper Saddle River, NJ: Prentice Hall, 1996).
10. R. Tannenbaum and W.H. Schmidt, "How To Choose a Leadership Pattern," *Harvard Business Review,* March–April 1958, 95–102.
11. K. Lewin and R. Lippitt, "An Experimental Approach to the Study of Autocracy and Democracy: A Preliminary Note," *Sociometry* 1 (1938): 292–300.
12. K. Lewin, "Field Theory and Experiment in Social Psychology," *American Journal of Sociology* 44 (1939): 868–896.
13. B.M. Bass, *Bass & Stogdill's Handbook of Leadership* (New York: The Free Press, 1990).
14. F.E. Fiedler, *A Theory of Leadership Effectiveness* (New York: McGraw-Hill, 1967).
15. P. Hersey et al., *Management of Organizational Behavior.*
16. R.M. Stogdill and A.E. Coons, eds., *Leader Behavior: Its Description and Measurement,* Research Monograph No. 88 (Columbus: Ohio State University, Bureau of Business Research, 1951).
17. R.J. House, "A Path-Goal Theory of Leadership," *Administrative Science Quarterly* 16 (1971): 321–338.
18. R.L. Kahn and D. Katz, "Leadership Practices in Relation to Productivity and Morale," in *Group Dynamics: Research and Theory,* eds. D. Cartwright and A. Zander (Evanston, IL: Peterson & Co., 1960).
19. B.M. Bass, *Bass & Stogdill's Handbook of Leadership.*
20. J.M. Kouzes and B.Z. Posner, *The Leadership Challenge,* 2d ed. (San Francisco: Jossey-Bass, 1995).
21. Hersey et al., *Management of Organizational Behavior.*
22. D. Coleman, *Working with Emotional Intelligence* (New York: Bantam, 1998).
23. M. Csikszentmihalyi, *Creativity* (New York: HarperCollins, 1996).
24. D. Osborne and T. Gaebler, *Reinventing Government* (Reading, MA: Addison-Wesley, 1992).
25. D.L. Kauffman Jr., *Systems 1: An Introduction to Systems Thinking* (Minneapolis: Future Systems, Inc., 1980).
26. P.M. Senge, *The Fifth Discipline: The Art and Practice of the Learning Organization* (New York: Dell, 1990).
27. Senge, *The Fifth Discipline.*
28. S.P. Robbins and M. Coulter, Management, 6th ed. (Upper Saddle River, NJ: Prentice-Hall, 1999).

Chapter 3

The Systems Approach to Organizational Change

Devote yourself to loving others, devote yourself to the community around you, and devote yourself to creating something that gives you purpose and meaning.

Morris Schwartz, *Morrie: In His Own Words*

Good leadership depends on systems thinking. This type of thinking focuses on ways to implement, in the short and long term, system components necessary for meeting identified needs. To ensure systems thinking is effective, public health agency leaders must support the systems perspective and make certain staff understand what is involved in a systems approach to change. Communication must be frequent enough to allow the staff to help manage the implementation of strategic policies. The leader is responsible for guiding the implementation activities and presenting to the community the steps being taken by the agency in response to local public health issues.

Team building is a critical part of leading a public health agency. The leader creates teams to address the programmatic needs of the agency. Once the members are appointed, the teams need to clarify the values that will guide their activities. Community coalitions and partnerships have basic similarities to teams, and their development resembles team development.

Public health leaders must

- think systemically and act strategically
- promote change
- support the values of the agency and the community
- understand the relationship between system inputs, program interventions, and outputs
- monitor and evaluate the effects of change
- practice systems thinking at the five levels of leadership (see Chapter 4)

The remainder of this chapter covers the main stages in the systems approach to organizational change (Figure 3–1). These stages include values clarification,

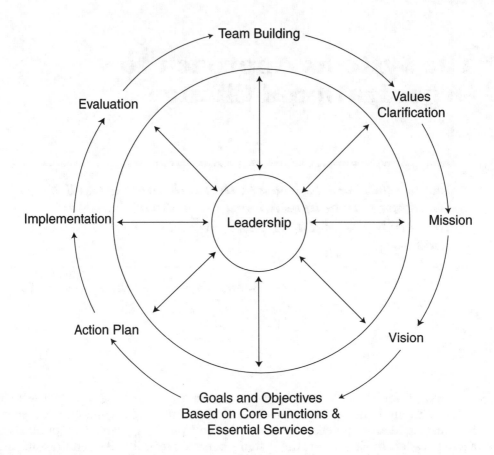

Figure 3–1 Systems approach to organizational change.

construction or revision of the agency's mission and vision, identification of goals and objectives, development of an action plan, implementation of the action plan, and assessment of the effects of the implementation.

VALUES CLARIFICATION

Blanchard and O'Connor make a distinction between the Fortune 500 and the Fortunate 500.[1] The latter are businesses in which management by values occurs. In the management-by-values process, which can take three years to complete, an agency goes through three stages. The first stage involves clarification of the agency's mission, values, and vision. The second stage involves communicating the agency's newly clarified mission, values, and vision to others. The final stage, which is the most complex, involves aligning the leadership and management practices of the agency with its stated values. In the case of public health leadership, the alignment of practices and values applies to the individual, team, agency, community, and professional level.

An agency's culture is made up, in part, of the values and beliefs that the members of the agency have in common.[2] These values and beliefs guide the members' individual and collective behavior. Also part of the agency's culture are the rituals and myths that have grown out of the agency's history. For example, a myth might be created about a former administrator, who, as an avid promoter of public health in the community, might be idealized as a public health hero. Treating the administrator as a hero has its benefits, since it reaffirms the importance of health promotion. Yet it can also have a downside. For one thing, it may lead to organizational stasis, for the myth suggests that everything the administrator did, every policy decision made, is above question, and thus the current members of the agency may be more reluctant to make necessary changes than if they viewed the administrator as praiseworthy but fallible.

Agency rituals might include a special public health award given to a community organization each year at an annual luncheon. If this award is named after the former administrator, the ritual supports the myth. A new public health administrator with new ideas and a new vision for the agency will need to work with the agency staff to redefine its values, and thus the current myths and rituals—and even the agency's physical layout, which is a component of organizational culture—may need to be changed.

A value, according to Rokeach, is "an enduring belief that a specific mode of conduct or end-state of existence is personally or socially preferable to an opposite or converse mode of conduct or end-state of existence."[3(p.5)] Each community has a unique configuration and a unique set of values, and the local public health agency is a reflection of these values. Societies that are geographically and politically separated from each other tend to develop different community approaches to dealing with their particular problems.[4] For example, a county with a mostly rural population will have different public health priorities than a county with a mostly urban population.

Some general truths about values are worth noting. First, certain values are universal while others occur only in specific locales. Second, values tend to be organized into value systems. Third, people generally have the values they do because of the socialization they have undergone. Fourth, values are present in every social situation.

The increasing diversification within many communities has led to changes in value systems and in some cases to a confusing diversity of values. To ensure that a system of shared values evolves, a community must undertake a process of value clarification. This type of process respects diversity but is aimed at elucidating the dominant values of the community. A vision cannot be realized unless it is built on an infrastructure of shared core values.

The question arises whether there are universal values. In the attempt to answer this question, 24 leaders from around the world and from various professions were asked to address the issue of universal human values.[5] They reached a consensus that the following values were universal: love, truthfulness, fairness, freedom, unity, tolerance, responsibility, and respect for life. Some widely shared values were nonetheless not universally shared, but these were listed as well. This group comprised courage, wisdom, hospitality, obedience, peace, stability, racial harmony, respect for women's place in society, and protection of the environment.

In the case of American culture, two other widely shared values should be added to the group. One is health protection and the second is quality of life. Americans, among others, are concerned about the effect that disease can have on quality of life. Public health leaders promote a public health agenda oriented toward improving the quality of life of people in their service communities.

Americans are also concerned about having a choice. In the health reform debate in the early 1990s, the potential for the loss of choice of medical provider (and loss of power over other aspects of medical care) was a critical factor in the defeat of the Clinton plan. It almost became more important than the potential benefits of universal health care. (To partially fill out the list of American cultural values, Americans are preoccupied with the biggest and newest consumer products, pursue dreams even when the chance of success is slight, are impatient, and tend to improvise in the making of changes. All these need to be taken into account in designing public health policies.)

Shared values play an important role in any reform of the public health system. Exercise 3–1 is intended to illuminate the relationship between personal, professional, organizational, and community values.

Public health leaders, as protectors of the values of the agency and the community, must stress the importance of maintaining high ethical standards inside the agency and in the community. One necessary task is to do an ethics check. Are the procedures being used in the agency and the community legal? And even if legal, are they consistent with the values of the agency and the community?

Public health leaders, besides identifying values, must consider how these values will affect the implementation of programs. They should be aware that the process of values clarification can simplify the solution of many local public health issues. Following is a list of strategies for clarifying values and promoting them in the agency and community:

- Learn which values are universal (or nearly universal) and promulgate them in the community.
- Learn which additional values prevail in the community and in the agency.
- In conjunction with agency members and community partners, integrate universal, community, and agency values.
- Evaluate prevailing values and revise those that need to be changed.
- Develop a shared values statement.

MISSION AND VISION

Leaders need to be oriented toward the future and help create the vision that guides the activities of the agency. They must also inspire their colleagues to share the vision and use it to guide their activities. Therefore, the next task after values clarification is to evaluate both the agency's mission and the current vision for the agency (or create a new one).

An agency's mission and the vision must reflect each other. A vision is a picture of what, according to its leaders, the agency's future should be like. The agency's mission is the role it sees itself playing in the community. If the vision and mission truly reflect each other, then the agency, in fulfilling its mission, will help realize its vision (i.e., help bring about the kind of future it desires).

In addition, public health, like other areas of society, is changing rapidly, and an agency's vision and mission must change in concert. For example, managed care, public-private partnerships, emerging infections, drug resistance, and community violence are issues, some newer than others, that public health must deal with. A public health agency's mission statement must be revised periodically to take into account new problems or other developments that have occurred in the public health arena.

An organization's mission defines its purpose—its reason for existing.[6] A standard mission for a public health agency is the promotion of health and the prevention of disease. If an agency views itself as having this mission, then it should not be primarily involved in providing direct services with a strong medical orientation.

A mission statement can be short or long. It can be a statement of the agency's general purpose or it can detail the agency's role in several areas. According to Wall, Solum, and Sober, a mission statement needs to answer four questions:[7]

1. What is the purpose of public health?
2. How does the public health agency intend to coordinate its values and actions?
3. Who makes up the constituencies of the agency?
4. How does the agency link the present with the future?

Pearce and David claim that a mission statement should address such things as the customer market (community), service-related issues, geographic concerns (global, national, state, or local), the level of technology, the requirements of agency survival, the personal concerns of the agency's leaders, the agency's philosophy, and the image of the agency in the community.[8] Albrecht recommended addressing the environment of competitors, economic concerns, political concerns, legal concerns, and social issues.[9] Wilson cautioned that a mission statement may leave out critical organizational activities, which sometimes shrivel financially and programmatically if not included in the mission.[10]

A mission statement should be inspiring, for the public health agency's work force needs to embrace the mission.[11] Getting the staff members to do this could be difficult, since many of them have a minimal background in public health. Many will have been hired to perform clinical functions rather than engage in community-oriented preventive activities.

The mission is an important determinant of the agency's goals and objectives and should be closely tied to the agency's action plan. Therefore, the agency leaders must communicate the mission to community partners and constituents as well as to the agency work force.[12] One strategy is to ask partners and constituents to read the mission statement in order to evaluate its clarity.

There is a question whether the mission or vision should be developed first. Typically, a public health agency has a clear idea of its mission but an undeveloped vision of its future. In a case like this, the mission is virtually given and the vision is what must be worked on. Sometimes an organization's mission and vision are both treated in a single statement that covers the present and the future. For example, the public health mission enunciated in *Healthy People in Healthy Communities* can also be viewed as a vision of the future.[13]

As pointed out earlier, managers are focused on protecting the integrity of their organization, whereas leaders are visionary and committed to change. Therefore, leaders can often benefit from developing their visioning skills. A vision can be likened to a blank canvas on which the leader sketches a possible future. Although a vision statement is about the future, it is often written in the present tense, which is one method of expressing the strong connection between the "now" and the "then."

Two cautionary notes: First, leaders are responsible for more than creating a vision. They need to motivate others and to play a major role in the development of action plans. Second, leaders may need to give up power in order to bring the vision into reality.[14] For example, they may be required to make changes in the organizational chart.

Following is a brief description of one method for developing a vision statement. First, the visioning team lays out the values and principles that will guide the visioning process. Second, the team develops a glossary of terms to go along with the shared mission statement. Third, it includes key constituents in the visioning process. Fourth, it describes the functions of a vision statement and how the vision statement to be created will be used. Fifth, the visioning team discusses the future and where it wants public health activities to go. (The team should consider scenarios likely to occur if the agency moves in certain directions. Scenario building is an important step in the visioning process.) Next, the team redefines terms and relates them to concepts in the glossary. Then it devises a vision statement based on the work it has done. The construction is followed by general editing, which occurs in smaller teams. The final step is to reach a consensus on the vision statement. Of course, once the vision statement is agreed upon, it is necessary to audit progress toward the implementation of the vision.

Below is a summary of the steps public health leaders need to take in order to develop a mission and vision for their agencies:

- Use a mission statement to guide the daily activities of the public health agency.
- Create a vision statement to guide the activities of the agency as it moves forward in time.
- Use visioning skills to create the vision.
- Involve colleagues and community partners in the development of a shared mission and vision.
- Develop a glossary of public health terms for colleagues and community partners.
- Review the mission and vision statements yearly.

GOALS AND OBJECTIVES

The next task in the systems approach to organizational change is to translate the mission and the vision into measurable goals and objectives. The mission statement is framed in general terms and does not contain the details of how the mission is to be fulfilled. Nor does the vision statement lay out how the vision is to be realized. Goals are more specific than either the mission or vision, and objectives are more specific still. They are, so to speak, the individual steps on the way to fulfilling the mission and realizing the vision.

Goals can be classified in several ways. One distinction is between organizational goals, which the activities of the organization are intended to achieve, and order goals, which are pursued as a means of preventing certain events from happening.[15] Organizational goals can be further divided into the stated goals of an organization and the actual, sometimes hidden, goals of the organization. Creating a fit between organizational goals and order goals is an important leadership activity. Goals can also be classified in terms of the areas of human activity to which they pertain, as seen in the division between economic, cultural, social, and political goals.

Objectives are the quantitatively and qualitatively measurable steps needed to achieve the goals of the organization. Along with the goals, they are used to guide the managerial processes. Public health agency leaders are responsible for

- translating the agency's mission and vision into programmatic goals and objectives
- discovering any hidden goals that may sabotage activities

Exercise 3–2 explores the relationship between an organization's mission, vision, and goals and objectives.

THE ACTION PLAN

The next step is to develop an action plan for achieving the goals and objectives identified in the preceding stage. The action plan consists of operational steps that, if performed, will lead to the attainment of the stated goals and objectives. In this step, the agency leaders are required to be especially creative, for the action plan will almost certainly demand innovative approaches to achieving the goals and objectives. Creativity is called for by the structural tension that exists between the vision and the current reality. A creative leader looks for ways of resolving the tension in order to move the organization forward.

Brainstorming is frequently used at this stage, for it is an effective way of discovering worthwhile ideas. In addition, the leaders, in creating an action plan, must take into account the environment (the agency and its community) and the resources needed to carry out the plan.[16]

The creative process can be divided into three stages.[17] First comes the germination phase, in which the leader uses personal excitement to address the problems that need to be dealt with. In the second stage, the organization and its employees begin to adapt to the leader's agenda. In stage 3, the process is completed. At the end of stage 3, the leader often starts the process over again.

Some management experts suggest that devising strategies for goal attainment is more effective than an action plan. Mintzberg, for example, argued that the action plan approach is too narrow.[18] For one thing, it divides strategic thinking from the goal-attainment process, and the separation prevents leaders from responding creatively to the changing environment. In Mintzberg's view, planning is an incremental process and is not something that can be done all at once. One way of proceeding is to create an action plan that addresses only a few important areas. If the plan is too complex, failure may result.[19] Note that if the strategic approach is used, the strategies chosen may in fact replace goals in the minds of the various constituencies.

One way of looking at an action plan is as a process of learning through action. Constant feedback is a necessary part of the process. If progress toward the goals is not occurring, revisions in the plan will need to be made. The leaders may have to go back to previous stages and repeat them.

According to Handy, an organization needs to learn the steps in action planning.[20] He felt that the learning part of action plans was harder in a traditional bureaucracy than in a partnership network.

One point to mention here is that government agencies tend to be highly bureaucratic owing to the legislative need for oversight and accountability. As may be expected, civil service requirements often work against organizational change, and networks are often difficult to form in bureaucratic organizations. Yet, an interesting phenomenon is occurring that may help in overcoming some of the barriers caused by bureaucratization. Over half of the states have an in-state or regional public health leadership institute, and such institutes are facilitating the development of leadership networks. Websites, forums, chat rooms, and other forms of electronic communication are making networking easier, and the Public Health Leadership Society has used the Internet to create a national network.

The structure of any organization is multilayered, and those devising an action plan need to take account of the hidden parts of the organization's structure.[21] Furthermore, they need to keep in mind that any stage in the implementation of the plan will be affected by all the previous stages. They also must pay attention to authority issues and the impact that the implementation of the plan will have on the work force, for major changes can alter a staff member's sense of identity.

A number of strategies, including the following four, can be used to reduce the problems likely to arise from a major change. First, resulting changes in roles and relationships should be determined as the action plan is being created. Staff will worry about no longer having a job when the process is completed—and in fact jobs may vanish as a result of the implementation. Second, the human resources office may have to be reorganized or its practices reformed in light of the proposed change. Third, an information system capable of monitoring the implementation process may have to be created. Finally, the financial management of the organization may have to be altered.

One way to measure the effectiveness of an action plan is to use the balanced scorecard model developed by Kaplan and Norton.[22] This model evaluates the degree of success from the financial, internal organization process, customer, and learning and growth perspectives. For an action plan to work, according to the authors, the leaders of the organization must communicate the mission and vision, the goals and objectives, and the action plan to all the relevant constituencies. Second, the leaders must understand and be able to explain to these constituencies the linkage between the action plan goals and the rewards associated with good performance—what might be called "encouraging the heart."[23] Third, the process of developing the plan must include target setting. Fourth, the action plan must include feedback and learning components.

An action plan can usher in a new era for the organization or be its death knell. It is more likely to benefit the organization if it is created by means of a well-thought-out method and is implemented using the strategies mentioned above. Below is a list of guidelines that public health leaders should follow when engaged in action planning:

- Develop an action plan tied to the agency's mission, vision, and goals and objectives.

- Use strategic planning techniques for action planning (see Chapter 10).
- Formulate operational steps or strategies for each goal and objective.
- Know the resources that are needed and the resources that available to implement the action plan.
- Explore existing barriers to successful action planning.
- Use the balanced scorecard model to measure the effectiveness of the action plan.

IMPLEMENTATION

The implementation of an action plan for the purpose of achieving goals and objectives and thereby realizing the agency's vision *is* the practice of public health, or at least part of it. During implementation, the leaders of the agency have the task of communicating the mission, vision, and goals and objectives of the agency to the staff and community constituents and doing this within the governing paradigm of the public health core functions of assessment, policy development, and assurance. In short, the leaders must become a bridge between the agency and the community.

Very little has been written about the implementation of action plans in the field of public health. Yet it is clear that implementation of an action plan can involve many of the same activities public health leaders normally engage in as part of their responsibilities. These include

- identifying community leaders
- delegating tasks to staff members and community partners
- establishing relationships with constituents
- communicating health information to the community
- working with the legislature
- working with the county board or local board of health

In a survey of California public health officers and executives, the respondents stated that their work encompassed budgeting, programming, disease control, staffing, environmental issues, health issues related to foreign nationals, and issues arising from undocumented care.[24] The researchers examined the lessons that the public health leaders had learned from their daily activities. These lessons included the importance of accuracy of information, flexibility, the total involvement of all stakeholders, action based on vision, patience, and providing information to the public.

EVALUATION

After an action plan is implemented, the results of the implementation need to be evaluated. The object of the evaluation is to determine to what degree the goals and objectives were achieved. Although the leaders of a public health agency will not be directly involved in gathering and analyzing the evaluation data, they will use the conclusions of the evaluation to determine what steps to take next to realize the agency's vision.

Leaders of an agency need data to foster a culture of evidence-based practice within the agency and among community constituents. For one thing, public health leaders are seen as sources of knowledge about community public health issues, and ensuring that evaluation data are gathered and publicized in some form confirms the legitimacy of their role as knowledge providers. In addition, the data will show the effects of the agency's activities on the residents of the community and, assuming they are mostly positive, will confirm the legitimacy of the agency's role as a protector of the community's health.

The evaluation process has been analyzed as consisting of six separate steps:[25]

1. posing questions about the program
2. setting effectiveness standards
3. designing the evaluation
4. collecting the data
5. analyzing the data
6. reporting the results

Not part of the evaluation process itself but an essential step nonetheless is the use of the results to determine further changes that need to be made.

Evaluation seems to frighten American health professionals, who tend to think evaluation data will jeopardize their jobs. In Great Britain, on the other hand, public health leaders seem convinced that evaluation helps strengthen programs.

SUMMARY

This chapter describes the main stages in the systems approach to organizational change. The first step is for the organization to clarify its values. Once it does that, it can more easily construct a mission for itself and create a vision of its own future. The next task is to determine which goals and objectives, if achieved, will lead to the fulfilling of the organization's mission and the realization of its vision. Then comes the development of an action plan designed to accomplish the goals and objectives. The action plan needs to be implemented, which constitutes the fifth step. The last step, of course, is to do an evaluation to determine whether the goals and objectives were accomplished and whether their accomplishment led to the realization of the organization's vision. Usually the evaluation uncovers changes that need to be made if the vision is to be realized.

Discussion Questions

1. What are the similarities and differences between systems thinking and strategic thinking?
2. What are the values that characterize public health in the United States or in your home country?
3. How do an organization's mission and its vision differ and how are they similar?

4. What is the relationship between goals and objectives?
5. What is an action plan and what is the typical purpose of such a plan?
6. What are four strategies for reducing the seriousness of problems resulting from major changes?
7. What are the six steps of the evaluation process?

Exercise 3–1

SHARED VALUES TEAM ASSIGNMENT

Purpose: to elucidate the relationships between personal values, community values, organizational values, and professional values

Key concepts: community coalition, community values, organizational values, personal values, professional values, value alignment

Procedure: The class should divide into teams of 4 or 5 members each. Each team pretends to be a community coalition charged with creating a shared values position statement intended to guide the coalition as it addresses the community's public health needs. The statement should integrate personal, organizational, community, and professional values—the values that guide our personal lives, the organization we work in, the community we live in, and the profession we are members of. Each team will perform the following steps:

1. Each team member writes down on a Post-it one of his or her personal values. The member acting as "mayor" (facilitator) collects the Post-its and sticks them on a poster board in a column. The team reviews the values to see if a pattern emerges.
2. Each team member writes down on a differently colored Post-it (one of another color than the Post-its used in step 1) a community value (the team members should choose from among the values held by the community in which they live). The mayor collects the Post-its and puts them on the poster board in a column next to the personal value Post-its. The team reviews the community values and compares them with the personal values.
3. Each team member writes down on a differently colored Post-it a professional value held by public health practitioners. The mayor collects the Post-its and puts them on the poster board in a third column. The team reviews these values and discusses the ways in which they are consistent or inconsistent with the values previously listed.
4. Each team member writes down on a differently colored Post-it an organizational value held by the organization in which he or she works. The mayor collects the Post-its and puts them on the poster board in a fourth column. The team reviews the values listed and discusses their relationship to the other sets of values.
5. The team reviews all the values listed and creates a values list that reflects the shared interests of all the team members (remember, the team members are pretending to be representatives of the organizations in a community coalition).
6. Each team presents its list of values to the whole group.

Exercise 3–2

THE VISION THING

Purpose: to elucidate the initial steps in the systems approach to organizational change; the role of a public health agency's mission, vision, and goals and objectives; and the connections between these

Key concepts: goals and objectives, mission, vision

Procedure: The class should divide into agency work teams of 5–10 members each. The first task is for each team to act as ad hoc committee assigned the job of drafting a mission statement for a public health agency. If a glossary of terms is necessary, one should be drafted. After the mission statements are completed, the teams present them to the group as a whole, which then develops a shared mission statement.

In the second task, each team acts as a committee that has been assigned the job of developing a vision statement utilizing the shared mission statement created in the first task. Some team members should be designated as senior staff and others as front-line staff. After the vision statements are completed, the teams present them to the group as a whole, which then develops a shared vision statement.

In the third and final task, each team develops goals and objectives statements that indicate what actions must be achieved in order to implement the agency's mission and vision.

REFERENCES

1. K. Blanchard and M. O'Connor, *Managing by Values* (San Francisco: Berrett-Koehler, 1997).
2. P. Hersey et al., *Management of Organizational Behavior*, 7th ed. (Upper Saddle River, NJ: Prentice Hall, 1996).
3. M. Rokeach, *The Nature of Human Values* (New York: The Free Press, 1973).
4. R.M. Williams Jr., *American Society: A Sociological Interpretation*, 3d ed. (New York: Knopf, 1970).
5. R.M. Kidder, "Universal Human Values: Findings on Ethical Common Ground," *Futurist* 28, no. 2 (1994): 8–13.
6. S.P. Robbins and M. Coulter, *Management*, 6th ed. (Upper Saddle River, NJ: Prentice Hall, 1999).
7. B. Wall et al., *The Visionary Leader* (Rocklin, CA: Prima Publishing & Communication, 1992).
8. J.A. Pearce Jr. and F.R. David, "Corporate Mission Statements: The Bottom Line," *Academy of Management Executives*, May 1992, 109–116.
9. K. Albrecht, *The Northbound Train* (New York: AMACOM [American Management Association], 1994).
10. J.Q. Wilson, *Bureaucracy* (New York: Basic Books, 1989).
11. N.M. Tichy, *The Leadership Engine* (New York: Harper Business, 1997).
12. E. Marzalek-Gaucher and R.J. Coffey, *Transforming Healthcare Organizations* (San Francisco: Jossey-Bass, 1990).
13. T. Norris and L. Howell, *Healthy People in Healthy Communities: A Dialogue Guide* (Chicago: Coalition for Healthy Cities and Communities, 1998).
14. Wall et al., *The Visionary Leader*.
15. A. Etzioni, *A Comparative Analysis of Complex Organizations* (New York: The Free Press, 1971).
16. E.E. Bobrow, *Ten Minute Guide to Planning* (New York: Macmillan, Spectrum, and Alpha Books, 1998).
17. R. Fritz, *The Path of Least Resistance* (New York: Fawcett, 1984).
18. H. Mintzberg, *Mintzberg on Management* (New York: The Free Press, 1989).
19. Albrecht, *The Northbound Train*.
20. C. Handy, *The Age of Unreason* (Boston: Harvard Business School Press, 1990).
21. P.M. Senge et al., *The Fifth Discipline Fieldbook* (New York: Bantam, 1994).
22. R.S. Kaplan and D.P. Norton, *The Balanced Scorecard* (Boston: Harvard Business School Press, 1996).

23. J.M. Kouzes and B.Z. Posner, *The Leadership Challenge,* 2d ed. (San Francisco: Jossey-Bass, 1995).
24. J.C. Lammers and V. Pandita, "Applying Systems Thinking to Public Health Leadership," *Journal of Public Health Management and Practice* 3, no. 4 (1997): 39–49.
25. A. Fink, *Evaluation Fundamentals* (Newbury Park, CA: Sage Publications, 1993).

Chapter 4

The Five Levels of Leadership

Effective leaders are capable of reframing the thinking of those whom they guide.

D.R. Conner, *Managing at the Speed of Change*

A leader is a person who inspires others to action and guides their undertakings. These others can be members of a team, employees of an agency, or heads of groups that have formed an alliance, for example. In other words, leadership, in public health as in other arenas, operates on different levels. This chapter discusses, first, the abilities that public health leaders need at any level, including the personal level (i.e., when dealing with another individual one on one), then goes on to consider the particular abilities and strategies that they put to use in heading a team, heading an agency, working within a community coalition, and guiding their profession toward improvement.

PERSONAL LEADERSHIP DEVELOPMENT

This section considers some of the prerequisites for being an effective public health leader at any level. These prerequisites include a commitment to social justice, an understanding of democracy, an understanding of the political process, communication skills, mentoring skills, decision-making skills, and the ability to balance work and life outside work.

Values

Public health leaders, to be fully effective, must be committed to the values that characterize public health, especially social justice. However, they need to be careful not to let the social justice agenda prevent them from doing the tasks that need to be done. Furthermore, social justice is a broad concept and encompasses a range of different issues. The predominant social justice issue of concern to

46

almost all public health leaders is equity in access to care. On the other hand, no consensus exists that, for instance, there should be a radical redistribution of wealth in the society at large.

A commitment to a value such as equity in access to care entails a willingness to challenge the political status quo and act as an advocate for the public health agenda. Leaders are supporters of organizational and community values and should be on the front lines in attempts to make public health practices and policies conform to these values.

Politics and Governance

Public health leaders need to understand the political system of the location in which their activities take place. In this country, they need to understand how the American version of democracy works at the local, state, and national levels and how to influence the political process. As an example, the author, on a visit to the office of a public health professional in a state health department, noticed *The Federalist Papers* and de Tocqueville's *Democracy in America* on the shelf. The public health leader said that he often referred to these books for guidance in making decisions.

One question that arises is whether there is a difference between government (or governance, the activity of governing) and politics. Governance, in large part, consists of administering programs and adjusting them to fit policies developed as part of the political process.[1] Unfortunately, these policies sometimes are not founded on the best available evidence but instead reflect the personal concerns (including the desire to get re-elected) of the politicians who vote them into existence. Several years ago, the author talked to a state legislator about having a school of public health supply data on specific health issues to the legislator. He refused the offer, because, according to him, he did not need data to make his decisions. (As someone has pointed out, politicians have spin doctors while government agencies have spokespeople.[2] That says something about the difference between politics and government.)

Public health agencies are government agencies, and public health leaders are implementers of policies set by politicians. This creates interesting possibilities for a partnership between the political and governmental sectors. Leadership theories often focus exclusively on organizational tasks, such as setting organizational policies and motivating the work force, but public health leaders need to develop the skills necessary for working with elected officials. Their role is to use the values, mission, vision, and goals and objectives of their agency to clarify public health issues and ensure that the policies created to deal with these issues will have a good chance of being effective.

Communication and Empowerment

The AIM Leadership Model is based on the idea that leaders have to learn to take *a*ction, learn how to *i*nfluence the field, and be *m*otivated by the process.[3] According to the model, the five building blocks of effective personal leadership are communication, the empowerment of followers, a focus on key issues, linkage to others, and life balance. Each of these building blocks is affected by leadership style and practices as well as the systems approach to organizational change.

Good communication skills are critical. Effective communication has several aspects, including slowing the thought processes, increasing understanding, testing conclusions, listening constructively, getting to the essence of things, and exploring areas of disagreement.[4] In addition, gender differences, racial or ethnic differences, and age differences can affect whether messages are received as intended.[5] Leaders need to understand all the factors that influence communication so that they can synthesize public health information into effective messages (see Chapter 9).

Leaders, in trying to empower work and community associates, often act as their mentors. Interaction between leaders and constituents is critical,[6] and leaders need to empower "followers" in ways that give them the chance to be more effective as well as to develop their own leadership skills. Followers are themselves people with exceptional talents, and, according to one study, 80 percent of the effectiveness of a project is due to the followers and only 20 percent to the leadership.[7]

Leading and Following

Also, followers in one situation become leaders in another, and many public health practitioners see themselves in both leadership and follower roles. Public health practitioners who work for public health agencies see themselves as professionals first and even leaders in their profession, but those who are part of a traditional public bureaucracy are frequently expected to be less leaders than followers, which can create a contentious work environment.

Members of a board of health often see themselves as powerful individuals and therefore as natural leaders. Health administrators also see themselves as leaders rather than followers. This may lead to conflict. For example, a health administrator addressing a group of public health professionals in a leadership program said that it was his job to protect board members from gossip and controversies. A local board of health president who was in the training program argued that if the health administrator kept information hidden from board members, someone in the community would give them the information instead. Board members need information and lose trust in health administrators who hold back information.

Another board of health president argued that the administrator of the health department was his employee, since he could fire the administrator and recommend cutting the local health department budget. This shows how important it is for the board of health members and the public health administrator to develop an understanding that they are partners. In this regard, governance has an important role to play.[8] A governance public health framework should include mechanisms for organizing values, carrying out the public health mission, formulating goals and objectives, developing realistic action plans, resolving conflicting agendas, determining the need for structural change, improving the relationship between the board and the health department, and developing mechanisms to share governance with the appropriate governmental body. As one public health leader stated,

> To create effective governing boards, we must examine our values and determine why our boards need to exist. Once we discover our common purpose, we can develop skills and processes to improve our effectiveness. Boards and administrators need a shared vision, commitment, and

leadership to make goals a reality. As public health leaders, it is our job to develop boards that are a part of our leadership teams and join us in creating healthy communities.[9(p.11)]

Agenda Setting

Public health leaders should learn about and use the systems approach to organizational change (see Chapter 3) and the public health core functions model (discussed in detail in Part II) to ensure that their agencies' agendas are tied to the core functions of public health. In addition, they need to master the art and science of public health. Leaders are the grand integrators of science and practice, and part of their job is to explain public health issues to health professional associates and community partners.

Leaders should acquire agenda-setting skills. An organization needs to prioritize the problems that it is facing and create action plans that deal with the largest problems first.[10] Figure 4–1 presents a model for agenda setting that includes the creation of a media agenda, a public agenda, and a policy agenda. The fact that public health leadership practice takes place in a government setting means that community realities impact the agenda-setting process. Also influencing the process are gatekeepers, the media, and spectacular news stories (e.g., a story about children becoming ill after eating in a fast-food restaurant).

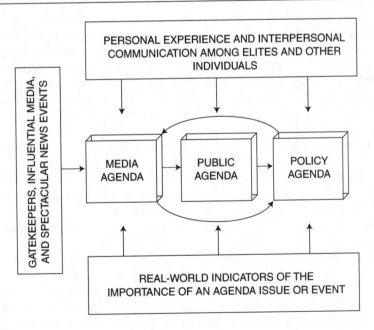

Figure 4–1 Three main components of the agenda-setting process: the media agenda, public agenda, and policy agenda.

Barriers to Effectiveness

In 1988, the Institute of Medicine issued a report that stated the public health system in the United States was in disarray. The report listed a number of barriers that reduce the ability of public health leaders to be effective, including the following:

- a lack of a consensus on the content of the public health mission
- inadequate capacity to carry out the essential public health functions of assessment, policy development, and assurance of services
- disjointed decision making uninformed by the necessary data and knowledge
- inequities in the distribution of services and the benefits of public health
- disharmony between the technical and political aspects of decisions
- rapid turnover of leaders
- an inadequate relationship between public health and the medical profession
- organizational fragmentation
- problems in relationships between layers of government
- an inadequate development of necessary knowledge across the full array of public health needs
- a poor public image of public health, inhibiting necessary support
- special problems that unduly limit the financial resources available to public health

Without question, the public health system in the United States needs to become more effective, and public health leaders will be at the forefront of attempts at reform.[11] One problem is that public health agencies are dealing with more complex problems today than previously, and the complexity of problems in the areas of infectious diseases and chronic diseases will probably continue to increase. Therefore, organizational stability may not be possible to achieve. In addition, public health professionals come from different disciplines with different approaches to problem solving, which leads to professional disagreements.[12] It will only be through collaboration that effective problem solving and decision making will occur.

In a speech before the Illinois Public Health Leadership Institute in 1992, George Pickett said that public health leaders need to increase their skills transorganizationally, that is, they need to be able to understand and communicate with others in community sectors with values and priorities different from theirs. Public health leaders are often deficient in collaboration skills,[13] and consequently they are sometimes prevented from cooperating effectively with leaders from important sectors, such as the business community and the religious community. Fortunately, obstacles to cooperation are becoming less frequent.

It should be noted that, in general, leaders who are extremely effective tend to be key players in rather than reactors to the change going on around them.[14] Effective leaders, when confronted with a problem, typically consider a wide range of options and seem to know how to select the important factors first. They also think in terms of win-win and try to arrange it so all parties are winners in a dispute. They are good listeners who try to understand others and their perspectives before trying to make themselves understood. They are excellent synthesizers who try to foster cooperation and collaboration. Finally, they constantly *renew* themselves through training, education, exercise, values clarification, and so on.

Leadership Style

Public health leaders need to develop an appropriate leadership style (see Chapter 2). Autocratic and directive styles work best when the leader structures the tasks and the workers are willing to do what the leader asks. In public health, the democratic style seems to work better.[15] Participative forms of leadership, in which staff members are involved in the problem-solving process, facilitate the building of a consensus and the acceptance by the staff of the decisions arrived at. Collaboration should be viewed as a creative process whose goal is to discover new approaches and new solutions for old problems.[16]

Dealing with Diversity

Professional diversity in public health brings its own set of problems.[17] Practitioners from different professions view public health differently. Public health leaders need to look at public health in its totality and develop strategies for integrating the different approaches. Exercise 4–1 provides an opportunity to consider the issue of professional diversity and its impact on public health strategies.

Public health leaders need to confront not only professional diversity but gender, race, ethnic, and age diversity. For example, the so-called glass ceiling for women still exists,[18] and therefore public health leaders must conscientiously promote gender equality. The first step is to gather the data necessary to determine whether gender inequalities exist and, if so, where they exist. The next step is to hire a consultant to evaluate the agency's environment and its receptiveness to gender equality. The third step is to use a benchmarking process (comparing the agency with the best agencies and not to the average ones) to identify best practices for achieving gender equality and taking full advantage of the skills that women bring into the workplace. The final step, so to speak, is to prepare oneself for a backlash. Case Study 4–A, at the end of this chapter, is an interview with Dr. Joyce Lashof, who has held a number of public health leadership posts. The interview explores some of the gender issues public health leaders typically confront.

Diversity encompasses gender, age, race, ethnicity, sexual orientation, work and family issues, education, work experiences, tenure within the agency or organization, personality, risk tolerance, geographic region, and religion.[19] A unified diversity enhancement program for public health professionals and clients may be difficult to construct because of the different issues that are prominent in each diversity category.

One way for public health leaders to deal with diversity issues is to empower staff so that they become advocates for themselves. It is important to understand how human beings in our society act and what needs they have. In his classic work *Motivation and Personality*, Maslow defined a hierarchy of needs.[20] At the most basic level, individuals want their physiologic needs met. Second in order of importance are their safety needs. In other words, issues of job security and amount of income are critical for most people. Next come social needs, including the need for recognition by colleagues. One level up, people want to experience a sense of self-esteem. They want to take pride in their work and hence want to be empowered to do a good job. A professional who works well and without the need of much direction will usually be allowed the freedom to design his or her own activities, an almost sure way of increasing self-esteem. Finally, people have a need for self-actualization—the ability to make personal dreams become reality.

Balancing Work and Play

Work has a tendency to take up most of a leader's waking hours, and family life can suffer as a result. O'Neil called this dilemma the paradox of success.[21] In his view, the myth of success is that success offers complete fulfillment, success is tied to how much money is made, and success increases freedom. In fact, success causes a constant craving for more success and hence can lead to a kind of bondage. Factors that can help a leader keep a balance between work life and private life include self-knowledge, managing conflicting pressures, and maintaining a concern for how others feel.[22]

Women seem to be very proficient at balancing personal and professional interests. For working women with a family, work and home are full-time jobs that they typically seem to handle equally well. At work, women, by redesigning their positions and demanding employee training and development, are helping to break traditional organizational molds.[23] They are also helping to break down the barriers between home and work by pushing for flex time, child care, and family leave.

This section raised and discussed many issues related to personal leadership development. Following is a list of leadership strategies that can be used to increase one's leadership skills and abilities:

- Be a value role model. Live the values that the community espouses.
- Understand the democratic process and how it affects the public health system.
- Translate political policy into action.
- Improve communication skills.
- Be a mentor to others.
- Learn to follow when appropriate.
- Be partners with the agency's governing board.
- Learn agenda-setting skills.
- Address barriers to effective public health practice.
- Explore community partnerships.
- Be creative in finding new funding sources.
- Balance work and family.
- Increase leadership opportunities for others.

LEADERSHIP AT THE TEAM LEVEL

Public health leaders do not work alone. Public health practice is a group activity. Therefore, among the most important skills a leader can possess are those that are necessary for building and maintaining teams and increasing their effectiveness.

A team is a group of people who come together to pursue a common purpose.[24] The results of the team's activities are often greater than the sum total of the results that would have occurred had each team member been acting alone.

Each team member should be viewed as leader although one person will generally become the official leader. The team leader will share information in an equitable manner with other team members.[25] The leader will build trust in the team process and share authority and power with other members. The leader will also intervene when necessary to move the team forward. The expectation is that all members will be involved in the performance of the team tasks.

Team members who are also members of the public health agency may need to act as a link between the team and the agency and community constituents. These team members, in particular, will need to learn the skills of conflict resolution and negotiation (see Chapter 11). When a skilled leader guides the team process, creativity and innovation are the result.

Reasons for Creating Teams

The reasons for creating teams include the following. First, a team allows an organization to use the leadership skills and talents and the multidisciplinary backgrounds of its staff. A multidisciplinary team that includes nurses, social workers, and environmental health specialists, among others, might be assembled, for example, to address the low level of prenatal care in the community. Second, creating a team allows the members time to get to know each other and to develop a sense of togetherness in the context of shared leadership. In general, team members find they can communicate with each other better even once they have left the team or the team has been disbanded. In addition, they learn how to cooperate and collaborate, and cooperation and collaboration increase productivity.[26] Finally, team decision making produces decisions that are supported by the majority of the team's members.

Teams that are created to lighten a supervisor's workload are often doomed to failure.[27] Teams are not a replacement for training and not a way for leaders to observe the opinions and working style of the staff. Teams do not necessarily increase the personal productivity of their members. They need leaders to clarify issues and set the parameters of their activities.[28] One of the strengths of teams is that they are flexible and can reorient themselves as roadblocks occur. Yet the freedom teams are given can be a weakness as well. Teams sometimes fail because they lack discipline and a sense of responsibility for achieving the desired outcomes. When team members realize that they will be completely in charge of their activities and will have the power to make decisions, they sometimes abuse this power, with negative results for the agency. This risk can be reduced if the agency leaders make clear to each team how they expect it to proceed and what results they expect it to achieve.

Leadership teams work differently than management teams. Management teams carry out the instructions of a supervisor. Their tasks are circumscribed, and there is very little room for creativity or innovation. Leadership teams share leadership with the public health administrator, who openly delegates decision-making power to them. In some leadership teams, the health administrator becomes a team member. If given the trust of the agency administrator, leadership team members become committed to the agency and lose their fear of reprisal. They feel that they are respected for their expertise and ability to innovate. They also know that their recommendations will be seriously considered.

Facts about Teams

Katzenbach and Smith did a study on teams in 30 organizations, including businesses, schools, and social agencies.[29] They found that teams were critical for building quality organizations and improving customer service. The authors came up with 10 findings about teams in general.

The first finding is that teams are created to address a performance challenge, and indeed a leadership team must have a purpose (mission) if it is to succeed. The second finding is that the team's composition and its purpose need to be thought through. Not every leadership team should be of the same size or professional composition. Third, leaders need to promote team performance opportunities. As the leaders view the organization, they will find these opportunities exist throughout. Fourth, many teams composed primarily of people at the top fail because of the other demands made on these individuals' time and energy. Fifth, organizations and their leaders find it easier to work with individuals than with teams. Everything, including the hiring of people, the determination of salary, the construction of career paths, and the monitoring of performance, is oriented toward the individual. Teamwork seems to go against the structure of individual responsibility.

The sixth finding is that organizations committed to high performance standards are more likely to use teams than organizations with lower performance standards. Seventh, very few high performance teams exist. High performance teams can be either leadership or management teams. However, leadership teams are generally clearer on the purpose for which they were created. They take control of their activities and promote the development of relationships between their members. They build team activities upon good communication. The leaders maintain their flexibility, work productively together, and recognize the accomplishments of their leader colleagues. Leadership teams also seem to have high morale. (High performance teams can be created using the PERFORM model, propounded by Blanchard, Carew, and Parisi-Carew.[30] The acronym stands for *p*urpose, *e*mpowerment, *r*elationships and communication, *f*lexibility, *o*ptimal productivity, *r*ecognition and appreciation, and *m*orale.)

The eighth finding is that teams do not replace organizational hierarchies. Instead, teams enhance these hierarchies, partly because they are able to cross over structural boundaries. Because of the strong community orientation of public health agencies, leadership teams can be used to address community concerns. These teams may include community partners among their membership.

The ninth finding is that teams are small learning organizations that integrate performance and learning. Typically a team will do research on a subject related to its purpose. Team members also learn team-building and leadership skills. They often learn that each member is a leader or potential leader. The conjoining of performance and learning in teams is generally a plus, since their conjunction throughout an organization is often a prerequisite for the organization to increase it effectiveness. This applies to public health agencies as well.

The final finding is that teams are effective in addressing new issues as well as old issues. In the case of old issues or problems, they often discover new solutions.

One reason teams are good at discovering solutions to problems is that they view the problems from a systems perspective rather than using the traditional cause and effect approach.[31] They are also experts at sharing information and coordinating actions, and members of one team frequently tie their activities to the activities of other teams working on different though related issues.

Team Classification

Many writers have attempted to classify teams. One helpful classification is as follows.[32] Natural work teams are made up primarily of individuals who work together as part of their regular activities. These teams, which can be either management or leadership teams, are usually given a set of designated activities to perform. Cross-functional teams, the second type, include members who have different functions within the organization. They are primarily leadership teams. Corrective action teams are management teams assigned to work on the solutions to problems that are already determined. Finally, hybrid teams address issues not addressed elsewhere in the organization. They may be either management or leadership teams, and they utilize the techniques associated with all the other types. Local public health departments use all four types of teams.

The Importance of Empowerment

Teams and their members need to be empowered by administrators to take active decision-making roles.[33] Empowerment, which gives team members the freedom to use their knowledge, experience, and skills to address important issues,[34] tends to increase their commitment to the agency and the level of their performance as well. Empowerment must come from the agency leader, and there appears to be a direct relationship between the amount of responsibility staff are given and the degree of their empowerment.[35]

The transfer of power to a team must be real and not merely nominal. A public health leadership team from a state public health leadership institute worked with a local health department to develop a lead-screening program for children. The administrator allowed the team to work on the creation of this new program because she had been told by the state to develop the program. However, the administrator viewed the team members as outsiders, and, though she told them that she had respect for them and would seriously review any recommendations they made, she used the team merely to show the state that she was complying with its request and had no intention of implementing the team's recommendations. This is an example of team activity subverted by a hidden agenda. The power to have an impact on the development of a program through recommendations was implied but was in fact an illusion.

As Figure 4–2 shows, empowerment is related to organizational values, leadership activities, human resource systems, and the structure and activities of the organization. Empowerment is often used as a tool for the improvement of programs and services.

Teams and Leadership Style

In Chapter 2, the situational leadership model was briefly discussed. The model identifies four leadership styles: directing, coaching, supporting, and delegating.

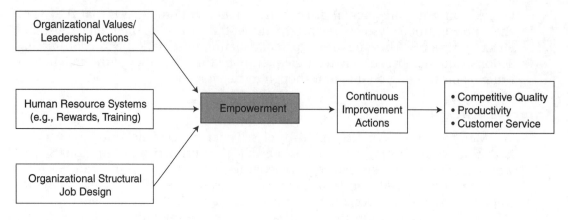

Figure 4–2 Empowerment in contemporary organizations.

This same classification can be applied to team-based activities (Figure 4–3). When a team is first created, the leader is involved in formulating the team's purpose and determining the activities to be performed. The leader, in other words, is using a directive style. During the next phase, the leader, acting as a coach, clarifies the team's activities. The leader then begins to involve team members in decision making, a process that falls into the category of providing support. In the final phase, the leader empowers the team members, and empowerment, as pointed out above, is closely related to the delegation of responsibility.

Team Preparedness

Of course, teams are at different places in their involvement in and commitment to the tasks they have been assigned, and leaders need to monitor team readiness, which ranges from unable and unwilling to carry out the team assignment to able and willing and confident (Figure 4–3). In some cases, leaders may have to utilize planning strategies for key team members as well as for the team as a whole.

One useful team technique, based on the so-called skunkworks model, is to send a team to a neutral place away from the organization to work on issues related to the team's activities.[36] The "skunkworks" is a subteam composed of experts on the topic that is the focus of the team activities. These team members tend to be transformational leaders who will move the organization forward.

Team Members

Mallory studied the characteristics of various types of team members.[37] Some members tried to take control of the activities of the team, and these he labeled *dominant* members. These individuals do well in structured situations with a well-defined purpose. The *influencers* tend to be creative and extremely talented in interpersonal relationships. They also tend to be optimistic and try to keep the team together. The *balancers* look at the big picture in an objective manner and try to reconcile the differences between the team members. The *loyalists* are committed

THE FOUR LEADERSHIP STYLES

INVOLVING
The team leader *involves* the team in setting its own goals and direction. Communication is multiway with the team leader acting as an active member.

S3

CLARIFYING
The leader *clarifies* team activities, fine-tuning roles and responsibilities. Communication is becoming more multiway between team leader and team members.

S2

S4

S1

EMPOWERING
The team leader *empowers* the team to be self-managing, letting the team establish and modify its own work processes. The team leader serves as a communication channel to the rest of the organization.

DEFINING
The team leader concentrates on focusing the team: *defining* goals, roles, and responsibilities. Communication is primarily one-way from team leader to team members.

TEAM READINESS

R4	R3	R2	R1
Able and Willing or Confident	Able but Unwilling or Insecure	Unable but Willing or Confident	Unable and Unwilling or Insecure

Figure 4–3 Leadership in a team environment.

to the status quo. Each actual team member, although mainly of one type, has at least a little of every personality characteristic associated with any of the four types. Exercise 4–2 is based on this personality typology. It is intended to get you to reflect on the type of team member you are likely to be.

Team members benefit in several ways from working on a team. First, they gain experience in working together with colleagues on a project.[38] They also learn problem-solving skills, interpersonal relationship skills, and new technological information. In addition, they learn about accountability from a personal perspective as well as a team perspective and become more committed to the team's goals and objectives.

The Life Cycle of Teams

Teams have a life cycle that is similar to the life cycle of human beings.[39] A team starts out as an infant and disbands as it ages and finishes its tasks. Organizational leaders must develop the ability to function as team leaders at each stage of the team life cycle. This is especially true in the public health field, where so many leadership activities occur in a team setting.

Following are guidelines that organizational leaders should use when creating and working with teams:

- Develop teams to address agency or community public health problems.
- Choose multidisciplinary team members for their expertise and leadership qualities.
- Allow teams to make decisions and recommendations for change. Share power and control.
- Share information.
- Intervene in the team process when necessary.
- Do not create teams to alleviate your workload.
- Use the skunkworks technique for dealing with team issues.
- Tie team development to performance standards.
- Put a time limit on the activities of the team.

LEADERSHIP AT THE AGENCY LEVEL

In a recent book on management in the health field, the authors claimed that nowadays managers have to integrate clinical practice skills and management skills.[40] The view propounded here is that public health leaders have to integrate public health practitioner skills and management and leadership skills (see Table 1–1).

Currently, public health agencies typically have a management orientation. In the 21st century they will need to become consumer and community driven.[41] The leadership expertise of agency staff will need to be increased if the agencies are to keep up with the speed of change. Figure 4–4 shows the relationship between management theories, the health care environment, clinical expertise, and consumer health care expectations. Most of the items listed are relevant to public health as well as medical care. Two missing items that pertain particularly to public health are building community coalitions and health promotion and disease prevention.

Public health agencies, along with other types of organizations, are undergoing many reforms but need to change further. For one thing, they have not fully incorporated the lessons of business. They are still run as traditional bureaucracies, although community groups are trying to take a role in the making of decisions about public health issues.

In a bureaucracy, the managers and leaders are often far removed from the daily activities of the staff,[42] yet they feel the need to control these activities. Perhaps this is one reason that Peters and Austin urged the importance of "managing by wandering around."[43] Of course it is true that leaders need to monitor operations, but they also need to delegate authority to managers and staff members.[44] By doing this, they can help make the professionals in their organization excited about coming to work in the morning. Leaders need to remember that associates are customers too.

In the late 1950s, Drucker noted that traditional bureaucratic organizations were gradually becoming knowledge-based organizations.[45] Public health agencies have always been knowledge based, and in fact the business community can learn much from the public health leaders about knowledge-based organizations and how they work.

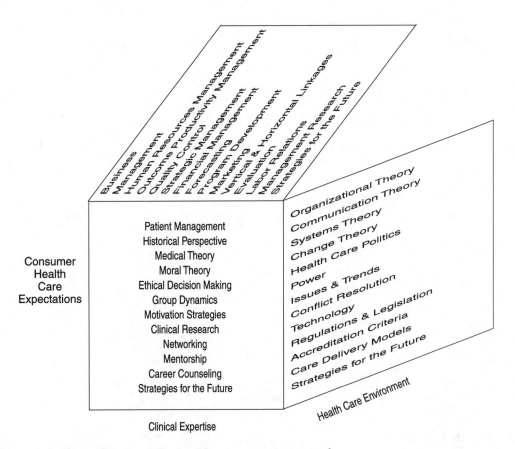

Figure 4–4 Characteristics of the health care management role.

Leaders, in order to thrive in the ever-changing environment, need to make a commitment to change and to focus on increasing customer satisfaction, fostering innovation, empowering staff, and instituting appropriate structural reforms.[46] Leadership is not just a matter of charisma; it is hard work.[47]

Nanus identified four main leadership roles (Figure 4–5).[48] First, public health leaders (to keep to the focus of this discussion) are spokespeople who present the contemporary public health issues to the community. Second, they are "direction setters" and involve community leaders in prevention activities and in the search for ways to increase the level of health in the community. Third, they act as coaches or mentors for agency associates as a means of improving the agency's effectiveness. Finally, they act as organizational change agents.

Looking into the Future

If public health leaders are oriented to change and want to become catalysts for change, they need to develop program scenarios for possible futures. This means that they should look for societal trends to guide agenda setting for the

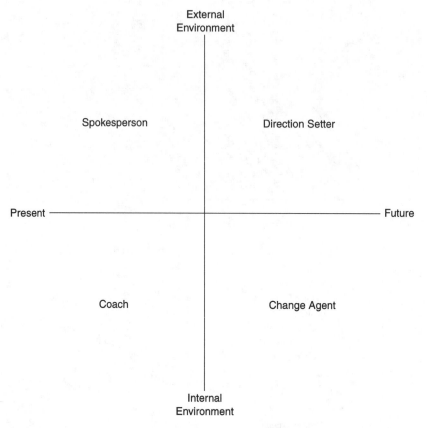

Figure 4–5 Leadership roles.

agency. They need to be students of change, in other words, and look closely at the predictions of futurists.

The social scientist Alvin Toffler tried to make sense of the changes that are occurring now by looking at past periods of vast social change.[49,50] Toffler identified three waves of societal and organizational change. The first wave was the agricultural revolution, the second was the industrial revolution, and the third, which is occurring now, is the information revolution.

Toffler developed what he called social wavefront analysis, by means of which a scientist can supposedly analyze the leading edge of a wave to predict its future. In *Creating a New Civilization,* he and Heidi Toffler examined the effects of the shift from the second wave to the third wave.[51] Political tensions have arisen between those whose thinking was formed during the industrial period and the new leaders of the information age. An interesting question can be framed regarding the present structure of government in this country. If government reflects its era, does this mean that the old governmental organizational structures, created prior to the industrial age but refashioned during that era, are now obsolete and need to be reworked to fit the information age?

If Alvin Toffler is correct, then public health will undergo major reforms in the 21st century. Even if he isn't, it is unimaginable that public health will remain perfectly static. The developments and trends likely to drive changes in public health agencies in the 21st century include the following:

- New models of public health. The direct service activities of local public health departments will continue to decline in the next 20 years.[52] New program and service models will emerge, and community-based public health activities will increase.
- Team-based problem solving. More multidisciplinary teams, both ad hoc and permanent, will be created to address public health concerns. Use of the team approach will lead to the structural leveling of organizations. Team success will empower the public health work force and increase the self-esteem of individual health professionals.
- Community health coalitions based on partnership. Public health activities take place in a community setting. Consequently, community partners as well as staff members need to be empowered. Also, partners need to have their expectations met and even exceeded.[53] If their expectations are exceeded, they will become "raving fans" of the agency.
- Privatization of assurance activities. Privatization of service provision and program development will become a reality in the future. One local health department struggled with running a mental health program in its county. It also owned the building where mental health services were provided. The program was being operated at a loss, and the health department decided to contract out the delivery of mental health services. A contract was signed (although the department kept oversight responsibility), the building was sold, and the deficit vanished.
- Decentralization of responsibilities. Community partners can do some of the work. If they become involved in public health, all sorts of activities will occur. Empowered communities address community issues.[54] Financial issues become less important because community volunteers will find a way to get things done even when the money is not there. Power must be shared to be effective.
- Communitywide governance. Governance will need to be incorporated into the activities of the agency and the activities of the community partnerships.
- Revision of values. Public health leaders not only will be protectors of the community's values but will help create new or revised value statements that reflect societal and cultural changes. It is interesting to note that politicians defend the status quo while organizational leaders support the generation of new values. Nonetheless, there seems to be a lag between the development of new values in the society and their adoption at the agency level.
- New political structures. There appears to be a trend on the horizon that may impact the future activities of agencies in the public sector. A number of states and local jurisdictions have combined public health departments with human services departments into superagencies. These mergers have caused some public health professionals to wonder whether public health has a future. However, the study of public health leaders done by the author indicated that these leaders are generally very hopeful about public health. Public health problems will not go away and will still have to be addressed by agencies headed by public health leaders.

- Third-wave leaders. The leaders of the new age are breaking down barriers to collaboration. These leaders know how to build their agencies using self-directed teams with high performance standards. Third-wave leaders also are expert at community building and empowerment. The goals of the agency become integrated with community goals. Third-wave leaders are innovative, creative, flexible, and adaptable to change.
- Integration of individual and community goals. Public health leaders must articulate the relevance of public health initiatives to the personal life of individual citizens. In an interview, one public health leader talked about an initiative designed to respond to the nationwide increase in tuberculosis cases. The leader, who worked for a congressional representative, pointed out that tuberculosis would need to be present in the representative's jurisdiction for him to be concerned about the problem. The unfortunate fact is that the societal perspective of public health practitioners—the attitude that protection of the public's health is a matter of social justice—has yet to be accepted by our elected officials.
- Complete community empowerment. Citizens as well as public health professionals need to be empowered to carry out public health activities. Empowerment leads to shared responsibility for addressing the public health needs of the local jurisdiction.
- Universal access to services. The service system of the future will be comprehensive. Programs will be integrated across agencies, and community coalitions will work together to address health needs. Leadership will be shared.

Public Health Functions

From the 1840s to the 1940s, six basic local health agency functions evolved: the collection and interpretation of vital statistics, sanitation, communicable disease control, the provision of maternal and child health programs, health education, and the provision of laboratory services.[55] In the period between 1940 and 1980, other functions were added, including the provision of environmental health services, the development and provision of personal health services, the coordination of community health services, the operation of medical care and public health facilities, areawide planning, and the assessment of the adequacy of health services. The year 1988 saw the release of the Institute of Medicine report on public health. This report promoted the use of core functions to organize the activities of public health at the community level.

Public health leaders have changed as public health has changed. They have adapted to new developments and devised innovative approaches to performing the standard public health functions. Exhibit 4–1 presents a comparison of the activities of a local health department in 1947 and 1995.

Not all states have local public health agencies. In states that do not, the state health department operates like a local agency. In states with local agencies, the activities of the state health department leaders are separate from the activities of the agency leaders. For example, state health departments have tended to stay away from the provision of direct services, especially in the case of services being provided by local public health agencies.[56] A state health department may provide

Exhibit 4–1 Comparison of Public Health Practice Performance Measures Used in 1947 and 1995

Examples of Performance Measures from Evaluation Schedule (1947)	*Consolidated Panel of Core Function–Related Performance Measures (1995)*
Hospital beds: percentage in approved hospitals	*Assessment*
Practicing physicians: population per physician	For the jurisdiction served by your local health department, is there a community needs assessment process that systematically describes the prevailing health status in the community?
Practicing dentists: population per dentist	In the past three years in your jurisdiction, has the local public health agency surveyed the population for behavioral risk factors?
Water: percentage of population in communities over 2,500 served with approved water	For the jurisdiction served by your local health agency, are timely investigations of adverse health events, including communicable disease outbreaks and environmental health hazards, conducted on an ongoing basis?
Sewerage: percentage of population in communities over 2,500 served with approved sewerage systems	Are the necessary laboratory services available to the local public health agency to support investigations of adverse health events and meet routine diagnostic and surveillance needs?
Water: percentage of rural school children served with approved water supplies	For the jurisdiction served by your local public health agency, has an analysis been completed of the determinants and contributing factors of priority health needs, adequacy of existing health resources, and the population groups most impacted?
Excreta disposal: percentage of rural school children served with approved means of excreta disposal	In the past three years in your jurisdiction, has the local public health agency conducted an analysis of age-specific participation in preventive and screening services?
Food: percentage of food handlers reached by group instruction program	
Food: percentage of restaurants and lunch counters with satisfactory facilities	*Policy Development*
Milk: percentage of bottled milk pasteurized	For the jurisdiction served by your local public health agency, is there a network of support and communication relationships that includes health-related organizations, the media, and the general public?
Diphtheria: percentage of children under 2 years given immunizing agent	In the past year in your jurisdiction, has there been a formal attempt by the local public health agency at informing elected officials about the potential public health impact of decisions under their consideration?
Smallpox: percentage of children under 2 years given immunizing agent	For the jurisdiction served by your local public health agency, has there been a prioritization of the community health needs that have been identified from a community needs assessment?
Whooping cough: percentage of children under 2 years given immunizing agent	In the past three years in your jurisdiction, has the local public health agency implemented community health initiatives consistent with established priorities?
Tuberculosis: newly reported cases per death, 5-year period	For the jurisdiction served by your local public health agency, has a community health action plan been developed with community participation to address priority community health needs?
Tuberculosis: deaths per 100,000 population, 5-year period	

continues

Exhibit 4–1 continued

Examples of Performance Measures from Evaluation Schedule (1947)	*Consolidated Panel of Core Function–Related Performance Measures (1995)*
Tuberculosis: percentage of cases reported by death certificate Syphilis: percentage of cases reported in primary, secondary, and early latent stage Syphilis: percentage of reported contacts examined Maternal: puerperal deaths per 1,000 total births, 5-year rate Maternal: percentage of antepartum cases under medical supervision seen before sixth month Maternal: percentage of women delivered at home under postpartum nursing supervision Maternal: percentage of births in hospital Infant: deaths under 1 year of age per 1,000 live births, 5-year rate Infant: deaths from diarrhea and enteritis under 1 year per 1,000 live births, 2-year rate Infant: percentage of infants under nursing supervision before 1 month School: percentage of elementary children with dental work neglected Accidents: deaths from motor accidents per 100,000 population, 5-year rate Health department budget: cents per capita spent by health department	During the past three years in your jurisdiction, has the local public health agency developed plans to allocate resources in a manner consistent with the community health action plan? *Assurance* For the jurisdiction served by your local public health agency, have resources been deployed as necessary to address the priority health needs identified in the community health needs assessment? In the past three years in your jurisdiction, has the local public health agency conducted an organizational self-assessment? For the jurisdiction served by your local public health agency, are age-specific priority health needs effectively addressed through the provision of or linkage to appropriate services? In the past three years in your jurisdiction, has there been an instance in which the local public health agency has failed to implement a mandated program or service? For the jurisdiction served by your local public health agency, have there been regular evaluations of the effect that public health services have on community health status? In the past three years in your jurisdiction, has the local public health agency used professionally recognized process and outcome measures to monitor programs and to redirect resources as appropriate? For the jurisdiction served by your local public health agency, is the public regularly provided with information about current health status, health care needs, positive health behaviors, and health care policy issues? In the past year in your jurisdiction, has the local public health agency provided reports to the media on a regular basis?

special services that the local agencies do not offer. It also is likely to be engaged in overseeing and coordinating public health activities in the state.

State health department functions include communicable disease control, tuberculosis control, venereal disease control, acquired immune deficiency syndrome (AIDS) monitoring, sanitation, industrial hygiene, dental health, laboratory services provision, public health nursing, case management, maternal and child health program provision, public health education, technical assistance, public health work force training, development of new local health departments, epidemiologic surveillance, regulation of health care facilities, licensure, inspection, cancer screening, and many more. The state health department also serves as the repository for state health data.

State health department leaders are responsible for organizing the state public health system to reflect its mission, vision, and goals and objectives. They need courage to carry out their action plans in the face of community opposition and must know how to reform the state public health system without overstepping the boundaries of the state political system, for, among other reasons, the state is the conduit for funding for local public health agency programs.

Responsibilities of Public Health Leaders

Leaders of local public health agencies have the responsibility to promote their agencies. They make sure the agencies are viewed as repositories of public health information as well as providers of high-quality programs and services. They develop relationships with the leaders of public health agencies throughout their state and also develop partnerships with community health providers.

Funding, of course, is critical for strengthening the public health system, and there is currently intense competition in the entire health industry for additional money.[57] Public health leaders need to be involved both in the allocation of public health funds and in the funding for related health service programs. They will need to make strong arguments for public revenues. Public health leaders became more entrepreneurial during the 1990s. They received grants from and developed contracts with public and private funding organizations to supplement their base budgets. Fund-raising needs to be tied to the mission and vision of the public health agency.

Public health leaders are concerned with excellence in public health. They act as role models for emerging public health leaders. They develop benchmarks for best practices. In their oversight role, they motivate community providers to improve their performance. They work with the leaders of other organizations to develop a comprehensive, integrative approach to improving public health in the community. Public health agencies do not want to duplicate programs or services adequately provided by others, although they might offer competing services if the quality of a community provider's services is open to question.

Public health agency leaders have important responsibilities toward agency staff. They must honestly monitor and evaluate job performance and job satisfaction.[58] If job evaluations are done fairly and regularly, staff will be able to learn their full job responsibilities and meet them more effectively. In addition, public health leaders must be enthusiastic about the task of protecting public health and be able to motivate their colleagues to be enthusiastic as well, by fostering collaboration and sharing power with them, for example.[59] They also should cheer colleagues and their progress. Einstein's formula $e = mc^2$ has been reinterpreted as enthusiasm equals mission times cash and congratulations. People have to be cheered and they also have to be paid for their efforts.

As noted already, leaders need to empower agency staff. Empowerment must occur at the team level, the agency level, and the community level. Exhibit 4–2 presents a list of principles of empowerment.

Exhibit 4–2 Ten Principles of Empowerment

1. Tell people what their responsibilities are.
2. Give them authority equal to the responsibilities assigned to them.
3. Set standards for excellence.
4. Provide them with training that will enable them to meet the standards.
5. Give them knowledge and information.
6. Provide them with feedback on their performance.
7. Recognize them for their achievements.
8. Trust them.
9. Give them permission to fail.
10. Treat them with dignity and respect.

In summation, at the agency level public health leaders have the responsibility to

- understand how the agency functions
- delegate authority whenever possible
- monitor client satisfaction
- make structural changes in the agency to accommodate new or emerging public health issues
- explore alternate futures for the agency
- apply the core functions model to agency activities
- empower the agency staff and the community residents

LEADERSHIP AT THE COMMUNITY LEVEL

Leadership at the community level requires skills that are not needed at the team and agency levels. At this level, public health leaders work to increase the visibility of the public health agency. In interviews with 100 American public health leaders, the author found consistent agreement that the public lacked in-depth knowledge about public health. Thus, public health leaders have a duty to provide public health information to the business community, the medical community, and the general public.

Figure 4–6 shows the dimensions of public health leadership. Public health leaders build on the core functions model regardless of the level of leadership while taking into account the political and social realities that impact the agency and the community. Public health agencies must take into consideration social and political issues if they are to survive. For one thing, they are mandated by funding sources to provide certain basic services and programs. (This raises the issue of the proper balance between mandated services and community-based services and programs not included in the mandated services protocol.)

The Nature of Community

Over the last couple of decades, business discovered community.[60] Business leaders now see that community involvement needs to be part of the practice of

Figure 4-6 Dimensions of public health leadership.

business. Public health agencies, by their nature, serve communities, but serving a group of citizens who live in a specified geographic area does not mean that community issues are being addressed. The author's study of public health leaders found that their efforts at developing community coalitions have been uneven at best. Almost all of the respondents stated that public health agencies have not been successful in getting the public to understand public health.

Community is more than bricks and mortar. It is more than a place to live. It is the place in which our dreams and aspirations are or are not fulfilled. When we talk about improvement in our quality of life, community is part of the improvement process. Community is the place where values are put into action. Community is a complex system made up of individuals, families, politicians, health organizations, human services agencies, churches, schools, businesses, business organizations, and so on (Figure 4-7). It is a system that accepts challenges, and to develop the resources to deal with them it needs to be built on the strengths of its constituent parts, not on their weaknesses.[61]

One view currently prevalent is that we need to rediscover civility.[62] Civility requires that community leaders be open to the opinions of other people and other organizations. Further, public health leaders must transfer the leadership skills they use at the team and organizational levels to the community level. Leaders build communities in all their leadership activities.

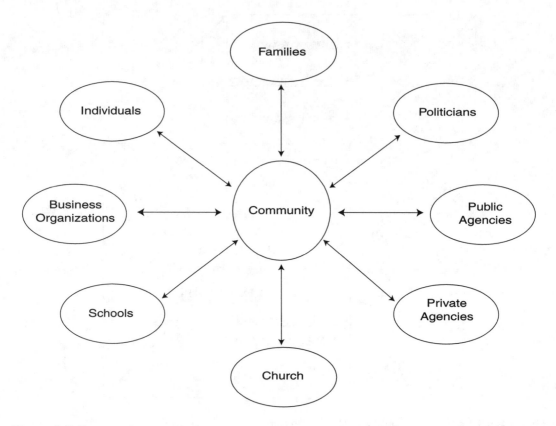

Figure 4–7 Community constituents.

It should be noted that public health concerns are part of almost every crisis that confronts a community. Exercise 4–3 is intended to explore what is likely to occur when a community experiences a natural disaster.

Advocacy through the Media

Media advocacy is an important way to promote public health programs and services.[63] Public health leaders should learn how to use the media to create support for agency goals. For example, they should consider sending letters on a regular basis to newspapers and other sources to increase the visibility of public health.

Think of the importance of using the media in the following situation: a public health leader in a conservative, middle-class community discovers that five cases of human immunodeficiency virus infection have recently been discovered. A statistic like this can hit the nerve center of a community. It is the public health leader who will have the skills to defuse the crisis and get community constituents to become partners in dealing with the problem.

One of the most important responsibilities of public health leaders is to promote prevention at the community level.[64] Our knowledge of health and disease is constantly growing, and new technologies and community-based prevention strategies are continually being developed to address public health concerns. The public needs to be convinced of the importance of using these technologies and strategies. It is the job of public health leaders to make the case.

Linking Programs

There is a good argument that public health programs should be linked together where possible.[65] The Centers for Disease Control and Prevention has helped create prevention research centers in a number of universities. Many if not all of these centers rely on community support to carry out their activities. Public health leaders, who see the future of their agencies as tied to primary prevention rather than direct services, know that linkage to academic programs will strengthen the infrastructure of public health in their communities.

Community Building

Community building is a complex process that does not occur overnight. Peck analyzed it into four stages.[66] In the first stage, various community representatives who have formed a coalition pretend to have the community's interests at heart in order to gain acceptance for their own agendas. Peck called this the pseudocommunity stage. The second stage, which begins when the coalition realizes that community concerns are not being addressed, is one of chaos. Next comes the stage of emptiness, in which the leaders have to empty themselves of all their preconceived notions about the community and its concerns. It is extremely difficult for the leaders to leave their agendas at the door. The fourth stage is when true community comes into being.

Organizations involved in building a community need leaders.[67] These leaders must be students of the community and its culture and be able to involve individuals with different power bases in community change. Since each community resident has an agenda to which he or she is committed, leaders have to find ways to reconcile the differing agendas.

Community coalitions ideally should be learning organizations.[68] The members of a coalition need to examine their predispositions and how these predispositions affect the community-building process. In addition, the scientific perspective needs to be incorporated into the group's deliberations.

Community building is best achieved through the use of collaborative leadership.[69] Following are 10 factors that can contribute to the success of collaboration and community building:

1. good timing and a clear need
2. strong stakeholder groups
3. broad-based involvement
4. credibility and openness of process
5. commitment and/or involvement of high-level leaders
6. support or acquiescence of "established" authorities or powers
7. overcoming mistrust and skepticism
8. strong leadership of the process
9. interim successes
10. a shift to broader concerns[70]

Coalition Building

Coalition building is an important part of empowering communities. Public health agencies can no longer work in isolation. Community leaders need to be involved in addressing public health issues. The major advantage of a coalition is that all voices are heard and programs can be developed that better reflect the health needs of the community. The major disadvantage is that being part of a coalition is time consuming.

Cohen, Baer, and Satterwhite developed an eight-step model for developing community coalitions (Exhibit 4–3).[71] The model is based on the experience of the Contra Costa County (California) Health Services Department Prevention Program. The authors define a coalition as a group of interested parties (individuals and organizations) that want to influence the attempt to solve a critical problem. The coalition members need to develop strategies for each of the eight steps and know when to move to the next step.

A coalition can have many advantages. It can help to save resources. It can influence a large number of people in a community through its diversified membership. It can create an agenda that is more comprehensive than the agenda of any single community organization. It can create a network for the sharing of information, a network that could be used beneficially by the local public health agency for purposes of marketing and fostering change in the community. In addition, coalition members gain satisfaction when they see positive things happen, and a coalition can influence emerging grass-roots organizations as they explore their roles in the community.

Building community through coalitions that are responsible and credible is an important goal of public health leaders. A recent report from the Centers for Disease Control and Prevention stated that public health should use a process called community engagement.[72] Community engagement involves collaboration between people who are in the same geographic area, share special interests, or are in similar situations. A mixture of social science and art, community engagement integrates the ideas of culture, community, coalition building, and collaboration. The report reviewed the literature for examples of successful engagement and presented a list of the principles of community engagement (Exhibit 4–4).

Partnerships are collaborative relationships that involve more than minimal cooperation. They tend to evolve through the same steps outlined in the systems

---

Exhibit 4–3 Eight Steps To Building an Effective Coalition

STEP 1   Analyze the program's objectives and determine whether to form a coalition.
STEP 2   Recruit the right people.
STEP 3   Devise a set of preliminary objectives and activities.
STEP 4   Convene the coalition.
STEP 5   Anticipate the necessary resources.
STEP 6   Define elements of a successful coalition structure.
STEP 7   Maintain coalition vitality.
STEP 8   Make improvements through evaluation.

Exhibit 4–4 Characteristics of Successful Community Engagement

- Community engagement efforts should address multiple levels of the social environment, rather than only individual behaviors, to bring about desired changes.
- Health behaviors are influenced by culture. To ensure that engagement efforts are culturally and linguistically appropriate, they must be developed from a knowledge and respect for the targeted community's culture.
- People participate when they feel a sense of community, see their involvement and the issues as relevant and worth their time, and view the process and organizational climate of participation as open and supportive of their right to have a voice in the process.
- While it cannot be externally imposed on a community, a sense of empowerment—the ability to take action, influence, and make decisions on critical issues—is crucial to successful engagement efforts.
- Community mobilization and self-determination frequently need nurturing. Before individuals and organizations can gain control and influence and become players and partners in community health decision making and action, they may need additional knowledge, skills, and resources.
- Coalitions, when adequately supported, can be useful vehicles for mobilizing and using community assets for health decision making and action.
- Participation is influenced by whether community members believe that the benefits of participation outweigh the costs. Community leaders can use their understanding of perceived costs to develop appropriate incentives for participation.

model of organizational change (see Chapter 3). Partnerships have a vision and a mission, they have goals and objectives, and they develop and implement action plans and evaluate their degree of success. The late Reverend Everett Hageman was a major supporter of leadership development in public health, and the author spent many hours talking to him about the importance of partnership. After Hageman's death, the author put together a list of principles based on discussions with him. The principles that pertain to partnerships are given below:

- Leave time to get to know your community partners on a personal level.
- Partnership is part of the human condition.
- Working together is better than fighting.
- Learn by listening to your partners.
- True partnership is the gourmet approach to organization.

Each community coalition needs to be revitalized on a regular basis. A community coalition often seems to work better when a community crisis is occurring.[73] When the crisis is over, people tend to move away from the coalition back to their own personal agendas. Thus, public health leaders need to be aware of this fact and make an extra effort to keep community coalitions alive after crises are resolved.

National and International Communities

Thus far the discussion has been on leadership in local communities, but there are also national and international communities that offer an arena for action by public health leaders. National leaders, like local leaders, act as advocates for public health. They keep the public informed about health issues. They work on the construction of a national mission and vision as well as public health goals for the future. They collaborate with leaders at the state level on the creation of a coordinated nationwide approach to public health. They collaborate with national elected officials to address key public health concerns, including the training of the public health work force.

On the international level, public health leaders implement public health programs in countries where public health is not a priority. These leaders need to develop skills to enhance their ability to improve the quality of life of people in these countries. Rather than reinvent public health, these leaders develop networks with public health leaders throughout the world to share model program methods for addressing specific public health problems. As already stated, public health leaders need to think globally about public health concerns while acting locally (to protect community residents from potential health crises). Building healthy communities is partially a matter of applying knowledge gained from all parts of the world to local conditions.

Most of the strategies and techniques discussed in this chapter have universal application. Below is a list of guidelines of special pertinence for public health leaders working at the community level:

- Build trust.
- Form coalitions.
- Develop partnerships.
- Teach community groups about the core public health functions.
- Do community building with partners.
- See the community as a system.
- Encourage coalitions or partnerships to continue after a public health crisis has been resolved.
- Use the media to promote best practices in public health.
- Push a prevention agenda.

LEADERSHIP AT THE PROFESSIONAL LEVEL

Despite the multidisciplinary nature of public health, its leaders need to speak with a unified voice. Public health as a profession takes precedence over the particular educational backgrounds of the public health work force. The following situation occurs much too often. A physician with almost no background in public health was appointed the administrator of a large county health department. He made decisions from a medical viewpoint and felt that physicians were the only ones who were qualified to do the department's work. He ran the department using a direct medical service approach and totally ignored the population-based approach to public health.

Public health practitioners tend not to travel to professional meetings or for professional development. Many local health departments have a small staff and are reluctant to let employees go to meetings. Funds for professional development are generally minimal, and paying for professional development is typically considered by taxpayers to be a waste of money. Yet public health leaders know that it is important to communicate with other public health professionals. Some of these leaders go to the annual meetings held by the various public health associations and even take a leadership role in these associations. They help to create public health policy that will trickle down to the local public health programs. Leadership development training seems to be a factor here. For example, the last nine presidents of the Illinois Public Health Association were either faculty members or fellows of the Illinois Public Health Leadership Institute.

Public health leaders need to become active participants of the American Public Health Association (APHA). This association represents all segments of the professional public health work force. It is at the annual meetings of the APHA that national public health policy tends to be made. Leaders should also consider taking key roles in the various associations for state and county public health directors. Board of health leaders can also become involved in a national organization for boards. Following is a list of guidelines for leaders who wish to make a mark in the profession of public health:

- Promote public health as a profession.
- Encourage staff to become involved in state and national public health associations.
- Be active in state and national public health associations.
- Run for office in these associations.

SUMMARY

Leaders need to operate on five different levels. On the most basic level, they need to know how to exert their influence as leaders on other individuals person to person. To do this, they need a whole range of skills and abilities, from communication skills to the ability to balance work and private life.

They also must be capable of functioning in teams, either as team leaders or as ordinary team members. Some of the leadership skills needed for teamwork are also needed on the personal level, but some are different.

Public health leaders are often the heads of public health departments or agencies, and so they need agency-level leadership skills as well. Their duties as agency heads include such things as mission and vision statement development, fund-raising, job performance evaluation, and role modeling.

Public health is obviously community oriented, and so public health leaders need to be able to play a major role in the community, by acting as advocates on public health issues and building coalitions to deal with such issues. They thus need advocacy skills and coalition-building skills, among others.

Finally, public health leaders, like other public health practitioners, have an obligation to try to improve the field of public health, by becoming involved, for instance, in professional organizations such as the APHA.

Discussion Questions

1. What is the difference between politics and governance?
2. What is the relationship between communication and empowerment?

3. What are several of the main barriers preventing public health leaders from being as effective as they could be?
4. What is one way public health leaders can deal with the increasing cultural diversity in the public health work force?
5. What are some of the main reasons for creating and using teams?
6. What are the main agency-related responsibilities of public health leaders?
7. What are the main community-related responsibilities of public health leaders?
8. How do partnerships differ from other types of collaborative relationships?
9. How can public health leaders further the interests of the public health profession?

Exercise 4–1

THE DRAWBACKS AND BENEFITS OF PROFESSIONAL DIVERSITY

Purpose: to explore how professional diversity impacts public health decision making

Key concepts: decision making, diversity, professionalism

Procedure: There has been an increase in teen gang violence in Midcity over the last 10 years. The mayor and the city council have asked the Midcity Department of Health to develop a plan to address this public health problem. The class should divide into teams to discuss the problem. Each team will have a designated leader from a different profession (e.g., physician, nurse, social scientist, environmental health specialist, or business expert). In addition to discussing the issue at hand, which should be done for half an hour, each team should reserve 5–10 minutes to examine how the professional background of the leader influenced the process and the outcome of the discussion. Each team will then report its conclusions and observations to the class as a whole.

Exercise 4–2

LEADERSHIP AND TEAM-BUILDING

Purpose: to explore leadership behavior in team situations

Key concepts: team building, leadership in teams, leadership style

Procedure: Using the Mallory's personality typology, each group member, using the worksheet, should classify him- or herself as one personality type or as a combination of types and analyze the degree to which he or she possesses the characteristics associated with all four types. The group should then break into teams and discuss the results of the self-evaluations, focusing on issues that are critical to team development, such as team communication, discussion facilitation, consensus development, priority setting, and conflict resolution.

Exhibit 4–2–A Worksheet for Team-building

Utilizing the personality typology for leaders, classify yourself relative to the percentage of each type that you may have. Fill out worksheet and discuss it with your team. The discussion will help you see issues that are critical to team development.

1. Name

2. Personality Type
                           % of this type
   Dominant
   Influencer
   Balancer
   Loyalist

3. Previous outstanding achievements in team activity, if applicable.

4. Previous problems in team activity, if applicable.

5. Outstanding achievements in overall job performance.

6. Problems in job performance.

7. How you act under pressure.

8. How you react to a lack of structure.

9. Ability to get along with others.

10. Potential future position in agency.

11. Current extracurricular activities requiring teamwork.

Exercise 4–3

A COMMUNITY IN CRISIS

Purpose: to explore the role public health leaders play in dealing with a natural disaster

Key concepts: collaboration, community crisis, strategic planning

Procedure: In February, California is hit by storm after storm. The town of Crisona is flooded for a two-week period, the entire town is evacuated, and eventually mudslides begin to occur in the surrounding hills.

The class should divide into teams of 6–10 members. In each team, half the members are assigned to play the role of Crisona City Council members, including the role of the mayor and of the head of the Crisona Department of Public Health. The remaining team members are to act as community leaders. These leaders and the head of the Department of Public Health testify about the disaster and offer suggestions for addressing it. The city council listens to the testimony and then works with the community leaders to develop a strategy for dealing with the crisis. The whole team should develop a one-page consensus statement outlining a strategy for responding to the crisis.

Case Study 4–A

A Leadership Interview with Joyce C. Lashof, MD

Shirley F. Randolph

Joyce C. Lashof, MD, is Dean Emeritus, School of Public Health, University of California at Berkeley. Her most recent previous positions include President of the American Public Health Association; Dean, School of Public Health, University of California at Berkeley; President, Association of Schools of Public Health; Assistant Director, Office of Technology Assessment, U.S. Congress; Senior Scholar in Residence, Institute of Medicine, National Academy of Sciences; Deputy Assistant Secretary for Health Programs and Deputy Assistant Secretary for Population Affairs, U.S. Department of Health, Education and Welfare; and Director, Illinois Department of Public Health.

The first name that comes to mind when one thinks of women leaders in the field of public health is Joyce C. Lashof, MD. Dr. Lashof has done it all. After three decades in public health leadership positions, she is, quite simply, the quintessential public health leader.

And she did it all while successfully integrating her workplace duties with her responsibilities as the wife of a university professor (her husband, Richard, is a well-known mathematician and the mother of three children (one son and two daughters)—two of whom have made Joyce and Richard grandparents, and all of whom are growing as young professionals in their chosen fields. Her insights into leadership issues, particularly as they apply to women, are perceptive and fascinating.

One of the first areas Dr. Lashof and I explored during a recent interview dealt with the challenge women often experience when faced with men as "gatekeepers" to upward mobility. Dr. Lashof was asked:

What have been your greatest challenges when confronting the male monopoly on power and men as gatekeepers on the upward path to leadership?

Her response: There was definitely a problem early in my career. Moving up depended a good deal on having a mentor who paved the way. At the beginning of my career, after I received my MD from Woman's Medical College of Pennsylvania and completed my residency in medicine at Montefiore Hospital in New York, I went to the University of Chicago first as a physician at the Student Health Services and then as an assistant professor in the Department of Medicine.

I served year to year on a one-year appointment for three years and then asked for a regular three-year appointment. I was told by the chairman of the Department of Medicine that he would never give a married woman a tenured track appointment because she would leave and go where her husband's career took him. Needless to say, I was unhappy about the situation and told him "thanks, but no thanks" to another one-year appointment. That was in 1960. At that time, of course, there were no laws about discrimination and affirmative action.

Luckily, colleagues referred me to Dr. Mark Lepper at the University of Illinois, College of Medicine, and Presbyterian-St. Luke's Hospital, Chicago. Mark offered me a faculty appointment in the Department of Preventive Medicine at the University of Illinois and arranged an appointment as assistant attending physician at Presbyterian-St. Luke's Hospital. This led to a series of succeeding appointments and long-term collaboration.

In many ways, Mark was a mentor who opened doors for me. Most specifically, he appointed me research director of a study of health needs of poverty populations funded by the Office of Equal Opportunity (OEO). It was this study that led to recommendations that health centers to serve the disadvantaged be opened in Chicago. The study was well received by OEO and resulted in the further development of a proposal to open a health center on Chicago's West Side. The West Side's Mile Square organization approached Presbyterian-St. Luke's about developing such a health center. We put together a proposal for an OEO-funded Mile Square health center. The proposal was successful and Mile Square Health Center was the second OEO-funded health center in the country. I served as its director for five years.

During this same period of time, I was promoted to attending physician and Director, Section of Community Medicine, at Presbyterian-St. Luke's Hospital. As the only woman to head up a section, during staff meetings I was the lone woman sitting around the table with all the men. They were more or less accepting of me, but I could sense that in their eyes I was not quite an equal. I walked a thin line between asserting myself and not being too assertive.

When Dan Walker became Illinois' government in 1973, he said he was going to appoint women to his cabinet. He did and I became the first woman to be named the director of a state public health department. I think I ought to thank the women's movement!

What changes in the male monopoly are occurring as we move into a new era with a new vision about women as leaders and managers?

Response: Things are certainly changing. Obviously there are now laws against overt discrimination against women. But just as important as the legal ramifications of discriminating against women (or anyone else), the fact is that women have proved themselves capable and are accepted as leaders and managers. In addition, women are networking more. Not being the only woman sitting around a table with a group of men makes a real difference in relationships with colleagues. And the younger generation of men are much more accepting of women in peer relationships. Men who are not comfortable with women as leaders and managers and who do not accept them as colleagues are a dying breed.

How did you counteract the obstacle of discrimination in the workplace because you are a woman? Was discrimination more or less a problem as you moved from mid-level management to top leadership roles?

Response: Of course the way I counteracted the first obstacle at the University of Chicago was by leaving. Beyond that, I think I just did the best job I knew how to do. I worked hard to be sure that I met *every* expectation and did not give anyone any excuses to criticize me because of my gender.

Then again, sometimes I just ignored the problems and sometimes I took little actions. For example, at Presbyterian-St. Luke's, we would sit around the table and select interns and residents. We would come to a woman applicant and the men would make comments like "Let's take her...she is really attractive." I would wait until we came to a likely male applicant and then I would say, "Yes, I think we should take him...he's quite a handsome fellow."

Problems related to discrimination because of my gender became less and less as I moved up. It was easier working with younger men and women. But, some of the "old-timers," both in terms of age and length of service in an agency, were still a problem that had to be faced.

Is it your sense that leadership opportunities are increasing or decreasing for top leadership positions for women?

Response: In many ways top leadership opportunities for women are increasing. For instance, more women are serving as directors of state health departments, as deans of schools of public health, and in high-level leadership positions at all levels of government. On the other hand, I look at medical school professorships and I'm not sure that the number of women professors has increased. I think people are looking for women to fill leadership roles, but it is still a problem when you look at the top jobs.

Are the opportunities for women to fill leadership positions greater or lesser in the field of public health?

Response: There are greater opportunities for women in public health. I think one reason for this is the more liberal nature of the public health field, the result being more opportunities and less discrimination. Public health professionals have a commitment to equality, social justice, women's rights, minority rights, etc. In addition, a career in public health often gives a woman the opportunity to be a leader in politics and in government by virtue of the position she holds.

Are the attributes and characteristics of successful women leaders different than they are for successful men leaders?

Response: Women's leadership styles tend to be different from men's to some degree. Whether those differences are the things that account for success is the question. Are women more successful as leaders because they have different values and styles? This is a research question and an issue that is currently being studied. In my experience, especially earlier on in my career, I found women to be more sympathetic, compassionate, much less aggressive, less domineering and more inclusive...all very valuable traits when one looks at leadership. We know now that research studies regarding capable leadership indicate that those who have an inclusive leadership style are more effective. Obviously, there are always exceptions to this rule. Taken as a whole, the inclusive leadership approach is lower key; it is more sharing and more "motherly." One of the best compliments I received as assistant director of the Office of Technology Assessment was that "I was good at 'mothering' them, but I could also kick their rears when I needed to!"

In addition to being a successful public health leader in a variety of fora, you are also a wife, mother, and grandmother. How did you integrate the workplace with your private life responsibilities and "juggle" the complexities that resulted from your various roles?

Response: It has been a real juggling act! Of course, things got easier as my three children grew up, but at times it was wild! One of the very conscious decisions I made early on in my career was to move toward public health and research in the medical care area because it was less competitive and that would result in a less intensive demand on my time, which gave me more time to be with my family. Before I made this decision, I had been working in infectious diseases. I observed how competitive this field was and felt that with three young children at home it wasn't what I wanted to do. I wanted to be home with my husband and children at night and on the weekends, holidays, etc. When the children were all in school and busy with their individual activities, the balancing act became easier. Also, I was very fortunate in having the same full-time housekeeper for over 20 years.

My need to spend time with my family was one of the main reasons why I decided to go into public health and medical care research. It was really serendipity...opportunity knocked through Mark Lepper's mentoring and I was there.

The present job market is very competitive for public health practitioners regardless of gender. What leadership skills are most important for women to cultivate who are presently at the lower and middle levels of a public health organization?

Response: First and foremost, one needs to know one's field. One has to be looked at as one who is a good problem solver. My advice is to learn how to be objective and analytical and how to be fair. Other important leadership skills include developing an inclusive leadership style, learning how to be a good listener and to reflect on what you hear. One leadership skill that is absolutely essential is knowing how to relate well to other people and to be honest in those relationships.

As public health redefines its role within a new health care delivery system that is likely to emerge as the result of some form of health care reform, will there be different or "new" opportunities for women in public health leadership positions?

Response: If the whole health care system becomes more and more competitive through a corporate approach, some women will be able to fit into that structure as leaders. If we move into a system that is accountable for populations (core functions included), opportunities for women to attain top leadership positions certainly should increase. As public health grows and strengthens its positions as an integral part of the health care delivery system, there will be increasing leadership opportunities for both women and men.

REFERENCES

1. P.M. Senge et al., *The Dance of Change* (New York: Bantam, 1999).
2. A. DeLaney, *Politics for Dummies* (Foster City, CA: IDG Books, 1995).

3. P. Capezio and D. Morehouse, *Secrets of Breakthrough Leadership* (Franklin Lakes, NJ: Career Press, 1997).
4. E. Tosca, *Communication Skills Profile* (San Francisco: Jossey-Bass, 1997).
5. D. Tannen, *You Just Don't Understand: Women and Men in Conversation* (New York: Morrow, 1990).
6. J.W. Gardner, *On Leadership* (New York: The Free Press, 1990).
7. R. Kelley, *The Power of Followership* (New York: Doubleday, 1992).
8. J. Carver, *Boards That Make a Difference*, 2d ed. (San Francisco: Jossey-Bass, 1997).
9. V. Mamlin-Upshaw, "Creating Effective Boards," *Leadership* 2, no. 3 (1993): 1, 11.
10. J.W. Dearing and E.M. Rogers, "Agenda-setting," *Communication Concepts* 6 (1992): 1–98.
11. B.J. Turnock, *Public Health: What It Is and How It Works* (Gaithersburg, MD: Aspen Publishers, 1997).
12. Turnock, *Public Health*.
13. Turnock, *Public Health*.
14. S.R. Covey, *The Seven Habits of Highly Effective People* (New York: Simon & Schuster, 1989).
15. M.M. Chemers, "Contemporary Leadership Theory," in *The Leader's Companion*, ed. J.T. Wren (New York: The Free Press, 1995).
16. R. Hargrove, *Mastering the Art of Creative Collaboration* (New York: McGraw-Hill Business Week Books, 1998).
17. Turnock, *Public Health*.
18. S. Wellington, "Breaking the Glass Ceiling," *Leader to Leader* 6 (1997): 37–42.
19. R.R. Thomas Jr., "Diversity and Organizations of the Future," in *The Organization of the Future*, ed. F. Hesselbein et al. (San Francisco: Jossey-Bass, 1997).
20. A.H. Maslow, *Motivation and Personality* (New York: Harper & Row, 1954).
21. J.R. O'Neil, *The Paradox of Success* (New York: Jeremy P. Tarcher and Putnam, 1993).
22. Capezio and Morehouse, *Secrets of Breakthrough Leadership*.
23. S. Helgesen, "Women and the New Economy," *Leader to Leader* 4 (1997): 34–39.
24. C. Mallory, *Team-Building* (Shawnee Mission, KS: National Press Publications, 1991).
25. S.P. Robbins and M. Coulter, *Management*, 6th ed. (Upper Saddle River, NJ: Prentice Hall, 1999).
26. Mallory, *Team-Building*.
27. Mallory, *Team-Building*.
28. P.F. Drucker, *Management: Tasks, Responsibilities, Practices* (New York: Harper & Row, 1985).
29. J.R. Katzenbach and D.K. Smith, *The Wisdom of Teams* (Boston: Harvard Business School Press, 1993).
30. K. Blanchard et al., *The One Minute Manager Builds High Performance Teams* (New York: Morrow, 1990).
31. P.M. Senge, *The Fifth Discipline Fieldbook* (New York: Doubleday, 1999).
32. P. Capezio, *Supreme Teams: How To Make Teams Really Work* (Shawnee Mission, KS: National Press Pub., 1996).
33. R.S. Wellins et al., *Empowered Teams* (San Francisco: Jossey-Bass, 1991).
34. K. Blanchard et al., *The Three Keys to Empowerment* (San Francisco: Berrett-Koehler, 1999).
35. Wellins et al., *Empowered Teams*.
36. T. Peters and N. Austin, *A Passion for Excellence* (New York: Random House, 1985).
37. Mallory, *Team-Building*.
38. J.R. Katzenbach and D.K. Smith, *The Wisdom of Teams* (Boston: Harvard Business School Press, 1993).
39. Capezio, *Supreme Teams*.
40. J.G. Liebler et al., *Management Principles for Health Professionals*, 2d ed. (Gaithersburg, MD: Aspen Publishers, 1992).
41. Liebler et al., *Management Principles for Health Professionals*.
42. J.Q. Wilson, *Bureaucracy* (New York: Basic Books, 1989).
43. Peters and Austin, *A Passion for Excellence*.
44. K. Blanchard and S. Bowles, *Gung Ho* (New York: Morrow, 1998).
45. P.F. Drucker, *Landmarks of Tomorrow* (New York: Harper & Row, 1957).
46. T. Peters, *Thriving on Chaos* (New York: Knopf, 1987).
47. P.F. Drucker, *Managing for the Future* (New York: Truman, Talley Books, and Dutton, 1992).
48. B. Nanus, *Visionary Leadership* (San Francisco: Jossey-Bass, 1992).
49. A. Toffler, *The Third Wave* (New York: Bantam, 1980).
50. A. Toffler and H. Toffler, *Creating a New Civilization* (Atlanta: Turner Publishing Co., 1994).
51. Toffler and Toffler, *Creating a New Civilization*.
52. P.K. Halverson et al., *Managed Care and Public Health* (Gaithersburg, MD: Aspen Publishers, 1998).
53. K. Blanchard and S. Bowles, *Raving Fans* (New York: Morrow, 1993).
54. M. DePree, *Leading without Power* (San Francisco: Jossey-Bass, 1997).
55. W. Shonick, *Government and Health Services* (New York: Oxford University Press, 1995).

56. Shonick, *Government and Health Services.*
57. Turnock, *Public Health.*
58. D.J. Breckon, *Managing Health Promotion Programs* (Gaithersburg, MD: Aspen Publishers, 1997).
59. J.M. Kouzes and B.Z. Posner, *The Leadership Challenge*, 2d ed. (San Francisco: Jossey-Bass, 1995).
60. F. Hesselbein et al., eds., *The Community of the Future* (San Francisco: Jossey-Bass, 1998).
61. J.P. Kretzman and J.L. McKnight, *Building Communities from the Inside Out* (Evanston, IL: Northwestern University Center for Urban Affairs, 1993).
62. M.S. Peck, *A World Waiting To Be Born* (New York: Bantam Books, 1993).
63. L. Wallack and L. Dorfman, "Media Advocacy: A Strategy for Advancing Policy and Promoting Health," *Health Education Quarterly* 23, no. 3 (1996): 293–317.
64. R.C. Brownson and E.A. Baker, "Prevention in the Community: Taking Stock," *Journal of Public Health Management and Practice* 4, no. 2 (1998): vi–vii.
65. R.C. Brownson et al., "Demonstration Projects in Community-based Prevention," *Journal of Public Health Management and Practice* 4, no. 2 (1998): 66–77.
66. M.S. Peck, *The Different Drum* (New York: Simon & Schuster, 1987).
67. R.H. Rosen, *Leading People* (New York: Viking, 1996).
68. P.M. Senge, "Creating Quality Communities," in *Community-building*, ed. K. Gozdz (San Francisco: New Leaders Press, 1995).
69. D.D. Chrislip and C.E. Larson, *Collaborative Leadership* (San Francisco: Jossey-Bass, 1994).
70. Chrislip and Larson, *Collaborative Leadership.*
71. L. Cohen et al., *Developing Effective Coalitions: An Eight Stage Guide* (Pleasant Hill, CA: Contra Costa County Health Services Department Prevention Programs, 1994).
72. Centers for Disease Control and Prevention, Agency for Toxic Substances and Disease Registry, *Principles of Community Engagement* (Atlanta: CDC Public Health Practice Program Office, 1997).
73. Peck, *A World Waiting To Be Born.*

Leadership Applications in Public Health

Chapter 5

Introduction to the Core Functions of Public Health

...The underlying premise of Healthy People 2010 is that the health of the individual is almost inseparable from the larger community and that the health of every community in every state and territory determines the overall health status of the Nation.

Healthy People 2010

Part II focuses on the core functions of public health—assessment, policy development, and assurance—and the role of leadership in ensuring that these functions are carried out effectively by public health organizations. This chapter introduces the core functions, and the next three chapters each discuss one of the functions in detail.

The overall mission of public health, as noted already, is to fulfill "society's interest in assuring the conditions in which people can be healthy."[1(p.4)] What this means, of course, needs to be spelled out, and one way of doing this is to divide the mission into its main parts, or core functions. There are various sets of core functions one might choose, but the trio mentioned above is certainly among the most defensible. Protecting and improving the general health of people in the community (the mission of public health) must begin with an evaluation of the current level of health and the current threats to health in the community (assessment). Following the assessment comes the step of developing policies to address the health threats or problems. Then the policies are implemented to improve the public's health (assurance). This step can be viewed as the last in a three-step process, but it must be followed by an evaluation of the effectiveness of the implementation, which evaluation will start the whole process over again, for the evaluation will undoubtedly uncover further problems or show the implementation was only partially successful, leading to further policy development and implementation (Figure 5–1).

CORE FUNCTIONS OF PUBLIC HEALTH

Many human service fields struggle with the issue of credibility. Part of the lack of credibility is due to the fact that the public often does not understand the

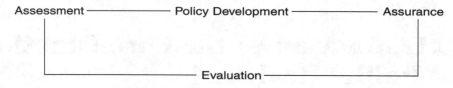

Figure 5–1 The government role in health.

---

nature of the services being provided. Developing a paradigm can help to increase public understanding. A paradigm of public health, for example, can define the structure and parameters of public health work. The core functions model of public health is such a paradigm.

A paradigm is a map that elucidates a major area of endeavor.[2] Public health leaders, to an extent, see the world in terms of core functions (or, in other words, a core functions paradigm). They also see it in terms of a leadership paradigm and a management paradigm. Sometimes leaders will substantially revise a paradigm or replace it with another. This is called a paradigm shift.[3] A paradigm shift, which usually takes a long time to be completed, creates a new set of rules.

The Future of Public Health first described the core functions paradigm.[4] The functions of assessment, policy development, and assurance are tied to the phases of public health practice. Assessment involves the identification of health problems, policy development involves the identification of possible solutions, and assurance involves the implementation of the supposed solutions (usually in the form of programs and services). Public health leaders have major responsibilities associated with each core function.

Policy development is seen as linking assessment to assurance. In reality, policy development is often an afterthought in the American public health system—that is, assurance activities sometimes occur before policies are developed. Many public health leaders with whom the author has spoken nevertheless have pointed out that leaders need to be effective in the policy development area if they are to create a comprehensive public health system.

One limitation of the core functions model is that it does not show the interaction between the functions. A second limitation is that "the concepts of assessment, policy development, and assurance, while useful in the public health community itself, have been difficult to translate into effective messages for key stakeholders, including elected officials and community groups. These concepts need to be translated into the vernacular that these groups understand."[5(p.50)]

It is worth viewing the core functions model as an interactive system rather than as linear. Figure 5–2 presents the core function model as a system, with the added element of governance. Governance is the glue that makes the entire interactive system cohere and function as it should, and it is therefore a central concern for leadership at all levels of the public health system.[6] Governance in public health is a community responsibility, which means that the community needs to be empowered to become more involved in policy development. If all people involved in public health become empowered, then governance will be part of the infrastructure of the entire public health system.

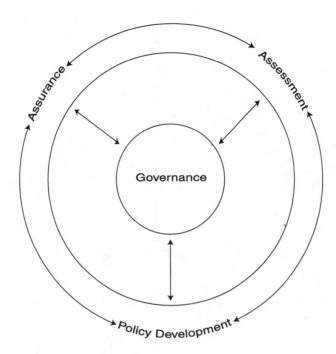

Figure 5–2 Core functions system paradigm.

Figure 5–3 combines the core functions model and the systems model of organizational change (Figure 3–1). The assessment of need in a community starts the system cycle, allowing leaders to think and act strategically as well as tactically. Leaders then decide on the best strategies for improving health and engage in action planning, which is oriented toward developing tactics for meeting the responsibilities of public health. Public health leaders also need to monitor public health activities to ensure they are effective.

Policy development plays a role throughout the process of protecting and improving the public's health. First, mission and vision development is a form of policy development. Second, whenever an evaluation is conducted, whether of a team, a community coalition, a program, or a service, the information gathered may suggest that policy revisions or entire new policies may need to be instituted. Obviously, though, assessment and policy development activities are pointless unless the policies chosen are implemented.

CORE ORGANIZATIONAL PRACTICES

Efforts have been made since the late 1980s to further define the role of government within the U.S. public health system. In 1989, the Public Health Practice Program Office of the Centers for Disease Control and Prevention initiated a process to identify the core organizational practices necessary for governmental agencies to carry out the mission of public health.[7] Representatives from government public health agencies and related associations identified 10 organizational practices that help illuminate the three core functions, which are obviously more

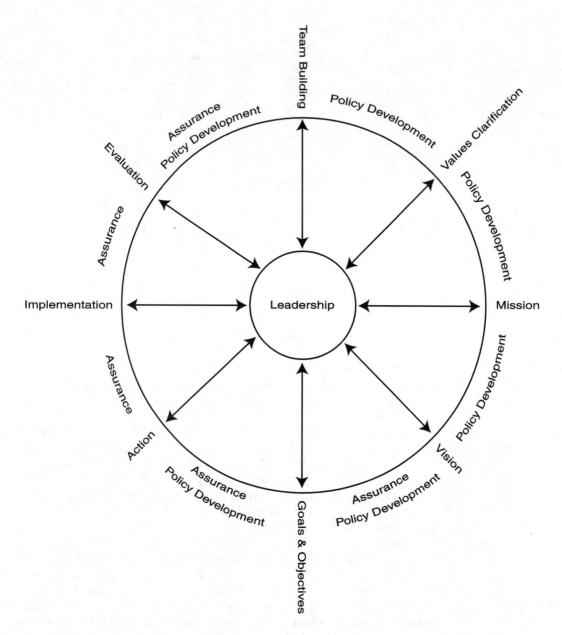

Figure 5–3 A system approach to public health leadership including the core functions.

general in nature (Table 5–1). These 10 organizational practices can be seen as providing an operational definition of the public health core functions.

Assessment Practices

There are three practices tied to the core function of assessment. The first, which concerns the health needs of the community, involves establishing a

Table 5–1 Leadership and the Organizational Practices

Core Functions	Organization Practices	Leadership Activities
Assessment	Assess the health needs of the community.	Lead the community assessment process.
	Investigate the occurrence of health effects and health hazards in the community.	Collect and utilize information to enhance the investigation.
	Analyze the determinants of identified health needs.	Integrate data with decision-making.
Policy development	Advocate for public health, build constituencies, and identify resources in the community.	Build coalitions; empower others; engage in public health advocacy; recognize community assets.
	Set priorities among health needs.	Clarify values; create a vision; tie vision to mission; use partners to set priorities.
	Develop plans and policies to address priority health needs.	Organize goals and objectives; translate goals into action.
Assurance	Manage resources and develop organizational structure.	Search for new resources; make organizational changes to better address community needs.
	Implement programs.	Stress innovation; delegate programmatic responsibility to others; oversee programs.
	Evaluate programs and provide quality assurance.	Support program evaluation; evaluate data collected; monitor performance.
	Inform and educate the public.	Use mentoring and training to educate work force; use social marketing and health communication to educate public.

systematic needs assessment process that is coordinated by the local health department and its leadership team and directed toward gathering data on the health status and health needs of the community. Although public health leaders initiate the process, community participation in the process is essential.

The second practice involves the investigation of health hazards in the community, especially timely epidemiologic research to identify the magnitude of the health problems, their duration and location, health trends, and populations at risk. As obvious as the importance of epidemiologic research is, it is not routinely done. A significant challenge for smaller health departments is doing investigations without an epidemiologist or behavioral scientist on the staff. Another significant challenge is finding the necessary funds. Public health leaders need to understand how data are collected to monitor health status and uncover health hazards.

The third practice is the analysis of identified etiologic and contributing factors that place certain segments of the population at risk for adverse health outcomes. The data generated by the assessment process are used as raw material for this type of analysis. Public health leaders need to understand how to analyze data and how to use data for decision making.

Policy Development Practices

There are three organizational practices identified for the policy development core function. The first of these (and the fourth total) involves the following activities: acting as an advocate for public health, building community constituencies, and identifying resources in the community. These activities are important because they help generate supportive and collaborative relationships with public and private agencies as well as with potential community partners and thereby create organizational mechanisms for the effective planning, implementation, and management of public health programs and services. These activities are also essential for developing action plans in cooperation with community partners.

The fifth practice is the setting of priorities. Criteria used in ranking health problems include the size and seriousness of the problems, the acceptability of the problems, the economic feasibility of solving them, and the effectiveness of the interventions developed to address them. Priority setting is not a completely objective process. For example, a concern about personal safety may exist even without a high community crime rate. If the community groups or politicians push hard enough, the community coalition in concert with the public health agency leader may designate violence as a key issue despite a lack of statistical validation. Public health leaders, in determining health priorities for the community, use value clarification skills, visioning skills, and partnership skills.

The sixth practice is the development of plans and policies to address the prioritized health needs of the community. The development process involves establishing goals and objectives to be accomplished by means of a systematic plan that focuses on local community health needs and the equitable distribution of financial and nonfinancial community resources. This practice requires the participation of the community stakeholders and representatives from other related agencies. Public health leaders will guide the development of goals and objectives and help translate them into action steps.

Assurance Practices

The final four organizational practices are associated with the assurance core function. The seventh involves managing resources and developing an organizational infrastructure to carry out the public health agenda. Critical leadership and management skills are necessary for the acquisition, allocation, and control of human, physical, cultural, and fiscal resources. Managing resources also encompasses maximizing the operational functioning of the local health system through the coordination of community agencies' efforts and the avoidance of the duplication of services. The issue of duplication is complicated by the professional protection of programs and resistance to the abolition of duplicative services. The seventh practice is unique in that it applies organizational considerations to the issue of public health agency operations. Public health leaders will search for new resources and alter their organizations to better reflect changing health priorities in the community.

The eighth organizational practice involves action plan implementation, which often involves the creation of services and programs. Plan implementation demands creativity and sound leadership, for legislative mandates must be interpreted and statutory responsibilities must be translated into programs. Public health agencies and health departments are usually given the task of providing population-based services, whereas personal services are seen as the responsibility of the medical care system. Public health leaders stress innovation in program development, delegate programmatic responsibility to others, and take an oversight role in monitoring program performance.

The ninth practice involves the evaluation of program activities. First, there is the issue of quality assurance—whether the program activities are being performed in accordance with professional and regulatory standards. Second, there is the issue of effectiveness—whether the program is achieving the intended goals and objectives. Third, there is the question of revision—whether the program needs to be reformed or resources need to be redirected. Given all the discussion in recent times on reinventing government, it makes sense for public health leaders to use evaluation data for purposes of reorganization. Leaders will need to support program evaluation, evaluate the data collected, and support performance monitoring.

The last assurance practice involves the provision of public health information to the community. Public health agencies have a responsibility to educate the residents of the community on ways to improve personal health—a responsibility they have not always fulfilled. They need to develop health education initiatives in order to increase health knowledge, change attitudes about unhealthy behaviors, and foster healthy habits. To meet their educational responsibility, public health leaders need to learn health communication skills, translate research intervention results into practice, and create linkages to academic institutions in order to develop health education strategies. They also need to use social marketing and health communication strategies to reach community residents and to use mentoring and training to educate the public health work force. The goal is to get the entire public to view public health issues as important. People must be made to realize that public health hazards put everyone at risk, not just the poor.

As can be seen from the discussion of the 10 practices, the public health model is extremely complex and needs a committed leadership to make it work. Turnock and colleagues, who have studied the core functions and organizational practices, claimed in an article that the 10 organizational practices have been applied in the local health department system as a way to build capacity.[8] It appears that public health leaders and other public health professionals understand the model and feel that it is applicable to their work.

In a follow-up article, Turnock and colleagues reported on current use of the 10 practices.[9] In a study of health departments, 50 percent of 208 respondents stated that they employed the 10 practices. Use was higher for the practices associated with the policy development core function, and it was also higher for departments serving a population of 50,000 or more and for smaller local health departments organized at the city or city-county level.

In a 1995 study, Turnock, Handler, and Miller investigated the relationship between the application of the core functions paradigm and the effectiveness of public health practice activities using a random sample of local health departments stratified by population size and type of jurisdiction.[10] They found that the U.S. public health system did not reach the proposed national health objectives for the year 2000 to a significant degree. In addition, the goal of having 90 percent of the population served by a local health department utilizing the core public health functions was not achieved. The researchers found that there was only 54-percent compliance on implementation of the core functions and organizational practices, about 4 percent higher than in the previous survey.

Voices have been raised that the core functions model is too abstract and needs to be replaced with a model that includes an emphasis on research activities in local public health departments. There seems to be general agreement about what public health does and little agreement about what public health is. The essential services approach to public health, which is discussed next, can be viewed as an evolutionary step toward a better understanding of what public health practitioners do and how they do it. Public health is at a crossroads because of all the changes and proposed reforms in the health system.[11] Yet it must be kept in mind that public health, since it is population based and community oriented, is importantly different than other health professions, whether at the local, state, or federal level.

ESSENTIAL SERVICES

The public health system will be affected by the implementation of any proposals for a national health system (Figure 5–4) or indeed by any substantial changes in the medical care system. Yet what the effects will be is largely a mystery, especially as the core functions paradigm is still confusing to policy makers and citizens, although the identification of organizational practices associated with the core functions helps to elucidate the paradigm. To offer further help, Baker and colleagues presented a list of essential public health services that are community based rather than organization based. This list, unlike the models of public health discussed thus far, includes research, enforcement of laws and regulations, and the assurance of a competent health services work force.

Table 5–2 lists not only essential services but also related leadership activities, and Exhibit 5–1 gives a brief description of each of the 10 services.[12] Leaders have key roles in the delivery of all of the essential services. There is a significant overlap in the leadership activities associated with the organizational practices approach and the essential services approach. The new leadership activities are associated with the three essential services not specifically covered in the organizational practices approach. With regard to enforcement of laws, public health leaders enforce laws and regulations that protect the health of the community. With regard to development of a competent work force, they build learning organizations based on systems thinking and support continuing education opportunities for the public health work force. With regard to research, they utilize research findings to guide program development.

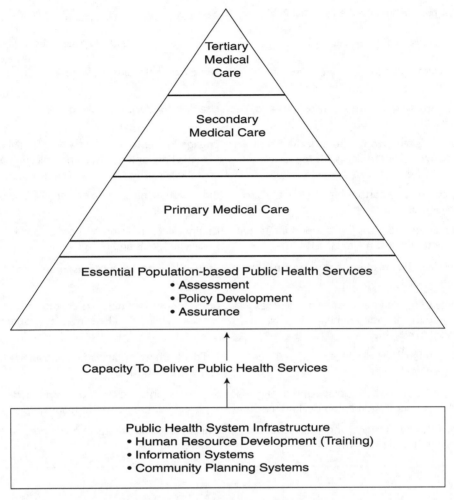

Figure 5–4 Public health: the foundation of a national health system.

If we think of the three core functions as the trunk of a tree, organizational practices constitute one of the branches and essential public health services constitute another. It is impossible to tell at this point whether either branch will be a dead end or whether a new offshoot will occur with an integration of the two approaches. The two approaches do have much in common, and if the essential services approach predominates, it can be modified to include the organizational practices that are not now part of it (i.e., setting priorities among health needs, managing resources, and developing organizational structure).

Following is a list of leadership activities related to the core functions paradigm:

• Put the core functions model into practice.

Table 5–2 Leadership and the Essential Public Health Services

Essential Public Health Services	Leadership Activities
Monitor health status to identify community problems.	Use data for decision making.
Diagnose and investigate health problems and health hazards in the community.	Use data for decision making.
Inform and educate people about health issues and empower them to deal with the issues.	Engage in mentoring and training, social marketing, and health communication activities; empower others.
Mobilize community partnerships to identify and solve health problems.	Build partnerships; share power; create workable action plans.
Develop policies and plans that support individual and community health efforts.	Clarify values; develop mission; create a vision; develop goals and objectives.
Enforce laws and regulations that protect health and ensure safety.	Protect laws and regulations; monitor adherence to laws.
Link people to needed personal health services and ensure the provision of health care when otherwise unavailable.	Stress innovation; delegate programmatic responsibility to others; oversee programs.
Ensure a competent public health and personal health care work force.	Build a learning organization; encourage training; mentor associates.
Evaluate effectiveness, accessibility, and quality of personal and population-based health services.	Support program evaluation; evaluate data collected; monitor performance.
Do research for new insights and innovative solutions to health problems.	Utilize research findings to guide program development.

- Develop leadership skills to carry out the organizational practices approach or the essential public health services approach.
- Increase commitment to the model and the two approaches by the public health work force and by community partners.

Exercise 5–1 is intended to help the readers explore the core functions paradigm and learn how the core functions are related to organizational practices and essential services.

SUMMARY

This chapter introduced the core functions of assessment, policy development, and assurance as a paradigm for the practice of public health. Public health leaders have roles and responsibilities related to each of the functions. As a way of illuminating the three functions, the chapter described 10 organizational practices

Exhibit 5–1 Essential Public Health Services

Monitor health status to identify and solve community health problems: This service includes accurate diagnosis of the community's health status; identification of threats to health and assessment of health service needs; timely collection, analysis, and publication of information on access, utilization, costs, and that are at higher risk than the total population; and collaboration to manage integrated information systems with private providers and health benefit plans.

Diagnose and investigate health problems and health hazards in the community: This service includes epidemiologic identification of emerging health threats; public health laboratory capability using modern technology to conduct rapid screening and high-volume testing; active infectious disease epidemiology programs; and technical capacity for epidemiologic investigation of disease outbreaks and patterns of chronic disease and injury.

Inform, educate, and empower people about health issues: This service involves social marketing and targeted media public communication; providing accessible health information resources at community levels; active collaboration with personal health care providers to reinforce health promotion messages and programs; and joint health education programs with schools, churches, and worksites.

Mobilize community partnerships and action to identify and solve health problems: This service involves convening and facilitating community groups and associations, including those not typically considered to be health-related, in undertaking defined preventive, screening, rehabilitation, and support programs; and skilled coalition-building ability in order to draw upon the full range of potential human and material resources in the cause of community health.

Develop policies and plans that support individual and community health efforts: This service requires leadership development at all levels of public health; systematic community-level and state-level planning for health improvement in all jurisdictions; development and tracking of measurable health objectives as a part of continuous quality improvement strategies; joint evaluation with the medical health care system to define consistent policy regarding prevention and treatment services; and development of codes, regulations, and legislation to guide the practice of public health.

Enforce laws and regulations that protect health and ensure safety: This service involves full enforcement of sanitary codes, especially in the food industry; full protection of drinking water supplies; enforcement of clean air standards; timely follow-up of hazards, preventable injuries, and exposure-related diseases identified in occupational and community settings; monitoring quality of medical services (e.g., laboratory, nursing homes, and home health care); and timely review of new drug, biologic, and medical device applications.

Link people to needed personal health services and ensure the provision of health care when otherwise unavailable: This service (often referred to as "outreach" or "enabling" services) includes ensuring effective entry for socially disadvantaged people into a coordinated system of clinical care; culturally and linguistically appropriate materials and staff to ensure linkage to services to special population groups; ongoing "care management"; transportation services; targeted health information to high-risk population groups; and technical assistance for effective worksite health promotion/disease prevention programs.

Ensure a competent public and personal health care work force: This service includes education and training for personnel to meet the needs for public and personal health service; efficient

continues

Exhibit 5–1 continued

processes for licensure of professionals and certification of facilities with regular verification and inspection follow-up; adoption of continuous quality improvement and lifelong learning within all licensure and certification programs; active partnerships with professional training programs to ensure community-relevant learning experiences for all students; and continuing education in management and leadership development programs for those charged with administrative/executive roles.

Evaluate effectiveness, accessibility, and quality of personal and population-based health services: This service calls for ongoing evaluation of health programs, based on analysis of health status and service utilization data, to assess program effectiveness and to provide information necessary for allocating resources and reshaping programs.

Research for new insights and innovative solutions to health problems: This service includes continuous linkage with appropriate institutions of higher learning and research and an internal capacity to mount timely epidemiologic and economic analyses and conduct needed health services research.

associated with the three functions and provided a list of essential public health services also associated with the functions.

Discussion Questions

1. What are the three core functions of public health?
2. What is a paradigm and what is a paradigm shift?
3. What are the similarities and differences between the organizational practices and the essential services of public health?
4. What leadership activities are required for priority setting?
5. What is one of the main criticisms of the core functions model of public health?
6. What is the main competitor of the core functions model and in what important way does it differ from this model?

Exercise 5–1

THE CORE FUNCTIONS DEBATE

Purpose: to explore the core functions of public health and their relationship to organizational practices and essential public health services

Key concepts: assessment, assurance, core functions, essential public health services, organizational practices, policy development

Procedure: The class should divide into teams of 5–10 members. Each team is assigned a core function and the task of constructing an argument that purports to show why this function is the most important of the three core functions. In constructing the argument, the team should use the organizational practices and the essential services associated with the core function to clarify the nature of the function. It should also discuss the leadership issues involved. One team should be given the task of preparing an argument favoring a model in which all three core functions are treated as equally important. Each team selects a spokesperson to present its argument, and then all the teams vote on the arguments to determine which is most persuasive.

REFERENCES

1. Institute of Medicine, *The Future of Public Health* (Washington, DC: National Academy Press, 1988).
2. S.R. Covey, *The 7 Habits of Highly Effective People* (New York: Simon & Schuster, 1989).
3. J.A. Barker, *Paradigm* (New York: Harper Business, 1992).
4. Institute of Medicine, *The Future of Public Health*.
5. M.A. Stoto et al., eds., *Healthy Communities: New Partnerships for the Future of Public Health* (Washington, DC: National Academy Press, 1996).
6. P. Block, *The Empowered Manager* (San Francisco: Jossey-Bass, 1987).
7. W.W. Dyal, *Public Health Infrastructure and Organizational Practice Definitions* (Atlanta: Centers for Disease Control, Division of Public Health Systems, Public Health Practice Program Office, 1991).
8. B. Turnock et al., "Implementing and Assessing Organizational Practice in Public Health," *Public Health Reports* 109, no. 4 (1994): 478–484.
9. B.J. Turnock et al., "Local Health Department Effectiveness in Addressing the Core Functions of Public Health," *Public Health Reports* 109, no. 5 (1994): 653–658.
10. B.J. Turnock et al., "Core Function-related Local Public Health Practice Effectiveness," *Journal of Public Health Management and Practice* 4, no. 5 (1998): 27–32.
11. E.L. Baker et al., "Health Reform and the Health of the Public," *JAMA* 272, no. 18 (1994): 1278–1282.
12. J. Harrell and E. Baker, *The Essential Services of Public Health* (Washington, DC: American Public Health Association, 1997).

Chapter 6

Leadership and Assessment

[Assessment] involves identifying and studying important data sources.

G. Pickett and J.J. Hanlon, *Public Health*

Assessment brings public health agencies and communities together as partners. Ideally, the leaders of a public health agency should work with a number of community groups to determine the health needs and health priorities of the community. Over the last century, public health has developed a number of methodologic approaches to studying the health status of a community. One important lesson is that the determination of community health needs and strategies for dealing with these needs must take into account community boundaries, community resources, and the local culture. Otherwise, intervention strategies risk being rejected by community residents and will then wind up being largely ineffective. Another important lesson is that public health agencies must not ignore community groups and individuals in determining the community's public health priorities. The tendency of all types of human service organizations to ignore community input may have contributed to making communities overly dependent on outside help.[1]

Public health agencies have long used epidemiologic methods and demographic and social science techniques to obtain an objective picture of community needs. The difficulty with this approach is that it is based on the assumption that problems exist. According to McKnight, human service organizations need to use an anti-diagnostic approach that focuses on evaluating the capacities and strengths of the community and the flexibility of community leaders.[2] In short, these organizations should first do an assets assessment. Once the strengths of the community are determined, the problems of the community can be addressed from a positive perspective.

THE ASSESSMENT PROCESS

Local health departments often view a complete community needs assessment as a burden rather than a tool for guiding their activities. The solution is for them to treat assessment as an ongoing dynamic process. If health department leaders incorporate assessment activities into everyday activities, assessment won't appear as a monumental task, for assessment data will be gathered as a matter of course.

Despite awareness on the part of public health professionals that assessment is a critical activity, they are often confused about the nature of assessment. Probably the best way to approach assessment is to focus on its basic component, which is problem identification.[3] It is with regard to this component that community research activities become especially important. Exercise 6–1 explores the issue of developing assessment strategies for an emerging gang problem in a small city.

The first step in the assessment process is to design a durable integrated public health information system.[4] The accomplishment of this step calls for a true partnership, based on public health leadership principles, between local and state health departments, national health-related agencies (including the Centers for Disease Control and Prevention [CDC]), and citizen groups and other agencies. The data systems must be designed to allow growth and the incorporation of new technologies and new databases as they become available.[5]

The second step is to identify community resources and evaluate their effectiveness.[6] Public health leaders need to be students of the community in which they work. They must examine the community health resources, such as health facilities, health professionals, available medicines and vaccines, and emergency medical transportation systems. They must also look at other community resources, such as sanitation programs, education programs, disaster response plans, and mental health and other counseling programs, to determine their availability and effectiveness. Their availability should be analyzed in terms of proximity, accessibility, affordability, acceptability, and appropriateness. The effectiveness measures should include such factors as population size relative to need, proportion of the population in need reached by existing community services, program effectiveness, program costs, and the cost to cover the population not covered. Finally, alternative program approaches should be evaluated.

The third step is to utilize the data that are collected.[7] These data need to be transformed into information that public health leaders can use for effective decision making. Indeed, assessment activities should lead directly to the policy development activities discussed in the next chapter. Public health leaders often fail to express information clearly, and they lose credibility with policy makers as a result. They should present the data simply and straightforwardly, not in a convoluted fashion. They should also orient the presentation to the specific audience receiving the information. The presentation should answer questions that have been posed. Public health leaders need to learn the art of presentation so that the recipients are educated by being given the information.

Case Study 6–A, which describes the leadership activities of a disease surveillance group, explores obstacles that can prevent an assessment from being successful and ways of overcoming these obstacles.

ORGANIZATIONAL PRACTICES ASSOCIATED WITH ASSESSMENT

As noted in the preceding chapter, three organizational practices are associated with the core function of assessment. The first involves assessing the health needs of the community. The researchers who defined the organizational practices also gave performance indicators for each practice. These indicators show whether the practice is actually in place. Five performance indicators were listed for this practice:[8]

1. A community health needs assessment planning process is in place.
2. Needs assessment includes community input.
3. Morbidity and mortality data are obtained from vital records.
4. Morbidity and mortality data are obtained from other sources.
5. Behavioral risk factors are included in the community needs assessment.

The second organizational practice involves investigating the occurrence of adverse health events and health hazards in the community. This practice has two performance indicators:

6. Epidemiologic surveillance systems are functioning.
7. No preventable mortality or morbidity occurs as a result of delays in surveillance.

The third assessment practice involves analyzing identified etiologic and contributing factors that place certain segments of the population at risk for adverse health outcomes and also determining the extent of available health resources. This practice has four performance indicators:

8. Health needs identified by the needs assessment are analyzed.
9. Determinants and contributing factors are identified.
10. Health needs of population groups are analyzed.
11. Existing health resources are analyzed.

The remainder of this chapter discusses the various approaches to needs assessment that have been developed in recent years. Public health has yet not built on the assets model, although community involvement is clearly a critical element in the approaches presented below. As soon as needs assessment becomes a leadership partnership activity, assessment and policy development move closer together, and it is out of the marriage of these two core functions that assurance activities come into being.

ASSESSMENT METHODOLOGIES

This section presents three methodologic approaches to community and organizational assessment. Each of these approaches, despite being analyzable into a set of operational steps, requires leaders to be creative in their supervision of assessment activities. The leaders, of course, must delegate many of the activities to managers and other professional staff.

APEXPH

In 1987, the Assessment Protocol for Excellence in Public Health (APEXPH) project was started under a cooperative agreement between the American Public Health Association (APHA), the Association of State and Territorial Health Officials, the CDC, the National Association of City and County Health Officials, and the National Association of County Health Officials.[9] Two major groups were established, a steering committee and an APEXPH working group. What eventually developed was a voluntary process for organizational and community self-assessment, a process for planned improvements, and methods for continuing evaluation and reassessment. The critical component is a set of procedures that local health departments can use to assess public health concerns. The final report and the manual created by the two working groups pointed to the differences between their approach and other approaches, some of which are indicated by the following outline of APEXPH:

1. APEXPH is a true self-assessment protocol that can be used by an agency to meet its needs and those of the community.
2. APEXPH leads to a practice-based plan of action.
3. APEXPH concentrates on a local health department's administrative and leadership capacity, the basic structure and organization of the local health department and its place in the community, and the community's actual and perceived problems instead of technical performance compliance with programmatic objectives by specific public health programs.
4. APEXPH offers opportunities for the local health department to assess its relationship with other local government agencies, with the community as a whole, and with state and federal agencies. The protocol can give guidance on ways to strengthen partnership relationships and obtain needed support.
5. APEXPH offers an approach by which the health department and its leadership will become accepted by the community as major players in the public health arena. It includes a community assessment process, health priority setting, policy development, and activities to ensure that the health needs of the public are being met.
6. APEXPH is adaptable to different local situations and different arrays of resources.

By following APEXPH, public health leaders will fulfill the responsibility of the local agency to perform a community assessment. They will also increase their and the agency's credibility within the community and foster strong partnerships with community groups. The principles of APEXPH include these:

1. Since government has a primary responsibility to ensure the health of the public, health departments need to provide direction for their communities in assessing health problems, developing policies, and addressing community health problems.
2. Because leadership and accountability go together, health departments must establish and meet competency and practice standards that are seen by their communities as appropriate to health protection and health promotion.
3. Since public health practitioners are often placed in difficult situations in which hard choices need to be made, health department leaders have to be risk takers who shape their programs to the communities that they serve in ways that the communities will find acceptable.

4. Because public health problems demand a strong, coordinated, authoritative response, state and local health departments need to discover techniques for working in partnership with each other so as to strengthen each other's resources and authority.
5. In order to set health priorities utilizing scientific knowledge, health department leaders must become health information experts. They must routinely provide information to their communities and aid their communities in the development of community-based health plans.
6. Owing to the multidimensional nature of public health problems, health departments have to find creative approaches to solving local health problems using a wide variety of community resources.
7. With a strong belief that improvements in the health of the public require active community ownership and commitment, health departments need to develop and maintain partnerships with community agencies, community leaders, interest groups, and representatives of high-risk population groups.

APEXPH is a three-part process. Part I is an organizational capacity assessment—an eight-step internal review of the health department itself (Figure 6–1). The object is to evaluate the health department's administrative structure and its capacity to undertake a community assessment (Part II of APEXPH). The internal review is performed by the health department director and a team of key staff members. As Figure 6–1 shows, the review includes preparing for further steps, scoring indicators in regard to importance and current status, identifying strengths and weaknesses, analyzing and reporting agency strengths, analyzing weaknesses, ranking problems, developing and implementing action plans, and institutionalizing the assessment process.

Part II of APEXPH is a community assessment. Public health leaders need to reach out and involve the community in the assessment process. The process involves evaluating the health of the community as well as identifying community strengths and the potential role of the health department in addressing health problems. (How community strengths are to be determined is not clearly laid out.) Part II also provides for the utilization of objective health data and the community's perceptions of community health problems. Those responsible for the community assessment gather demographic data, socioeconomic data, environmental data, and data on years of potential life lost, access to primary health care, other health indices, perinatal indicators, the leading causes of mortality, the estimated prevalence of disease, and the leading causes of hospitalization. They then construct a community health problem summary, rank the top 10 contributors to years of productive life lost, and develop a community health plan.

The final part of the APEXPH process is called "completing the cycle." In this part, public health leaders integrate the plans developed previously into the ongoing activities of the health department and the community it serves. This part involves policy development, assurance, monitoring, and evaluation of plans developed in Parts I and II. As a result of the total APEXPH process, the leaders make recommendations for changes in current services or the development of new services. They also usually find ways of improving the functioning of the local health department (capacity building). The protocol guidelines are quite comprehensive and allow for assessment to be an ongoing agency process.

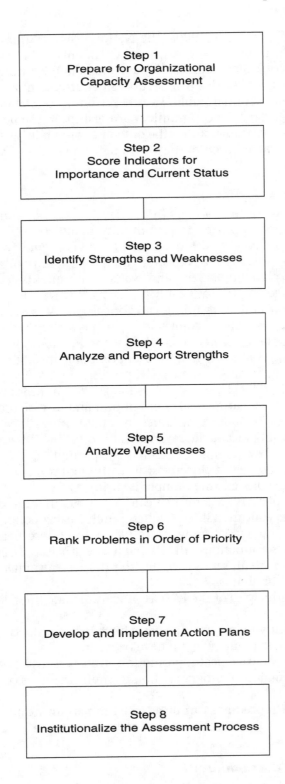

Figure 6–1 Flowchart of steps in assessing organizational capacity.

Beginning in the late 1990s, the National Association of County and City Health Officials, in partnership with the CDC, engaged in a revision of APEXPH. The new protocol, called APEX-CPH (Assessment and Planning Excellence through Community Partners for Health), ties assessment to essential public health services as well as to the National Public Health Performance Standards (set by CDC). It stresses the importance of community partnerships in the public health enterprise and the importance of measuring the outcomes of public health programs. Leadership is necessary at all levels of the assessment process.

PATCH

CDC was one of the partners in the development of another assessment protocol, the Planned Approach to Community Health (PATCH). Other participants included state and local health departments and community groups. The protocol was designed in the mid-1980s to strengthen the capacity of state and local health departments to plan, implement, and evaluate community-level health promotion activities targeted at priority health problems.[10] It was developed in response to a shift in federal policy regarding categorical grants to states. Although PATCH includes strong assessment components, it has strong policy development and assurance components as well. It can be used to link local, state, and federal public health agencies, yet it is oriented toward local public health initiatives. Consumers are also essential partners in the PATCH process.

PATCH, like APEXPH, has a methodology communities can use for planning, conducting, and evaluating health promotion and disease prevention programs.[11] The methodology includes procedures for establishing a health promotion team, collecting and using local data, setting health priorities, planning and implementing programs, and evaluating the results. The promotion of PATCH was tied to the *Healthy People 2000* health objectives, and although some health departments still utilize the PATCH process, the number is shrinking.

The object of PATCH is to inculcate behaviors that are conducive to health. The process uses educational techniques, public health policy, and environmental strategies to encourage community residents to choose healthy lifestyles. Each community, in conjunction with its public health leaders, needs to do its own community assessment, set its own health priorities, formulate solutions, and take ownership of its programs.

The main principles of the PATCH process include these:[12]

1. Community members must participate in the process.
2. Data should guide program development.
3. A comprehensive health promotion strategy must be developed.
4. The evaluation of programs should emphasize ways of improving them.

The PATCH procedures can be adapted to various health problems and communities. The whole process can be analyzed into five phases, which are summarized below.

Phase I: Mobilizing the Community

Public health leaders must use their coalition-building skills to involve the community in the PATCH process. They first need to complete a demographic profile of the community so as to identify the best community leaders and organizations to recruit. During this phase, the public health leaders must also work at informing the community about the PATCH process.

Phase II: Collecting and Organizing Data

The community workgroup, which includes community leaders, obtains and analyzes data on mortality and morbidity and their causes. It also collects behavioral data. Community groups may identify other sources of data that might be useful. The data are then analyzed in order to determine the leading health problems in the community.

The community workgroup should collect extensive data on the community and compare its community's statistics with state and national statistics. The addition of data from multiple sources will aid the group in other phases of the PATCH process. The assessment should include data on the causes of death and disability and identify ways of preventing premature death and disability (Table 6–1).

Both quantitative and qualitative data are collected. Among the quantitative data are mortality and morbidity data gathered from state and local health departments, state and local social service departments, the state department of highway safety, state and local police departments, boards of education, voluntary agencies, hospitals, major employers or the chamber of commerce, and colleges and universities. Among the qualitative data are community opinion data. In order to get this type of information, it is necessary to identify community leaders, develop a series of survey questions, train interviewers, conduct interviews, collate and analyze data, and prepare a report of the results. The survey results will allow problems to be ranked according to the number of times they were mentioned. Public health leaders need to discuss the survey results report with community groups.

Phase III: Choosing Health Priorities and Target Groups

Behavioral data as well as other relevant data are presented to the community workgroup, which then analyzes the behavioral, social, economic, political, and environmental factors that impact behaviors and thereby put community residents at risk for disease, death, and injury. After reviewing all the behavioral data, the community group sets health priorities and appropriate community objectives and decides which priorities are to be addressed initially.

Phase IV: Developing a Comprehensive Intervention Strategy

In this phase, interventions are chosen, designed, and eventually implemented. Existing health resources, policies, environmental supports, and programs need to be identified before new programs are created so that duplication of services can be avoided. The workgroup begins to explore the assurance function of public health and develops a comprehensive health promotion intervention plan, including strategies, a timetable, and a schedule for completing tasks.

Phase V: Evaluating PATCH

In this phase, an evaluation working group is set up by the public health leaders. The working group's job is to evaluate progress, including improvements in the health of community residents, through the use of standard evaluation methods.

Table 6–1 Contributors to the Leading Causes of Death

	Heart Disease	Cancers	Stroke	Injuries (Nonvehicular)	Influenza Pneumonia	Injuries (Vehicular)	Diabetes	Cirrhosis	Suicide	Homicide
Behavioral risk factor										
Tobacco use	•	•	•	•	•					
High blood pressure	•		•							
High blood cholesterol	•		P							
Diet	•	•	P					•		
Obesity	•	•						•		
Lack of exercise	•	•	•					•		
Stress	P		P	•		•				•
Alcohol abuse	•	•	•	•		•		•	•	•
Drug misuse	P	•	P	•		•				•
Seatbelt nonuse						•				
Handgun possession				•						•
Nonbehavioral risk factor										
Biological factors	•	•	•		•			•	•	•
Radiation		•								
Workplace hazards		•		•		•				
Environmental		•				•				
Infectious agents	P	•			•				•	
Home hazards				•						
Auto/road design						•				
Speed limits						•				
Health care access	•	•	•	•	•	•		•	•	•

Note: P = possible.

The purpose of the evaluation is to provide feedback to program participants and the public health leaders so that they can enhance the effectiveness of the interventions.

Steckler and colleagues evaluated 27 PATCH sites that had been functioning in 13 states for one to three years.[13] Figure 6–2 shows a presumptive PATCH model containing the steps that 72 percent of the sites had completed. All 25 sites had completed a behavioral risk factor survey, which is discussed later in this chapter.

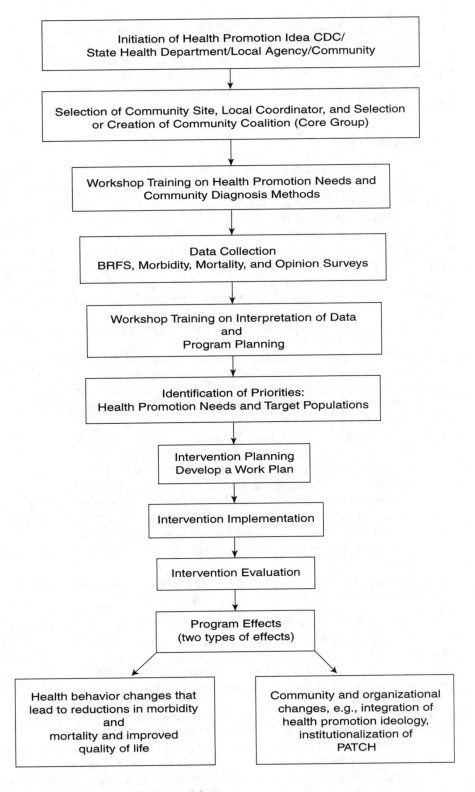

Figure 6–2 The presumptive PATCH model.

Of the 18 sites that had completed the six CDC training workshops, 55.6 percent had completed most of the PATCH processes. The researchers found that PATCH was well liked by the participants. Funding for the process, however, tended to be a problem. Finally, PATCH was perceived to be effective as a community organization process by almost half of all state and local coordinators as well as by community leaders.

Model Standards

A third major assessment methodology is based on model standards.[14] The model standards project, developed under the auspices of APHA, was an attempt to bring together the various approaches to community assessment and apply the tools of assessment to the *Healthy People 2000* health objectives as a way of determining how and to what extent the objectives were being achieved. It was assumed that communities would adapt the national health objectives to local needs, in particular by a process in which community leaders and agencies, under the guidance of public health leaders, would set health priorities. Eventually, plans would need to be developed for programs designed to achieve the local health objectives.

The following principles are intended to guide the use of model standards:[15]

1. The health objectives should be measurable and reality based.
2. Plans should be flexible, and community coalitions should quantify their objectives and develop local strategies for addressing problems.
3. Communitywide partnerships that focus on the community as a whole should be fostered.
4. Government is the "residual guarantor" of health services, which means that a government agency provides the services directly or ensures their delivery by a public or private community-based organization.
5. Negotiation is the secret to relationships between agencies.
6. The use of the term "standards" implies that the objectives are uniform (in the interests of equity and social justice), and the use of "guidelines" suggests the existence of local decision-making discretion.
7. Assurance and accessibility to services are requirements of model standards.
8. Program development is emphasized rather than professional practice considerations.

In August 1990, a meeting was held at the CDC headquarters in Atlanta. The meeting, attended by representatives from the major U.S. public health organizations, focused on how local communities could best use planning methods in order to meet the objectives for the nation for the year 2000. Out of the discussion came the 11 steps of the model standards process:[16,17]

1. Determine and assess the role of one's health agency.
2. Assess the lead health agency's organizational capacity.
3. Develop an agency plan to build the necessary organizational capacity.
4. Assess the community's organizational and power structures.
5. Organize the community to build a stronger constituency for public health and establish a partnership for public health.

6. Assess the health needs of the community and its available resources.
7. Determine local priorities.
8. Select outcome and process objectives that are compatible with local priorities and the *Healthy People 2000* objectives.
9. Develop communitywide intervention strategies.
10. Develop and implement a plan of action.
11. Monitor and evaluate the effort on a continuing basis.

The model standards methodology can be used in conjunction with other assessment methodologies, such as APEXPH or PATCH. In *The Guide to Implemented Model Standards,* it was argued that APEXPH improves the public health infrastructure in the community by enhancing the community's capacity to perform the core functions of assessment, policy development, and assurance.[18] PATCH was seen more as a generic planning and implementation tool geared toward chronic diseases prevention and health promotion programs. The guide recommended that a community choose either APEXPH or PATCH but not both, although there are overlaps and connections between the two methodologies. The model standards process is oriented toward the health priorities for the nation, and model standards are organized into four categories within each of the 22 priority areas of *Healthy People 2000:* health status, risk reduction, services and protection, and community surveillance. In essence, the model standards approach creates a blueprint (with extensive fill-in-the-blank forms) for addressing the health priorities at the local level. The integration of either APEXPH or PATCH with the model standards approach would provide a comprehensive tool for discovering what a community needs to reach its goals.

An interesting extension of the model standards approach was presented in a recent report by Randolph and Ford.[19] A model standards workgroup worked with the model standards project staff to design and review community strategies for public health. The strategies were developed for the purpose of training staff to involve the community in the model standards process. A series of steps for "putting it all together" was also constructed. The first step is to choose the head of a lead agency to serve as coordinator of activities and meetings, collector and disseminator of data and information, and overall moderator and reporter for each of the various activities. The local health department head should take on this leadership role if possible. The role will allow the health department head to help improve public health in the community by

- aiding the community in the assessment of local health problems by using health education methods
- establishing appropriate laws, regulations, and policies to protect the health of the public
- establishing and maintaining practice standards that encourage public confidence
- involving community residents in the planning of communitywide programs
- developing partnerships through linkage with the state health department and other local government agencies also involved in activities related to public health
- developing community resources to address problems

- acting as a trustee and guarantor (leadership roles) that the health needs of the public are being addressed
- encouraging flexibility in the development, adaptation, and elimination of programs based on the health needs of the community
- following the 11 steps for implementing the model standards[20]

The model standards project attempts to integrate the various assessment procedures. All three assessment methodologies are oriented toward collecting health status information about the residents of a community. They all require public health leaders to implement the assessment process. They just do it in different ways. The role of public health leaders in any kind of assessment is to

- lead the community assessment process
- use health information data in decision making
- carry out the assessment using one of the assessment methodologies
- communicate the assessment results to the community

OTHER ASSESSMENT APPROACHES

Assessment is one of the major responsibilities of public health. The public health system is organized to provide needed programs and services, and public health leaders therefore constantly look for innovative assessment techniques that can help gauge community health status. This section discusses several assessment techniques that can be used in conjunction with the methodologies described above.

Since the mid-1980s, telephone surveys have been conducted in the United States as a means of estimating the prevalence of specific behaviors associated with health problems.[21] For example, telephone survey data have been collected on cigarette smoking, dietary fat intake, level of physical activity and exercise, seatbelt use, and screening tests for early detection of disease. The information obtained has then been used by states to develop state and local health interventions.[22,23]

For instance, a San Francisco study used the behavior risk factor survey to evaluate differences between Latino and non-Latino white adults.[24] Telephone interviews were done with 652 Latinos and 584 non-Latino whites selected by random digit dialing. The researchers found that Latino men and women were less likely to consume alcoholic beverages and consumed fewer drinks per week than non-Latinos. The Latinos were more likely to be sedentary. Latino women were less likely to smoke and to have had a Pap smear or a clinical breast examination than their non-Latino counterparts. The researchers argued that the data showed that health programs targeted at Latinos would be beneficial. They also stressed the importance of providing information in Spanish.

In recent years, the value of community health report cards that provide an overall picture of community health status has been debated. Their advantages are clear. Community health report cards can help public health leaders monitor the overall health of the community in a straightforward way, and if they are written in easy-to-understand language, they provide a means of informing the community of its health status over time.

One type of report card can be created using CATCH (Comprehensive Assessment for Tracking Community Health), a system developed at the University of South Florida School of Public Health.[25] CATCH was used to produce a ranking of community health problems in 11 Florida counties by combining information on more than 200 indicators that was drawn from multiple data sources. The system allows public health agencies to compare their health indicator scores with those of other agencies. Trends over time can be identified so that an agency can check its progress in improving community health.

The report card approach has been explored by managed care systems. Both managed care and public health use population-based approaches to health.[26] Both are concerned with the cost of health care. Managed care organizations (MCOs) use population-based assessments of their membership groups to deliver the most cost-effective quality care at the lowest price. Public health professionals are taking leadership roles in the managed care sector, for they have long supported a population-based approach to community health improvement.

The survival of MCOs depends on their evaluating the health needs of their membership. The Health Care Financing Administration and private health care systems use Health Plan Employer Data and Information Set (HEDIS) to compare the quality of care delivered by health maintenance organizations. HEDIS, which monitors the effectiveness of care provided, is essentially an assessment tool. Some MCOs use a life care plan model oriented toward helping members increase their health potential by stressing prevention, wellness, better management of chronic conditions, and increased personal responsibility for health.[27] MCOs also conduct market research to determine whether their services are perceived to be of high quality, and they assess their programs to see if the programs reflect their mission.

MCOs and public health agencies both engage in some of the same monitoring and assessment activities.[28] They both do health risk assessments, community health assessments, health policy assessments, health systems assessments, and comparative analyses of populations and systems; they also both monitor adherence to quality standards, health outcomes, planning effectiveness, and cost-effectiveness. Leadership is critical in all of these activities. Leaders from the public and private sectors need to develop partnerships to create integrated systems of assessment and care in communities.

Attempts have been made to build leadership activities directly into the assessment process. The Healthy Communities approach is an example. The goal is to foster healthy lifestyle choices by community residents from birth to death and to share the responsibility for community health among residents, public health practitioners, and community leaders.[29] The community as a whole explores health issues in detail, and the dialogues between community residents and public health practitioners are part of an overall community assessment. Communities that have implemented the Health Communities approach may use any of the earlier discussed assessment techniques.

In assessing the health status of a community, public health leaders

- use national databases when appropriate
- coordinate the use of assessment techniques in the public and private health care sectors
- explore the pluses and minuses of regularly released community report cards
- explain community health report cards to the community
- work to integrate HEDIS with public health assessment techniques so as to better identify the needs of the community

PUBLIC HEALTH INFORMATICS

Assessment depends on data collection and the use of information system techniques, and therefore public health leaders need to know how to design data collection activities, employ the latest information technologies, interpret data, translate data into useful information, and build data systems that utilize an evidence-based approach. Public health informatics is a new specialty designed to give leaders the necessary knowledge to perform these tasks.[30]

Public health informatics uses analytical tools such as meta-analysis, risk assessment, economic evaluation, public health surveillance, expert panels, and consensus conferences. It also uses new tools associated with geographic information systems (GISs). GISs are user-friendly data representations (in the form of spatial maps) that provide leaders with information on health risks, underlying causes of disease transmission, and the effectiveness of public health interventions and can demonstrate needed structural changes in the health system at the community level.[31]

Data are the raw facts of public health. Collected according to objective criteria, they tend to be quantitative in nature, although there is increasing support for collecting qualitative information, which can sometimes provide especially deep insights into public health issues. Information is processed data.[32] The translation of usable quantitative data into useful information involves computer-related information technology.[33] Qualitative information may also be computer analyzed, but such information often takes the form of stories, focus group findings, or anthropologic field materials. Public health leaders use information to inform and educate the public, make decisions, develop policy, and implement appropriate public health interventions.

Following are six principles that pertain to the use of information systems by public health leaders:[34]

- Public health leaders need to use data from two different data systems. One data system reports on the delivery of direct services and on program encounters (e.g., a case management meeting or a home visit). The second system collects population-based data.
- Public health leaders need to remember that people are complex, integrated beings but that programs are fragmentary (i.e., each program focuses on just one part of the whole person). Leaders need to advocate for information that integrates different types of data so that they can better understand the health concerns of community residents.
- Public health consumers must get something back from data collectors. They need to know why data are being collected and must be given feedback.
- Data systems need to be flexible and should be designed to meet the needs of local health leaders as they monitor the health of community residents.
- Information systems need to be compatible so that leaders can access different data sources using just one computer. (The Internet is becoming a very useful data source for public health leaders because all the data on Websites are accessible by anyone with Internet software.)
- Public health leaders need to respect confidentiality. The public wants to be assured that personal information will be kept private.

Since public health draws data from multiple sources, including sources from different disciplines, public health leaders need to understand the different perspectives of the various professions and learn how to synthesize data from different sources. Information science, computer science, and computer technology are advancing, and public health leaders need to keep up with the changes. Leaders may not be personally responsible for data collection, but they must be able to define the data they need to make effective policy decisions. They must also be involved in the development and design of the information system.

An interesting example of cooperative sharing of information is the community health status indicators project supported by the National Association of County and City Health Officials, the Association of State and Territorial Health Officials, and the Public Health Foundation. The goal of the project is to regularly provide community-specific public health data reports to local public health leaders in counties across the United States. The reports will include information on actual causes of death, risk factors for premature death, access to care, preventive services use, and county demographics. They will also summarize health measures and compare data from counties with similar demographics.

Another example is the CDC's Information Network for Public Health Officials (INPHO). INPHO has several goals, including improving communication among public health leaders throughout the United States, increasing the accessibility of information, and utilizing information technology to expedite the exchange of information.[35] CDC funded several INPHO projects to create networks and investigate the barriers to access within present data systems.

Illinois is one state that has struggled with the issue of how to create useful and integrated information systems. Case Study 6–B, a review of the history of the development of the Illinois Cornerstone project, describes the development of an integrated system for providing information on maternal and child health to health professionals. Public health leaders need information if they are to positively impact the communities that they serve. To ensure they receive the necessary information, they should

- take training courses in informatics
- learn techniques for the collection of health status indicators
- learn how to interpret data and turn them into useful information
- learn how to access information on the Internet
- explore different analytic tools for better understanding data
- utilize quantitative and qualitative information
- become involved in the development of information systems
- integrate conflicting data systems

SUMMARY

This chapter discussed the key elements of the core function of assessment. It began by describing the assessment process and then went on to consider three assessment methodologies, APEXPH, PATCH, and the model standards approach. These three methodologies, though they overlap, are not mutually exclusive, and elements from all three can be combined. Other assessment methodologies were then discussed but not in as much detail. Finally, the chapter considered public health informatics, which involves the collection of data and the use of information system techniques to turn the data into information.

Discussion Questions

1. What is the relationship between core functions, organizational practices, and performance indicators?
2. What leadership skills are needed for community assessment activities?
3. Why does assessment start the change process?
4. What are the three parts of the APEXPH process?
5. What are the five phases of the PATCH process?
6. What role can model standards play in evaluation?
7. What are community health report cards?
8. What is public health informatics?

Exercise 6–1

THE TRAINERVILLE GANG

Purpose: to assess a potential community health problem utilizing community groups

Key concepts: assessment, board of health, community advisory board, data protocols

Procedure: Trainerville is a small city of 100,000 on the Mentor River in the northwestern United States. There are 10,000 children under the age of 10. There are also 10,000 young people between the ages of 11 and 18. Citizens have reported that there is a gang presence in the community. Data on gangs are not presently available unless a gang member gets arrested.

Mayor John Snow asked the Trainerville Health Department to develop strategies for getting data on gangs in the community. The Director of the health department convenes a community health advisory group to work with him on the mayor's request. The charge to the group is to assess the extent of the gang problem in Trainerville.

Divide into groups of 5–10. Each group will develop strategies for determining the extent of the problem in the community. Each group will then present its assessment protocol to the Trainerville Board of Health. The Board of Health includes a representative from each of the groups. The Board will then select the protocol that they think will best assess the gang problem. Since the open meetings act is operative, all group members can attend the deliberations and offer citizen comments.

Case Study 6–A

Removing Obstacles for Assessment: the MSDH Disease Surveillance System

Kate Wright, Mahree Fuller Skala, Ronald Gribbons, and Adelaide Merkle

The following case study reviews a selection of problems faced by many disease- or risk factor–oriented public health surveillance systems. Some surveillance systems may not be comprehensive or may contain fragmented disease registries, holding large quantities of surveillance data not utilized to their full potential. This ultimately affects not only local public health and well-being but also state, regional, and national efforts to identify public health problems and implement interventions to control and prevent them.

MIDDLE STATE HEALTH DEPARTMENT

Surveillance System Problems

Surveillance for communicable diseases has been one of the most visible and critical assessment functions of the Middle State Department of Health (MSDH). Like other state health departments, MSDH reacted to the need for assessment of communicable diseases by designating for itself which diseases were necessary to track.

The department developed its own requirements for collecting data on both individual and outbreak cases and added them to the federal report list. Various reporting procedures were developed by six different MSDH programs responsible for surveillance of various reportable diseases. Program-specific procedural differences resulted in the development of different report forms, several targeted reporting sources, and six separate surveillance databases.

Required information was provided to MSDH by various health providers, who could report directly to their local health departments or to MSDH. Most reports were forwarded by local agencies intending to maintain control over "local" surveillance functions. Even if accurate data were forwarded by some local authorities in an efficient manner, this did not create a "real-time" data system available to MSDH for critical decision support when needed. The largest cities in the state were exempted from state reporting requirements, which resulted in additional complications, including the existence of different local ordinances, report forms, and procedures.

As a result of the lack of systemwide tools and procedures and policies, the problem of underreporting of communicable diseases became increasingly apparent during the late 1980s and early 1990s. Depending on the seriousness and rarity of the disease and the accessibility of the reporting system, a range of from 10 to 90 percent of diagnosed disease cases were reported, annually. Many factors were blamed for the underreporting of communicable disease surveillance data.

These included misunderstandings by providers regarding reporting requirements and confidentiality and the inconvenience of compliance given the wide range of reporting procedures and forms. Analysis of surveillance data did not present complete or accurate conclusions regarding disease trends, with the result that policy development and prevention and control measures to reduce public health risks were less than optimal.

History and Background Information

Historically, the public health system in Middle State was based on cooperation between autonomous local health departments and the state health department. The relationship was formalized through contractual arrangements that provided state general revenue funds to the local jurisdictions for core public health activities, including disease surveillance. Most local health departments received the majority of their funding from local taxes, Medicaid charges, and federal funding for nutritional and other services for mothers and children. These departments reported to local governing boards and set their priorities based on local constituent demands and funding source requirements.

Local health departments in cities with less than 75,000 residents were governed by MSDH administrative rules regarding the list of and procedures for reporting disease and health conditions. Larger cities were exempted from these rules by law but were required to establish their own reportable disease lists and submit surveillance data to MSDH. In practice, most cities used the state list along with their own versions of the report form and the processes and procedures. Over time, additional diseases were added to the state report list but rarely were any diseases deleted. The criteria for adding a reportable disease included disease severity, the number of individuals affected by it, and the availability of public health measures to prevent or control it. In 1994, there were 49 diseases and conditions listed in the U.S. Centers for Disease Control and Prevention list of nationally reportable diseases, of which most were included the MSDH list of designated diseases.

The location where a disease case entered the surveillance system depended on the disease, the patient's residence, and the initial recipient of the information. State administrative rules defined those responsible for reporting requirements, although there were no penalties for failure to comply. The list included physicians, laboratories, school nurses, day-care providers, and nursing homes. Hospitals were not included on the list, although they often completed reporting requirements for physicians. In practice, laboratories were the chief source for disease reporting, followed by hospitals and physicians.

Both local and state jurisdictions were responsible for disease control activities, and the locus of responsibility depended on the disease. Local health authorities were responsible for investigating and controlling most reportable diseases, but state authorities would step in when local control was not assumed. MSDH policy specified the need for cooperation with local authorities in cases requiring state involvement. In fact, many smaller local health departments did not have full-time disease control personnel, and these often requested MSDH to assist with surveillance and follow-up activities.

The complexity of the MSDH surveillance system grew over time. Within the Division of Epidemiology, six of the seven programs maintained their own disease registries. Three of these programs (STD/AIDS, TB, and Immunization) received most of their funding from categorical federal grants. Program managers and supervisory staff were CDC employees assigned to MSDH as advisors; CDC determined most aspects of their operations, including the diseases tracked, the data reported to CDC, and even the computer database programs and record format used. Local and district data were transmitted weekly, through computer-modem transmission, to the Miscellaneous Diseases Program Office, where they were aggregated and sent to the appropriate registries, including national reportable data, which were also transmitted to CDC.

The largest of the division's registries, the STD database, received 18,500 case reports in 1994. The TB registry added approximately 10,000 tuberculosis infections and 270 cases per year. The Immunization database added fewer than a hundred cases per year to several hundred per year, varying with the occurrence of outbreaks. The Miscellaneous Diseases and Zoonotic Diseases programs, supported by meager state general revenue funds, shared one centralized disease registry, which in 1994 received approximately 9,000 case reports. The Environmental Health program had two established registries, one for occupational fatalities and one for blood lead–screening results. Each used specialized methods and database formats mandated by federal funding agencies and entered and analyzed data in the program office. About 160 occupational fatalities and 30,000 blood lead–levels were annually recorded.

MSDH distributed specialized case report forms for STDs, TB infection, TB disease, miscellaneous diseases (also used by Zoonotic Diseases and Immunization), miscellaneous diseases reported by laboratories (used by several programs), HIV infection, AIDS, occupational fatalities, and lead screening. In 1994, a new set of specialized forms was being developed by the Environmental Health program for additional reportable conditions. The major metropolitan health departments developed their own case report forms for most of the reportable diseases. A few MSDH forms were universally accepted, most notably for HIV and AIDS. As a result of the variances in report form acceptance and use, physicians, pediatricians, internists, and emergency department physicians, who initially diagnosed most reportable diseases, used at least 10 different report forms to meet surveillance obligations. In addition, each reportable disease had requirements regarding whether it should be reported immediately, by telephone or by mail, and whether the form should be sent to the local health department, district office, or directly to MSDH.

The division's largely decentralized system had positive and negative attributes. Local control allowed physicians and other sources to report to their city or county health department, which helped minimize delays in local case investigation and implementation of control measures. Each large urban and suburban health department and each MSDH district office had access to its own database to track workloads, complete investigations, analyze for local assessment and planning purposes, such as determining trends, identifying high-risk populations, and generating report source feedback reports to local agencies. Localized data entry also reduced the workload burden for MSDH disease registry clerical staff. Although local authorities with investigation resources preferred to maintain control, local control resulted in variations in local policies, procedures, and report forms. These variations affected the quality and accuracy of surveillance procedures, data analyses, report transmissions, and timely disease investigations and follow-up.

THE CHALLENGE

In July 1994, three opportunities for change created visibility for those wanting to address problems and begin reinventing the surveillance system. First, MSDH's capacity in the area of environmental epidemiology was expanded. This created an opportunity for allocation of new resources to expand the surveillance system to include environmental and occupational conditions that were not previously reported and increase the accuracy of and number of reporting sources for surveillance data. The Division Director, Mr. Jenkins, realized the importance of not dedicating new resources to perpetuate and further complicate the existing system. Other individuals supporting the need for change included the state epidemiologist and the program chiefs of the following programs: Sexually Transmitted Diseases/HIV/AIDS, Tuberculosis, Immunization, Zoonotic Diseases, Environmental Epidemiology, and Miscellaneous Diseases. At the local level, the Communicable Disease directors from West City, East City, Suburban East City, and Southwest City, the largest cities in the state, expressed similar concerns.

While these needs were surfacing, the Middle State agency for licensing of physicians offered its newsletter as a forum for informing physicians about disease surveillance reporting obligations. They asked the division to provide their newsletter staff with a precise and succinct description of the state's system and reporting requirements. During the same period, the MSDH director's office identified population health measurement as a priority and created an initiative to assist local health departments in developing community assessment and strategic-planning activities. Local support for this initiative was based on increasing demand for consumable and accurate data on the health status and needs of local populations. Local departments wishing to access all data for community assessment had to request surveillance data from each MSDH program.

As a result of these developments, Mr. Jenkins became more aware of the complexity of the disease-reporting system in Middle State and identified a pressing need to expand surveillance for environmentally induced conditions, teach physicians how to use the reporting system, and make local disease data accessible for local community assessment projects. His challenge, as a leader, was to simplify the system in order to improve its efficiency, accuracy, sensitivity, and ability to have an impact on the continuous improvement of disease-preventing investigation and follow-up policies and procedures. In general, the challenges confronting the division were complicated by

- the variety of division programs involved
- different categorical funding sources
- different federal requirements due to ties to CDC, including different data criteria for each program
- lack of a centralized database
- the obligation of various report sources to submit disease reports, complicated by different disease-specific requirements and report forms
- the involvement of different levels of the public health system in surveillance data management and response

POSTSCRIPT: TAKING ACTION

In October 1994, Mr. Jenkins called a meeting of the program chiefs to discuss possible solutions to the problems facing the division. The following suggestions were made:

- Develop a generic report form. This was supported by Immunization, Miscellaneous Diseases, and Environmental Health but rejected by STD/AIDS and TB. The program chiefs believed that specific, detailed information about clinical history and treatment was essential to determine the appropriate follow-up procedures for each case.
- Utilize electronic disease-reporting methods. The Miscellaneous Diseases program advocated the use of fax and computer bulletin board technology to make reporting easier. This would require development of a simple generic form that could be faxed and scanned.
- Centralize the reporting locus or "target." Some of the larger, well-funded programs advocated centralization of reporting requirements. They requested that all reports be sent directly to MSDH. Others warned that additional (unavailable) resources would be required to handle the increased workload and that centralized reporting could delay local response and investigation. There were additional concerns that transmission of all reports to MSDH would erode communication lines between local health providers and public health departments.

Next, Mr. Jenkins contacted the local communicable disease directors to solicit their input. They were supportive of the concept of a generic report form; West City and Suburban East City already had generic forms in local use and would continue to use them regardless of any changes MSDH implemented. All local directors insisted that local disease reports should be sent directly to them to prevent unacceptable delays in investigation and creation of a negative impact on local reporting relationships. Opinions on fax reporting were divided; some sites were already receiving most of their reports by fax.

A division disease surveillance work group was established that included members from each of the disease control programs, the four city communicable disease directors, and three other members from local health agencies involved in surveillance and follow-up. The committee chose simplification of reporting requirements as its first priority. Its tasks included

- updating the disease report list
- reducing the report categories to two
- eliminating outdated report requirements
- expanding the categories of sources required to submit disease reports (it added hospitals to the list) and defining group practice requirements
- developing a generic disease report form

The committee accomplished these objectives during the spring of 1995 and received board approval the following August. In October 1995, these policy changes were published in the Middle State Register for public comment. It was expected that policies recommended by the committee would go into effect by April 1996.

All jurisdictions involved were in agreement over the use of the new generic report form as well as other policy-simplifying report requirements. These changes represented a major shift in collaboration at all levels to ensure meeting public health needs. However, the remaining challenges were formidable. The fundamental problem regarding the locus of responsibility for reports entering the system and local jurisdiction over local disease surveillance continued to raise concerns. Providers remained unclear as to where reports should be sent. The issue of managing disease surveillance data from customer source to an electronic system that could transmit information to the appropriate locus and ensure disease investigation and follow-up also remained a challenge.

Case Study 6–B

Cornerstone: Illinois' Approach to Service Integration

James R. Nelson

BACKGROUND

As federal and state governmental agencies became more involved in community health services, funding was increasingly offered through grants for specific diseases and other public health issues. Over a 20-year period, this funding approach resulted in numerous discreet, single-purpose programs, each with its own reporting requirements and information system. Unintended consequences of this phenomenon were fragmented, episodic, and incomplete service delivery; repetitive registration processes; redundant data collection and reporting; nonstandard assessments; incomplete understanding of clients' service history; and inconsistent documentation of services. Fundamentally, the core functions of public health—assessment, policy development, and assurance—were undermined by the continued proliferation of discreet and separate services.

Recognizing the significance and extent of discreet service delivery, the Illinois Department of Public Health and now the Illinois Department of Human Services, moved to integrate the services of several health programs. At the heart of the issue was the need for a mechanism that would facilitate and encourage service integration and, ultimately, improve the health outcomes of Illinois residents. After considerable research and development, as well as the active participation of a diverse group of health care and human service providers, the department implemented a package of tools that redesigned community service delivery into an integrated system of care. That package of tools was Cornerstone.

At the beginning of the process, in 1992, the department offered several different maternal and child health programs. These included WIC; Healthy Moms/Healthy Kids; EPSDT, pediatric primary care, immunizations, Families with a Future, Drug Free Families with a Future, and Parents Too Soon, a teen pregnancy program; and a prenatal smoking cessation program. Statewide, 173 WIC clinics, 104 Healthy Moms/Healthy Kids agencies, 115 immunization sites, and 91 primary pediatric care programs offered services. At that time, several data systems supported the information needs of many of these programs, including the following:

- A statewide WIC system developed in 1989. This system operated on a PC-based network, using a mainframe for support. The system automated the nutritional risk assessment and food coupon issuance functions of the WIC program.
- A case management information system (CMIS) originally developed for the Medicaid-eligible client population. The CMIS was a PC-based, batch-oriented system for which data were entered locally and submitted for update on disk via mail.
- A HM/HK case management system. The system had limited functionality and insufficient hardware resources.
- Distributed immunization databases. As an enhancement to the WIC system, several screens specific to immunization history and current status were created. The immunization data were collected locally and not compiled into a central registry.

The selection of Chicago as a federal Healthy Start Infant Mortality Reduction project site provided an opportunity for Illinois to initiate an integrated information system to support greater coordination, standardization, and sharing of information among community health programs. The requirement of the Healthy Start project to design an information system for collecting evaluation data was also viewed as a way to integrate MCH-related information systems that were not integrated with respect to clients or front-line practitioners and thus led to duplicative intake processes and information collection.

The development of the integrated information system was approached from several key philosophical points of reference. First, to the extent that potential system users were invested in the system from its inception, they would be more likely to use it. Second, to the extent that system developers understood program service delivery, they would better be able to customize it to provider needs. To facilitate this understanding, an individual with a social sciences background served as a liaison between service providers and technical staff during the design process.

An executive steering committee was formed to facilitate planning and ensure diverse representation and contributions to the project. The committee included representatives from the then state Departments of Public Health; Alcohol and Substance Abuse; Public Aid; Mental Health and Developmental Disabilities; and Children and Family Services as well as advocates and members of the provider community. The committee met frequently, and several subcommittees and standing committees were responsible for addressing specific areas, such as legal issues, local implementation, program implementation, system support, and funding. As many as 40 individuals participated in the committee work and reviewed the project design.

CORNERSTONE

One result of these efforts was Cornerstone. A management information system, Cornerstone supported a case management framework that ensures delivery of prenatal care, well-child visits, nutrition products and education, and immunizations in over 300 separate locations across the state. Its design capitalized on the original WIC service delivery and information system. Cornerstone's features included combined registration, standardized risk assessment, automated care plan development, and consolidated referral and scheduling. Demographic and eligibility information specific to a client was captured once and shared with all other service providers that used the system when caring for the client. The system also provided a client's service history to the various providers responsible for that client. Following is a brief overview of the systems features from the perspective of a system user.

REGISTRATION

When registering a client, a case manager checked the client's enrollment status by searching a locally based statewide index. In this checking process, the case manager could have used the client's identification numbers assigned through Medicaid, WIC, or other community health programs. Potential matches were pulled into the local system and displayed. If no match was found, the case manager enrolled the client and created a Cornerstone participant identification number. During the matching process, the case manager also obtained critical client information through the system (e.g., previously identified medical problems, MCH program status, and contact information).

ASSESSMENT

During an assessment interview, case managers accessed a table of standardized questions designed to assess a client's medical and/or psycho/social risk and prompt either "yes" or "no" or numeric responses. The system compared the responses to a table of normative values for that assessment type, generating a list of goals and recommended services. For example, a "yes" response to the question "Are you pregnant?" automatically generated the goal of adequate prenatal care and a list of recommended services (i.e., prenatal care, prenatal education, WIC, and prepared childbirth education).

GOALS

The risk factors were linked to a set of goals associated with specific services and outlined a recommended care plan. The case manager reviewed the goals and services for appropriateness and had the option, based on professional judgment, to modify these recommendations. The care plan highlighted two dimensions: (1) adult/child services that incorporated MCH elements, prenatal care, well-child care, and injury prevention and (2) a risk assessment that included information on transportation, child care needs, and other requirements.

ACTIVITIES AND SERVICES

Based on the care plan, a tickler file generated a list of activities and services requiring follow-up or monitoring. To facilitate the referral process, the system offered a localized provider database organized by type of service. The case manager could have selected services based on provider address, volume, or client preference. Provider selection was linked to the client record and documented in the care plan, reminding case managers to follow up to ensure receipt of services.

REFERRAL AND SCHEDULING

Scheduling within a clinic consisted of matching the client's service needs with the available internal and external providers. The case manager accessed the family's schedule to coordinate all appointments.

Cornerstone technical architecture was based on a PC local area network (LAN) that supported activities in the community health services clinic. The activities, particularly the ones that relied on information sharing between various program providers, were supported by a technical architecture consisting of LANs, wide area networks (WANs), and the state's central computing operation. The LANs supported 2 to 30 workstations (one for each case manager) per service location. Locally collected client information was transmitted to the state nightly for central processing. The WAN enabled local agencies to share appropriate data about clients among themselves. Access to WAN data was accomplished through a "read-only" mode; it can be read but not modified. Access was available on an as-needed basis and was accomplished by a function (or "hot") key built into specific screens. This protocol ensured the autonomy of agency operations in the event of a WAN failure.

As designed, the system consisted of approximately 150 screens and generated as many pre-established reports. It was written in FoxPro, a DOS-based software language, and utilized pulldown menus.

The development and design work was completed in 1995. In May of that year, the long process of installing the system in 300 service locations began. The Healthy Start agencies served as pilot sites where the software and installation processes were tested, reviewed, and documented. The enormousness of deploying Cornerstone across the state—which entailed supplying, installing, and maintaining equipment; providing training on system procedures; and encouraging local program providers unaccustomed to the intricacies of an integrated computer system to accept the new system—prompted a partnership with the Illinois Primary Health Care Association (IPHCA). The association was uniquely qualified for this partnership role because of its widely recognized role as advocate for community health services in Illinois. For the next two years, until December 1997, IPHCA worked side by side with state staff to install over 3,000 computer workstations in 300 locations.

The development of Cornerstone represented an effective response to a situation that was weakening the core functions of public health. Community-based programs provided in a discreet fashion were making uniform assessment, system-wide policy development, and accurate assurance nearly impossible. Underlying Cornerstone's development were a series of guiding principles that in the end ensured the system's successful deployment. These principles included the desirability of listening to diverse viewpoints through a process of inclusion; the benefits of forging partnerships among those involved in service delivery; the interrelatedness of health care problems and social service needs; the necessity of comprehensive solutions rather than "bandage" remedies; and the need to promote service integration wherever possible. By adhering to such principles and by incorporating modern technology, the department has operationalized a model that strengthens community health management through efficient and optimal use of available information.

REFERENCES

1. J. McKnight, *The Careless Society* (New York: Basic Books, 1995).
2. McKnight, *The Careless Society*.
3. K.G. Keppel and M.A. Freedman, "What Is Assessment?" *Journal of Public Health Management and Practice* 1, no. 2 (1995): 1–7.
4. L. Novick, "Public Health Assessment in a New Context," *Journal of Public Health Management and Practice* 1, no. 2 (1995): v.
5. P.C. Nasca, "Public Health Assessment in the 1990s," *Journal of Public Health Management and Practice* 1, no. 2 (1995): vii–viii.
6. Keppel and Freedman, "What Is Assessment?"
7. Keppel and Freedman, "What Is Assessment?"
8. B.J. Turnock et al., "Implementing and Assessing Organizational Practice in Public Health," *Public Health Reports* 109, no. 4 (1994): 478–484.
9. *Assessment Protocol for Excellence in Public Health* (Atlanta: Centers for Disease Control and National Association of County Health Officials, 1991).
10. M.W. Kreuter, "PATCH: Its Origin, Basic Concepts, and Links to Contemporary Public Health Policy," *Journal of Health Education* 23, no. 3 (1992): 135–139.
11. Centers for Disease Control and Prevention, "PATCH: Planned Approach to Community Health," draft (Atlanta: Centers for Disease Control and Prevention, 1994).
12. Centers for Disease Control and Prevention, "PATCH: Planned Approach to Community Health."
13. A. Steckler et al., "Summary of a Formative Evaluation of PATCH," *Journal of Health Education* 23, no. 3 (1992): 174–178.
14. American Public Health Association, *Healthy Communities 2000: Model Standards*, 3d ed. (Washington, DC: American Public Health Association, 1991).

15. American Public Health Association, *Healthy Communities 2000: Model Standards*.
16. American Public Health Association, *Healthy Communities 2000: Model Standards*.
17. American Public Health Association, *The Guide to Implemented Model Standards* (Washington, DC: American Public Health Association, 1993).
18. American Public Health Association, *The Guide to Implemented Model Standards*.
19. S. Randolph and J. Ford, *Community Strategies for Health: Fitting in the Pieces* (Washington, DC: American Public Health Association, 1994).
20. Randolph and Ford, *Community Strategies for Health*.
21. L.M. Anderson et al., "Design and Use of the Behavioral Risk Factor Surveillance System," *Illinois Morbidity and Mortality Quarterly* 1, no. 3 (1994): 16–23.
22. J.M. Bacon et al., "A Consortium Approach to Local Behavioral Risk Factor Assessment," *Illinois Morbidity and Mortality Quarterly* 1, no. 3 (1994): 1–3.
23. J.I. Staff and J. Zimmerman, "Adams County Behavioral Risk Factor Survey Project," *Illinois Morbidity and Mortality Quarterly* 1, no. 3 (1994): 9–11.
24. E. Prez-Stable et al., "Behavioral Risk Factors: A Comparison of Latinos and Non-Latino Whites in San Francisco," *American Journal of Public Health* 84, no. 6 (1994): 971–976.
25. J. Studinicki et al., "A Community Health Report Card: Comprehensive Assessment for Tracking Community Health (CATCH)," *Best Practices and Benchmarking in Healthcare* 2, no. 5 (1997): 196–207.
26. L. Potts et al., *The Growth of Managed Care* (Washington, DC: Association of Schools of Public Health, 1998).
27. K. Jennings et al., *Changing Health Care* (Santa Monica, CA: Knowledge Exchange, 1997).
28. Potts et al., *The Growth of Managed Care*.
29. T. Norris and L. Howell, *Healthy People in Healthy Communities: A Dialogue Guide* (Chicago: Coalition for Healthy Cities and Communities, 1998).
30. A. Friede et al., "Public Health Informatics: How Information Age Technology Can Strengthen Public Health," *Annual Review of Public Health* 16 (1995): 239–252.
31. W.L. Roper and G.P. Mays, "GIS and Public Health Policy: A New Frontier for Improving Community Health," *Journal of Public Health Management and Practice* 5, no. 2 (1999): vi–vii.
32. J.K.H. Tan, *Health Management Information Systems* (Gaithersburg, MD: Aspen Publishers, 1995).
33. Friede et al., "Public Health Informatics."
34. J.R. Lumpkin, "Six Principles of Public Health Information," *Journal of Public Health Management and Practice* 1, no. 1 (1995): 40–41.
35. E.L. Baker et al., CDC's Information Network for Public Health Officials (INPHO): A Framework for Integrated Public Health Information and Practice," *Journal of Public Health Management and Practice* 1, no. 1 (1995): 43–47.

Chapter 7

Leadership and Policy Development

Leaders are willing to take the blame.

William Foege, Speech to Public Health Leadership Society

Through assessment activities, public health leaders evaluate the community's health status and identify health problems and risks that need to be addressed. The task they next face is to determine how to deal with the identified problems and risks. The activity of devising effective courses of action (or plans) for problem resolution and risk reduction is known as "policy development," and it constitutes the second core function of public health. The final task is to implement the policies that have been designed. This task is known as "assurance," for by implementing effective policies and enforcing laws and regulations, public health leaders help to assure the health of community residents.

All state health departments are involved with policy formulation at some level. State health department activities related to policy development include health planning; policy analysis; and the setting of regulations, standards, health objectives, and disaster and emergency public health procedures. Peripheral activities include building coalitions, empowering community organizations, and determining health priorities.

In his 1991 presidential address to the American Public Health Association (APHA), William Keck argued that the public health community must change its thinking about policy if it is ever to meet the health needs of the American public. The public health community has tended to let market forces and political expediency shape American public health policy rather than look for techniques for maximizing health status. Keck also claimed that American political leaders have a responsibility to develop sound public health policies for the nation. When they fail in their responsibility, they must be held accountable. Methods must be found for getting our leaders to move in different directions. Finally, Keck emphasized the importance of creating linkages between academics, practitioners, and the public in order to empower communities to assess their health status and set health priorities and in order to foster community-based demands for humane decision making.

In her 1992 APHA presidential address, Joyce Lashof stated that public health has made its greatest advances through its commitment to the common good and its strong support for the principles of social justice.[1] Despite these commitments, progress has been erratic, and there continue to be disparities in the health status of socioeconomically, racially, and ethnically diverse communities. The American economic policies of the 1980s and early 1990s have made these disparities worse. Lashof also said that health reform is needed in our society to improve its record in the areas of health promotion, health protection, and disease prevention.

Exercise 7–1 is an experiment in policy development. It concerns an issue that a local health department and the county board may both have an interest in trying to resolve through the creation of a new policy. Public health departments often recognize potential problems before they become fully mature, giving public health and community leaders the opportunity to deal with the problems before they become unmanageable.

INSTITUTE OF MEDICINE POLICY DEVELOPMENT RECOMMENDATIONS

In 1988, the Institute of Medicine issued a report entitled *The Future of Public Health.*[2] The report, which listed recommendations regarding policy development, emphasized that public health agencies, in constructing policies, need to balance political realities and professional practice concerns and should always try to serve the interests of community constituents. They also need to provide leadership in policy development, promote the use of scientific knowledge in decision making, and use a strategic planning approach based on the democratic principles. Specific recommendations contained in the report include the following:

1. Public health leaders need to develop relationships and positive partnerships with legislators. They also need to inform politicians and other public officials of the community assessment results. The education of public officials should include an explanation of the strategies being employed by the health department to address health priorities.
2. Agency personnel need to learn the skills of constituency building as well as citizen participation techniques. Citizen involvement in program development needs to be encouraged.
3. It is important to create partnerships between the public health agency leaders, the medical community, and other private sector health entities.
4. Agencies need to cultivate relationships with other professional and citizen groups involved with public health. Such groups might include voluntary health organizations, groups concerned with improving social services, environmental organizations, and economic development organizations.
5. Public health agencies must educate the public on public health issues.
6. Public health agencies need to ensure that the quality of their contacts with grass-roots organizations and community residents is cooperative in nature as well as productive.

ORGANIZATIONAL PRACTICES

Three organizational practices are associated with the policy development core function. The first involves acting as an advocate for public health, building coalitions, and developing community resources. Four performance indicators were given by Turnock and colleagues:[3]

1. The local health department meets regularly with health-related organizations.
2. The local health department disseminates information on public health to the community on a regular basis.
3. The local health department disseminates information on public health to the local media on a regular basis.
4. The local health department mission is given a public review every five years or less.

The second organizational practice involves setting health priorities based on the size and severity of the problems and the acceptability, economic feasibility, and effectiveness of the possible interventions. The three performance indicators were these:

5. The local health department prioritizes community health needs based on the size and severity of the needs.
6. The local health department prioritizes needs based on the possible interventions.
7. The local health department takes into account community input when prioritizing needs.

The third organizational practice involves the development of action plans to deal with the health priorities. It includes the establishment of goals and objectives to be achieved by implementation of the plans. Four performance indicators were given for this practice:

8. The local health department develops action plans to address priority health needs.
9. The local health department fosters public participation in the development of the action plans.
10. The local health department incorporates policy analysis into the development of the action plans.
11. The local health department develops a long-range strategic plan that is linked to community action plans.

Below are listed policy development guidelines for public health leaders:

- Stress the importance of governance and its implications for the effectiveness of the public health system.
- Develop policies that build the core functions and essential services of public health into a community-based public health program.
- Learn to share power.
- Put policies into action.

THE POLITICS OF PUBLIC HEALTH POLICY

Policy development is a complex process in which the participants consider alternatives for action and decide which alternatives to implement. It is a team process, and many individuals and organizations can be involved, including state and local boards of health, elected officials, community groups, public health professionals, health care providers, and private citizens. Factors that the participants typically need to take into account in their decision making include budgetary considerations; federal, state, and local regulations; and program and organizational operating procedures.

The infrastructure of public health is currently at risk because of the general attack on social programs in Congress and in state legislatures throughout the United States. The discontent with social programs in the United States can be traced back to the 1960s, when many of them were created. Since then, the American public seems to have grown increasingly disenchanted with such programs, largely because of the supposed negative effects of the welfare state as well as doubts about the effectiveness of current programs.[4] There is evidence that the public will no longer tolerate increases in taxation to support social programs, including public health programs, and indeed in the mid-1990s public health programs appeared to have come under special assault.

Part of the discontent with federally operated social programs is based on skepticism regarding the competency of the federal government. "Decentralization" was a watchword of the 1990s, and states and local governments took over many programs that had been run by the federal government. On the other hand, part of the discontent is probably based on the idea that social programs act as replacements for traditional groups devoted to problem solving and helping people live better lives.[5] Furthermore, so goes the thinking, social programs, by weakening the authority of traditional groups and encouraging people to become dependent on the government for help, create a demand for more social programs, which foster a higher level of dependency, and on and on in a vicious circle.

It is easy to see the appeal of the view that communities should redefine themselves, re-establish traditional values, and become less dependent on government. Yet it is also easy to see that public health programs are importantly different from other programs. Whereas individuals arguably should assume more responsibility for protecting their own health, surely some type of public health system is necessary to assess health hazards, educate the public about these hazards, and provide population-based services designed to help individuals shed harmful behaviors. Public health leaders need to become advocates for their own agencies and for a population-based approach to health promotion and disease prevention. They also need to distinguish public health programs from other types of social programs and make a strong case that public health programs should be supported no matter what other programs the public chooses to dispense with.

According to one definition, politics is the process of putting the moral consensus of the community into practice.[6] In democratic politics at its best, interested parties discuss the issues face to face, reach a consensus, and develop and implement policies. Yet in this country conflict always enters the picture, because the ideology of self-interest (the American ethic of individualism and search for personal success) is at odds with the strong concern Americans have for promoting and protecting the community. The ideology of self-interest leads to the development of special interest coalitions, and one of the challenges faced by public health leaders is to find ways to promote the community and satisfy special interest groups at the same time.

Among the strategies that can be used to meet this challenge are the following:[7]

- Community leaders and organizations and special interest groups should be involved in policy development.
- The policies developed and implemented should include some that tie together medical care and public health activities. Health promotion is a shared responsibility and calls for interagency collaboration in the pursuit of population-based goals.
- The policies should also include some that will help build a community-oriented continuum of care. Primary prevention programs clearly need to be community based. Examples include programs to reduce the prevalence of lead paint, provide acquired immune deficiency syndrome (AIDS) education, and get people to stop smoking.

Below are some guidelines related to the politics of public health policy development:

- Consider national health and social policy trends when developing local policies.
- Make a case for the importance of having a governmental public health presence in the community.
- Use special public health interest groups in public health policy development.
- Develop integrated and interdependent health and social policies for the community.

POLICY TRENDS

Policy development, far from being a modern invention, is a universal requirement of community living, and it is affected by the historical circumstances in which it occurs. Many social science theorists have looked at historical trends and studied the social and cultural principles tied to these trends. Indeed, with the coming of the new millennium, there has been increasing interest in understanding where we are and where we are headed.

As discussed in Chapter 4, Alvin Toffler claimed that civilization had undergone three major periods of change, which he referred to as three waves. Assuming this is a defensible way of looking at human history, the third wave (the information age) will probably be followed by a fourth wave, which, according to Maynard and Mehrtens, will be a period in which humans will attempt to integrate all aspects of life and show an increased concern and sense of responsibility for the whole.[8] People will also attempt to tap into their full range of perceptual and cognitive abilities. The concepts of global stewardship and cultural diversity will grow in importance. Organizations will become strongly oriented toward service, they will become collaborative systems in which power is shared by everyone, and partnership development will be the key to organizational success.[9]

Toffler's theories became extremely influential in the mid-1990s. In early 1995, Newt Gingrich, speaker of the House of Representatives, assigned the recently published *Creating a New Civilization*,[10] by Alvin Toffler and Heidi Toffler, to newly elected congressional representatives. This book appeared to influence congressional agendas over the next few years, although the prestige of the Toffler model seems to have waned recently.

In the preface to *Creating a New Civilization,* Gingrich stated that the present structure of the federal government is tied too closely to the industrialism of the past. The government needs to redefine itself in light of third-wave changes. In his own book, *To Renew America,* Gingrich said that America needs to move forward into the information age and to recognize how technology has changed our lives.[11] If the United States does not change the way it does its work, the standard of living of the American people will deteriorate. Whether or not everyone agrees with Toffler's theory of historical waves, no one can escape from the fact that change is a constant.

Furthermore, the way problems are handled changes as the rules of the game change. This means that the field of public health will need to change as well. In all likelihood, the relationship between personal health care issues and population-based services will be expanded and redefined. Some local health departments will become managed care entities. Most public health activities will be team based. The horizontal organization will become a reality, and the old vertical bureaucracies will continue to break down. Community health coalitions will encompass all stakeholders. Public-private partnerships will increase in number, and privatization will become more prevalent. Public health responsibilities will become increasingly decentralized. Public health will be viewed as the community's business, and different groups will take responsibility for different activities. Governance will finally become communitywide, not just limited to the few stakeholders or politicians at the top.

Public health leaders, besides acting as protectors of community values, will need to help the community redefine its values and generate new values that reflect current realities. Political structures will change as more people become involved in political activities. Public health leaders will work in the community more and be less agency-bound than in the past. The community will become stronger and its residents more empowered. Universal access to a multitude of services will be the rule rather than the exception. The quality of life for most people will improve.

In order to increase their understanding of social and economic trends, public health leaders will need to learn the techniques of forecasting. Public health leaders are seen as experts on the health issues of their communities, and public health agency governing boards look to them for guidance on what the future is likely to hold and how to prepare for future developments.

Quantitative forecasting involves applying a set of statistical techniques to present data sets. Statisticians usually do the actual manipulation of numbers. Quantitative forecasting techniques include regression and time series analysis, which can be used to predict public health trends over a period of time and into the future.[12] A regression model mathematically predicts the effect of change in one factor on other factors. For example, immunization compliance for children under two years of age increased during the 1990s. A regression model could help determine the impact of immunization compliance on other health status indicators. Finally, econometric techniques can be used to forecast future program costs.

Qualitative forecasting uses experts to make predictions.[13] One qualitative forecasting method is to survey a number of experts (a so-called opinion jury) and analyze their responses statistically. Another method is to survey clients and evaluate their responses. Reviewing similar case studies to identify trends is a third method. As an example of qualitative forecasting, imagine a local health department in a rural area is concerned about the potential impact of a new managed care organization. The health department administrator might hire a consulting organization with expertise in managed care organization development and the effects that the entry of a managed care organization is likely to have on existing health care and public health service providers in the community.

Futurists are experts in predicting the future, or at least experts in painting pictures of different possible futures, and considering the scenarios they devise can be helpful for "testing" alternative policies. Public health leaders can see what will be the overall outcome if one policy is chosen and one scenario occurs, if the same policy is chosen and a second scenario occurs, and so on. Together with estimations of the likelihood of the various scenarios, this type of review of different outcomes can help public health leaders make rational decisions as to which policies to implement.

In order to make good policy decisions, public health leaders need to

- study their community's past
- understand how local and state public health agencies have affected health outcomes over time
- learn forecasting techniques
- explore national trends and compare them with local and state trends
- apply forecasting techniques in a rational way to best reflect social and economic realities
- develop policies that take cost into account
- modify forecasts or develop new ones if new information becomes available

ADVOCACY AND EMPOWERMENT

During the 1970s and 1980s, public health advocacy was viewed as an important tool for social change. The assumption was that people with all types of problems benefited from having professionals speak for them and protect their rights. Public health leaders took on the responsibility of protecting the health of community residents and pushing for the appropriate interventions to be made available to residents facing health problems or health risks. In recent years, the advocacy movement has been criticized for being too paternalistic. Community leaders have argued that they understand their communities better than the health professionals who work there (partly because the latter often live elsewhere). Advocacy without personal community involvement leads to credibility loss within the population supposedly being protected.

Public health leaders have reduced their advocacy efforts not only because they have become frustrated by their inability to gain acceptance within the communities they serve but also because advocacy has been confused with lobbying.[14] Lobbying is an activity pursued by special interests—usually an organization or group of related organizations—in order to influence the enactment or administration of laws. Advocacy is much broader in scope. Advocacy in support of public policy change involves research, policy statement development, action planning, implementation, and evaluation.

Advocacy activities are also to be distinguished from the enforcement of rules and regulations. Advocacy focuses on policy changes necessary to improve the health of the public, not the administration of existing policies. Public health leaders thus need to balance their advocacy efforts, in which there is room for passion, and their enforcement efforts, which should be dispassionate. If they have been successful in building trust and credibility in the local community, they will be able to involve the community in both health regulation and advocacy. One requisite for engaging the community in advocacy for policy changes is to communicate the reasons the changes are necessary.

Another disadvantage of advocacy by professionals is that they tend to be oriented toward the weaknesses of the community rather than its strengths.[15] Stressing the negatives often leads to fragmented problem-solving and partial solutions. In addition, the community's culture, which is typically intertwined with its problems and will have an effect on attempted solutions, is often neglected. Thus, there is a strong argument that people need to become self-advocates and not rely on third parties to protect their interests. Additional support for this conclusion is that policies developed and implemented without community involvement have historically failed. Therefore, at the very least, professional advocacy and community self-advocacy need to be combined. Each group—the professionals and the community residents—brings different strengths to the partnership and contributes to the total impact of the advocacy on the policy makers they are trying to influence.

In their efforts to empower community residents to become self-advocates, public health leaders need to understand that empowerment will not work if it is treated as a fad.[16] Empowerment means that someone will have to give up power and dominance. Public health leaders, by virtue of their skills and their leadership positions in public health organizations, tend to have more prestige as public health advocates and more control than community residents. They need to give up some of their power if empowerment is to occur. Furthermore, empowerment should be systemwide and not restricted to the community leadership. The object is to give all residents in the community a sense that they have some say over public health policy.

There are four aspects to personal empowerment. First, each individual must have a vision for him- or herself and for the local community. Second, the individual needs to identify and manage the other constituencies with which the individual has a relationship. Third, the individual needs to give up a personal wish for dependency on others (this is exceedingly important). Finally, the individual has to have the courage to make the community vision come to life. In empowerment, there is a belief that change is possible and that, through strength, problems will be solved. Empowered people believe that they can make a difference and affect policy decisions.

Exhibit 4–2 presented a list of 10 principles of empowerment that public health leaders can use in their attempts to empower community residents. Public health leaders should also consider taking on a mentoring role in the community. The people they are trying to empower have not, for the most part, exercised power before, at least in the public health area, and they will need guidance as they learn new behaviors.

People to be empowered need to be given authority equal to the responsibilities that they have accepted or that have been assigned to them.[17] Next, they need to learn the appropriate standards of excellence and the skills they must have to meet these standards. Mediocrity is not the goal. Public health professionals and community residents can clearly work together to improve the quality of life but the residents need information on healthy lifestyles and the skills to bring these healthy lifestyles into reality.

Public health leaders must provide community residents with feedback on the progress they have made toward meeting their goals. They could, for instance, develop a community report card or some other mechanism to report back to the residents public health successes and failures. They should also recognize the community's successes in some special way. If the teenage pregnancy rate were to drop significantly in a community, this should be publicized or otherwise specially noted.

The issue of trust plays an important role in community empowerment. Not only must community residents be given the power to make decisions on their own behalf, but they must be trusted to make good decisions. Community leaders often have difficulty recognizing that all residents are entitled to trust. Residents are also entitled to make mistakes. Life includes good decisions as well as bad. Finally, residents have the right to be respected and to be able to maintain their dignity in the community. Public health agencies sometimes struggle to respect these citizen rights fully, especially in situations where cultural diversity is present.

Social and behavioral scientists often wince at the softness of the issues being raised here. A better reaction would be for them to study the advocacy and empowerment process and determine whether empowerment increases the chance of attaining health objectives in a community. They could also investigate whether people with severe mental and physical disabilities, immigrants who do not speak English, homebound individuals, high-risk mothers, chronically ill individuals, persons with AIDS, alcohol or substance abusers, suicide- or homicide-prone individuals, abusive families, or the homeless can become successful self-advocates? These issues need to be studied in order to understand the complexities of empowerment.

Following are advocacy guidelines for public health leaders:

- Build trust and credibility with community constituents.
- Empower others to be advocates.
- Do background research on health issues and draft policy statements in the form of legislative bills.
- Work with elected or appointed officials on the enactment of appropriate legislation.

COLLABORATION

Citizen and community empowerment lays the groundwork for the collaboration between organizations, constituencies, and individuals to influence the policy development process. Collaboration can take many forms, and collaborative groups come in many types. Cohen and colleagues identified five.[18] Advisory committees offer suggestions and provide technical assistance to leaders, programs, or organizations. Commissions are usually composed of citizens appointed by official bodies. (The problem with commissions is that the appointments are often political.) Consortia (or alliances) are semi-official in nature. They tend to have broad policy-oriented goals and may cover large geographic areas. A single consortium may include several coalitions. Networks, which are fairly loose in organization, are created for the purpose of resource or information sharing. Finally, task forces are short-lived groups created to address a specific issue.

For our purposes, we will divide collaborative groups into coalitions, which are loosely structured; alliances, which are structured around a specific organizational agenda; and partnerships, which are highly structured (and often contractual). Each type of collaborative group is discussed in turn.

Coalitions

A coalition is the coming together of people and organizations to influence outcomes related to a specific problem or set of problems.[19] The synergism of joint action allows a coalition to accomplish a broader array of goals than could the participants acting on their own. (See Chapter 4 for a discussion of the importance of coalitions for the assessment core function. Exhibit 4–3 presents an eight-step approach to coalition building.)

The collaborative relationship that sometimes forms between a public health agency, other health and human service–related organizations, and various community constituencies is typically coalition-like.[20] Such coalitions are created to get the organizations and constituencies involved in addressing community health needs and issues. They tend to be less structured than other types of collaborative groupings, and participants move in and out of the coalition as situations and priorities change.

To establish a coalition, a public health agency must make use of a number of strategies, including the following three.[21] First, it needs to establish a dialogue on health service delivery and policy with possible partners. Second, it needs to create a pool of groups willing to collaborate on the resolution of public health issues. This pool might include

- at-risk groups affected by the health issues
- allies with whom the agency shares common interests
- experts knowledgeable about the issues
- associates that the agency works with on a day-to-day basis
- opposition groups that may challenge agency positions on the issues
- third-party groups indirectly affected by the issues
- state and local government officials who have influence on public policy
- media organizations

Third, the agency needs to establish a communication network for the purpose of exchanging information. Communication is essential for promoting the coalition and mobilizing the members to take action to meet the community's health needs, which is, after all, the whole purpose of creating the coalition.

Coalitions have several significant advantages, which are listed below:[22]

- A coalition can conserve resources, because the participants cooperate in promoting the coalition's agenda and avoid duplication of efforts.
- A coalition is an excellent communication tool, for its member organizations can send out its message to many more people than any single organization can.

- A coalition, through synergy, can achieve more objectives than could the participant organizations acting alone. For example, it possesses greater power to influence political decision makers.
- A coalition has a credibility advantage over its individual members. There is clearly strength in numbers.
- A coalition provides a mechanism for sharing information. For instance, one coalition member can provide information to others not able to attend a meeting, and the entire coalition or individual members can develop releases to provide to the media.
- A coalition typically has a lead agency that most of the coalition members provide with advice, guidance, and direction. In the case of public health coalitions, the lead agency is usually the local health department or public health agency.
- A coalition helps the representatives from member organizations by improving their self-esteem, giving them personal satisfaction, and developing their understanding of their organizations' roles in improving the health of the public.
- Finally, a coalition can foster cooperation among the members and can strengthen the community by concentrating on the community's strengths.

On the downside, a public health coalition takes some effort to sustain. Over time, the community and the community's health needs will change, and the coalition must change in concert. In addition, conflicts over turf occasionally occur, and schisms within the coalition can make it more difficult to deal with public health issues than if the coalition did not exist.

Alliances

A community health alliance is a group of health care and public health organizations that have combined forces to address key public health risks and problems for the population of a specific geographic area.[23] Although the participating organizations may benefit from the alliance, the purpose of the alliance is to meet the needs of the community residents. A community health alliance might include the local public health agency, health care providers, payers, purchasers of services, advocacy groups, community social service agencies, and neighborhood groups.

Alliances can be divided into three types.[24] An opportunistic alliance is created to increase the knowledge and expertise of organizations in a new field of operation. This new information may be used to develop a new type of program in a community. For example, a local public health agency may collaborate with a number of health maintenance organizations to learn how their managed care programs work and then use this information to develop a Medicaid managed care program of its own.

A resource dependency alliance is created to provide a needed service or resource for multiple health care organizations. For example, a local health department may agree to immunize all children less than two years of age in the community, preventing other health care organizations from having to develop immunization programs.

A stakeholder alliance is developed by organizations willing to work together to achieve a common objective. For example, the alliance members may jointly develop a trauma registry to better document trauma-related problems in the community.

Partnerships

In the early 1990s, partnership became a favored type of collaborative relationship. The partnering process requires each partner to show respect for the other partners and put personal or organizational agendas aside. The partners, whether from the public or private sector, treat each other as equals. That means, not that all issues are raised and dealt with at once, but rather that all partners engage as equals in the decision-making process. In an effective partnership, the partners share a vision, are committed to the integrity of the partnership, agree on specific goals, and develop a plan of action to accomplish the goals. A partnership may have a partnering agreement, which is like a contract, to guide its activities.

Summary

Case Study 7–A looks at a coalition created to develop a policy on leaf burning. Parents of asthmatic children, county public officials, and concerned citizens wanted an ordinance passed that would restrict leaf burning in the county, and by working together they were able to achieve their goal, although not all members of the coalition were perfectly happy with the regulations resulting from their efforts.

To promote the public health agenda, public health leaders should

- identify potential collaborators among community organizations
- engage in discussion with potential collaborators to determine whether enough commonality of interest exists to justify creating a coalition, alliance, or partnership
- for each collaborative relationship, establish goals that all parties in the relationship are committed to achieving
- use the type of collaborative relationship that is most appropriate for addressing the issues of concern
- show respect for the other members of a collaborative relationship

PRIORITY SETTING

The community assessment process ends with the setting of priorities. In fact, priority setting is a link between assessment and policy development, since which policy issues are chosen to be worked on is determined by the priority-setting process.[25]

Setting local public health priorities should be a communitywide activity.[26] The process should include major health agencies, community organizations, key community constituencies, and individuals. Elected and appointed officials will need to put their stamp of approval on the chosen list of priorities, and they might demand changes in the list. For example, public health leaders concerned about an increase in teenage pregnancy in the community may recommend the distribution of condoms in high school clinics. If the community is politically conservative, the condom distribution recommendation may be overridden by elected or school officials.

According to one author, those engaged in priority setting should follow these eight guidelines:

1. Set realistic goals to maintain credibility.
2. Formulate the goals in understandable terms for the public at large.
3. Set goals that combine process and outcome.
4. Set quantitative and qualitative goals that are able to be evaluated.
5. Evaluate progress toward the achievement of health goals at regular intervals.
6. Set goals that can be pursued in compatible ways across geographic boundaries.
7. Develop techniques to handle data constraints.
8. Set goals that reflect the concerns of all interested parties.[27]

Three other guidelines are worth considering. First, those who are establishing the priorities must determine the magnitude of each problem and the ability of the public health agency to address the problem given the existing staff and budgetary constraints. Second, they must estimate the seriousness of the consequences if the problem was not addressed or only partially addressed. Third, they must decide whether it is feasible to resolve the problem at all.

In the priority-setting process, public health leaders have the responsibility to

- work with coalitions, alliances, or partnerships
- set health priorities that will be acceptable to elected and appointed officials
- set realistic goals and objectives
- make goals and objectives measurable
- tie action plans to the budget

LEADERSHIP CHALLENGES

Researchers who have investigated the advances in clinical medicine over the past 50 years estimate that only 5 of the 30 years of increase in life expectancy can be tied to clinical breakthroughs.[28] Most of the increase in life expectancy instead is due to changes in public health policy. The last half of the 20th century has seen the virtual elimination of polio, the elimination of smallpox, declines in dental decay due to fluoridation in water supplies, and reductions in childhood blood lead levels. If society continues to invest in the public health system, substantial financial savings will accrue, assuming past history is any guide. It is the public health system that prevents epidemics; protects the environment, workplaces, housing, food, and water; promotes healthy behaviors; monitors the health status of the population; mobilizes communities to take remedial action; responds to disasters; ensures the quality, accessibility, and accountability of medical care; reaches out to link high-risk and hard-to-reach people to needed services; performs research to develop new insights and innovative solutions; and leads the development of sound health policy and planning.[29]

In spite of the impressive record of achievement by the public health system, financial support for public health programs has recently declined. The result is likely to be an increase in disease and injury—and an increase in health care costs. Major public health problems, including human immunodeficiency virus (HIV)/AIDS, cancer, cardiovascular diseases and stroke, diabetes, teenage pregnancy, substance abuse, and community violence, remain to be dealt with. Following are several examples of the impact that public health agencies, in collaboration with other organizations, can have on public health issues.

Public health professionals have consistently argued that tobacco use is the greatest single preventable cause of premature mortality in the United States.[30] With the harmful effects of tobacco use in mind, the *Healthy People 2000* objectives called for the development, enactment, and enforcement of laws prohibiting the sale of tobacco products to adolescents. Further, the report stated that, in order to reduce access to tobacco by adolescents, vending machine sales should not be allowed.

The tobacco industry fought the *Healthy People 2000* proposals and came up with a proposal for requiring electronic locking devices. In 1990, Forster, Hourigan, and Kelder drew a random sample of vending machine locations in St. Paul, Minnesota, where a law mandating the use of locking devices on cigarette vending machines had been passed.[31] The researchers found that the rate of noncompliance by merchants was 34 percent after three months and 30 percent after one year. For sites in which a locking device was installed, the purchase rate of cigarette packages from the machines dropped from 86 percent before the law went into effect to 30 percent after three months. However, the rate rose again to 48 percent after one year. The effectiveness of the law deteriorated in all types of businesses over the course of the year. The researchers demonstrated that banning cigarette vending machines, together with other methods to improve compliance, will be necessary in the future. If businesspeople are not committed to a change in policy, its level of effectiveness will be low.

In a second example, a local health advisory board in a small Illinois city decided in 1997 that it was no longer willing to tolerate cigarette vending machines near the local high school. The board recommended a bill to the local city council, who not only agreed with the board but passed a more comprehensive antismoking law. This story indicates how leadership can be required in different places if a policy is to be developed and put into action. It was first needed in the health department (which addressed the question of how to reduce access to tobacco by adolescents), then on the board (which took action on a potentially volatile issue), and then on the city council (which passed a bill that had the potential to be unpopular).

The challenge for public health leaders is to bring different groups in a community together when a critical public health issue needs to be addressed. There are clearly risks involved in trying to influence the political process. The public health community and local, state, and federal governments may have conflicting agendas. Special interest groups often try to undermine the public health agenda through contributions to the political parties as well as by lobbying to prevent a bill from getting passed.

In cases where public health leaders have been instrumental in passing a bill, they need to monitor the effects of the legislation. In 1989, a cigarette tax increase of 25 cents per package went into effect in California, partly because of a public health campaign.[32] Flewelling and colleagues evaluated the impact of this increase one year after its implementation.[33] Comparing adult per capita consumption data from 1980 to 1989 in California and the United States, they showed that a sharp decline in cigarette consumption in California had occurred at the same time as the tax increase. They concluded that a 5- to 7-percent decline in consumption was attributable to the tax increase.

What will be the long-term effect of the legislation is, of course, hard to determine. Undoubtedly, educational strategies and other policy mechanisms will be required if further reductions in tobacco use are to occur. Public health leaders must continue to take an active role in the antismoking movement. The battle against tobacco use will not get any easier, since the tobacco industry has more money to spend on promoting smoking than public health agencies have to spend on antismoking activities.

Another example of public health–driven policy development consists of the efforts to deal with the HIV/AIDS epidemic of the 1980s and 1990s. Reducing HIV transmission is still entirely a matter of changing behavior, since no vaccine or cure is yet available. Since changing behavior is such a difficult process, the challenges for public health are significant. Although the public health community has been criticized for what it has done and when it has done it, public health practitioners have been on the front lines in the education of the public about HIV and AIDS. The only other critical advocacy group has been made up of people with AIDS.

The Ryan White Act stands as a premier example of what legislation can do. However, mustering the resources to deal with the mounting crisis has not been easy. During the 1980s, many policy makers, for political reasons, tried to play down the AIDS epidemic. For example, the evidence is strong that budget considerations were put before the health needs of the American public and that research scientists were sometimes more concerned with their personal reputations than with saving lives.[34]

Public health leaders at the local, state, and federal levels have taken leadership roles in promoting better methods of AIDS surveillance, creating policies to help the afflicted, raising concerns about the cost and accessibility of new treatments, and promoting an increasing number of programs to prevent the disease from spreading. Public health leaders took a strong position in favor of confronting the crisis head on, even when it was not popular to do so. The result is that the quality of life of many people with AIDS has improved substantially.

Success sometimes creates political enemies. Public health leaders need to take risks for the important health issues they think need to be addressed. The consequences for them could include political retaliation, budget cuts, and loss of leadership positions. Public health leaders may also find themselves in conflict with community leaders. To reduce the risk of conflict, they need to work with community leaders, lobbyists, and special interest groups on common agendas. At the same time, they need to realize that deal making has its own risks, for collaboration with lobbyists and special interest groups in particular may compromise their community oversight activities.

Community leaders have a strong voice in community affairs. They usually have a vision of what the community should be like and want others to share it. They may, therefore, be unwilling to accept the public health leaders' view of the community, especially its health priorities. Yet without the support of community leaders, public health leaders may find it impossible to implement the health policies they think are needed. As much as possible, health policies should emanate directly from community groups. When community leaders with credibility join forces, they are usually able to convince most community residents that there is a problem that must be addressed immediately.[35] Unless the community leadership, the public health leadership, and the political leadership come together and work collaboratively, change will not be possible.

Public health leaders are often in a situation in which they have to increase their own knowledge as a prerequisite to policy development. Case Study 7–B describes a possible biological disaster and the community politics and coalition building that were necessary to avert it. All individuals involved needed to learn new things to better understand the nature of disaster planning.

Judicial decisions have increasingly played a major role in the area of health policy. Public health leaders have found themselves as witnesses in trials or proponents of health policies being evaluated by the courts. Since courts must interpret the law, the outcomes are not always predictable. During the 1990s, class action suits were brought against tobacco companies, and the courts have ruled that these companies must pay enormous damages to the states. How to use the tobacco settlement money has become a new issue. The public health leaders want the money used to prevent smoking and promote smoking cessation programs, but many states see this tobacco money as a windfall and want to spend large amounts of it on other state priorities. Dealing with the courts and even the happy results of court decisions thus constitutes another challenge faced by public health leadership.

In the area of policy development, public health leaders must

- collaborate with managed care organizations
- collaborate with state legislatures and the U.S. Congress
- create policy agendas in conjunction with community leaders
- work to implement policies even if they are opposed by special interest groups
- understand the relationship between politics and policy
- encourage cooperation between local, state, and federal health organizations
- prepare for retaliation when pushing unpopular issues
- incorporate judicial decisions into policy development

SUMMARY

Policy development is the core function that, in a sense, follows assessment, for only after public health problems have been identified can policies be created to deal with them. Yet in the normal course of agency operations assessment and policy development are occurring continually and often simultaneously.

The chapter first presented policy development recommendations publicized by the Institute of Medicine in a 1988 report. It then discussed organizational practices associated with policy development and listed performance indicators for each practice. Additional topics covered included policy trends, advocacy and empowerment, and collaboration. Finally, the chapter discussed leadership challenges related to policy development, including the challenge of bringing diverse groups together to address significant public health risks and the challenge of preparing for retaliation when pushing unpopular positions.

Discussion Questions

1. What are the three organizational practices associated with policy development? How do these practices relate to the essential services of informing, educating, empowering, and mobilizing community partnerships and developing policies?
2. What leadership skills are required for developing policies?
3. What is the difference between politics and policy development?
4. In what ways can politics influence policy development?
5. What is a futurist and why should public health leaders pay attention to what futurists say?
6. How do advocacy and collaboration contribute to empowerment?
7. What are similarities and differences between the three main types of collaborative relationship?
8. What are the main advantages of a collaborative relationship?
9. What is the role of priority setting in policy development?

Exercise 7–1

TATTOOING IN MID-AMERICA

Purpose: to explore how policy development occurs and how a policy can affect the relationship between a local public health agency and the county health board

Key concepts: board of health, policy development, strategic planning

Procedure: The number of tattoo parlors in Tolbert County has grown. Tolbert High School Superintendent Violet Davis calls Tolbert Health Department Director Doris Martinez about the significant increase in tattoos among high school students—an increase that has understandably upset the students' parents. Martinez researches the subject and comes up with similar findings. There is no law in the county related to tattooing.

The class should divide into teams of 8–10 members. Half the members of each team will act the role of Tolbert County Health Department professionals and stakeholders. The other half will act the role of members of the Tolbert County Board of Health. The health department members, as a way of addressing the issue of tattooing, develop a proposed anti-tattooing law and devise a strategy for convincing the board of health to support the proposed law. The board members invite the health department representatives to a board meeting to present their arguments favoring the proposed law, and the two groups debate the merits and limitations of the proposal, ultimately focusing on whether it should be enacted.

Leaf-Burning Policy

Helene Gottesmann and Michael Tryon

BACKGROUND

Previous leaf burning legislation in Acorn state had neither been enforced properly nor validated by the courts. In 1974, Tree County Board approved the Nuisance Section of the County Public Health Ordinance, which limited open burning only when adverse health effects could be demonstrated. This was hard to enforce. The state of Acorn also had an open-burning law for counties over 400,000, which was challenged in the courts in 1986, after which any municipality could burn. The state environmental protection agency's stance was that open burning was a local decision. Until January 1995, one could burn any kind of landscape anywhere in the unincorporated areas of Tree County as close as 25 feet from neighboring houses.

HEALTH EFFECTS OF LEAF BURNING

The ban on the disposal of yardwaste in landfills in 1990, the subsequent increasing costs of solid waste disposal, and an increase in the county population have all contributed to the increased air pollution in Tree County. Air pollution accounts for as many as 60,000 deaths a year. Open leaf burning has been established as a significant source of air pollution and causes a significant increase in carbon monoxide levels, hydrocarbons, and total suspended particulates, which are injurious to the population.

Open leaf burning represents a significant health hazard for asthmatics and other high risk groups—newborn infants, children, the elderly, and people with chronic respiratory, cardiovascular, and allergy problems. In 1986 and 1987, in Tree County, respiratory diseases, such as emphysema, bronchitis, and asthma, became the third leading cause of death, while they were the fourth leading cause of death in the United States. Bronchitis and asthma were the second leading causes of hospitalization in the 0–14 age group in Tree County during the same time period.

In the fall of 1991, a 14-year-old girl died as a result of an allergic reaction to leaf burning. The following February, another young girl died from asthma when moldy yard waste from the previous fall was being burned. During this same season, another child almost died of an asthmatic attack after being exposed to the smoke from burning leaves and had to live with relatives in another town until the air cleared. With support and facts from other parents of asthmatic children in neighboring towns with leaf-burning bans, parents attended several Smokey village board meetings to express their worries about the health hazards of open burning. As a result, in the fall of 1992 a total burn ban was passed by one vote after it was vetoed by the village president. Simultaneously, another parent with an asthmatic child in a neighboring town of Ashes went to her village board with a packet of information concerning the health hazards of leaf burning. The board decided to form a committee to investigate the issue. Not taking no for an answer, mothers continued attending village meetings, networking, and educating the community about the health hazards of leaf burning. Parents also received TV and news coverage.

COALITION BUILDING

Frustrated by the lack of action by the village board, in the spring of 1992 the concerned parents from Ashes and neighboring towns formed a coalition. In October, the Ashes village board said they wanted to wait 5 to 10 years to investigate and decide the matter.

In the response to this, the coalition circulated a petition and wanted a burning ban by the state pollution control board. "Please don't burn your leaves" fliers were distributed. In November 1992, the burning ban failed. The coalition grew larger, began publishing a newsletter and called a meeting to devise a plan of action. Individuals from the local and state lung associations and councils, public health workers, emergency room nurses, state and local environmental groups, and lawyers joined forces. The parents received some support from the board of health, who were willing to write letters on their behalf, but it was not known whether the county board members supported the ban and how they stood on the leaf-burning matter.

LOBBYING ON THE STATE LEVEL

The coalition felt a policy or law banning leaf burning was needed at the state level because villages and towns with leaf-burning bans were being affected by smoke from unincorporated areas and municipalities without bans. A former state pollution control board member who had received yearly complaints about leaf burning instructed the coalition on how to introduce a state bill. In the spring of 1993, the senate and house introduced a bill against leaf burning that included the 17 counties in Acorn. Dedicated coalition members actively lobbied their senators and representatives. Opponents of the bill tried to kill the legislation but it finally passed. However, the governor vetoed it in December 1993, claiming it was an "unfunded mandate."

COUNTY LEVEL INVOLVEMENT

Simultaneously, in 1993 leaf-burning ban activists expressed their concerns not only to local and state officials but also to Tree County board representatives, members of the county board public health services committee, and members of the county board of health. County board members decided not to impose an open-burning restriction on municipalities and the rural areas. Both the board of health and the public health services committee planned to address the leaf-burning issue in the future. The president of the board of health thought the county should launch a massive education effort about the health hazards of leaf burning and alternative disposal methods and start encouraging residents to voluntarily stop burning leaves. The Tree County public health services committee was scheduled to consider a "voluntary ban," but the politicians said the proposal would be ineffective since it had no enforcement measures. In November 1993, the Tree County public health services committee tabled the issue, since the general assembly was considering this legislation. (In the fall of 1993, while parents were in the midst of lobbying the state for a leaf-burning ban, the village of Ashes finally voted to ban leaf burning.)

In January 1994, in response to the governor's veto of the leaf-burning bill in December 1993, lobbyists pressured the county board of health to consider a countywide ban on open burning. In the spring of 1994, the county board of health sought a voluntary burning ban; however, lobbyists against leaf burning continued to pressure board members to oppose it.

POLICY CONTROVERSIES

In developing a policy (or ordinance) for leaf-burning, the chair of the public health services committee of the county board acted as a bridge between the county board of health and the county board, the legislative body. His main objectives were to build a consensus around the various opinions of the county representatives and develop a balanced policy. In order to develop a balanced policy, the committee needed to consider the following issues: (1) Should grass and other yardwaste be included with leaves? (2) What months or days can individuals burn leaves? (3) What educational efforts are needed? (4) What are enforcement alternatives? In addition, the chair wanted to communicate and share his vision of the challenges of a rapidly growing community: "Tree County is the fastest growing county in the state and the issue of open burning will not go away. As the county continues to grow, the issue of open burning will become more serious" (Minutes of May 11, 1994, committee meeting).

Policy development and consensus building were done gradually and methodically. The chair of the public health services committee was very specific about steps he had to pursue to accomplish his goal. His first objective was to listen to all conflicting points of view concerning leaf burning before a policy was drafted. For this purpose, the public health services committee held open meetings in the spring and summer of 1994 to obtain the public's input as well as that of the various county officials. In addition, the chair tried to determine what type of ordinance could be passed by the county board by personally talking to every county board member and other significant individuals.

The public health administrator of Tree County health department provided assistance to the public health services committee chair in developing a leaf-burning policy. The board of health had as one of its goals to reduce respiratory diseases in the county by addressing the issue of open burning. The public health administrator participated in the public meetings held by the public health services committee and presented morbidity and mortality statistics regarding respiratory diseases in the county. He pointed out that the board of health is "an organization that exists in most counties throughout the state for the primary purpose of preventing diseases in the county by addressing the issue of open burning. The board of health had as one of its goals to reduce respiratory disease and disability and improve the health status of the community. In this role, the board of health needs to know what the disease problems are" (minutes of May 11, 1994, committee meeting). In view of this, the provision of epidemiologic data becomes critical in policy development.

PUBLIC MEETINGS ON LEAF BURNING

The following section briefly summarizes opposing viewpoints shared at the Tree County board public health services committee public meetings on leaf burning. Developing a policy based on these opposing views was a challenge for the chair of the health services committee and required effective leadership skills.

OPPONENTS TO THE BAN

The following are issues raised by those opposed to the leaf-burning ban.

Big Government versus Individual Freedom

Being one of the most politically conservative counties in the nation, Tree County citizens did not want the government interfering in their lives. They felt that the leaf-burning ban was an "unfunded mandate." The main issue was their right to burn leaves.

Local versus State Government

If there had to be a ban, individuals felt that it should be imposed locally and not by the county or the state.

High versus Low Density Areas

Individuals felt that the committee needed to differentiate between high- and low-density areas. People were opposed to banning leaf burning in the rural areas or the country because the smoke dissipated before it reached any of the neighbors. Also, unincorporated areas do not have the same waste disposal options as city residents.

Incorporated versus Unincorporated Areas

The ordinance should not include incorporated areas, only unincorporated areas. Municipalities wanted to decide for themselves.

Expense of Waste Disposal

Opponents were against the additional cost for waste disposal if leaf burning was banned. Some cities include leaf pickup with garbage pickup at no additional cost.

No Adverse Health Effects

Some opponents did not believe that the smoke from leaf burning had any ill effect. One individual noted that other allergens (such as ragweed) have not been eradicated.

PROPONENTS OF THE BAN

The following are issues raised by proponents of the leaf-burning ban.

Individual Property Rights versus Right To Breathe

Opponents of leaf burning expressed the need to act on behalf of one's fellow humans—and the right to breathe. It was pointed out that the constitution of Illinois requires the government to protect the health, safety, and welfare of the citizens and provide a healthful environment. Therefore, leaf burning, a health hazard, should not be allowed.

Adverse Health Effects versus No Effect

Citizens with asthma and parents of asthmatic children testified as to the adverse health effects leaf burning has had on their lives and their children's lives. Some opponents of the ban did not believe leaf burning caused asthma and wanted "proof." Medical personnel reported the increasing number of children and adults they treated with respiratory diseases and concluded that a ban on leaf burning would save medical costs as well as lives. It must be noted that some opponents of the ban and their children also had asthma, but apparently they did not feel a ban was necessary.

County or State Legislation versus a Local Piecemeal Solution

Proponents felt a countywide solution was needed. Though some towns have burning ordinances, people live along borders where leaf burning is allowed. Children may live in one village with a ban but go to a school in a town with leaf burning and are exposed to the air pollution.

Education or Referendum versus Legislation

Proponents of the leaf-burning ban felt education was extremely important but not a substitute for legislation. They were also against holding a referendum, for they felt people would vote according to their emotions and not the facts.

OTHER BURNING ISSUES

The following are some additional concerns expressed at the public meetings on leaf burning.

What kind of waste disposal would there be? How much would it cost and how much responsibility would the county take for doing it? How much would bagging leaves cost? Citizens wanted to be provided with alternatives such as composting, vacuuming of leaves, or collecting leaves for farmers. Highschoolers reported that they picked up leaves for free and delivered them to farmers.

People wanted to know how the county would respond to complaint calls (the fire department would respond to the calls) and who would enforce the ban.

They also wanted to know whether overnight campfires and bonfires would be prohibited.

In May 1994, another open-burning meeting was held by the public health and human services committee of the Tree County board to discover how individual communities and fire districts felt about open-burning regulations. Invited were representatives of the 27 municipalities, 17 townships, and 16 fire districts. The issues brought up were similar to those that had been discussed at the April meeting: assurance of leaf disposal before a ban was enacted and methods of enforcement. Individuals felt the leaf-burning problem should be resolved by local units of government.

CONSENSUS BUILDING: DRAFTING A BALANCED POLICY

In June 1994, county board members met to discuss and then vote on whether to draft a leaf-burning ordinance. The chair of the public health services committee felt he needed the board to reach a consensus in order to devote staff time and energy to drafting an ordinance. County board members said they wanted options, facts, and documentation of the health effects of leaf burning and of large composting sites. One of the members wanted it stated that the right to clean air had precedence over the right to burn leaves. Another member felt people should be more sensitive to the needs of their neighbors. Some individuals supported extensive educational efforts. A county ban may give locals more control if and when the state passes legislation. County board members voted 19 to 5 for the public health committee staff to draft a balanced policy regulating leaf burning.

At this point, the board was far from a consensus on how to regulate leaf burning. Some board members wanted a total ban, others a partial ban only in the unincorporated areas, and others regulation rather than a ban. They did not want to adopt legislation for municipalities that already had an ordinance. They felt the county could not enforce a ban anyway.

The chair felt he had to resolve the clash of conflicting opinions by means of a compromise. He knew he did not have the votes for a total ban. The committee used a conservative approach in formulating the proposal (a "balanced" policy). In order to develop a balanced, integrated policy, the staff addressed the following issues: (1) density (distance between homes), (2) type of waste, (3) disposal alternatives, (4) enforcement, and (5) time of day and months.

In January 1995, the committee presented the following ordinance to the county board for a vote (it passed 13 to 10). It would restrict burning to assigned weekends. The burning ordinance is an amendment of the National Fire Prevention Code, BOCA Ordinance. The amendment limits burning of yardwaste to weekends between dawn and dusk during the months of October, November, April, and May. Open fires would not be allowed within 30 feet of a structure or within 500 feet of a neighbor's home. The ordinance excluded municipalities.

The leaf-burning policy is an example of governance sharing and collaborative policy development, for three different departments were involved: the health department, the fire department, and the building department. Assurance or enforcement of the BOCA amendment would be provided by all three departments, with the fire department taking the lead. The health department would educate citizens on alternatives to leaf burning and already has a burning ordinance that can ban leaf and yardwaste burning if it affects the health of the citizens. The building department would also be responsible for enforcing a fire and safety code that would include the leaf-burning regulation.

The BOCA amendment had a good chance to pass the county board because it is a regulation, not a ban. It provides a mechanism to let people know when the burning is occurring so they can take precautions and adjust their schedules accordingly. The BOCA amendment also exempts municipalities whereas a public health ordinance would not. A leaf ban would not have passed because the county had no mechanism for leaf pickup. If the chair would have submitted a pickup cost of $75,000, the ordinance would never have passed.

CONCLUSION

In 1993, after the leaf-burning ban was vetoed by the governor, concerned parents and citizens went to the Tree County board and board of health for a countywide ban. The public health services committee of the Tree County board held two open meetings to allow the public to air their opinions on this matter. After receiving the "go ahead" from the county board, the public health services committee researched the matter and developed what they considered was a "balanced" policy on leaf burning.

The parent activists have mixed feelings about this ordinance, since it still allows leaf burning on weekends in the fall and spring in densely populated areas. They feel the regulation should be a health ordinance rather than an amendment to the BOCA (fire) ordinance. The proposed ban treats burning as a fire hazard, not a health hazard. Burning supporters say it was a compromise. The chair says that the BOCA compromise "is the best way of protecting the public by reducing fire hazards without also denying individual property rights." He feels that this is an effective ordinance, for it limits the amount of days leaf burning is permitted.

The coalition has introduced a bill to the state legislature that would give the state pollution control board authority over open burning in the state. Parents say they will continue to try to get stricter measures passed. Concerned citizens have noted the approach used by parents in the Quad Cities, where they plan to argue that local governments that allow leaf burning discriminate against residents with breathing ailments and thus infringe on the Americans with Disabilities Act (ADA).

Case Study 7–B

A Department of Health Learns about Its Role in Emergency Public Health

Linda Young Landesman

In the spring of 1995, the commissioner of health of a large metropolis was informed by federal officials that massive amounts of biological chemicals might be released somewhere in his community. This agent was highly toxic and had the potential to cause high levels of morbidity and mortality among those exposed. While the Smithtown Department of Health had a disaster plan, the plan was inadequate to meet the needs that would follow such a release. Further, there was a range of interest among the leadership in the department regarding the need to prepare for and respond to disasters.

BACKGROUND

Tom Asher, MD, MPH, commissioner of health in Smithtown for five years, hung up the phone and closed his eyes to think. He wasn't sure if he had heard correctly. There were stockpiles of biological chemicals here in Smithtown. Millions could be killed if there was an accidental release. As health officer, he was responsible for protecting the public's health. Protecting public health against a hidden enemy was not an easy task, especially in this time of shrinking resources.

Smithtown was a large metropolis in the northern section of the country. It was a hub of activity, and millions of people came in and out of the city every day. They came in to work, to shop, to play. Controlling egress within the city was difficult on a good day. There were hundreds of transportation routes involving bridges, trains, buses, ferries, and airplanes. It was an international port of entry by land, sea, and air. A terrorist could slip through easily.

John Thompkins had been elected mayor of Smithtown by a slim margin the year before. His vocal constituency was demanding cutbacks in government service. The mayor was particularly sensitive to this message, because his political adversaries were eager to see his tenure limited to one term. Betsy Reardon, his predecessor, had been a popular mayor. She had served three terms as head of Smithtown, and the local "spin doctors" felt that she lost the election because the city was paralyzed by a major winter storm the previous December. It didn't matter that the citizens of Smithtown had voted down the last two transportation bond issues or that it was a 100-year storm. Betsy was blamed because it took almost a week for transportation to move smoothly again. The situation was made worse because the storm occurred the week before the Christmas holiday. Retailers suffered throughout the city. But Betsy was still a political heavyweight in the region. And she and Thompkins had never been friends.

The impetus to "do more with less" came at a time when the state and federal governments were also retrenching and reducing support for government programs. The department of health had already been hit hard. When Tom and his deputies met six months earlier to review the implications of the cuts, they realized that they had to eliminate 10 percent of their staff and programs. Most of these reductions had already taken place. So resources in the department were scarce.

The health commissioner believed that he was fortunate in other ways. During their mayor-commissioner get-togethers, Tom felt that the mayor was responsive to his message. In these meetings, Tom highlighted how public health professionals were really part of the public safety network. In this city, where public officials were used to dealing with the "crisis of the week," there had even been a recent opportunity for the commissioner of health to educate the mayor about the importance of vigilance against biological agents.

A strain of the bubonic plague had erupted in India. Villagers, fearful of getting sick and trying to avoid the illness, moved from one village to another. It was days before the public health officials there issued a quarantine. As a result, it was very difficult to contain the epidemic. Thousands of people had died. Indian officials suspected that exposed villagers had boarded planes and traveled aboard. Health officers around the world went on alert. When Tom learned about the possibility of plague being brought to the United States by an international traveler, he met with the mayor to discuss what should be done to protect Smithtown.

"This is the end of the 20th century. What do you mean we could have an outbreak of bubonic plague in Smithtown?" asked the major.

"We both realize that Smithtown is an international port," Tom said. We have visitors coming here from countries where the public health laws are not as vigorous as ours. We need to take a defensive stand by increasing surveillance at all ports of entry and by alerting hospitals and clinics around the region. If we learn of any patients with plague, we'll jump on it immediately."

Mayor Thompkins was insistent: "Do whatever it takes. We cannot have an outbreak happen here."

Tom Asher left that meeting feeling relieved that he had administrative support for an all-out effort to contain an outbreak of the plague if it appeared necessary. At the time, he didn't realize that he'd be calling on that support so soon.

SOLUTIONS

The next day he returned to his office and was hoping to spend the morning responding to correspondence and returning phone calls when he received the call about the biological agents stockpiled in Smithtown.

"Get Jayne, Jack, and Sid on the phone stat," Tom ordered. "Tell them that I need them in my office in 30 minutes." His secretary, Glen Oaks, ran into the room.

"Only Sid is in the building. What's up?" Glen asked.

"We may have a potential terrorist situation on our hands. We've got to come up with a plan as soon as possible."

"Jayne's at a meeting at the chancellor's office downtown," Glen reported. "Jack took a few hours leave to take his daughter to the dentist. It may be awhile before they can get back."

"Beep them. Tell them to get back here now!"

Glen hurried back to his desk and hoped that Jayne and Jack could get back soon. Jack was at least two hours away if he traveled by public transportation. It would be prohibitively costly for him to take a taxi back to the office. Besides there was a city rule that travel by taxi was strictly forbidden except in a municipal emergency. Glen wasn't sure that this qualified as an emergency. He was used to the commissioner calling these types of meetings with his deputies. Last month there was that TB scare. The month before the media reported that the water wasn't safe to drink because of a death due to *Cryptosporidium*. It turned out that the patient was immunosuppressed and had been living in Milwaukee during the outbreak in that city. He had just come home to die. But the resources of the department sure rallied around until the facts were clear.

So how important was this threat? Glen couldn't tell from the commissioner's demeanor, but he felt that he had to do his best to bring the deputies back to the office. And he was in luck: both were on their way and able to meet with the commissioner within the hour.

Tom started the meeting by asking if there was anybody in the department who knew about disaster planning for biologicals. The deputies looked at each other and shook their heads. They knew about monitoring for infectious disease in shelters and guaranteeing the safety of the water supply, but they knew nothing about preparing for biologicals.

The department had a disaster plan, as required by law, but they all knew that it hadn't been tested in the types of event happening around the country. Perhaps more importantly, Jayne, the deputy commissioner for environmental affairs, had come to realize that the health department should be more involved in planning with other agencies in the city than it currently was. Emergency medical services (EMS) had a lock on responding to disasters. Yet EMS didn't have the expertise that was needed to assess and respond to public health issues. They couldn't identify hazardous materials. They couldn't identify infectious agents. They didn't have the skills to conduct surveillance or monitor the safety of those who responded to an event. With EMS as the lead health agency, there were lots of limitations in the current city plan. It was clear to Jayne that EMS was not the agency that should have lead responsibility. She had told Tom that this was a potential problem for the department. But federal dollars for disaster preparedness and response seemed to be flowing to EMS. And so the commissioner and his deputies planned the best that they could and tried to increase their influence in the system.

"What are we dealing with?" Sid asked.

"I received a call from the chief medical officer of the Office of Foreign Disaster Assistance. Remember him? We met him at the public health annual meeting last November. He called to say that he'd just returned from investigating the Sarin release in the subway in Japan. While investigating the extent of the cache of chemicals over there, the U.S. team learned that there is a stockpile of hundreds of gallons of Sarin somewhere in the Smithtown metropolitan area. There could be a release at any time."

"That would be disastrous," exclaimed Sid, the deputy for infectious disease. "How can we get ready for a Bhopal type accident? All of our available staff are working round the clock as it is, just trying to keep up. Besides, what do we know about planning for these things?"

"I think that we should call Dan Nickels, chief of EMS. They have the man-power and the resources to respond to this thing," Jack insisted. Jack, deputy director for maternal and child health, could be depended on to support only those efforts that affected mothers and infants. He felt that with shrinking resources, he had to fight to ensure that services weren't diverted form this group.

"That's not a bad idea," Sid agreed.

"Wait a minute. Why should we shove this thing over to EMS?" Jayne asked. "We all know that they can't do the job that is needed to guarantee public health. Besides, if we don't know how to prepare for this thing, there must be people across the country that we can use as resources. This can't be the first time any health department in the country has had to deal with this. Besides, I don't think we should work in isolation. We should be sitting at the table where the interagency response is discussed."

Jack used this as an opportunity to complain about his current staffing. "I don't have enough staff to monitor the child health stations. We can't get newborns in for their first checkup until they are 10 weeks old, and you are talking about using staff to scrounge around the country for someone who knows something about preparing for a Bhopal here in Smithtown. I say call Dan Nickels. If you don't want to call him, then call the CDC. But let's not get over our heads."

"Jack's got a point. If we let another agency do it, it's their problem if something goes wrong," echoed Sid.

"I'm not sure I agree," said the Commissioner. I think that our responsibility is very clear. EMS doesn't have the capability to handle the public health issues. And if this thing blows, it will be our necks out there. It happens that I met with the mayor about the plague threat just yesterday. He was very clear. He wants the city prepared, and that means us. If we need to be prepared for plague, we need to be prepared for biologicals."

Jack asked, "Who's going to do it? I don't have anyone to spare."

Sid and Jayne agreed that there was no one on their staff who could be released from current responsibilities to develop a disaster plan for biologicals.

CONCLUSION

Tom looked around the room and pondered what to do. He knew that Jayne would find the time to supervise someone so that the department could better prepare for this thing. But how could he make this happen? More importantly, should he use valuable resources—resources that could be used to meet other public health responsibilities—to become an active player in citywide disaster preparedness?

REFERENCES

1. J.C. Lashof, "Commitment to the Common Good," *American Journal of Public Health* 83, no. 9 (1993): 1222–1225.
2. Institute of Medicine, *The Future of Public Health* (Washington, DC: National Academy Press, 1988).
3. B.J. Turnock et al., "Implementing and Assessing Organizational Practices," *Public Health Reports* 109, no. 4 (1994): 478–484.
4. N. Glaser, *The Limits of Social Policy* (Cambridge, MA: Harvard University Press, 1988).
5. Glaser, *The Limits of Social Policy.*
6. R.N. Bellah, "The Quest for the Self," in *Interpretive Social Science*, eds. P. Rubinow and W.M. Sullivan (Berkeley: University of California Press, 1987).
7. L.A. Aday, *At Risk In America* (San Francisco: Jossey-Bass, 1993).
8. H.B. Maynard Jr. and S.E. Mehrtens, *The Fourth Wave: Business in the 21st Century* (San Francisco: Berrett-Koehler, 1993).
9. J.L. Marrioti, *The Power of Partnerships* (Cambridge, MA: Blackwell Publishers, 1996).
10. A. Toffler and H. Toffler, *Creating a New Civilization* (Atlanta: Turner Publishing, 1994).
11. N. Gingrich, *To Renew America* (New York: Harper Collins, 1995).
12. S.P. Robbins and M. Coulter, *Management*, 6th ed. (Upper Saddle River, NJ: Prentice Hall, 1999).
13. Robbins and Coulter, *Management.*
14. M. Siegel and L. Doner, *Marketing Public Health: Strategies To Promote Social Change* (Gaithersburg, MD: Aspen Publishers, 1998).
15. J.P. Kretzmann and J.L. McKnight, *Building Communities from the Inside Out* (Evanston, IL: Northwestern University Center for Urban Affairs and Policy Research, 1993).
16. P. Block, *The Empowered Manager* (San Francisco: Jossey-Bass, 1987).
17. D. Tracy, *Ten Steps to Empowerment* (New York: Morrow, 1990).
18. L. Cohen et al., *Developing Effective Coalitions: An Eight Step Guide* (Pleasant Hill, CA: Contra Costa County Health Services Department Prevention Program, 1994).
19. Cohen et al., *Developing Effective Coalitions.*
20. M.T. Hatcher and J.K. McDonald, "The Constituency Development Practice in Public Health Agencies" (Centers for Disease Control and Prevention, Atlanta, 1994).
21. Hatcher and McDonald, "The Constituency Development Practice in Public Health Agencies."
22. Cohen et al., *Developing Effective Coalitions.*
23. G.P. Mays et al., "Collaboration To Improve Community Health: Trends and Alternative Models," *Joint Commission Journal of Qualitative Improvement* 25, no. 10 (1998): 518–565.
24. Mays et al., "Collaboration To Improve Community Health."
25. Public Health Service, *Healthy People 2000* (Washington, DC: U.S. Department of Health and Human Services, 1991).
26. Public Health Service, *Healthy People 2000.*
27. G.E.A. Dever, *Community Health Analysis* (Gaithersburg, MD: Aspen Publishers, 1991).
28. Public Health Service, *For a Healthy Nation: Returns on Investment in Public Health* (Washington, DC: U.S. Department of Health and Human Services, 1994).
29. Public Health Service, *For a Healthy Nation.*
30. Centers for Disease Control, *Reducing the Health Consequences of Smoking: 25 Years of Progress*, Report of the Surgeon General (Washington, DC: U.S. Department of Health and Human Services, 1989).
31. J.L. Forster et al., "Locking Devices on Cigarette Vending Machines: Evaluation of a City Ordinance," *American Journal of Public Health* 82, no. 9 (1992): 1217–1219.
32. M. Siegel and L. Doner, *Marketing Public Health: Strategies To Promote Social Change* (Gaithersburg, MD: Aspen Publishers, 1998).
33. R.L. Flewelling et al., "First Year Impact of the 1989 California Cigarette Tax Increase on Cigarette Consumption," *American Journal of Public Health* 82, no. 6 (1992): 867–869.
34. R. Shilts, *And the Band Played On* (New York: St. Martin's Press, 1987).
35. D.D. Chrislip and C.E. Larsen, *Collaborative Leadership* (San Francisco: Jossey-Bass, 1994).

Chapter 8

Leadership and Assurance

Be sure it's done well by you or others.

K. Gebbie, Speech to the Illinois Public Health Leadership Institute

The core functions of public health, for the sake of explanation, can be viewed as a series of steps. First comes assessment—the evaluation of the health status of a community, including the health risks it is facing. Next comes policy development—the creation of plans to deal with the community's health problems, or at least those that are given a high priority because they have serious consequences and can be dealt with effectively. Finally comes assurance, which largely consists of the implementation of the plans developed during the second stage. Assurance, in a phrase, involves ensuring that the public's health is protected and, hopefully, even improved.

Of course, these three core functions are all ongoing and thus overlap. Changes occur in a community and new problems arise, so evaluations of the community's health status must occur regularly. Newly uncovered problems call for new solutions, so policies must be developed continually as well. And assurance is obviously a continuous function, for it involves the implementation and *maintenance* of public health programs.

OVERVIEW

Prevention

Assurance activities focus on disease prevention and health promotion. Primary prevention involves creating an environment in which disease will not come into being—the ultimate public health goal. Secondary prevention involves intervening when problems occur and implementing major initiatives to prevent the consequences from becoming worse. Tertiary prevention involves stopping the progression of a disease or disability in order to prevent dependency. As one writer put it, prevention of health problems is essentially equivalent to public health.[1]

The three levels of prevention are usually presented linearly, but a circular representation would seem to be more appropriate (Figure 8–1), for an intervention initiated at one level will impact activities at the other two levels. For example, the discovery of a new vaccine to prevent a childhood disease will lead to an immunization strategy at the primary prevention level. If the strategy is successful, the disease will become less prevalent, making secondary and tertiary strategies for dealing with the disease less important, perhaps to the point where they can be abandoned. A new treatment for a disease (secondary prevention) may lead to the discovery of a vaccine to prevent the disease (primary prevention) as well as reduce the long-term harmful effects of the disease, lessening the need for rehabilitation (tertiary prevention). The virtual eradication of polio shows how scientific research, leadership, and prevention can work together creatively.

Infrastructure

Public health agencies provide services to their communities on a regular basis but they also are responsible for maintaining the capacity to respond to critical situations and emergencies. The term "capacity" is used extensively in public health. In the Washington State Department of Health's *Public Health Improvement Plan,* capacity is defined as the ability to perform the core functions of assessment, policy development, and assurance on a continuous, consistent basis, made possible by maintenance of the basic infrastructure of the public health system, including human, capital, and technology resources.[2]

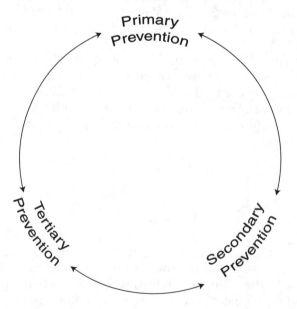

Figure 8–1 The cycle of prevention.

A public health charter was presented in a 1990 report that laid out an agenda for strengthening the infrastructure of public health in Illinois. Two articles of the charter[3] are relevant to the assurance function:

Article III: Categories of Public Health Services To Be Assured

Public health workers in Illinois have established five categories of public health services that further the mission of public health and are appropriate to the governmental role in public health. These are: Health Promotion; Primary Care; Environmental Health; Infectious Disease Control; and Health Care Regulation.

Article IV: Guiding Principles for Restructuring the Public Health System in Illinois

The following principles . . . should guide the restructuring of governmental public health responsibilities in Illinois. The principles enumerated below are predicated on the belief that most services to public health clients are most efficiently and effectively provided at the local level by local health units:

1. The delivery of public health services in the State of Illinois should be improved.
2. The societal benefits derived from public health services should be more effectively communicated.
3. The quality of public health services provided in Illinois should be improved and standardized.
4. The funding of public health services should be increased.

Barriers

The Institute of Medicine report on public health described a number of barriers to carrying out the assurance function.[4] To begin with, the roles of the state and local health departments vary from state to state, and the patterns of assurance activities performed by these departments differ as well. Four states do not even have official local health departments (Delaware, Hawaii, Rhode Island, and Vermont).[5] In seven states, the state health department operates all the local health departments (Arkansas, Florida, Louisiana, Mississippi, New Mexico, South Carolina, and Virginia), whereas the remaining states either possess completely decentralized systems or use a mixed approach.

Differences in funding sources also contribute to the variation in the types of assurance activities performed.[6] One result of the variation in assurance activities is that universal access to services is not a reality for many segments of the population. Even in the case of population-based initiatives, such as communicable disease control, the benefits are inequitably distributed.

Public health agencies and their leaders need to be proactive rather than reactive in the area of assurance. Public health leaders often seem to sit on their hands and allow other entities to decide what the role of public health agencies is to be. One difficulty they face is that, in the United States at least, public health and politics are so intertwined that it is often impossible to know which is which.

Nonetheless, they need to make certain that the communities they serve receive the services that are needed to attain agreed health objectives,[7] either by having the public health agencies provide the services or ensuring, through regulation, that they are provided by other public or private health organizations. Assurance of adequate services is guaranteed by social contract. Living up to the guarantee can be difficult, for it often requires subsidization or direct provision of personal health services for those who cannot afford them.

At the federal level, assurance involves making services available that are needed to deal with nationwide problems, such as human immunodeficiency virus (HIV) transmission, and, at the state level, it involves providing public health services that are needed statewide. Local public health agencies have the responsibility of ensuring "that high quality services, including personal health services, needed for the protection of public health in the community are available and accessible to all persons; that the community receives proper consideration in the allocation of federal and state as well as local resources for public health, and that the community is informed about how to obtain public health, including personal health, services, or how to comply with public health requirements."[8(p.145)]

Public health leaders must

- ensure the development of priority public health programs
- explore multiple public and private funding sources for programs
- stress population-based program development
- start programs with a primary prevention focus
- use governance to support prevention activities
- encourage capacity-building activities in local health departments
- build community partnerships to support programs

THE ROLE OF LEADERSHIP IN ASSURANCE

There are four organizational practices associated with the assurance core function (see Table 5–1 for a list of practices associated with all three of the core functions). The first involves searching for new resources and restructuring the public health agency to better meet community health needs. Turnock and colleagues defined four performance indicators for this organizational practice:[9]

1. The local public health agency has an organizational chart that includes all its functional elements.
2. The agency has completed a self-assessment and has developed a plan to identify capacity needs.
3. The agency has written job descriptions that describe necessary qualifications.
4. The agency has identified the funds required to address priority needs.

The second organizational practice involves the implementation of programs—the translation of plans and policies into services. In each state, certain programs and services are mandated, and other programs are either provided or made available on a priority basis. All programs are expected to be provided in accordance with applicable professional and regulatory standards. Public health leaders need to stress innovative program development, learn to delegate managerial responsibilities to others, and develop protocols for program oversight. There are two performance indicators associated with this organizational practice:

5. The local public health agency addresses its programs.
6. The agency provides services to meet priority health needs.

The third organizational practice involves evaluating programs and performing quality assurance activities. Feedback data are gathered and looked at to determine if programs need to be revised or resources redirected in order to deal with problems that have arisen during implementation. The behavioral and social sciences have developed many methodologic techniques for evaluating public agencies. Public health leaders need to support program evaluation, be involved in evaluating data, and adopt a system of performance monitoring. All these activities will strengthen the functioning of the local agency. There are three program indicators for this organizational practice:

7. The local public health agency demonstrates compliance with professional and regulatory standards.
8. The agency's programs are monitored to assess compliance with standards and objectives.
9. If changes in programs are necessary, the agency revises programs based on evaluation and quality assurance activities.

The final organizational practice concerns education and training. Public health agencies have a responsibility to inform the public about community health care concerns and available public health services. They need to develop health education initiatives to help people get rid of unhealthy behaviors and learn important public health information. They also need to ensure their work force is properly trained. Public health leaders must take on mentoring and training roles, encourage social marketing, and develop health communication initiatives. Only one performance indicator is listed for this practice:

10. The public is informed about health status, healthy and unhealthy behaviors, and policy issues.

Whether a public health agency engages in the organizational practices described here indicates whether it is meeting its public mandate. Of course, it can be questioned whether the practices are comprehensive and properly defined and whether the performance indicators are a good gauge of the extent to which the practices are being adhered to. For one thing, the practices seem to overlap, in the sense that some of the activities associated with a given practice are associated with others as well.[10]

Furthermore, since program implementation demands more than two-thirds of the resources of local public health agencies, it might be beneficial to subdivide the practices in order to take account of the diversity of programs provided. Another issue is the allocation of staff time to the activities associated with each practice.[11] For example, not much staff time and not many financial resources are devoted to the practices associated with assessment or policy development, and the role of technical assistance is not clearly defined in the core function practices model. These issues need to be addressed if the model is to be workable over the long run. Many of these criticisms are also applicable to the essential services approach.

In a national sample of local health departments, Turnock and colleagues investigated the rate of use for the 10 organizational practices.[12] The overall rate was 50 percent (this figure was calculated using weighted responses from 208 local health departments). The rate of use was highest for the practices associated with assurance and lowest for practices related to policy development. The researchers also found that about 40 percent of the U.S. population was being served by health departments utilizing the core functions approach to public health during the year of 1993. The rate of use for the essential services model is presently unknown.

Illinois has become so committed to the core function practices model that the Illinois administrative code was changed in 1993 to reflect the new commitment.[13-15] Exhibit 8–1 shows the activities required for the certification of local health departments prior to and following adoption of the 10 organizational practices as part of the administrative code.

Case Study 8–A shows the benefits of creating community partnerships—including a partnership between the local state university and the community—as a way to enhance the implementation of community health activities. (Note that the neighborhood health advisors program described in the case study is oriented toward leadership development, an added plus.)

Public health leadership activities tied to assurance include

- building a strong agency managerial team
- delegating authority for programmatic decisions
- restructuring agency activities to address health priority needs
- encouraging feedback to all constituents
- supporting program evaluation on an ongoing basis
- mentoring and training staff
- developing a technical assistance team

POPULATION-BASED SERVICES AND PERSONAL HEALTH SERVICES

Public health leaders and their professional colleagues are often confronted with the question of how public health differs from health care. The usual answer

---

Exhibit 8–1 Activities Required for Certification of Local Health Departments in Illinois, Before and After July 1993

Before July 1993	July 1993 and later
1. Food sanitation	1. Assess the health needs of the community
2. Potable water	2. Investigate health effects and hazards
3. Maternal health and family planning	3. Advocate and build constituencies
4. Child health	4. Develop plans and policies to address needs (includes analyzing for determinants and setting priorities)
5. Communicable disease control	
6. Private sewage	
7. Solid waste	5. Manage resources
8. Nuisance control	6. Implement programs
9. Chronic disease	7. Evaluate and provide quality assurance
10. Administration	8. Inform and educate the public

is that public health practitioners provide services oriented toward the population at large and do not routinely provide personal or direct services to individuals. Population-based services are programs intended to promote health and prevent disease in a community or a larger geographic entity. Public health practitioners are concerned about the factors that affect health. Some of these factors are in the control of each person in a community and some are not.

The major determinants of health are biology, environment, lifestyle, degree of wealth, and health organizational matters.[16] All of these key determinants have psychosocial components, such as social status; ties between people (e.g., family ties), social networks, and ties to voluntary organizations; and relationships to the neighborhood or community.[17]

The relationship between the provision of population-based services and the provision of direct health services is complicated. The medical care system in the United States reserves the right to provide personal health- and illness-based direct services, and the medical care infrastructure has been built up to support this medical care approach. Yet, although the public health system often takes a backseat to the medical care system in the United States, many people who need help cannot get services, even when government financial support is available, and as a consequence public health agencies sometimes act as service providers of last resort.[18]

Table 8–1 shows some of the population-based services that local public health agencies provide, such as surveillance, environmental health and control, communicable disease control, aging programs, and maternal and child health programs. Personal health services include community health clinical services, primary health care, case management services, dental health services, and clinical counseling programs. Some services mix elements of both, such as immunization, health-screening, and dental sealant programs.

Regardless of the changes that occur in the health care field in the future, population-based programs will probably still mainly be a public health responsibility. The configuration of personal health services constantly changes in response to changes in health policy. The mixed services may remain unchanged or become reconfigured in some way. Assurance is interconnected with the whole public health system, so it causes changes and also responds to changes in other parts of the system. Currently, the three major areas of assurance arguably are personal health service provision, environmental control, and behavior modification,[19] but undoubtedly a new list will be needed for the 21st century, since local public health agencies will probably be less involved in the direct delivery of personal health services.

Public health surveillance is a marriage between the core functions of assessment and assurance, and epidemiology serves as the minister who joins these two functions together.[20] In turn, surveillance connects research to service needs and monitors the linkage routinely.[21] Public health surveillance involves the collection, interpretation, and use of data (for purposes of policy development and decision making). One author listed 11 reasons for surveillance:

1. health planning
2. monitoring changes in public health practice
3. quantitatively estimating the extensiveness of a health problem in a community

Table 8–1 Examples of Assurance Activities in State and Local Health Departments and Leadership

Population-based	Mixed	Personal Health-based	Leadership Activities
Public health surveillance	Community health nursing	Community health clinical services	Delegation of programmatic responsibilities to others Evaluation of collected data for decision making
Environmental health and control (air and water quality, waste disposal, toxic substances control, etc.)	Health screening programs	Clinical services for children with lead toxicity	Program oversight Translation of environmental health goals into action
Occupational health and safety	Immunization Substance abuse screening Accidents	Clinical services for workers	Development of treatment partnerships with other health providers
Injury control	Infant car seat laws Violence prevention Teen peer support	Deliver donated car seats to people who cannot afford them	Education of the public Enforcement of laws and regulations
HIV/AIDs surveillance	Screening programs Reporting laws	AIDS counseling	Enforcement of laws and regulations Use of data for decision making
Communicable disease control	Immunization programs	Primary health care	Monitoring of health issues in the community Study of global health trends Education of the public
Family planning	Statistical monitoring of lack of prenatal care by pregnant teens	School clinics	Education of the public Development of partnerships with the community
Maternal and child health programs	Metabolic/genetic screening programs WIC eligibility	Case management services	Enforcement of laws and regulations
Aging programs	Medicaid eligibility	Long-term care	Collaboration with other agencies that serve older populations
Nutrition programs	WIC eligibility	Nutrition counseling	Placement of emphasis on innovation Program oversight

continues

Table 8–1 continued

Population-based	Mixed	Personal Health-based	Leadership Activities
Disaster preparedness	Community disaster plans	Disaster clinics (emergency public health)	Advocacy of a role for public health in disasters Creation of disaster teams
Health promotion and disease prevention	Educational programs	Clinical counseling	Creation of a vision and mission based on primary prevention Development of goals Translation of goals into action Development of academic linkages
Dental health	Dental sealant programs	Dental health clinics	Delegation of responsibility to dentists Program oversight
Vector/animal control	Observation of community health standards	Maintenance of animal shelters	Enforcement of laws and regulations Delegation of responsibility to other professional staff
Restaurant inspection	Monitoring of food-borne health problems	Community health clinic services	Enforcement of laws and regulations Creation of partnership with local restaurant association
Health hazard appraisal	Evaluation of community health hazards	Community health clinic services	Placement of emphasis on innovative program development Support and evaluation of data collected
Train and educate the work force	Leadership development programs	Application of learning to clinical programs	Mentoring and training Health communication Social marketing
Population-based managed care	Development of managed care model(s) for all community residents	Running of public HMO by a local health department	Development of partnerships with local health providers
Laboratory activities	Privatization of some laboratory activities	Personal testing for problems	Support for laboratory directors' involvement in public health decision-making

4. determining the natural history of a disease
5. detecting epidemics and disasters
6. determining the spread of disease in a population
7. facilitating epidemiologic and laboratory investigations
8. hypothesis testing
9. evaluating assurance activities
10. monitoring changes in infectious agents
11. monitoring isolation activities

It is imperative to link the population-based health objectives to the assurance activities of the local public health agency at the community level.[22] Assurance of vital services is a governmental function. However, the community needs to define its own process for tying goals to services.

The state of Washington ties the population-based assurance activities of local health agencies to capacity standards that identify what the agencies and their governmental and community partners need to do on a regular basis to protect and promote health and prevent disease.[23] Appendix 8–A presents the list of health promotion, health protection, and quality assurance activities contained in the Washington State *Public Health Improvement Plan*.[24] Quality assurance is defined in the plan as monitoring and maintaining the quality of public health programs and services. Quality assurance includes licensing and training health professionals, licensing health facilities, and enforcing standards and regulations. Quality assurance is discussed in detail in the next section.

Public health leaders must

- utilize creative techniques to maintain population-based programs during a downsizing period
- provide clinical services that are not accessible to segments of the population for lack of insurance or other reasons
- tie public health issues to personal health issues
- learn to interrelate surveillance to program development
- support quality assurance

QUALITY ASSURANCE

The U.S. General Accounting Office (GAO) was asked in 1989 to review the issue of quality assurance in health care.[25] In a briefing report to the chair of the U.S. Bipartisan Commission on Comprehensive Health Care, the GAO pointed out the multidimensional factors associated with quality measures. Part of the difficulty in quality assurance is that quality means different things to different people and organizations. For the individual, health improvement is the measure of quality. If the improvement can be tied to a particular treatment intervention, then quality is implied in the techniques used. For health care leaders and providers, such factors as accurate diagnosis and treatment, the clinical content of care, and technical skill are viewed as related to quality. Purchasers tie quality to factors such as cost-effectiveness, the appropriateness of the care setting, and the frequency and duration of services. For the public health leadership, quality can be tied to meeting health objectives, declines in rates of disease and infant mortality, and increases in healthy behaviors.

The GAO report also argued that quality assessment and quality assurance are sometimes confused with each other:

> Quality assessment involves the use of measures of quality, based on either explicit or implicit criteria, to assess the structure, process, and outcomes of care and to monitor levels of quality over time. Quality assurance goes beyond the simple assessment of quality to include its improvement. This requires identifying and confirming problems in the quality of medical care, planning interventions to lessen or eliminate the problems, monitoring the effectiveness of the interventions, and instituting additional changes and monitoring where warranted. . . . Quality assessment is a prerequisite to quality assurance.[26(p.7)]

Since quality assurance is an important part of the core function of assurance, developing a national strategy to address concerns about quality assurance may be required. The GAO report raised the issue of equity and people's need to gain access to services that are able to improve their well-being. Equitable access to services depends to a degree on how services get reimbursed. It is also related to the different health needs of different subpopulations. Older people, for example, have different concerns than young mothers with sick children. A national strategy may also be required to deal with the issue of comprehensiveness of health care services.[27] The services available in a community are partially determined by the service models in use in the community.

A comprehensive national strategy for quality assurance would likely include

- national practice guidelines and standards of care
- enhanced data to support quality assurance activities
- improved approaches to quality assessment and assurance at the local level
- a national focus for developing, implementing, and monitoring a national system[28]

Quality of care is affected by a number of factors, including demographic factors, such as the age, gender, race or ethnicity, socioeconomic status, education, and occupation of those who use the services. Poor people, for instance, tend to be sicker and have more trouble getting the services they need. Economic factors, of course, play a role in determining the quality of care as well. It is common to hear that there is not enough money to provide universal access to services, keep the quality of care at a high level, or hire enough health professionals to provide the needed services. Finally, politics, including the political orientation of the party in office, can have an impact on the quality of the health care system. Indeed, the direction of health care policy may be largely determined by the lobbying of powerful groups such as the American Medical Association or the various managed care organizations (MCOs).

One of the keys to quality assurance is the accreditation process, in which special review organizations, most notably the Joint Commission on Accreditation of Healthcare Organizations, evaluate the care provided by health care organizations. One problem with present accreditation procedures is that the focus is on structural and staff performance requirements rather than treatment outcomes. Moreover, health care organizations, in order to improve their services, must be motivated by more than a desire to receive accreditation; they must be motivated to engage in improvement efforts out of an inner need to offer the public the best care they are capable of providing.

Public health agencies may undergo an accreditation review for some of their clinical programs, such as home care or ambulatory care services. Also, state and federal money is given to local agencies to provide certain mandated programs, and sanctions, including loss of funds, are applied if the mandated programs are not implemented, although the use of sanctions is inconsistent.

There is a built-in quality assurance process related to health objectives. If one of a local public health agency's objectives is to increase the immunization rate to the point where 90 percent of children under a certain age are receiving immunizations, the agency, by developing indicators of success, can determine the extent to which the objective is being achieved and also which segments of the population are being reached effectively. Partnerships with academia are useful in evaluating progress toward the attainment of objectives, and business techniques associated with continuous quality improvement or total quality management can be applied to uncover the reasons for the failure to meet objectives. Also, publicizing the success of community programs can strengthen the local public health infrastructure by demonstrating to residents that the public health agency is an effective social service organization.

Public health agencies need to monitor community assurance activities. The fear among public health professionals is that MCOs will take over the assurance function from local agencies. Public health leaders need to make sure that all public health agency and private health organization programs are of high quality.

Public health and mental health agencies have become program partners in many communities. Quality assurance is an important issue for mental health agencies as well, and it is likely to become even more important with the likely continued growth in third-party payers, governmental regulations, and national organization involvement.[29] Quality assurance methods need to be used not only in program operations but also in the training of public health and mental health professionals. Agency leaders need to support the training of the public health and mental health work force in innovative approaches to solving problems and making decisions.

In the area of quality assurance, public health leaders must

- develop local guidelines for practice
- promote high-quality programs
- meet or surpass proposed health objectives
- increase access to care for underinsured and underserved populations
- engage in quality assurance activities, such as those necessary to gain accreditation
- support continuous quality improvement procedures
- promote a consumer- and community-driven public health system
- train the public health work force in quality techniques
- work to integrate public health and mental health quality assurance activities

THE GREATEST LEADERSHIP CHALLENGE

The greatest challenge for public health leaders in the coming years will be to work out a viable relationship between governmental public health agencies and MCOs. Public health leaders have become defensive on the issue of partnering with MCOs and in fact have tended to ignore the MCOs in their communities under the mistaken assumption that they will eventually disappear.[30] As pointed out above, public health leaders are concerned that MCOs will take over many of the assurance responsibilities that presently belong to health departments. They are also concerned that MCOs will increase their community penetration by serving more and more community residents, with the result that public health agencies will suffer a reduction in operating funds for mandated services and core function activities.

It is important to point out that the assurance activities of government public health agencies will not diminish but will rather expand. These agencies will continue to have the responsibility of ensuring that necessary programs and services are available to all residents of the community. Each local public health agency will need to come up with unique solutions for meeting this responsibility. For example, an agency in some cases may be the managed care provider for certain segments of its community. Case Study 8–B presents an interview with Dr. Jean Malecki, who as a director of a Florida public health unit helped to develop a unique managed care program for her county. This interview shows the importance of creativity in leadership and how a local health unit can benefit from collaborating with local service providers.

Managed care can be defined as "a system of administrative controls intended to reduce costs through managing the utilization of services. Managed care can also mean an integrated system of health insurance, financing, and service delivery that focuses on the appropriate and cost-effective use of health services delivered through defined networks of providers and with allocation of financial risk."[31(p.371)] This definition does not entail that public health agencies will be without a direct service role in the future. Strong partnerships between public- and private-sector organizations will provide a synergy that could well lead to more effective public health initiatives at the community level—with more citizens being served as a result of the collaboration.

Strong leadership on both sides is necessary if improvement in the community's health is to occur, and everyone involved with improvement efforts needs to be aware that public health leaders, managed care leaders, and legislators have different priorities.[32] The highest priority for managed care leaders and legislators is to keep costs down. The highest priority for public health leaders is to increase access to services, the next highest is to ensure the services are of high quality, and third in rank is keeping costs low. Managed care leaders put quality second and access third. Legislators put access before quality. Thus, partnership is sometimes difficult because of the differences in priorities.

One thing that public health leaders and managed care leaders can agree on is the importance of prevention, for preventive activities are essential for keeping the demand for managed care services low (which of course keeps MCO costs low). Novick[33] reported on an interesting partnership between the public health agency in Onondaga County, New York, and the four Medicaid MCOs that were providing services to county residents. The partners

- set up a system for monitoring the delivery of preventive services in the MCOs and in the community at large
- created linkages between managed care clinical services and population-

based prevention services (e.g., programs to reduce the prevalence of sexually transmitted diseases, tuberculosis, and HIV infection)
- worked together to facilitate disease surveillance, health promotion and disease prevention programs, and behavioral and environmental interventions

The relationship between public health agencies and MCOs can take many forms. It can range from complete independence through various levels of interaction to complete integration. In the author's study of public health leaders, most of the leaders believed that governmental public health agencies need to remain independent if they are to serve their communities well, perhaps because it is not possible to delegate responsibility for program oversight to nongovernment organizations.

Whatever the relationship between a public health agency and local MCOs (except for complete independence), public health leaders need to create a process for creating and maintaining it. One such process, developed by Leviss and Hurtig, encompasses the following 10 steps:[34]

1. Conduct assessments of both the inside and outside of the organization.
2. Evaluate and redefine the mission and vision of the agency in order to create viable assurance activities.
3. Review partnership models and start implementation.
4. Create collaborative relationships with MCOs.
5. Develop formal structures to undergird the collaboration.
6. Create new policies and regulations to support the collaboration.
7. Market materials to demonstrate the partnership.
8. Build an infrastructure to support the partnership.
9. Not only choose models of collaboration, implement the models.
10. Evaluate the process.

The Institute of Medicine report on *Healthy Communities* discusses the evolving relationship between government public health agencies and the MCOs.[35] Three recommendations from the report are relevant to the present discussion:

1. Local public health agencies should ensure that there are high-quality services and programs available in their jurisdiction, including personal health services, and that these are accessible to all residents.
2. The leadership of local public health agencies, MCOs, and other stakeholder organizations must agree on their proper roles and responsibilities.
3. Public health agencies need to increase the level of their oversight of the health services system in their jurisdiction. For purposes of oversight, they need to collaborate with insurance regulators and state Medicaid agencies. If they perform their oversight activities effectively, they will have the opportunity to define the integrated health care system of the future.

The evolving relationships between public health agencies and MCOs will continue to present formidable challenges. Whether public health leaders like it or not, managed care will not go away. Furthermore, putting your head in the sand is never a good strategy. It is clear that managed care will be part of any comprehensive system of health services.

Public health leaders must

- make public health promotion the number one community action priority
- work proactively with MCOs and not ignore them
- redefine the health care delivery system to include primary prevention programs
- reorganize local public health agencies (e.g., by creating new programs and revising current ones)
- develop a public health leadership toolkit

Public health leaders need to take an active role in developing assurance programs and services. Exercise 8–1 is based on a leadership credo exercise discussed by Kouzes and Posner.[36] Discuss your credo in relation to the percentage of time that you allocate to each of the three core public health functions.

SUMMARY

Finding out what problems exist (assessment) and figuring out what to do about them (policy development planning) would be pointless without the final step: doing what needs to be done (assurance). In public health, the overall goal of assurance is to prevent disease and promote health in the community. This chapter began with a discussion of disease prevention and the barriers to carrying the assurance function. It then went on to discuss the organizational practices associated with assurance. These include organizational restructuring, the implementation of programs, the performance of quality assurance activities, and the education of the public.

Oddly, even though managed care may become more prevalent and take over the provision of direct services in most communities, the assurance activities of government public health agencies will expand rather than diminish. These agencies will continue to have oversight duties and will need to come up with new ways of meeting their responsibility to ensure necessary programs and services are available to every community resident. Indeed, working out a viable relationship between public health agencies and MCOs will be one of the main challenges for public health leaders in the early part of the new century.

Discussion Questions

1. What are the differences between primary, secondary, and tertiary prevention?
2. What are the program responsibilities of public health agencies in primary, secondary, and tertiary prevention?
3. What are some of the main barriers that public health leaders face in meeting their assurance responsibilities?
4. What are the four organizational practices associated with assurance? How

do these practices relate to the essential services of enforcing laws, linkage and provision of care, assurance of a competent workforce, and evaluation?

5. Are the assurance activities of government public health agencies likely to diminish or increase? Explain why.
6. How do public health agencies benefit from creating community partnerships?
7. What are the differences between population-based services and personal health services?
8. What are some of the factors that affect quality of care?
9. The greatest challenge that public health leaders will face in the immediate future is dealing with the growing prevalence of managed care. How can public health leaders meet this challenge?
10. Why is prevention likely to play a large role in the relationship between public health agencies and managed care organizations?

Exercise 8–1

LEADERSHIP CREDO

Purpose: to develop a set of guidelines for agency staff that reflect the agency leader's beliefs, values, and concerns

Key concepts: core public health functions, delegation of responsibility, leadership credo, leadership values

Procedure: Each student is to pretend that he or she is the head of a public health agency and has been given a six-month leave of absence to luxuriate on a tropical island that lacks all modern means of communication, including mail service. Before departing, the leader of the agency must give general guidance to the staff. The staff need to know the leader's values and beliefs—in short, the leader's credo. The leader must write a one-page memorandum that expresses that credo. After the credos are written, they are read to and discussed by the entire class.

Case Study 8–A

Big City Neighborhood Health Advisors

Adam B. Becker, Barbara A. Israel, and Rose Hollis

In today's context of decreasing budgets and increasing disparities in health status among U.S. population groups, health departments are faced with a serious challenge in trying to ensure the delivery of adequate and appropriate services to communities. Given the complex needs of communities and the differences between professional and lay experiences and perceptions, health department services often fail to be as relevant to community issues as they could be. To create more relevant services, some health departments are finding creative ways to involve community members in meeting the diverse needs in the community.

The Big City Health Department (BCHD) developed the Big City Neighborhood Health Advisor (BCNHA) project with the assistance of a local community-based organization (CBO) and a nearby school of public health. The project was funded for four years under the umbrella of a larger, multi-site project aimed at increasing the capacity of communities, bringing stronger community influence into the practice of public health, and changing the public health curriculum in universities to strengthen the community focus. Developing the BCNHA project was one strategy adopted by the BCHD to meet community needs and ensure that appropriate quality services were available locally.

ABOUT BIG CITY: THE PROJECT SETTING

Big City is one of the largest cities in the United States and has a population well over 1,000,000. Among the 77 U.S. cities with populations above 200,000, Big City has at times been ranked first in the percentage of people below the poverty level (as high as 32 percent). Big City has also been ranked first in unemployment rate (as high as 13 percent overall). In certain sections of the city, the unemployment rate is as high as 36 percent. Within Big City, 19 percent of all households are female headed, and 55 percent of these live below the poverty level. In addition, more than 40 percent of all children under the age of 18 live below the poverty level.

There is an increasing amount of racial and ethnic segregation in Big City, with extreme differences in health and income status between European Americans and people of color. Racial and economic segregation in Big City is linked to decreasing access to social and structural supports within the local communities, as jobs, stores, and other community institutions relocate to suburban areas and as the city's major industries downsize or disappear altogether.

"BIG CITY HEALTH DEPARTMENT: YOUR PARTNER IN GOOD HEALTH"

As federal, state, and local budgets for health and human services decline, the BCHD finds it more and more difficult to ensure that quality services are available to the residents. Many residents are not aware of the services that are available, nor how to access them. Those services that are available, because they are fewer in number and spread out, are often hard to reach for those who need the services the most.

In attempting to fulfill the three core functions of public health as defined by the Institute of Medicine (assessment, assurance, and policy development), the BCHD made an intensive effort to form partnerships with the communities it serves. The BCNHA project was one means by which the BCHD formed such partnerships. This kind of relationship with the communities was not new for the BCHD, nor was the BCNHA project the only example of a project it had implemented. The health department's openness to such partnerships was one of the factors that contributed to the success of the BCNHA program. This openness is evident in the BCHD's motto—"Big City Health Department, Your Partner in Good Health"—and its mission statement: "The overall role of the department is to prevent disease, promote health, and protect the environment. This is accomplished through partnerships and other types of collaboration with schools, hospitals, churches, physicians, health insurers, businesses and other community-based agencies...."

When university faculty, members of a major community-based organization, and staff of the BCHD sat down to determine the role of the health department in the umbrella project in which they were all engaged and the project activities it would take on, the BCNHA project seemed a natural fit for the BCHD. The BCNHA project would help the BCHD to achieve its mission by strengthening and expanding the role of Big City community members in the delivery of services aimed at meeting community needs.

DEVELOPING THE BIG CITY NEIGHBORHOOD HEALTH ADVISORS PROJECT

The first step in developing the BCNHA project was to establish a steering committee to oversee the project. This committee consisted of university faculty and students, community members, and staff from the CBO partner and the health department. The committee developed criteria for identifying and recruiting neighborhood health advisors (NHAs), established goals and approaches for training NHAs, and determined the relationship of the NHAs to the health department.

The steering committee based the BCNHA project on the lay health advisor (LHA) concept. Within communities, there have always been people who are trusted and respected and whom others rely upon for care, advice, and support. The support given is often informal, spontaneous, and so much a part of everyday life that it may go unrecognized. In most cases, the informal support is given by one person to another within a pre-existing relationship: friend to friend, coworker to coworker, neighbor to neighbor, or family member to family member. These special community members are knowledgeable about their community and well respected by friends, family, and neighbors. Others frequently turn to them for advice and assistance, and they are responsive to the strengths and needs of others. The NHA Steering Committee established these characteristics as the criteria for identifying potential NHAs.

In determining the relationship between the NHAs and the BCHD, the steering committee wanted to differentiate the roles of the NHAs from the roles that community members played in other BCHD projects. Health departments and other types of health and human service agencies often rely on members of their target populations to assist in the provision of services. Community members may provide information and education to others with similar backgrounds and life experiences (e.g., peer educators), extend the agency's access into the community and increase community awareness of agencies and services available to them (e.g., community outreach workers), or provide agencies with input into the types and quality of health services available (e.g., community advisory boards). These roles are extremely helpful in improving services and breaking down barriers to care.

The steering committee felt that the NHA role should be broad enough that the NHAs could provide services to their community in some or all of the capacities mentioned above. The distinction made between NHAs and other community members in BCHD projects was that NHAs would be identified, not created; would work with the BCHD and according to their own perceptions of priorities within their communities and not *for* the BCHD and according to its objectives; would not be paid employees of the health department; and would live or work in the settings in which they would provide help and assistance, perhaps facing issues similar to those faced by the people who would receive their support.

THE ROLE OF THE BIG CITY HEALTH DEPARTMENT

While the NHAs would not be employees of the BCHD, the steering committee decided that the BCNHA project headquarters should be housed at the health department. The health department's role, therefore, would be to hire a program coordinator and provide support and resources wherever possible. The BCHD hired Sue Siloh as the program coordinator. At first, Ms. Siloh felt out of place at the BCHD. The characteristics that made her a perfect fit for the job of coordinator meant that she was a unique health department employee. Ms. Siloh lived in the community served by the BCNHA project, had spent some time living in public housing, and did not have public health training. Initially, Ms. Siloh often felt that others did not take her or her program seriously.

The BCHD's deputy director, who was a strong supporter of both the BCNHA project and Ms. Siloh, saw that something needed to be done to create a support system for the project within the health department. Ms. Siloh was made a member of the administrative team of the BCHD, which had traditionally consisted only of the director, deputy director, and division heads. As a result of her inclusion on the team, Ms. Siloh was able to develop personal relationships with all the division heads, and they in turn learned more about the BCNHA project, how they could help support the project, and how the project could help the community and thus strengthen the department's relationship with the community, benefiting all of BCHD's programs. As needs arose for training or delivery of services (e.g., satellite immunization clinics, health screenings in community centers or churches), Ms. Siloh could now personally contact those in the BCHD who could help her to meet those needs.

THE ROLE OF THE COORDINATOR: RECRUITING, TRAINING, AND SUPPORTING NHAs

Sue Siloh's official title was community health coordinator. As coordinator of the BCNHA project, she was given many responsibilities. Ms. Siloh was responsible for recruiting and selecting NHAs, training new NHAs (she coordinated the eight-week training programs and additional in-service trainings and also served as a trainer for some sessions), supporting the trained NHAs (she coordinated monthly meetings, assisted NHAs with special projects, and maintained contact with each individual NHA), and starting up new NHA projects in other target areas of the city as requested (she assisted several community-based organizations in developing similar projects). In addition, Ms. Siloh presented the BCNHA project at professional meetings and conferences, advised other agencies in the development of NHA projects, and worked with members of the university on publications about the BCNHA project. Ms. Siloh also participated in grant-writing activities to bring in new money to sustain the project.

RECRUITING NHAs

The recruiting process for NHAs was somewhat informal and combined several strategies. The coordinator contacted local block clubs, churches, and other community groups in order to spread the word about the project. Flyers were posted throughout the community. Ms. Siloh also contacted community members she knew from her work as a community organizer and advocate. For subsequent cohorts, previously trained NHAs played a recruiting role by bringing in interesting friends and neighbors. As for qualifications, NHAs were expected to have the trust and respect of people in the community, an interest in learning about the community, and an eagerness to work to improve the health and quality of life of community members.

TRAINING THE NHAs

Once the NHAs were identified, they participated in eight sessions of "core" training. This initial training covered three broad areas: health education, community resources and referrals, and community problem-solving and organizing. Health department staff provided most of the training in health education (topics included diabetes, high blood pressure, and HIV/AIDS). Representatives from local agencies provided information about the resources available to the NHAs and their neighbors, and faculty from the university provided the community problem-solving and organizing training.

Once trained, NHAs also participated in training subsequent cohorts. They worked in teams with trainers to give the NHA perspective on the training topic and to provide "real-life" examples of how NHAs could put their skills to work.

Although the initial training content was, for the most part, determined by the steering committee, the trainees determined the training schedule as a group to fit their needs. They also had opportunities to select priority areas on which to focus during the core training. After the core training, NHAs had opportunities to go on to specialized training in areas they selected, such as CPR, organizing block clubs, substance abuse, and parenting. Over 40 NHAs participated in three core trainings.

NEIGHBORHOOD HEALTH ADVISORS AT WORK

Once they graduated from the training program, NHAs had increased skills to continue the help they were providing in their communities. NHAs became involved on a daily basis with individuals and groups in their own neighborhoods—helping friends and family to access needed services, assisting block clubs to organize and address community issues, providing day care to families, transporting neighbors to appointments, and providing education on health issues to church and community organizations and businesses.

Health was not the only human service sector with which BCNHAs were involved. Several NHAs began to work with a local police precinct through the Safe and Healthy Neighborhoods Program to educate neighborhood residents about crime and safety and to assist police in learning to work with community members in a way that would foster trust and cooperation.

In addition to these helping roles, NHAs developed some dynamic programs in their neighborhoods. Examples include the Community Cupboard, a neighborhood food and clothing pantry; Together We Can, a grief support group for those experiencing loss; and Facing the Challenge, a parenting program that builds skills and provides support for pregnant women. In addition to these programs, NHAs participated in other ongoing programs, such as the Peterson Clinic Advisory council, a community board that assisted a local health clinic in developing programs for the community, and the Violence Task Force, a group that worked to provide alternative activities for youths at risk. NHAs participated in these projects according to their interests and the needs in their neighborhoods. In addition to these projects, the NHAs distributed a monthly newsletter to over 5,000 individuals and families in Big City. The newsletter included information about health issues and services, local business news, and community events.

SPECIAL PROGRAM ISSUES

RECOGNITION AND REIMBURSEMENT

Given the number of activities in which NHAs were involved and the limited resources available to the program, the question of reimbursement was one that continued to arise for the BCNHA project. Many of the NHAs had full- or part-time jobs. They considered helping friends and family as part of their responsibility to the community or to God or as part of being a member of a family and community and did not want to be paid. There were other NHAs who wanted to have a full- or part-time job, and their hope was that the training and activities they did in conjunction with this program would lead them to a job. Regardless of whether NHAs wished to be paid, their work needed to be recognized. Whenever possible, portions of new grant monies brought in to sustain the NHA project were designated for reimbursement for travel (e.g., gas and mileage), reimbursement for meals (e.g., dinner during training sessions), to provide incentives (each NHA received a printed cloth carrying bag with the NHA logo), or as stipends for hourly work on special neighborhood projects. For most of the NHAs, these forms of compensation were enough to support and encourage them as they engaged in their work.

In a few cases, NHAs were hired by the BCHD or affiliated organizations for full- or part-time positions. While employment was welcomed by these NHAs, formalizing their work as NHAs was not without challenges. Along with a salary came an obligation to the paying agency. Some of the NHAs who received jobs found that they had less time to work with groups in their own neighborhoods. Others found that they were limited in the scope of health issues with which they could work, as their training was specialized to fit their new jobs.

To some extent, those who became employed through their work as NHAs lost a modicum of the community's trust when they became agency employees. They were seen by some as "part of the system" rather than part of the community, and their loyalties became suspect. Because an open, trusting relationship between an NHA and the local community was essential to the work of the NHA, employment actually decreased the ability of some to provide individualized support and assistance.

Though the steering committee and the program coordinator had varying opinions on the subject of compensating NHAs, decisions about paying stipends to BCNHAs or hiring them into agencies followed two basic principles: (1) the work of NHAs had to be recognized and compensated in some way, and (2) NHAs themselves had to be involved in the decision regarding their compensation.

EVALUATING THE WORK OF THE NHAs

Assurance of service delivery and the quality of those services requires public health departments to evaluate programs to determine whether they are meeting community needs appropriately and sufficiently. Several challenges faced the BCNHA program when it came to evaluation. First, designing an evaluation plan for such a diverse set of activities was extremely difficult. Some NHAs worked more with individuals and others more with groups, some worked with certain agencies and others worked independently, some participated in all monthly meetings and others attended only when they needed materials or to meet with the coordinator. In addition, all NHAs possessed unique styles of helping. Given the diversity, could an evaluation plan be developed that would be appropriate to all NHAs?

Second, collecting data on BCNHA activities was a challenge. The often spontaneous and informal nature of the work of NHAs made observation by evaluators difficult if not impossible. Likewise, NHAs found it difficult to keep records of their activities because they took place during a phone call from a friend or a chance meeting in the grocery store. Much of the "helping work" done by NHAs was seen by project staff and evaluators as program-related work. NHAs, however, saw their work as part of daily life and therefore not appropriate for documenting. Confidentiality and trust issues, as well as the sheer number of people in contact with NHAs, make "client" interviewing a challenge as well.

Given the above challenges, the steering committee, the coordinator, the evaluator, and the NHAs themselves knew that whatever evaluation methods were used would not be able to capture an entire picture of the BCNHA project. Talking with NHA "clients" who were willing to be interviewed helped the program evaluators form an idea of how the NHAs were interacting with other community members and what that interaction meant for the community. Community members were less likely, however, to talk about weaknesses of the program because of the relationships they had with the NHAs.

Looking at community outcomes was also extremely difficult. Could NHAs be credited with a drop in infant mortality rates or a decrease in visits to the emergency room? Could they be held accountable for a rise in criminal activity or incomplete immunization rates? With so many other activities going on in Big City, how would evaluators determine what changes were effects of the project? The steering committee felt that using communities without NHAs as comparisons was also a problematic strategy. The ethical responsibility of the BCHD to all the communities in which it works, the difficulty of matching diverse communities, and a shortage of resources were among the reasons why the project chose not to implement a quasi-experimental evaluation design.

The effects of participation on the NHAs themselves were, however, assessed through the evaluation. NHAs completed a profile form when they joined the program. They were asked to indicate employment status, education level, skills and talents, interest in and commitment to empowering their neighborhoods, organizational affiliations, and availability. Changes in these items for each NHA were assessed either through having the NHA complete a profile form after a certain amount of time or through an interview.

In addition, documentation gave those involved with the project a good idea of how program activities were being carried out. The program coordinator used several strategies to encourage NHAs to document their work. NHAs were given documentation forms to keep track of activities, needs, challenges, and ideas for priority projects in the community. Once a month the NHAs jointly met with the coordinator to discuss project ideas and challenges, to learn about new resources in the community, to give each other support, and sometimes to receive additional training. The first portion of these meetings was devoted to discussing and providing assistance in completing the documentation forms.

THE NHAs AND ASSURANCE

The BCHD takes very seriously its responsibility to the community. In order to fulfill part of the assurance function, the BCHD implemented and supported the BCNHA project. The project helped the BCHD to carry out assurance activities in several ways:

- by disseminating information throughout the target area regarding health issues, resources, and services available
- by strengthening the connection between the health department and the community and expanding the role that community members play in the delivery of health services
- by providing training to community members that strengthened their ability to solve problems, gain access to resources, voice their needs and concerns, and transfer these skills on to other community members.

This program is an excellent example of how one health department approached the function of ensuring the delivery of quality services to the community in a time of decreasing budgets and increasing needs for services.

Case Study 8–B

A Leadership Interview with Jean M. Malecki

Louis Rowitz

Jean M. Malecki, MD, MPH, is the director of the HRS/Palm Beach County Health Unit. She holds a Doctor of Medicine degree from New York Medical College and a Master of Public Health degree from the University of Miami. Dr. Malecki is also a graduate of the Public Health Leadership Institute in California. She has been one of the leaders in the development of unique models for public health service at the county level and talks about these programs during the interview, which occurred on February 17, 1995.

How have you helped your health unit reinvent public health for the county?

We have begun a countywide total quality improvement project where we initially used APEX as our tool and then brought in outside consultants on visioning and team building for all staff. In so doing, we decided as a health department that we would continue to do traditional public health but that would be the foundation for a major effort in prevention and primary care in the managed care arena. Currently, we are putting in an application for a commercial HMO, which would use only public dollars—both Medicaid and tax dollars. The HMO will be called Healthy Palm Beach. It will be housed in the health department. We presently have a Medicaid HMO. We are thus applying for a commercial HMO so that we can use some of the same tax dollars that are currently received to a taxing entity to provide the same level of care to the working poor that we provide to the Medicaid clients. It will be a single payer. Any willing provider can be part of the system. This proposed program provides a healthy competition environment.

Are the three core functions still relevant in a reinvention environment?

The core functions are even more relevant in a reinvention environment. You have to have the core functions in place whether the health department directly provides the care or not. The health department has to oversee healthy outcomes. It is necessary to ensure that any health care reform that takes place achieves what it is supposed to. In Florida, what we are seeing, unfortunately, is that the cost factor is number one to policy makers. Costs—and not quality—are driving the system. Having the core functions are extremely important if we are going to work out what we need to on the local level. Both the new model of essential public health services and the model of core functions are needed. They need to be integrated. The critical issue relates to a continuum of services and functions that need to be applied in a rational manner.

Where is public health going during the next five years?

The answer to your question depends on how rapidly and influentially we can educate our policymakers. We got a reprieve last year (1994) when national and state health care reform legislation was not passed. We need to intensively educate our public because education was neglected at the national and state level. First, we need to educate our policymakers one on one in terms of what public health is. The idea of core functions is not part of the message to policy makers because the terms are misleading. It is necessary to be very concrete rather than abstract with policy makers. The arguments need to not only be concrete, but also the messages given must be very simple and strong. For example, we might say that the mission of public health is to prevent epidemics and the spread of disease, protect against environmental hazards, prevent injury, promote and encourage healthy behaviors, respond to disasters and assist communities in recovery, and ensure the quality and accessibility of health services. Specific local examples will strengthen the arguments. The important message to give is that the health reform plans will not work unless we have a strong public health foundation.

How do we do more with less money?

This depends on the decisions of the organization. In Florida, health departments are doing three things. First, they are downsizing completely and doing nothing except traditional public health activities totally out of the prevention/primary care arena. Other health departments are downsizing but are doing things in the contractual arena with local HMOs to provide some prevention and some primary care. There are other departments like us that are competitive, entrepreneurial, and will compete for the primary care dollar in just as businesslike a manner as the private entrepreneur. The money that we get and save goes into public health. There may be less money through categorical funding, block grant funding, or whatever, but there is a way to make money to fund public health. We chose the latter road.

How do we become more entrepreneurial?

Public health professionals need to learn how to be more creative. They need to learn how to create a vision that defines what public health should be. This needs to be done by working with the community as well as other colleagues in the health department. Then, it is necessary for the public health department leader to market itself. You first create the vision. To achieve it, you must become more businesslike and accountable. You don't market yourself only to get more business, but market in terms of health promotion activities and successes. Thus, you need to market yourself to the community and all the way up to the policy makers. I can tell you what we did to attract the attention of our entire legislative delegation. They are impressed with our mobile clinics that go to migrant camps, as well as the fact that we serve clients at night and on weekends. We are not always as good at tooting our horns as we should be. That is a mindset that hasn't been in public health.

What is public health's role in managed care?

I look at it in three ways. Number one is you are doing it yourself. Number two is that you are participating with other managed care groups. Third, if you are not in the business yourself or participating with other managed care entities, you do have to oversee the assurance piece. If you are in the business, you are going to have to monitor assurance anyhow. Assurance of the managed care activities in your jurisdiction is a critical public health activity for the health department whether the department is doing the managed care or not.

What aspects of health care reform will pass Congress in the near future?

I don't think anything is going to pass soon. If anything does pass, it will probably be something related to insurance reform. It will be tough because the insurance lobby is strong. With a great amount of discussion now on welfare reform, we are more likely to see action here that might relate to the tightening up of Medicaid benefits. I don't see that much change is going to occur in Florida either.

What is the relationship between strong leadership and restructuring the field of public health?

It's everything. We can't stress this more. How come we don't have a public health political action committee? Everybody else does. Public health professionals don't seem to fight for public health like other special interest groups do. Leadership development should not be separated out from professional education. It should be part of the educational experience of our public health students. Leadership training should also be available for residency training directors. Leadership training is clearly important for preventive medicine residents. Fellowship training is good, but leadership development needs to occur earlier in the educational process.

REFERENCES

1. B.J. Turnock, *Public Health: What It Is and How It Works* (Gaithersburg, MD: Aspen Publishers, 1997).
2. Washington State Department of Health, *Public Health Improvement Plan: A Progress Report* (Olympia, WA: State of Washington Department of Health, 1994).
3. Roadmap Implementation Task Force, *The Road to Better Health for All of Illinois* (Springfield, IL: State of Illinois, 1990).
4. Institute of Medicine, *The Future of Public Health* (Washington, DC: National Academy Press, 1988).
5. G. Pickett and J.J. Hanlon, *Public Health: Administration and Practice,* 9th ed. (St. Louis: Times Mirror and Mosby College Pub., 1990).
6. Institute of Medicine, *The Future of Public Health.*
7. Institute of Medicine, *The Future of Public Health.*
8. Institute of Medicine, *The Future of Public Health.*
9. B.J. Turnock et al., "Implementing and Assessing Organizational Practices in Local Health Departments," *Public Health Reports* 109, no. 4 (1994): 478–484.
10. J. Studinicki et al., "Analyzing Organizational Practices in Local Health Departments," *Public Health Reports* 109, no. 4 (1994): 485–490.
11. Studinicki et al., "Analyzing Organizational Practices in Local Health Departments."
12. B.J. Turnock et al., "Local Health Department Effectiveness in Addressing the Core Functions of Public Health," *Public Health Reports* 109, no. 5 (1994): 653–658.
13. Illinois Administrative Code, title 77, sec. 600.
14. Turnock et al., "Implementing and Assessing Organizational Practices in Local Health Departments."
15. Turnock et al., "Local Health Department Effectiveness in Addressing the Core Functions of Public Health."
16. Pickett and Hanlon, *Public Health.*
17. L.A. Aday, *At Risk in America* (San Francisco: Jossey-Bass, 1993).
18. L. Breslow et al., Preface, in *Annual Review of Public Health 1,* eds. L. Breslow et al. (Palo Alto, CA: Annual Reviews, Inc., 1980).
19. Breslow et al., Preface.
20. K. Gebbie, *Redefining the Assurance Function (Speech)* (Chicago: Illinois Public Health Leadership Institute, 1995).
21. S.B. Thacker, "Historical Development," in *Principles and Practice of Public Health Surveillance,* eds. S.M. Teutsch and R.E. Churchill (New York: Oxford University Press, 1994).
22. American Public Health Association, *Healthy Communities 2000: Model Standards* (Washington, DC: American Public Health Association, 1991).

23. Washington State Core Government Public Health Functions Task Force, *Core Public Health Functions* (Olympia, WA: State of Washington Department of Health, 1993).

24. Washington State Department of Health, *Public Health Improvement Plan: A Progress Report* (Olympia, WA.: State of Washington Department of Health, 1994).

25. U.S. General Accounting Office, *Quality Assurance: A Comprehensive National Strategy for Health Care Is Needed* (Gaithersburg, MD: U.S. General Accounting Office, 1990).

26. U.S. General Accounting Office, *Quality Assurance.*

27. U.S. General Accounting Office, *Quality Assurance.*

28. U.S. General Accounting Office, *Quality Assurance.*

29. J. Zusman, "Quality Assurance in Mental Health Care," *Hospital and Community Psychiatry* 39, no. 12 (1988): 1286–1290.

30. G.P. Mays et al., "Managed Care, Public Health, and Privatization: A Typology of Interorganizational Arrangements," in *Managed Care and Public Health,* eds. P.K. Halverson et al. (Gaithersburg, MD: Aspen Publishers, 1998).

31. Turnock, *Public Health.*

32. C.P. McLaughlin, "Managed Care and Its Relationship to Public Health: Barriers and Opportunities," in *Managed Care and Public Health,* eds. P.K. Halverson et al. (Gaithersburg, MD: Aspen Publishers, 1998).

33. L.F. Novick, "Managed Care and Public Health," *Journal of Public Health Management and Practice* 4, no. 1 (1998):vi.

34. P.S. Leviss and L. Hurtig, "The Role of Local Health Units in a Managed Care Environment: A Case Study of New York City," *Journal of Public Health Management and Practice* 4, no. 1 (1998): 12–20.

35. M.A. Stoto et al., eds., *Healthy Communities: New Partnerships for the Future of Public Health* (Washington, DC: National Academy Press, 1996).

36. J.M. Kouzes and B.Z. Posner, *Credibility* (San Francisco: Jossey-Bass, 1993).

Appendix 8–A

State of Washington Assurance Capacity Standards

HEALTH PROMOTION CAPACITY STANDARDS

All public health jurisdictions, both state and local, must:

- Bring about needed changes in laws, regulations, ordinances, and policies.
- Develop health promotion programs that are culturally and linguistically appropriate for the community.
- Provide education about and intervention to prevent specific infectious and noninfectious diseases such as dental caries, vaccine-preventable diseases, hypertension, cancer, and heart disease.
- Provide education about and intervention to address specific personal and environmental risk factors such as substance abuse and hazardous materials in the home.
- Provide assessment data to the community about the incidence and causes of intentional and unintentional injury.
- Provide education in the community to help create healthy living environments.
- Provide public and professional education and other interventions to reduce intentional and unintentional injury.
- Provide services and education that enhance the formation of healthy family relationships, promote normal child growth and development, and foster appropriate child health care practices.
- Provide education about reproductive health and family planning methods and strategies.
- Provide education about noninfectious disease to affected individuals and their families, especially regarding disease progression, treatment, and support services.
- Provide publications, presentations, programs, and media releases on a routine basis that inform and educate the public on the health status of the community, relevant health issues, and positive health behavior.

Each local public health jurisdiction must:

- Address prioritized public health risk factors in the community through a planning process, developed in collaboration with the community, that identifies appropriate intervention strategies for specific issues and populations.
- Maintain an information and referral system concerning available health facilities, resources, and services.
- Give community members access to information and training regarding appropriate actions that enhance their living, working, school, and recreational environments.

The state must:

- Help agencies develop education strategies, including media releases and hotlines, aimed at reducing behavioral and environmental public health risk factors.
- Provide staff and technical expertise and support where local level resources are temporarily or permanently unavailable to ensure health promotion plans and programs addressing health risk factors are fully implemented statewide.
- Serve as the lead agency for coordinating public health activities during emergencies.
- Develop intervention strategies, education materials, and classes for specific needs of caregivers, health professionals, and other public and private partners on a statewide basis.
- Design model health education and related organizational, environmental, and economic interventions to address public health risk factors.
- Help develop public health curricula in K–12 school health education.
- Develop or provide information and referral mechanisms, including hotlines, for statewide services (for example, oral health, mental health, and environmental health issues).
- Coordinate with local health agencies and other state organizations to draft and promote statewide legislation aimed at reducing public health risk factors and promoting healthy behaviors.
- Work with the higher education system to ensure health education/promotion personnel and training are available to address health promotion needs in local and state agencies.

HEALTH PROTECTION CAPACITY STANDARDS

All public health jurisdictions, both state and local, must:

- Maintain appropriate monitoring, inspection, intervention, and enforcement activities that eliminate or reduce the exposure of citizens to communicable disease, environmental health, and emergency hazards.
- Coordinate protection efforts with many other local, state, and federal agencies and groups.
- Develop protection programs, in accordance with federal guidelines and scientifically identified risk factors, that address prioritized health risk factors.
- Ensure that communicable disease contact investigation and follow-up are done in a timely and appropriate manner, in adherence to guidelines of the federal Centers for Disease Control and Prevention.
- Ensure that persons with communicable diseases are identified, treated in a timely, appropriate manner, and given information regarding treatment protocols and appropriate behavior to reduce the spread of disease.
- Take appropriate legal or other action if treatment protocols or behavior changes are not followed through.
- Ensure that individuals, especially children, are immunized according to recommended public health schedules.
- Provide surveillance, diagnosis, and treatment of infectious diseases of public health significance.

- Analyze and interpret data regarding environmental and personal risk factors.
- Provide maternity services such as outreach, case management, and support services.
- Provide nutrition intervention services for children and childbearing women that include education and provision of specific foods.
- Regularly screen and assess children who are at risk or who live in high-risk families.

Each local public health jurisdiction must:

- Conduct ongoing inspections and provide oversight consistent with state and local board of health rules and regulations.
- Respond to concerns expressed by the public regarding health problems.
- Conduct surveillance and manage the data generated so that program efforts can address community needs and problems.
- Enforce compliance with public health regulations whenever a voluntary compliance strategy is not effective or appropriate.
- Train operators of facilities (for example, water treatment plants and food service establishments) in order to ensure that facilities are properly operated and maintained on a day-to-day basis.
- Identify and control small animal, insect, and rodent populations that present potential and actual hazards to public health.
- Determine the nature and impact of public health emergencies and mobilize resources to control or prevent additional illness, injury, or death.
- Provide public health information services on a 24-hour basis to inform and help coordinate responses of local, state, and federal organizations to public health emergencies.
- Maintain an inventory of local medical and health personnel, medical equipment, facilities, and other resources that might be needed during emergencies, noting availability and response criteria.
- Provide or have access to laboratory services that can, during emergencies, support the local detection, identification, and analysis of hazardous substances that may present threats to public health.
- Maintain required potability and quality of domestic water supplies affected by emergencies.
- Provide for the public health concerns of the rescue workers and care providers in emergency situations, including needs for shelter, food, and sanitation equipment.
- Provide ongoing public health staff training in emergency response plans, including participation in practice exercises on a routine basis.

The state must:

- Facilitate and provide periodic training to local health agency staff and operators of facilities (for example, hotels, hospitals, restaurants, water treatment plants, public swimming pools, sewage disposal plants) on new and emerging issues.
- Routinely coordinate with federal rule making agencies and the Congress to

ensure that they take into account the effects of federal rules and statutes on the health risks, protection needs, and resources of Washington State.

- Develop, in cooperation with local health agencies, consistent uniform statewide regulations and policies that guide the public health activities of direct service providers, the local public health jurisdictions, and state agencies.
- Support the day-to-day efforts and provide assistance in the crisis response efforts of local agencies.
- Carry out the direct regulatory responsibilities over the largest public water supplies and certain community on-site sewage disposal systems.
- Assume appropriate service, consultative, and coordination responsibilities for emergency response efforts.
- Serve as the lead agency for coordinating all public health activities during emergencies in the State Emergency Operations Center.
- Provide public information support to the Office of the Governor and to other state or federal emergency management agencies during emergency and disaster recovery operations.
- Support local health agencies in the provision of laboratory services, food and water inspection, radiological assessment, and disease identification and testing during emergencies.
- Help coordinate and incorporate local emergency response plans into a statewide plan.
- Help coordinate the transfer of needed personnel, resources, and equipment to emergency sites.

QUALITY ASSURANCE CAPACITY STANDARDS

Each local public health jurisdiction must:

- Ensure that communicable diseases are being appropriately treated in the community.
- Ensure that prevention and intervention efforts for communicable diseases are being appropriately implemented, including tracking the immunization status of children in the community.
- Evaluate the health status of populations who receive public health services and the impact of those services on their health status.
- Recognize and respond to unmet community needs, especially those related to high-risk conditions or behaviors.
- Gain access to data systems to provide long-term trend analyses, including being a participant in the Health Services Information System (HSIS).
- Monitor and ensure the competence of people such as food handlers whose activities can affect the health of the public and who are not otherwise licensed or monitored by the state.
- Develop strategies to ensure individuals and families can be linked with needed providers.
- Help inform providers regarding public health interventions, areas of concern, and recommended standards of care.
- Evaluate access to personal health services, especially for low-income and

special populations. Where applicable, the evaluation should include a measure of the cultural appropriateness of services.

- Educate providers about specific public health interventions or areas of concern and recommended standards of care.
- Support strategies to ensure linkages between providers, families, and individuals.
- Evaluate the efficacy, costs, and benefits of prevention services as compared to medical treatment.
- Recognize the need for and establish criteria for competency assessment and assurance of health professionals.
- Design, implement, and evaluate licensing and certification programs and methods for health professionals and facilities and providers of other public services.
- Ensure compliance with appropriate regulations and standards in health care sites and facilities.
- Periodically review local health agency and community programs to ensure compliance with state standards.
- Assess and monitor state-funded public health programs for outcome results.
- Conduct quality assurance activities and operate state-mandated regulatory programs necessary to ensure that all laboratories produce high-quality outcomes. Work with agencies to correct deficiencies and provide appropriate training programs.
- Ensure that laboratories that provide data for public health purposes are linked through a common information management system that ensures consistent laboratory performance and ready access to analytical and diagnostic data.

Leadership Skills and Competencies

Chapter 9

Leadership and Communication

There was an inimitable cadence, an emphasis on certain words, an exaggeration of certain phrases, a kind of intoning here and there which made his telling unforgettable.

A. Thirkell on Rudyard Kipling, *Three Houses*

Part III of this book looks at the tools and skills that leaders need to apply in carrying out their responsibilities. This chapter is concerned with communication skills. Leading, after all, is an interactive process involving leaders and followers, and obviously good communication between all participants in the process is absolutely essential.

Communication is the transfer of information,[1] and it has become even more important over the last decades—the start of the so-called information age—than it was previously. Information makes situations orderly, promotes change and growth, and defines reality. It plays an important part in the leadership process, as does the communication of information in all the various forms that such communication takes, from face-to-face conversation to electronic transfer of data.

THE COMMUNICATION PROCESS

It may be difficult to communicate effectively, but it is impossible not to communicate at all.[2] Each person's life is based on developing and using language to interact with other people.

A communicative act involves the transmission of two messages. The first message is about the topic of the communication. The second message concerns the hidden or real agenda of the parties to the communicative act.

Communication is an ongoing process throughout our personal and professional lives. It does not solve all our problems itself but must be accompanied by action.[3]

189

Barriers to Communication

There are many barriers to effective communication.[4] Communication can be blocked by forces within the participants as well as external forces. Nonverbal behavior—in the form of facial and hand gestures—can influence how a message is received, as can conscious and unconscious thoughts and distractions such as noise and motion. In addition, men and women have different conversational styles that can either enhance communication or create barriers to communication.

The intended recipient's state of mind can be a major barrier to receiving a message. How many of us have found ourselves daydreaming in a public health agency staff meeting when the agency director asks our opinion on an issue. Other reasons for not listening to a conversation include anxiety about talking, lack of interest in the topic, thinking about what to say, confusion from trying to make sense of overly complicated discourse, lack of understanding of the professional lexicon, dislike of the speaker and his or her principles, and a desire to be somewhere else.[5]

Sometimes a person says things in order to upset the listener, and the message does not completely reflect the ideas of the sender.[6] This type of behavior can create tensions in a marriage—or an agency. Suppose the director of a program says to a staff member, "John, I need further infant mortality data from the state. Please call the state statistician and get me the infant mortality data for the last five years for our county. Would you also ask her to evaluate the data for us?" The true message might be this: "I don't trust John's interpretation of the data. John probably did it wrong." John may understand the underlying message, and his response—"I'll do it immediately"—might have as its underlying message, "Why doesn't he do it himself? I did the analysis correctly."

Other barriers include injecting into the communicative process a judgment that discredits the other party to the process and avoiding the concerns of the other party.[7]

An Interactionist Model of Communication

Hulett[8,9] built a communication model based on the symbolic interactionist approach used by some social scientists, including Robert Sears, who had developed a model of communication as a dyadic action system.[10] According to Sears, each individual brings a personal history to each communicative interaction. Hulett, who thought that most communication models were simplistic, claimed that communication needs to be seen as a natural social process that encompasses what takes place within each participant as well as what takes place between the participants and that every act of communication occurs within a multilevel social system that it influences and is influenced by.

Hulett analyzed an act of communication into a number of steps, which he called the "instigation action sequence." Each step involves one of five types of act or event: a motivating stimulus, a covert rehearsal, an instrumental act, an environmental event, or a goal response (Figure 9–1). Each participant in a communicative act brings to the act a cognitive map that affects the motivating stimulus. The initiator of the act evaluates the stimulus and mentally rehearses the proposed communication (covert rehearsal; see Figure 9–2). The initiator then performs some action or says something (instrumental act) that triggers the

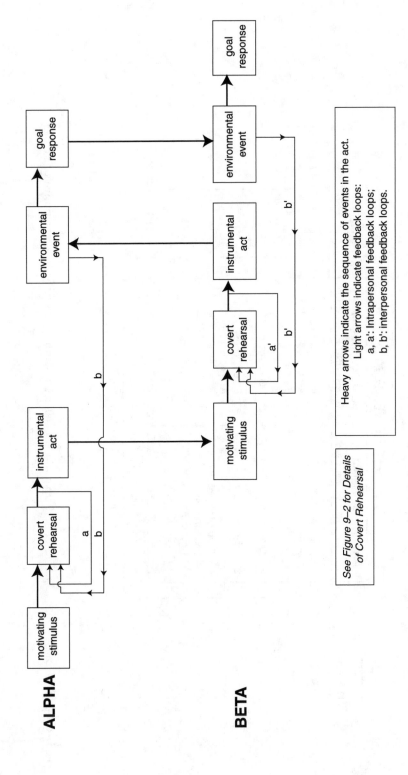

ALPHA

motivating stimulus → covert rehearsal → instrumental act → environmental event → goal response

a, b (feedback loops)

b

BETA

motivating stimulus → covert rehearsal → instrumental act → environmental event → goal response

a', b'

b'

See Figure 9–2 for Details of Covert Rehearsal

Heavy arrows indicate the sequence of events in the act.
Light arrows indicate feedback loops:
a, a': Intrapersonal feedback loops;
b, b': interpersonal feedback loops.

Figure 9–1 Block diagram of a social act between two interacting individuals, according to symbolic interactionist principles.

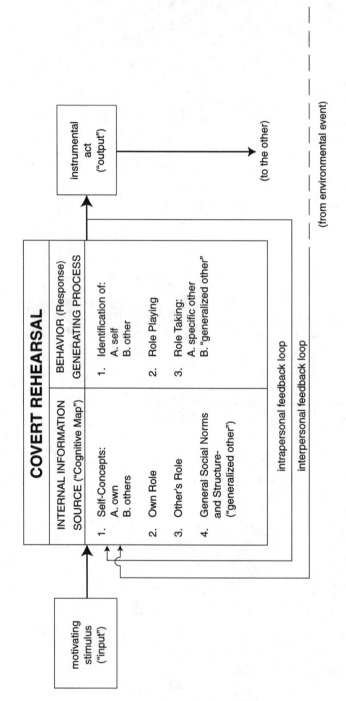

Figure 9–2 The covert rehearsal of either participant in a social act, according to symbolic interactionist principles.

motivating stimulus for the recipient of the interaction, who then mentally goes through the covert rehearsal phase. The recipient performs an instrumental act (answers the sender), which becomes the environmental act for the initiator. If the initiator is satisfied, then the goal response will be positive. If the recipient sees the response as positive, the interaction is complete. Feedback loops in the process allow the initiator and the sender to clarify issues and then finish the process.

According to Hulett, the covert rehearsal is the stage at which the individual role-plays his or her actions and tries to determine how the other person will respond. The self-concept of each participant, the values that guide each person, and the person's perceptions of the other's role influence the communicative process. For example, a public health leader will approach communication differently depending on whether the intended recipient is an agency staff member, the leader of another agency, or the president of the board of health. Further, a public health leader from a middle-class, suburban background will likely have different expectations when dealing with the residents of a working-class community than would a public health leader from a working-class background.

The model devised by Hulett concerns personal communication between two people. However, leadership also occurs at the team, agency, community, and professional levels, and the communicative process at each of these levels is complicated by the fact that a multitude of individuals are involved, each of whom comes to the process with a unique agenda and a unique interpretation of the same set of facts. A public health leader addressing a coalition, for instance, must discuss the issues with each coalition member individually at another time to ensure the communication of ideas or information is successful.

Communication Skills

Table 9–1 lists the communication skills needed by leaders at the five levels of leadership. It indicates that a public health leader requires at least 18 communication skills. Most are discussed in this chapter, but conflict resolution and negotiation are discussed in Chapter 11, and cultural sensitivity is discussed in a wider context in Chapter 12.

To be effective communicators, public health leaders must

- fully develop their communication skills as part of their lifelong learning agenda
- respect the different agendas that coalition members or partners bring to the table
- use the core functions of public health to guide communication with others
- use their communication skills to guide the transfer of knowledge
- be on the lookout for barriers to communication

INTERPERSONAL COMMUNICATION

According to Hulett, interaction between two individuals is the basic unit of communication. In the workplace, critical communicative interactions include giving instructions, asking and answering questions, listening to the concerns of others, and, especially in the case of leaders, publicizing the organization's mission and vision.[11]

Table 9–1 Communication Skills and Levels of Leadership

Skill Categories	Personal Leadership	Team Leadership	Agency Leadership	Community Leadership	Professional Leadership
Interpersonal communication	X	X	X	X	X
Active listening	X	X	X	X	X
Public speaking	X	—	X	X	X
Interviewing	X	X	X	X	X
Written communication	X	X	X	X	X
Computer skills	X	X	X	X	X
Media advocacy	X	X	X	X	X
Cultural sensitivity	X	X	X	X	X
Feedback	X	X	X	X	X
Delegation	X	X	X	X	X
Framing	X	X	X	X	X
Dialogue, discussion, and debate	X	X	X	X	X
Meeting skills	X	X	X	X	X
Health communications	X	X	X	X	X
Social marketing	X	X	X	X	X
Mentoring and facilitation	X	X	X	X	X
Conflict resolution	X	X	X	X	X
Negotiation	X	X	X	X	X

There are advantages to oral communication.[12] First, talking is the quickest form of communication. Ideas and thoughts can be relayed in a simple form that others can understand. Quick feedback is also possible. An important disadvantage is that the potential for distortion is great. Even with the best of intentions, community leaders may misinterpret the statements of public health agency leaders. Communication will have to be continuous if agreement on goals and programmatic interventions is to occur.

Communication Styles

Different conversational styles exist, and the differences in style can have social ramifications.[13] It is not uncommon for residents in a nursing home to be called by their first names by the staff, but this kind of informality may disturb some older residents, who might see the use of first names as indicative of a lack of respect. Also, major differences in conversational style exist between men and women, shown by the fact that men and women often seem to talk at cross-purposes. In addition, although the public health work force is mostly female, most of the agency heads are men, and this may have something to do with the fact that women have different public speaking styles than men. Women must speak without the appearance of submission or of lack of a strong position. Women tend to not be overly aggressive,[14] but they will need to face conflict squarely in order to convince others of the truth of their beliefs.

In general, leaders need to avoid being too submissive or too aggressive in their communications.[15] Assertiveness is the most effective strategy. Assertive leaders fight for their beliefs and thus gain the respect of others without antagonizing them by being aggressive. Many public health leaders believe that they possess finely honed interpersonal skills, but in fact observation shows that these leaders frequently have trouble communicating with their staff and with community partners. Learning interpersonal skills is a lifelong process.

Types of Formal Communication

There are three types of formal communication within an organization.[16] The first type is downward communication, from a superior to a subordinate. Among its benefits, it allows a supervisor to correct problems, and it keeps communication channels open, which tends to increase employee satisfaction. The second is upward communication, in which a subordinate initiates a conversation with someone at a higher level. This type of communication has the potential of preventing problems as well as solving existing problems. The final type of communication is horizontal or lateral, as occurs when colleagues at the same level communicate among themselves. The benefits include cooperation across sections of the organization. Cooperation between public health leaders and community leaders involves the last type of communication.

Informal communication networks are based on personal friendships, similar personal interests, shared career interests, and the closeness of working together in the same organization.[17] Informal communication networks focused on community health issues can be built on love of community and a desire to help the community by strengthening the infrastructure of public health.

Interpersonal Communication Guidelines

Effective interpersonal communication requires talking to people in a way that will be meaningful and about topics that will be meaningful for them. For example, public health leaders might talk to agency staff about the importance of the core functions of public health. In talking to a community group, on the other hand, they might discuss putting on a health fair or implementing a Healthy Communities 2010 program.

Leaders need to be careful not to let hostile feelings interfere with their judgment. Expertise should drive their conversation, not their organization titles. And they should always respect those with whom they are talking. Each conversation needs to be based on mutual trust.

They should use language that is understandable to their audience, which in many cases means forsaking the specialized language of public health. They should speak from the heart and take a positive perspective. Credibility is important to communication, which may fail without it. Sometimes the maintenance of credibility requires a leader to abandon his or her own agenda and replace it with an agenda favored by others.[18]

To ensure that their interpersonal communication is effective, public health leaders should

- converse with other people in a meaningful way and on meaningful topics
- be assertive, not aggressive
- control hostile feelings
- allow their expertise, not their titles, to be the basis for paying attention to what they say

- be open to considering new ideas
- respect the agendas of others and know when to abandon their own agenda
- use understandable language, speak from the heart, and take a positive perspective

Personal communication is the most important means of sharing a mission and vision with others. In the 21st century, it will be impossible for leaders without personal communication skills to sustain their credibility with colleagues, teams, agency staff, and community stakeholders.

ACTIVE LISTENING

Public health leaders must be not only proficient speakers but also active listeners. Active listening takes concentration. The goal is to understand what the other person is saying and what it entails. Four critical skills are needed for active listening:

1. intensity of involvement in the interaction
2. empathy for the other's message and meaning
3. acceptance of the message of the other person without judgment until the other person finishes talking
4. willingness to get all the information needed to make a decision[19]

Passive listening is listening without much involvement.[20] How many of us have taken courses or attended conferences where we were talked at rather than with? Yet passive listening is sometimes the appropriate listening style, as when, at a public presentation, a speaker is interrupted by questions from the audience.[21]

The classification of listening styles into active and passive is somewhat simplistic. Alessandra and Hunsaker divide listeners into four types.[22] First comes the nonlistener, who does not pay attention to the message being sent. The second type is the listener who only marginally listens to the message. This listener is always rehearsing what to say or is preoccupied with other thoughts. The evaluative listener, the third type, listens to the entire message but misses the intent. The final type is the active listener.

To be an active listener, a person must ask good questions that will clarify both the content and the intent of the message.[23] Open-ended questions allow the respondent to go into detail about the meaning and intent of the message, whereas close-ended questions are meant to elicit short answers that will illuminate specific comments. One strategy, the so-called funnel technique, involves starting with global, open-ended questions and then gradually moving toward focused, close-ended questions.[24]

Consider this example. A new health department administrator is asked by the local board of health to explain the core functions and essential services of public health and why they are important. The administrator gives a 15-minute informal presentation on the topic. Board members start with broad questions, indicating that they still do not understand the core functions model, or why the administrator favors this model. The administrator answers these broad questions as best she can. As she clarifies her position, the board members narrow in on specific details by asking close-ended questions.

A listener can use questions to offer advice or attack the speaker for holding a position contrary to the listener's. In addition, the listener, in asking questions, may have a hidden agenda of which the speaker is unaware. The questions asked should be sincere and intended to elicit information the questioner truly needs in order to understand the speaker's meaning.

Walton listed five rules governing conversational etiquette:

1. Don't hog the floor.
2. Don't change the subject.
3. Don't step on the sentences of others.
4. Do hold your tongue.
5. Don't forget—there's always tomorrow.[25]

In active listening, the listener should make eye contact with the speaker and pay close attention to the speaker's words as well as any nonverbal message the speaker is conveying. Active listening is intense and requires an expenditure of energy. The speaker expects the listener to pay attention and not do distracting things, like answering the telephone or shuffling papers. When the speaker is finished, the listener should ask questions that show that attention was paid to the speaker's comments. The questions, however, should be as brief and to the point as possible. The author has been to talks in which an audience member got up and gave a 10-minute exegesis on his or her personal views—hardly a sign of active listening.

Active listeners

- make eye contact and listen with all their senses
- avoid distracting actions, like answering the telephone or shuffling papers
- ask questions
- do not interrupt
- do not talk too much
- use positive gestures as part of their listening behavior

PUBLIC SPEAKING

Public health leaders may have a clear vision of the future, but the effort they spent developing the vision will be all for naught unless they can publicize their vision and inspire others to share it. One of the best ways of publicizing it is to speak in different public venues, from local PTA meetings to national conferences, such as the annual meeting of the American Public Health Association. And to speak effectively, no matter what the venue, additional skills are needed beyond those required for effective personal communication.

At some state universities, public speaking is a university curriculum requirement. But even in these states, students tend not to understand the benefits to be gained by acquiring public-speaking skills. Public speaking helps teach the individual not only how to conceptualize an issue concisely but also how to integrate words with gestures to make a more effective argument in support of a particular point of view. Further, the more a person speaks in public forums, the easier public speaking tends to become.

Leaders know how to use language that strengthens the message given. Leaders tell stories. President Reagan always added inspirational stories to his talks, and

President Clinton does the same. Leaders also use analogies and metaphors in their talks. A public health leader might say, for example, "We must be careful not to let the ship of public health founder in the stormy debate over proposed cuts in federal programs." Body language is important. Holding on to the podium, for instance, does not communicate confidence. A speaker's nonverbal language should correspond with the speaker's words. In addition, the speaker should be aware of the pitch of his or her voice, especially when using a microphone.

Speakers should tailor each speech to the needs of the audience.[26] If the members of the audience cannot identify with the issues raised, they will tune out or forget the message fairly quickly. Speakers need to have a message that is realistic and focused. Unfocused presentations confuse the audience. Speakers also need to include supporting information.

Speakers need to appear credible to the audience.[27] They can maximize their acceptance by proving they are competent to discuss the chosen topic. They also need to earn the trust of the audience, which they can do partly by impressing the audience with the fact that they and the audience are basically alike and partly by appearing sincere. Also, using names of people in the audience sometimes increases the degree of acceptance of both the speaker and the speech.

Speakers are often viewed as mentors or teachers[28] and as entertainers. It has been suggested that public speaking is 25 percent knowledge and 75 percent charisma. Consequently, a speaker may find it worthwhile to rehearse the presentation ahead of time.[29] Dressing appropriately is important as well. A speaker in blue jeans does not go over well when the audience is in suits and dresses. If possible, speakers should leave time for questions, which is a good strategy for appearing human before the audience and gaining its acceptance. Of course, in some cases acceptance is hard to obtain, and so speakers should develop the skills necessary for dealing with a hostile audience. Humor usually helps when confronting hostility—and in most other cases as well.

Speakers need to know their audience but also be flexible enough to modify the prepared text if it is not appropriate for a particular audience. They also need to take note of the layout of the room, since it can have an effect on the acceptance of the message.

Public health leaders who are required to do a lot of public speaking should familiarize themselves with the speaker aids that are currently available. Overhead projectors, for instance, allow speakers to present information concisely. One danger with overheads is that they often contain so much information in such small type that they cannot be read beyond the second row or in a reasonable amount of time. (The so-called six-second rule is that every overhead or slide should be able to be read by the audience in six seconds.) Another danger is that, when many overheads are displayed, the audience may become frustrated trying to keep up with the overheads or make notes on what they contain. A good solution is to provide copies of the overheads to the audience in order to lessen the information overload. Slides tend to be better in large groups, at least if the remote control switch works. Handouts can be used in conjunction with slides to good effect, for they help the audience to remember the information after the talk is over. Running a short video may enhance a presentation. New computer presentation software and new projection devices can be useful, though buying or renting the necessary equipment can be costly. Further, since this equipment may break down, it is important to have a backup set of slides or overheads.

Which are the best speaker aids to use in a given situation depends to a degree on the speaker's speaking technique. If the speaker reads from a prepared draft, slides can be easily coordinated with the words. When using an overhead projector, the speaker may have to leave the podium and come down to the projector. This kind of interruption can lend the presentation an informality that some audiences seem to prefer, but it can also act as an irritant.

In preparing a speech and giving it in front of an audience (Exercise 9–2), a public health leader should

- become extremely knowledgeable about the topic of the speech
- find out the nature of the audience
- make the speech informative, persuasive, and entertaining
- integrate feelings and facts
- be candid and tell stories
- harmonize the verbal message and the message conveyed by body language
- blend theory and practice

INTERVIEWING

Interviewing skills are used by public health leaders when interviewing job seekers, agency staff for membership on self-directed work teams, and representatives of community organizations for partnership development.

As regards job recruitment, public health leaders must develop not only protocols for recruitment but also strategies for helping selected candidates keep their jobs.[30] Those responsible for job interviewing need to specify the qualifications for each job and follow a schedule in interviewing candidates so that all candidates are evaluated objectively.

A distinction can be made between direct and indirect recruiting. Direct recruitment is tied to defined positions that are currently vacant. Indirect recruitment is aimed at expanding the pool of potential job candidates through internships, school presentations, community health promotion programs, community lectures, and so on.

When interviewing a job candidate, the interviewer should cover a range of topics, from the job description to the way the candidate might fit into the agency. Exhibit 9–1 lists 12 topics that should be explored in an interview.

The interview format can be structured or open-ended. In a structured interview, the interviewer works from a set of standardized questions. The problem with this strategy is that the set of questions lacks application beyond the selection of a candidate for the particular job. An open-ended interview uses a general outline and allows the interviewee to structure his or her responses. The two format types can be combined to create an instrument that includes some of the best features of each.

Where the interview is conducted is also important. Interview questions asked from behind a desk will elicit different responses than if asked in a conference room or a more casual setting. In conducting the interview, the interviewer needs to establish rapport with the interviewee and control the direction of the conversation so that the necessary topics are covered.[31] The interviewer should urge the interviewee to give concise and thoughtful answers and make clear what his or her goals are. In addition, the interviewer should indicate to the interviewee the basis on which he or she will be evaluated.

Exhibit 9–1 Issues in Interviewing Job Applicants

---

1. Job requirements and expectations
2. Department and institution characteristics (including patient and staff demographics)
3. Department and institution strengths
4. Management's unique vision of health care delivery
5. Mission of the institution
6. Applicant's technical level of skill
7. Opportunities for advancement within the department and institution
8. Applicant's career goals
9. Salary expectations
10. Applicant's personal and professional assets and liabilities as they relate to the worker role
11. "Fit" between the institution and the individual
12. Benefits

The interviewer should either take notes during the interview or, if the interviewee agrees, audiotape the interview.[32]

Checking the candidate's references is essential, as not all resumes are accurate and not all letters of recommendation are truthful.[33] Telephone reference checks are especially useful if done after the interview, since they then allow the interviewer to delve into issues raised during the interview. In fact, the author has found telephone conversations with references to be more useful than letters of recommendation. Candidates sometimes develop fears about reference checks, whether or not those fears are legitimate. They also can be concerned to keep their present employers from finding out that they are applying for other jobs.

Public health leaders, though usually acting as the interviewer, do occasionally take the role of interviewee, such as when applying for a job as administrator at another agency and being questioned by the agency's governing board.[34] In interviews for leadership positions, the board must define the relationship between the administrator and the board as well as the boundaries of the administrator's authority. A candidate should not accept a position if convinced that he or she will not be able to function within the parameters set by the board.

One cautionary note: board members rotate off the board and some of today's members may not be on the board in a year. A candidate for a position as administrator should try to identify the challenges that exist and determine whether it is worth accepting the appointment on the chance that things will improve in the future.

Interviewers need to follow these guidelines:

- Prepare a series of questions ahead of time.
- Select the appropriate interview structure.
- Arrange the setting for the interview.
- Learn different interviewing techniques and when each is appropriate.
- Maintain high ethical standards.
- Keep each job candidate informed about the process of selection.

WRITTEN COMMUNICATION

Leaders need to be masters of all types of communication. The written word can have a major impact on readers. Leaders sometimes use the words of others to guide their vision and actions. The Declaration of Independence and the United States Constitution, both written more than 200 years ago, still provide the framework for political and social life in the United States.

Written communication in a modern organization encompasses, among other things, memoranda, letters, periodicals and books, e-mail, electronic bulletin boards, personal notes, grants, contracts, statistical and technical reports, over-heads and informational slides, and performance appraisals. One of the major advantages of written communication is that it contributes to the creation of a permanent tangible record[35] and thus allows verification of past activities and events. Another advantage is that the written word is often clearer than the spoken word, largely because it can be reviewed and revised until the author is satisfied.

On the negative side, good written communication takes time. A telephone call takes but a moment and the feedback is immediate, whereas a letter takes time to write and reception of the response can be delayed for days or weeks. Of course, a telephone call leaves no permanent record unless it is followed up with a memo or letter. One-day mail delivery service and facsimile transmission do speed up the process of getting written feedback more quickly, but the process still lasts many times longer than a phone conversation.

Successful written communication demands preparation. The writer needs to plan the communication by organizing the underlying facts and developing the message prior to putting down words. If the organizing step is left out, the communication will almost certainly fail to be clear, specific, accurate, and concise.

Some writers find outlining a useful technique. Some can do this mentally. Wycoff suggested using a technique called "mindmapping."[36] This technique, in which possible approaches to an issue are diagrammed, can clarify the purpose of a written communication and provide a focus (a focus is important for the reader).

In the actual writing, choosing the right words is of the utmost importance. The use of jargon may undermine the effectiveness of the written communication and obscure the information to be disseminated. The promotion of health among community residents through written materials requires language that the residents understand. The writer should always keep in mind the recipients and how the message may be received. It is also important to follow up on the impact of the written materials over time.

Writers usually possess more facts than they are able to use. Part of the task of writing is to winnow out those facts that are unnecessary and focus on those that are critical to the intended message. The written product should of course be grammatically correct and contain no typographical errors—an easily attainable goal now that virtually all word-processing programs have a spelling checker. The importance of writing coherently cannot be overemphasized, and it is a good idea to have a peer check the writing for clarity. The reviewer should point out places where the writing is obscure or confusing and should offer any other advice he or she thinks might be helpful.

Public health leaders engaged in producing written health promotion materials or any other kind of writing should pay attention to the following guidelines:

- Use proper English and restrict yourself to a vocabulary that the intended audience understands.
- Master different writing techniques and use the appropriate technique for each piece of writing.
- Create an outline for a piece of writing prior to writing it.
- Check spelling and correct typographical errors.
- Avoid the incorporation of extraneous material into written materials.
- Write in the same way you talk, although choose your words more carefully.

COMPUTER COMMUNICATION SKILLS

The personal computer has added some new wrinkles to communication and the transfer of information. Now we trade e-mail messages rather than letters. One advantage is that send-and-respond times are appreciably reduced. Further, although most e-mail messages are short, informal, and limited in scope, e-mail programs allow the sender of a message to attach large document files, such as for a report or research paper.[37] Personal computers can now also be used to do research on the Internet, by using search engines or by tapping into various databases.

One of the latest trends in high technology is the integration of personal computers, fax machines, cellular phones, and pagers.[38] The integration of computer technology and communications technology is allowing organizations to become even more interconnected than previously. For example, any person hooked up to the Internet can create a network of colleagues around the world devoted to discussing topics of common interest.

The new technologies have some negative consequences, however.[39] One problem is the difficulty of ensuring the security of the messages that are sent. Another is e-mail overload and the decrease in responsiveness that sometimes results. How many of us go on a one-day business-related trip to come back to 100 e-mail messages. All of them have to be at least perused to see which are worthwhile reading and which need a response—a time-consuming process. Reviewing and answering messages on a daily basis can eat into valuable work time, as can listening to and answering phone messages. The transfer of e-mail or phone messages over the phone lines occurs virtually instantaneously, yet it is still the same old sluggish human brain that has to interpret each message and figure what to do in response.

Public health agencies are struggling to acquire the technology necessary to enter the information age. Small rural health departments with limited budgets may not be able to purchase more than one or two personal computers, which will need to be shared. Even when computers are available, public health professionals complain that the necessary training is not. Public health leaders need to convince their governing boards of the importance of computer technology, including new advances.

One recommended strategy is to chart communication activities in order to determine how much time is spent talking, listening, reading, and sending e-mail messages.[40] Public health leaders may find it necessary to reorganize their communication activities so as not to impair their ability to carry out their main responsibilities. Leaders need to remember that computers are tools for dealing with problems, not complete solutions to them. And something else they should remember is that computer communication systems are not substitutes for personal communication.

Any important new tool brings with it a need to redefine work. The advent of computer and communications technology has made it necessary, for instance, to change interorganizational and intraorganizational structures,[41] and changes in technology will continue to impact the field of public health and the way public health leaders go about doing their job. To keep pace with the computer and communications revolution, public health leaders must

- learn how to use electronic mail and the Internet to increase effectiveness
- understand the advantages and disadvantages of e-mail as compared with other forms of communication
- learn e-mail etiquette
- monitor advances in computer hardware and software
- train staff in the use of personal computers and the Internet

MEDIA ADVOCACY

During the 1980s and early 1990s, public health leaders had to learn how to talk to the media. They had to learn, for instance, how to condense a message into a 20-second sound byte, how to use letter-writing campaigns, and how to dress for television—all with the goal of promoting the goals and objectives of public health by using the media to bring pressure on policy makers in order to influence policy.[42] Public health leaders are the leaders most likely to view public health issues from a systems perspective, taking into account social, cultural, psychological, economic, and political dimensions, and they have a duty to use media advocacy to get the message out.[43] Media advocacy can be viewed as a form of empowerment in which public health leaders galvanize the community residents to fight for policies that will directly benefit them.

Major planning efforts need to be undertaken to create a coordinated approach to using the media to help solve community health problems. Public health leaders, in publicizing a public health concern, should urge the importance of developing a policy to deal with it and should involve community partners in any publicizing and policy development activities. In promoting a given policy, public health leaders must make sure the facts are researched and verified and must get key stakeholders to support the policy.[44] One of the tasks required for media advocacy is to foster good relationships with media representatives so that channels are open for important public health messages to get out to the community.[45] In developing support for public health initiatives, the use of each of the various media should at least be considered.

There are important differences between traditional public education and media advocacy (Table 9–2).[46] In traditional health promotion programs, the individual is the target, and the goal is to alter the individual's behavior. In media advocacy, the individual becomes empowered by becoming involved in the push for health policy changes. Advocacy is aimed at policy makers, and the goal of advocacy is to get beneficial policies legislated and put into action. The advocates, besides public health practitioners, are people who are affected by the health problem at issue and are willing to fight to ensure the necessary changes are made.[47]

Table 9–2 Comparison of Media Advocacy and Public Education

Media Advocacy	Public Education
Individual as advocate	Individual as audience
Advances healthy public policies	Develops health messages
Decentralized and opportunistic	Problem and approach fixed
Changes the environment	Changes the individual
News and paid advertising	Relies on public service
Target is person with power to make change	Target is person with problem or at risk
Addresses the power gap	Addresses the information gap

Media advocacy is most effective when it is community based. At its best it includes collaborative efforts at framing issues, setting agendas, developing talking (or writing) points, and monitoring the progress of policy proposals. Those collaborating in the media advocacy process must also keep the general public up to date on the various happenings.

A caution regarding media advocacy needs to be raised here. According to Fallows, the media often undermine the American political system by generating a sense of hopelessness about the future.[48] He argues that the media need to become more public spirited, support the American political system, and empower the public to influence policy. Those who use the media must recognize their limitations and the difficulty of controlling media reactions to local health problems. Case Study 9–A describes a situation in which the press overreacted to a potential private-well contamination problem. It shows how the media need to be handled in the context of public health surveillance activities and how public health leaders should communicate these activities to policy makers and the public.

One media advocacy issue is how to publicize health risks. Public health leaders should involve key stakeholders in discussions of the technical aspects of health risks. For one thing, a given risk must be evaluated from social, psychological, economic, and political perspectives.[49]

In publicizing a health risk, public health leaders should explore the various media options and choose a presentation format appropriate to the level of concern. All the media should be used to inform the community about a health risk. See Exhibit 9–2 for a list of risk communication rules.

Public health leaders should

- use their media advocacy skills to influence policy makers
- include key stakeholders in the media advocacy process
- follow the seven cardinal rules of risk communication
- write a letter on a public health issue to the local newspaper twice a month
- dress conservatively for television events
- learn to present messages concisely
- select appropriate communication channels for advocacy and risk communication
- rehearse before any oral presentation of advocacy positions
- make sure they are the appropriate spokesperson for a media interview

Exhibit 9–2 Seven Cardinal Rules of Risk Communication

1. Accept and involve the public as a partner. Your goal is to produce an informed public, not to defuse public concerns or replace actions.
2. Plan carefully and evaluate your efforts. Different goals, audiences, and media require different actions.
3. Listen to the public's specific concerns. People often care more about trust, credibility, competence, fairness, and empathy than about statistics and details.
4. Be honest, frank, and open. Trust and credibility are difficult to obtain; once lost, they are almost impossible to regain.
5. Work with other credible sources. Conflicts and disagreements among organizations make communication with the public much more difficult.
6. Meet the needs of the media. The media are usually more interested in politics than risk, simplicity than complexity, danger than safety.
7. Speak clearly and with compassion. Never let your efforts prevent your acknowledging the tragedy of an illness, injury, or death. People can understand risk information, but they may still not agree with you; some people will not be satisfied.

COMMUNICATION AND CULTURAL SENSITIVITY

American society has always been diverse, ethnically and racially as well as in other ways, but it is becoming even more so. For example, women and minorities are increasingly assuming leadership roles in the workplace. Since protection against health risks is a right of all citizens, the makeup of public health programs should reflect the makeup of the larger society. This entails that public health leaders need to learn to be students of culture and develop the interpersonal skills needed for relating to staff and community residents of different social and cultural backgrounds.[50]

A culture is a type of social system that encompasses a shared language, shared values, and a shared set of behaviors. A person's culture to a large extent determines how the person acts and reacts, and thus public health leaders need to understand the cultures of the community they serve and eliminate their prejudices if they want to work for the good of the community.

Diversity can be an obstacle to communication and cooperation among agency staff or with community partners.[51] Fortunately, public health leaders can use a number of techniques to evaluate how an agency is responding to the issue of diversity. First, they need to study how the agency treats job applicants from different backgrounds as well as clients or community partners from different backgrounds. They also need to explore the power relationships that exist between staff from diverse backgrounds and to read all printed materials related to the organization in order to determine if the messages given are discriminatory. They should walk around the agency to see how people from diverse backgrounds are treated by staff and interview staff about instances of mistreatment that may have occurred or patterns of discrimination that may have developed. Finally, they should build a "web of inclusion."[52] As a prerequisite, they need to ensure that a system of open communication is in place and that information flows freely throughout the organization, allowing, among other things, power relationships to become realigned.

With regard to gender differences, the increase of women in the workplace has led to an increase in sexual harassment laws and new approaches to affirmative action.[53] In the late 1990s, there was a backlash against affirmative action laws and regulations that will affect organizations well into the 21st century. One thing to keep in mind is that many Americans believe that the only way to create change is through opposition. As one author put it, ours is an "argument culture."[54] Yet it is best to move away from debate to more of a dialogue between equal partners. Equality and dialogue are critical if we are to understand each person, no matter what gender, race, or ethnicity, and be able to listen to him or her with an open mind.

Public health leaders will need to become multicultural in the 21st century,[55] which is to say that they will need the skills to communicate effectively with diverse social groups. In general, they will need to increase their cultural sensitivity by investigating the reasons diverse groups act in certain ways. Cultural sensitivity leads to mutual respect and to the empowerment of previously marginalized groups. It also allows public health leaders to find innovative ways to increase the health literacy of people from different backgrounds.[56]

Culturally sensitive public health leaders

- remain objective
- learn to control gender, racial, and ethnic prejudices by clarifying values
- understand the different expectations that men and women bring to leadership
- learn the spoken and gestural languages and behavior patterns of different racial and ethnic groups
- adjust the way in which they convey messages in light of the culture of the audience and the situation
- build a web of inclusion
- become familiar with sexual harassment laws, affirmative action laws, and other laws and regulations relevant to the issue of diversity

FEEDBACK

Completion of an act of communication requires feedback from the respondent, whether in the form of a spoken statement, printed data, graphics, or a videotape. Communication strategies, including strategies for giving feedback, change to reflect the expansion of technology,[57] but certain principles remain unaltered. For example, feedback may be positive or negative, but most people seem to respond better to positive messages than to negative ones.[58] Negative feedback, however, can lead to positive results when there is potential resistance. The response is affected by the credibility of the person giving the feedback and the ability of the person receiving the feedback to evaluate what has been said objectively.

In the case of a group, such as a team or even a whole organization, the receivers of a message can engage in a conspiracy of silence in which they subvert the message without informing the sender. Leaders need to become expert at determining whether lack of feedback is a reflection of acquiescence or silent resistance.

The solicitation of feedback should be planned and not left to chance.[59] In fact, leaders need to develop continuous feedback loops between themselves and staff and organizational and community stakeholders.[60]

Feedback can be divided into various types.[61] Verbal feedback is extremely interactive, and it often impacts the total process of communication. Nonverbal feedback involves the use of body language and facial gestures. Fact-based feedback presents relevant information for dealing with a specific situation. In a fourth variety of feedback, the receiver of the message expresses his or her feelings, sometimes nonverbally, about the message. Public health leaders need to be empathetic and pay attention to the feelings of those they are communicating with.

The symbolic interactionist model developed by Hulett (see Figure 9–1) includes feedback control.[62] The person initiating a communicative process performs an instrumental act that motivates the other person to become involved in the communicative process and eventually perform his or her own instrumental act, which can be viewed as a response to the message (or as feedback). The person receiving the return message may then go through the covert rehearsal phase for a second time in order to clarify the message received and perform another instrumental act, leading to further feedback. Hulett identifies two feedback loops: an intrapersonal loop (part of the covert rehearsal stage) and an interpersonal loop. The interpersonal feedback loop is used to relay information from the receiver of a message back to the sender.

In performance evaluations, feedback on specific behaviors is preferable to feedback on general behaviors.[63] Specificity makes the feedback seem more personal, as if the individual giving the feedback took an active interest in the individual receiving the feedback. At the same time, the feedback should be objective. It should not consist of criticisms of the person, but of an evaluation of job-related behaviors. If the evaluator must give criticism (negative feedback), the critique needs to focus on behaviors that the individual can change. Feedback on performance should be oriented toward the goal of improving the person's performance and achieving desired outcomes, which of course means that the message must be understandable to the receiver. The timing of feedback is important as well. It should be given to an individual as soon as possible after the occurrence of the behaviors being evaluated.

In giving feedback, including feedback on a person's work performance, public health leaders should

- accentuate the positive but point out ways in which performance could be improved
- concentrate on specific rather than general behaviors
- be objective and goal oriented (aim at improving work performance)
- provide the feedback in a timely fashion
- offer negative feedback only in regard to behavior that is controllable
- create ongoing feedback loops

DELEGATION OF AUTHORITY

To delegate is to give others, including individuals and teams, both the responsibility for certain actions and the power to ensure the actions are performed. There is a strong communication component in delegation, and the delegators need to be cognizant of the communication factors that can enhance the delegation of responsibility and the factors that can obstruct its delegation. One way to look at delegation is that it is a shift in the power to make decisions and to act from one level to a lower level of the organizational hierarchy.[64] Delegation is not shared decision making. Rather, if decision-making authority is truly delegated, the decision made by the delegatee will be put into force. This entails that the boundaries of the delegated authority must be made clear to the delegatee, which of course requires good communication between the delegator and the delegatee.

When responsibility is delegated, the delegator must nonetheless act as an overseer to ensure the delegatees are moving in the right direction. If the delegator loses confidence in the ability of the delegatees to carry out their assigned responsibilities, the delegator may accept their recommendations while taking back final decision-making authority.

Since a public health agency usually has many specialized public health programs, the agency leaders tend to delegate responsibility for these programs. Sharing power can increase agency effectiveness and can generate trust and credibility.[65] Among the best activities to delegate are those that a leader has done over and over but that are still needed for the smooth functioning of the organization.[66] Because the leader has extensive experience with these tasks, he or she can give detailed instructions to staff members on how to perform them. Also, since a leader cannot attain expertise in all areas under his or her purview, he or she would do well to delegate certain specialty areas to the appropriate experts. In the information age, the need for delegating responsibilities will increase in line with the expansion of technology, including information-processing technology.

Leaders should not delegate the responsibility for attending meetings that require their presence, nor responsibility for activities related to personnel or other confidential matters. They need to control the policy-making function, and although delegatees may influence policy development, the leaders need to make the final policy recommendations. All organizations occasionally face crises, and the leaders need to monitor any mounting crisis and maintain tight control over the efforts to resolve it.

All leaders struggle with the issue of too much responsibility and too little time. Each new task that a leader accepts brings with it new duties and often a new set of constituents. As the number of tasks grows, the leader experiences role overload.[67] On the other hand, sometimes staff members feel that they do not have enough to do—an example of role underload. Thus, delegation can lead to interesting results. If assignments are delegated to public health practitioners lower down in the organization, those staff members will experience a reduction in role underload. Conversely, the leader should feel relief since pressure is being removed. The leader, however, might also feel insecure as a result of the transfer of responsibility. Hopefully, the leader will gradually become more secure as he or she sees the positive results of the delegation of activities. Delegation involves a balance between trust and control.

Hersey, Blanchard, and Johnson treat delegation as one of four leadership styles.[68] The ability of a leader to delegate authority is determined by the abilities and backgrounds of others in the organization. New employees may need specific instructions on how to perform tasks as well as supervision during the learning process. Gradually the leader moves from discussing decisions with the staff to delegating decision-making authority. During this process, the leader should provide continual feedback.[69] Empowered staff members need information on how they are doing, and good performance should always be recognized.

As mentioned earlier, the delegator of an activity needs to make the assignment clear to the delegatees. The best strategy is to be as specific as possible and yet leave room for the delegatees to use their creativity to address the problems presented by the assignment. If a whole task is not within the realm of authority of delegatees, they need to know the limits of their authority. Further, the delegator should inform others in the organization or community about the delegation of responsibility. This is another place where communication plays an essential role in delegation.

In delegating authority and responsibility for activities and outcomes, public health leaders must

- define the dimensions of the assignment
- specify how much freedom the delegatees possess to do the task
- delegate the whole task to an individual or a team
- include potential delegatees in the whole decision process
- let other staff or partners know about the delegation
- set up feedback channels

FRAMING

A paradigm is a set of rules that define boundaries and act as guidelines for action.[70] Followers of a professional paradigm are generally accepted by other professionals in their field. Given that science and practice continue to change, paradigms do not last forever. If a paradigm reaches its operational limits, then a new paradigm will evolve to take its place.

There is a strong communication component in paradigm building. Once the new paradigm has been constructed, the leader has to communicate it to the various public health stakeholders. Their response to it is a form of test. Below is a set of guidelines for creating a new paradigm for public health:

- Create a mission and vision or adopt existing ones.
- In developing the paradigm, take into account the perspective of key stakeholders.
- Promote individual leadership development.
- Promote organizational change on the basis of core functions and organizational practices or essential public health services.
- Develop public health coalitions built on a team-based model and a community-defined agenda.
- Improve transorganizational relationships.
- Move toward an integrated communitywide model with strong prevention components.
- Increase interaction between local governmental boards, local agencies, state health and health-related agencies, and the local health department.

According to Goffman, framing consists of a series of acts that integrate primary frameworks (or paradigms) and actions.[71] Primary frameworks, which create a culture of understanding in teams, organizations, and communities, include such things as values and beliefs. Communication is the mechanism for monitoring the framing process. In addition, communication, as well as new perceptions, can add new information to past experience and thus clarify a current framework or require a reframing.[72]

A framework is a tool, and like any tool it can be used well or poorly.[73] If the right framework is used in a given situation, the framework will be supported or extended. If the wrong framework is used, it may become undermined.

If a crisis occurs, mechanisms must be found for renewing the organization.[74] The leaders of an organization might even precipitate a crisis in order to break down the frameworks that do not work. Since the leadership role includes acting as a change agent, leaders need to master transformational change methodologies, people management skills, and framing skills.

It is through framing that reality gets defined.[75] Framing creates an action language that serves as an aid to understanding situations. This language helps in classifying information within the context of the framework used. Leaders tend to be more effective when they recognize framing opportunities and take advantage of them to create frameworks for self-guidance and the guidance of others. Table 9–3 identifies several types of framework, describes their functions, indicates when to use them and when not to use them, and gives examples of each.

Public health leaders need to

- develop or adopt frameworks (paradigms) to guide action
- become familiar with the frameworks of those with whom they interact
- learn reframing techniques
- coordinate their vision and their primary frameworks (governing paradigms)
- learn how to use metaphors, jargon, contrast, spin, and stories for purposes of framing

DIALOGUE, DISCUSSION, AND DEBATE

Imagine that a group of public health leaders come into a room and take chairs organized in a circle. All preconceived notions and professional credentials are left at the door. The rules governing the ensuing conversation are that each person gets to talk without interruption and that no one should be concerned about the output of the group process. The kind of discussion that will result—if the leaders talk freely—is what has been called dialogue. It can be a means of uncovering hidden values and agendas[76] and exploring the way these values and agendas control the behavior of the participants. Further, it can change the way people work because it diffuses information throughout the dialogue group and eventually throughout the organization and community.[77]

Dialogue, because of the group's synergism, is a communication process in which everyone can win.[78] The participants often find out things they were unaware of, such as the fact that they share patterns of thought. They might also identify shared areas of concern, common causes of conflict, ways to heal fragmented perspectives, and new approaches to personal and organizational development.[79] However, a dialogue group might find itself struggling because of the lack of objectives, even to the point where emotions flare up. Therefore, a facilitator is often used to guide the dialogue process. The goal is to prevent par-

Table 9–3 Framing Techniques

	Metaphors	Jargon/Catch-phrases	Contrast	Spin	Stories
Function	They show a subject's likeness with something else.	They frame a subject in familiar terms.	It describes a subject in terms of its opposite.	It puts a subject in a positive or negative light.	They frame a subject by example.
Use it because	You want a subject to take on new meaning.	Familiar references can enhance meaning. Jargon and catchphrases help communicate a vision's "god" and "devil" terms.	It is sometimes easier to define what your subject is not than state what it is.	It can reveal your subject's strengths or weaknesses.	Stories attract attention and can build rapport.
Avoid it when	They mask important alternative meanings.	A word or phrase is in danger of overuse.	Meaning can be skewed by a poor contrast.	The ratio of spin to reality is excessive.	They mask important alternative meanings.
Example	"I feel our relationship is formal, like punching a ticket."	"We've got to break the squares today."	"It's a choice between raising my hand for the teacher to ask if it's okay or just telling it like it is."	"Which Ray will show up? The one who's cooperative and generous, or the egotist who constantly reminds others of his successes and what is due him."	"In my first three or four years here, I was a lot like you. I thought…"

ticipants from getting angry at each other and instead get them to feel enthusiasm for the process.

The first step in holding a dialogue session is to contact potential invitees to gauge their willingness to attend a session. The invitees should be apprised of the guidelines for the session. For example, in order for the dialogue process to be effective, the participants must actively listen to what others are saying and must observe themselves as well as the other participants. In addition, the participants should suspend assumptions and judgments for the period set aside for the dialogue (usually two hours). One recommendation to give participants is that they should try to provide concrete examples of what they are talking about. Concrete examples clarify abstract language and aid in coming to a shared understanding.[80]

Following a dialogue session, the participants can begin discussing ways to implement ideas coming out of the session. Discussion is perhaps the primary mechanism for problem solving and decision making. One of the dangers of discussion is that personal agendas can undermine the activity.[81] Another is that the participants might not listen respectfully (or at all) to the opinions of others and might tend to interrupt each other. If a dialogue session is held first, the participants would have a better chance of using discussion to develop and implement action plans, since their different perspectives would have already been addressed. Further, discussion is the form of discourse in which attempts are made to come to agreement on the issues, whereas dialogue is intended to be only exploratory.

We live in a society full of turmoil and change.[82] There are arguments and stresses related to all our communication. A debate allows extreme views to be presented and evaluated in a controlled forum, reducing the chance of emotional flare-ups. A good example of a debating forum is the television show *Crossfire* on the CNN network, where parties on both sides of a controversy can present their views. A debate can help to clarify positions and change opinions, but, despite its value, debating as a technique for acquiring information is often ignored in organizations.

As an example of the appropriate use of debate, imagine a group of community residents come to a county board meeting to convince the board to do something about the contaminated water supply. Their testimony might be followed by the testimony of a local chemical company claiming that it cannot clean up the local river because of the high expense. The board thus hears both sides of the story and is in a better position to make a rational decision as to what to do.

Table 9–4 contrasts dialogue on the one hand and discussion and debate on the other. All three types of discourse are valuable if used appropriately.

Public health leaders should

- engage in dialogue rather than discussion or debate at the first level of interaction whenever possible
- be open to changing their views as a result of dialogue, discussion, or debate
- invite, not force, potential participants to come to a dialogue session
- use dialogue to strengthen relationships

Table 9–4 The Conversation Continuum

Dialogue	Discussion/Debate
Seeing the *whole* among the parts	Breaking issues/problems into *parts*
Seeing the *connections* between the parts	Seeing *distinctions* between the parts
Inquiring into assumptions	*Justifying/defending* assumptions
Learning through inquiry and disclosure	*Persuading, selling, telling*
Treating *shared* meaning among many	Gaining agreement on *one* meaning

- use discussion to problem solve
- use debate to explore both sides of an issue

MEETING SKILLS

Public health leaders spend a large amount of their time in meetings. When the author held a university administrative position, more than 30 committees required his time. It is amazing how little time 30 committee assignments leave to get noncommittee work done.

Most public health leaders attend internal staff committee meetings, team meetings, board meetings (which are often open meetings), community meetings, partnership and coalition meetings, and professional meetings, among others. One way they can increase their effectiveness as leaders is to cut down the number of meetings they attend, and they can do this by delegating committee assignments to staff members who exhibit leadership ability.

For a meeting that a leader does have to attend, the goal is to run the meeting as efficiently as possible. A good strategy for preparing for a meeting is to review the results of the previous meeting as soon after it occurs as possible.[83] The idea is to review successes as well as the failures in order to judge whether improvements need to be made.

Problems that arise need to be addressed from a systems perspective.[84] For example, one problem may be that there are too many meetings. If so, consolidation or elimination of some committees needs to occur. Another problem may be that attendees are seldom prepared, forcing those who are prepared to educate those who are not, thereby wasting valuable meeting time. Still another common problem is the tendency of a small number of attendees to try to take over meetings. And another is the tendency of meetings to drag on past the scheduled time. It is important to set an end time and stick to it.

Each meeting should have, besides a chairperson, a facilitator (to help the group to maintain its focus) and a recorder (who should remain objective so as to be able to record what happens accurately). The other participants should be actively engaged in what is going on. The regular chair may decide to delegate the role if it will lead to a more successful outcome or if he or she prefers to take an active part in the discussion of issues. It is the chair's responsibility to create a sociable climate in which sharing of thoughts can occur and objective decisions can be made. Good minutes will remind members of where the group is in dealing with the issues before it. Members may find that a review of several months of minutes will provide insights into the meeting process as well as the specific issues. Participation by all members is important. Passive members may silently disagree with decisions that are made and subvert these decisions in the normal course of their work.

The purpose of an official meeting is to solve problems, make decisions, and meet organizational challenges. Thus, the facilitator must keep the meeting on track while encouraging members to present all sides of an issue and argue in favor of the positions they sincerely hold. The facilitator's other main task, of course, is to get the members to reach a decision on each issue (even if the decision is merely to continue consideration of the issue at the next meeting).

Not all meetings are the same, and public health leaders need to adjust their role according to the type. Organizational meetings deal with issues related to the running of the agency and its programs, and they should cover the diversity of activities in which the agency is engaged. In a team meeting, the agency director may transfer the role of chair to a staff member who is expert in the issues under examination. In a meeting of the governing board, the agency director may collaborate with the board chair in running the meeting. At a community meeting (or any open meeting), the director will have the task of listening carefully to issues raised by community residents.

In carrying out their meeting-related responsibilities, public health leaders should follow these guidelines:

- Keep committee meetings to a minimum.
- Make community and other extraorganizational meetings as information based as possible.
- Use communication skills appropriate to the meeting format.
- Hold extraorganizational meetings in a neutral place if possible.
- Use round tables to increase interaction, and do not assign seats.
- Keep the number of attendees to less than 15 if possible.
- Plan the agenda carefully.
- Encourage both dialogue (exploratory discourse) and discussion (problem-solving discourse) in meetings.
- Start meetings on time and end them on time.
- Keep meetings focused on the issues.

HEALTH COMMUNICATION

Specific skills must be learned to translate health information into understandable messages. Not only must these messages be developed, but they must be marketed. There is controversy over the relationship between health communications and social marketing. In this book, these two communication activities are presented separately. In an interview with the media expert Robert Howard, Shirley Randolph explored some of these issues (Case Study 9–B).[85] Howard said that the concepts of health communication and social marketing are closely related. In health communication, the target audience is typically the community or population at risk, and the long-term goal is to help people in this population increase control over and improve their health. Social marketing, which is discussed in the next section, is aimed at increasing the acceptability of an idea, social practice, or social cause among the target audience. The desired goal of public health–oriented social marketing is to induce the public and policy makers to support disease prevention and health promotion concepts and programs.

The Centers for Disease Control and Prevention (CDC) perspective on health communication is that it "is the crafting and delivery of messages and strategies, based on consumer research, to promote the health of individuals and communities. . . . Effective health communication activities will be an integral component of all programs designed to promote health, improve quality of life, and foster healthful environments."[86(p.2)] CDC developed 10 guidelines for increasing the effectiveness of health communication. They are as follows:

1. Review background information. (What is out there?)
2. Set communication objectives. (What do we want to accomplish?)

3. Analyze and segment target audiences. (Whom do we want to reach?)
4. Develop and pretest message concepts. (What do we want to say?)
5. Select communication channels. (Where do we want to say it?)
6. Create and pretest messages and products. (How do we want to say it?)
7. Develop promotion plan/production. (How do we get it used?)
8. Implement communication strategies and conduct process evaluation. (Let's do it!)
9. Conduct outcome and impact evaluation. (How well did we do?)
10. Feedback to improve communication. (Where do we go from here?)[87(pp.2–4)]

These 10 guidelines can be applied in Exercise 9–2, which concerns the development of a team-based health communication strategy.

Despite the fact that more than 500,000 individuals are employed in public health programs nationally, the public health system is not routinely promoted as an essential provider of health-related services of importance to all constituencies. As a result, public health practitioners are at a disadvantage in getting funds for programs in the highly competitive health services arena. It is almost as if they do not want to talk to the various media and broadcast their accomplishments.

Because of the restructuring in health service delivery and financing, the future role and functions of public health are now uncertain. The uncertainty is not necessarily to be decried. New opportunities for public health agencies to address community health issues are becoming apparent. Primary among these are opportunities to promote healthy behavior through health communication initiatives. The first step in creating an initiative is to build a coalition of equal partners for the purpose of defining, planning, operationalizing, and evaluating health communication (and social marketing) strategies. The second step is to acknowledge existing barriers to full operationalization of the coalition, including the difficulty of creating a coalition in which no one partner controls the components of the process or its outcomes.

Figure 9–3 shows the essential components and partners in any action partnership for health. Each partner has a vested interest in ensuring that the health communication initiatives will succeed. In addition, each partner brings unique resources and expertise to the coalition. Once the action partnership is established and the responsibilities of the partners are negotiated, the first order of business should be to achieve a consensus on the initiatives to be pursued and to develop action plans for implementing the initiatives at the community level.

Creating action partnerships for health is one of the best ways available to public health agencies of addressing community health issues. Further, by establishing such coalitions, public health agencies can maintain an important leadership role. On the other hand, if they fail to work with community partners, they may face a future of lost opportunities.

Public health leaders must

• build coalitions of equal partners capable of defining, planning, operationalizing, and developing health communication strategies

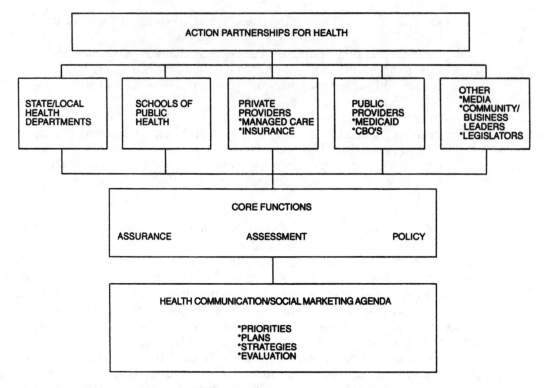

Figure 9–3 Coalition components and partners.

- set communication objectives, select communication channels, and determine how to use programs
- identify single overriding communication objects
- identify and respond to barriers to full operationalization of coalitions

SOCIAL MARKETING

Social marketing has been defined as "the application of commercial marketing technologies to the analysis, planning, execution, and evaluation of programs designed to influence the voluntary behavior of target audiences in order to improve their personal welfare and that of their society."[88(p.7)] The purpose of public health–oriented social marketing is to increase the general acceptance of certain health practices so as to induce the public and policy makers to support health promotion and disease prevention concepts and programs. This kind of social marketing depends on mass communication, for mass communication is the easiest and surest means of informing the public of the behavior changes that are necessary to improve the health status of the community.[89]

A social marketing campaign, according to Winett and Wallack, has seven essential characteristics:[90]

1. It possesses a consumer orientation geared toward meeting the needs and values of the target audience.

2. It places an emphasis on the audience's voluntary exchange of resources for products.
3. It rests on a strong research base, including audience analyses and market segmentation studies that indicate the needs, preferences, and values of various target populations.
4. It uses formative research to test the audience's acceptance of messages, concepts, campaign design, and products prior to full implementation.
5. It seeks an optimum balance among the four P's of marketing (product, price, place, and promotion).
6. It uses channel analyses to test the appropriateness and effectiveness of the campaign delivery systems.
7. It evaluates campaign components using built-in feedback systems in order to discover how to modify them during implementation (if necessary).

To understand how the four P's of marketing apply to social marketing, consider a situation in which public health practitioners are trying to promote dietary changes to reduce fat intake.[91] *Product* encompasses the foods that the public will have to give up or consume in a different form. If people are addicted to pizza, they might have to give up pizza altogether or convince the local pizzerias to offer low-fat varieties. *Price* relates to the cost to the public of making the necessary changes. Will people be willing to pay three dollars extra for a low-fat pizza and put up with the loss in flavor? *Place* is where the activities occur. Perhaps the only place to get low-fat pizza is at the supermarket, so that reducing fat intake means eating at home. *Promotion* involves activities intended to convince the public to accept the message and alter their behavior. (Note that social marketing has a fifth P, *politics*. Part of a social marketing campaign may be devoted to convincing politicians to pass or revise a law.)

Case Study 9–C is intended to clarify the relationship between health communication and social marketing. Note that it is possible to have a health communication success and a marketing failure. It will be hard, for instance, to convince pizza lovers to give up the high-fat food. Public health issues tend to be controversial, and people's views are closely related to the values that they hold dear. Think of the pipe smoker who believes that smoking a pipe is safer than smoking cigarettes. Also, people do not see the results of lifestyle change for years and do not project forward their increased risk for disease as a result of present activities. Another social marketing challenge is that priorities differ in different segments of our communities, such as among the affluent and the poor. And still another is that local public health agency leaders have limited budgets for social marketing and must choose their battles carefully.

Kotler and Roberto developed a hierarchy-of-effects model (Figure 9–4) that takes into account that not all of the target audience will accept the message of a social marketing campaign.[92] It is important, therefore, to provide reinforcement for people who have made a commitment to change or have assimilated the new knowledge gained from the campaign.

Public health leaders need to know how to develop health communication programs and monitor the effectiveness of these programs. Creating effective programs is complicated by the fact that many communities want to maintain the status quo or at least contain community groups hostile to the message of such programs.[93] In order to market public health information more effectively, public

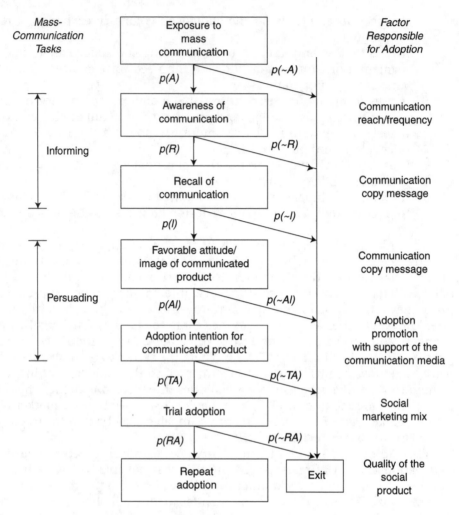

Figure 9–4 Hierarchy-of-effects model of the mass-communication process.

health leaders need to conduct surveys on consumer health knowledge, investigate different behavior change strategies, target programs at appropriate population segments, and modify programs as necessary.

Public health leaders should

- use social marketing as a process to increase the acceptance of an idea, social practice, or social cause among a specific audience
- develop strategies for promoting health promotion and disease prevention initiatives in the community
- learn techniques for fostering behavioral change
- identify the various population segments within the overall population

- conduct research on the use of different strategies and their outcomes
- create innovative funding mechanisms for health communication and social marketing campaigns

SUMMARY

Communication is central to leadership. For example, the leader of an organization may be able to develop a compelling organizational vision, but if that leader is unable to communicate the vision to others in the organization in a way that inspires them, the work of visioning will have been all for nought.

This chapter began by discussing the nature of the communication process and the barriers to communication, which include the fact that people in a communicative situation can have different communication styles. As was pointed out, one means of getting around the barriers that exist, at least in the case of oral communication, is to engage in active listening. Of course, not all communication is oral, and the chapter presented the advantages and disadvantages of oral communication and those of written communication as well.

Advancements in communication technology bring with them new communication skills that need to be learned. The most obvious example is the widespread use of computers for the transfer of data and for sending messages in a timely fashion and the corresponding need to master computer skills. Technological advancements also typically bring with them new problems, such as the e-mail overload that public health leaders frequently experience.

Public health leaders must communicate not only with their colleagues but also with the public, for part of their responsibility is to educate the public about public health issues and act as advocates for public health. In short, they need to publicize pertinent information and promote the public health agenda. The only way to do the latter is to communicate the agenda to policy makers who have a direct say in whether the agenda gets implemented or not. Therefore, among the communication skills that public health leaders need are media advocacy skills. They also need to learn the various skills associated with health communication and social marketing.

Discussion Questions

1. As a public health leader, how would you develop a health education program to increase the health literacy of the people in your service area?
2. What are the barriers to successful communication and how have you personally overcome them?
3. What would be a workable communication strategy to get more funds for an expanded childhood immunization program?
4. What strategies might you use to increase your interpersonal communication skills?
5. What are the advantages and disadvantages of oral communication as opposed to written communication?

6. What are the characteristics of active listening?
7. What are Walton's five rules of conversational etiquette?
8. What speaker aids can be used to enhance a public talk and what are their advantages and disadvantages?
9. What are some guidelines for interviewing job candidates?
10. What are the differences between media advocacy and public education?
11. What are the advantages of engaging in dialogue before engaging in discussion or debate?
12. What are the differences between health communication and social marketing?

Exercise 9–1

USING PERSUASION

Purpose: to learn how to use public speaking for purposes of persuasion
Key concepts: persuasion, public speaking, strategic planning, team consensus
Procedure: The class should divide into teams of 8–10 members. Each team has the task of preparing a speech intended to persuade community residents of the benefits of a particular project. It seems likely that federal funds will become available to the community for the development of a teen clinic at Margaret Sanger High School. The team, during 30 minutes of discussion, should first identify a strategy for convincing an audience made up of community residents that the teen clinic will benefit the community and should then develop a speech based on that strategy. After the speech is completed, the team selects a spokesperson to give a 5-minute presentation at a community meeting in support of the teen clinic.

Exercise 9–2

CREATING A HEALTH COMMUNICATION STRATEGY

Purpose: to understand the process of developing a health communication strategy to address a local health problem
Key concepts: epidemiology, health communication
Procedure: A group of children who had eaten hamburgers and drunk milk-shakes at a local fast-food restaurant, Old Mother Hubbard Eatery, become seriously ill. The health department calls in the state epidemiologist, who investigates the problem and determines that a *Salmonella* outbreak has occurred. The epidemiologist also finds evidence of *E. coli* contamination. The local health department is called in to develop a health communication strategy to get the word out to the public. The class should divide into teams of 8–10 to develop the communication strategy. Following the CDC guidelines, each team should draft a brief document that outlines this strategy, including the communication skills to be used by each team member during the process.

Leadership Opportunities in Private Well Contamination with Volatile Organic Compounds

Lillian Mood

INTRODUCTION

One of the emerging public health problems of our time is the actual or perceived risk of disease, particularly cancer, as a result of exposure to toxins in the environment. Two factors make protecting the health of the public from the dangers of environmental toxins particularly difficult. One is that the science of acceptable risk is still young; standards are developed as chemical compounds are identified as being harmful or potentially harmful to human health. The second factor is that the period of time between exposure and illness is measured in years and sometimes decades rather than the few hours to several days which has been the norm for communicable diseases.

The whole concept of "acceptable risk" is a dilemma in itself. Persons who willingly take risks like not wearing a seat belt, exceeding the speed limit, living a sedentary life, even smoking, want and expect their environment to be free of any contamination from sources outside their own home. To them, any chemical which can be detected at any level is harmful and must be eliminated; many insist on limits for chemical compounds in air, water, and soil which are below detectable levels. The assessments are made in parts per billion, a quantity hard for the average citizen to conceptualize. Making the acceptance of reasonable risk even more complicated is the feeling people have about risks over which they have no control. The thoughts are something like this: "I can choose to eat a diet filled with foods that increase my risk of heart disease, but I have a horrible fear of and outrage about what that industry down the road is putting into the air or into the nearby river. Someone may be doing something to harm me that I can't see or feel, and I'm not at all sure that I can trust the government to protect me."

This is the general climate in which the state health department works toward its goals of minimizing health risks, preserving the quality and safety of the environment, and being responsive to citizens' concerns.

CASE CHRONOLOGY

In early September 1990, a resident of the Regal Oaks community contacted Al Brown, director of the Midlands Environmental Quality Control (EQC) District of the state health department, to register a complaint about his water. The resident, Mr. Bell, was experiencing itching and a skin rash that he was sure was due to contamination of his well from a nearby industry. Since Regal Oaks is not on Capital City's public water system, groundwater is the source of water from the private wells in the neighborhood.

Surveillance (Assessment)

Because contaminated groundwater could affect the quality of water in the Regal Oaks' wells, on September 12, 1990, scientists from the Midlands EQC District took groundwater samples in response to the resident's complaint. Samples were taken from the complainant's home on the 700 block of Fore Avenue and at another home, on the 200 block of Fore Avenue. They were analyzed for volatile organic compounds (VOCs), pesticides, and herbicides, drinking water metals, and general water chemistry.

Analytical data received September 14 indicated the presence of three VOCs, including tetrachloroethene, trichloroethene, and cis-1,2-dichloroethene from one well in the 200 block of Fore Avenue. The level of tetrachloroethene was 5.04 parts per billion (ppb), exceeding the maximum contaminant level (MCL) of 5.0 ppb which has been proposed for this compound and is in the process of negotiation by the federal Environmental Protection Agency (EPA).

The sample from the 700 block of Fore Avenue, Mr. Bell's home, was clean. More samples were taken from the 200 block of Fore Avenue and four other homes upgradient of that location. Analytical results from these samples confirmed VOCs above MCLs on the 200 block of Fore Avenue and identified detectable levels on the 100 block of Fore Avenue. A detectable level does not necessarily mean that levels are unsafe but shows the need for more testing. For this reason, the staff began an ongoing sampling program at Regal Oaks to determine the extent and source of the groundwater contamination and the resulting risk to the resident population.

On September 17, 1990, confirmatory sampling for VOCs was conducted at the previously sampled private well in the 200 block of Fore Avenue and four wells which appeared to be upgradient of the contaminated well. Analytical data received September 26, 1990, confirmed previous sampling results of tetrachloroethene at 5.09 ppb and identified these same VOCs below established or proposed MCLs at a second well. The other wells sampled were free of contamination.

Political Inquiry

Meanwhile Lee Steele, the deputy commissioner for environmental quality control at the state health department, received a letter from the Reed County Council chair, Jim Moore, dated September 18, 1990. Mr. Moore asked for an assessment of the air and water in Regal Oaks because residents were complaining to him that "the drinking water was often green in color and that an unpleasant smell can be frequently found in the air." The residents suspected that the air and water were being contaminated by the Woodbranch Subdivision's wastewater treatment plant, which was adjacent to Regal Oaks. Mr. Steele's response of September 25 indicated that inspectors had found problems at the treatment plant which accounted for the odors, and corrective action was being taken with the operator. Bacterial analyses of the groundwater, however, did not show contamination indicative of the presence of sewage. He also updated Mr. Moore on the status of the sampling for the VOCs.

Surveillance Follow-up

On October 3, 1990, department personnel obtained groundwater samples for VOC analysis from 17 additional wells. Analytical data received October 19, 1990, found 3 additional wells with the identified VOCs above the MCLs. Two other wells had detectable levels of VOCs but below the MCLs.

When the results were received for each sampling, each resident received a letter giving the analytical data for his or her well. If an MCL was exceeded, the resident was advised not to use the water for drinking or cooking.

Between September 1990 and February 1991, concurrent with the private well samplings, EQC personnel pursued identification of a potential source, or sources, for the identified contamination. Activities included review of project files and monitoring data, site inspections and interviews with staff personnel, and review of tax maps and property records. Review of the file for Diamond Board, Inc. (formerly Wheeler Trace, Inc.) indicated that Mitchell Jones, state health officer, had responded on September 19 to an August inquiry from Mr. Moore on behalf of his constituents in Regal Oaks.

The residents were concerned that an industry (Wheeler Trace, Inc.), formerly located adjacent to the subdivision, was believed to have used or disposed of hazardous chemicals at its site, and if this were true, those chemicals may have contaminated the environment. The state health officer's reply indicated that a consent order in January 1990 required the present industry on the site (Diamond Board, Inc.) to install two groundwater monitoring wells. Two rounds of samples from these wells allowed department staff to determine that groundwater was not adversely affected by the historical discharge of wastewater.

Media Response

A local newspaper reported the investigations on November 1, 1990. The options for well owners with water problems included digging new wells, treating their existing wells, using bottled water for drinking, or tapping into the city lines. Some residents had begun using bottled water, and Mr. Moore had approached city officials about extending the city's water system to the area. The city's estimate of the cost at that time was approximately $1 million; the cost to each resident would be slightly over $3,000 for the tap-in fee.

On November 2, 1990, two existing monitoring wells located on the former Roberts and Mixon facility property were sampled for VOCs, general water chemistry, and drinking water metals. Analytical data received December 7, 1990, revealed no detectable levels of VOCs from these wells.

On February 28, 1991, EQC personnel installed a temporary well on the property at 10260 Two Notch Road located apparently upgradient of private wells previously identified as being contaminated. Sampling results received April 18, 1991, revealed no detectable levels of VOCs.

On April 25, 1991, a news article reported the status of the investigation to the public.

Department Action

A May 10, 1991, internal department memo to the managers of the Facilities Compliance Section and the Assessment and Development Section of the Bureau of Drinking Water Protection from Pat Bissell, Midlands District hydrologist, summarized the activities and findings of the investigation and requested additional sampling between residences #144 and #224 along Fore Avenue. It was Mr. Bissell's opinion that, given the configuration of the impacted wells, if a single source of contamination existed, it should manifest itself in that area.

On July 3, 1991, two additional private wells were sampled for VOCs (161 Fore Avenue and 232 Wynnette Way). Analytical data received August 8, 1991, indicated both wells had detectable levels of the identified compounds, with one well exceeding the MCL for tetrachloroethene (11 ppb).

On August 22, 1991, an EQC district memorandum to the Bureau of Drinking Water Protection summarized the analytical data obtained to date: "Groundwater contamination appears to approximate an elongate plume which has (or is) emanating from an unidentified point south-southwest of the subdivision. Currently, the apparent contaminate plume is undefined both in vertical and lateral extent, which indicates additional receptors may be utilizing impacted groundwater at this subdivision."

Mr. Bissell urged a meeting as soon as possible to discuss actions necessary to resolve the matter expeditiously. On August 27, 1991, Mr. Bissell met with the director of the Division of Drinking Water Quality and Enforcement, three staff members from the Groundwater Protection Division, and a representative of the Enforcement Section of the Bureau of Drinking Water Protection. The staff agreed to continue efforts to identify the source of contamination and to extend the sampling to additional wells to determine if they were impacted. The division director agreed to contact the state health department's legislative liaison to discuss funding alternatives for city water in this subdivision.

On August 29, 1991, a site discovery form listing the Regal Oaks subdivision was sent from the Bureau of Drinking Water Protection to the manager of site screening at the Bureau of Solid and Hazardous Waste. The Site Screening Section is funded by the U.S. Environmental Protection Agency (EPA) to conduct investigations at sites that may potentially qualify for the National Priorities List (NPL) for federal "Superfund" action. If Regal Oaks site qualified for the NPL, federal monies might be available to assist in remediation of the plume.

In September and October of 1991, additional water samples were collected from individual wells in an effort to identify all potential receptors of impacted groundwater; 19 samples were obtained on September 4, 1991; 7 samples on September 12, 1991; 19 samples on September 30, 1991; and 8 confirmation samples on October 8, 1991. Analytical results indicated that 7 samples exceeded the MCL for tetrachloroethene or the MCL for trichloroethene.

On October 22, 1991, seeking more information about potential sources of the groundwater contamination, EQC personnel sampled the sanitary septic tank (sludge bottom) at Diamond Board for VOCs. Analytical data identified three VOCs normally associated with petroleum products. None of the VOCs found in groundwater within Regal Oaks were detected by this sampling. In another attempt to locate a possible source, on October 23 Midlands EQC District hydrogeologists met with university agricultural experiment station employees to explore the history of use of the station property. Experimental station employees of many years (15 and 32 years) were not aware of any spills, landfills, or landfilling activities on the station property during their tenure.

On October 25, 1991, health department staff met with state, county, and city officials to discuss the necessity for an alternative water source for the subdivision. In addition to providing an update on the status of the investigation, department personnel informed attending officials that the department has no funding, nor does it know of any funding source, to assist in the development of an alternative water supply.

On November 15, 1991, EQC staff installed and sampled three temporary wells, two on property directly across Two Notch Road from the subdivision and one on the corner of Two Notch Road and Fore Avenue. Detectable levels of two VOCs were identified in the two wells across Two Notch Road, but the compounds and levels needed to be substantiated through additional sampling. No VOCs were found in the sample collected from the corner of Two Notch Road and Fore Avenue.

Legal Interest

On December 3, 1991, Pat Bissell wrote a letter to Jim Moore updating him on the status of the well sampling and enclosed maps of the area. Mr. Bissell also wrote a letter to the Perdy law firm in response to a Freedom of Information Act request for information on the investigation. The Perdy law firm was also referenced in a letter sent by a resident of Regal Oaks to other residents on January 17, 1992. The law firm had been retained for a class action suit. Other citizen initiatives to get action on their concerns were described.

Informally, citizens reported that persons indicating they represented a law firm were knocking on doors in the neighborhood and asking if residents were experiencing health problems and needed legal assistance.

Funding for a Public Water Supply

On January 30, 1992, EPA officials informed the health department that no source of funding was available to assist in providing a public water system for the Regal Oaks subdivision.

On January 31, 1992, Department personnel met again with state, county, and city officials to provide additional information in an effort to assist in obtaining grants to fund a public water source for the affected area of Regal Oaks.

On February 5, 1992, 15 additional water samples were collected from individual wells in an effort to track the location of the suspected contaminant plume. As of February 12, 1992, the department had collected 94 samples from 73 water supply wells in the Regal Oaks subdivision. Also the department had installed and sampled four temporary monitoring wells and sampled four existing monitoring wells at two facilities in the immediate area. Of the 73 wells sampled, data indicated that 30 wells exhibited detectable levels of VOCs, principally tetrachloroethene (PCE) and trichloroethene (TCE). Twelve of the wells exceeded the established and/or proposed maximum contaminant levels for PCR and/or TCE, which are 5.0 ppb.

Communication with Residents

Each time sampling was done, a copy of the results and a letter of explanation were provided to each resident whose well was sampled. Residents were invited by the Midlands EQC District director and the Reed County Council chair to a public meeting on February 12, 1992. A large number of Regal Oaks residents attended. Al Brown, EQC District director, welcomed the group, introduced the others who would be speaking, and explained a number of the terms (e.g., ppb, VOC, and TCE) in a fact sheet furnished to each attendee. Overhead projections of maps were used to show exactly the area affected and the points beyond which no contamination had been found.

Pat Bissell, hydrologist, described the patterns of groundwater migration in the area, which provided the basis for ruling out certain industries as potential sources of the contamination.

Mac Monroe, division director of the Drinking Water Protection Bureau, explained how standards for maximum contaminant levels are reached and the boundaries of authority of the drinking water program. Bill Marks, MD, director of Health Hazard Evaluation, talked about what is known and not known about exposures to VOCs and what people can do to minimize their risk of exposure.

There were a number of questions from residents about health symptoms ranging from itching to rashes and about some residents' impression that the neighborhood had too many cases of cancer. Information was given on the usual effects of toxic doses of the VOCs identified. Liver damage and tumors of the liver occurred but only after long exposure to high concentrations. Well samples had been taken from the residences of persons with health complaints and no VOCs were found.

Jim Moore, county council chair, spoke of the efforts of elected officials to find funding to provide city water to Regal Oaks. He explained the availability of funds from the governor's office if the subdivision qualified. Since qualifying was dependent on the income levels of residents, attendees were given forms to fill out documenting their income. They were assured that the confidentiality of the information provided would be maintained.

The Media Turn up the Volume

The meeting and some of the residents' reactions were reported in the local newspaper. A letter to the editor dated February 20, 1992, cited the Regal Oaks investigation as an example of "Power Failure," a term coined by the newspaper to support the governor's initiative to restructure state government into a cabinet organization of state agencies. One part of the proposal was to separate the health and governmental protection functions into two separate departments.

A March 25 letter to the editor from the district EQC director attempted to clear up some misunderstandings of the department's actions.

Interim Measures

On March 30, 1992, residents with contaminated wells were notified that money had been made available through the Superfund program to install granular activated charcoal filters in their homes as a temporary measure. The filters would allow residents to use their well water safely until the city water system was extended to the subdivision. The filters would then be moved by the health department staff.

Obtaining a filter was voluntary; residents were told how to request a filter. After some follow-up, 7 of the 11 residents contacted requested filters, 1 said he would give permission for additional monitoring, and 1 declined the filter. No reply was received from 2 residents.

About the same time Reed County provided a single tap into the city water system with a faucet so residents would have access to safe water, making it no longer necessary for them either to buy bottled water or go outside the area to fill bottles of water.

On May 14, 1992, a letter was sent to all Regal Oaks residents giving them current information, and on August 6, 1992, a news article reported the status as of that date.

PRESENT STATUS

The last sampling by Midlands EQC District staff occurred in March 1992. Sampling by the state Superfund staff is scheduled to begin on September 22, 1992.

Funding for the public water supply is progressing. A public hearing on funding through the community block grant is scheduled for September 23, 1992. A meeting with county officials is scheduled in order to pursue the local matching funds required by the block grant.

There has been no further word on the class action suit. The resident who made reference to the suit in her letter to other residents has sold her property in Regal Oaks and moved out of the neighborhood.

The news media has been relatively silent on the issue recently. There was one recent TV news spot which presented a very negative view of the situation. The emphasis of the story was on funding a public water supply, and the implication was that people were suffering severe health problems. The health department was not contacted by the TV news prior to or for comment on the story. The spot generated only one follow-up call to the department from a citizen.

Jim Moore was defeated in his primary bid for re-election to the Reed County Council in August 1992. He had served on the council since 1984 and as its chair for one year.

Case Study 9–B

A Leadership Interview with Robert Howard

Shirley F. Randolph

Robert Howard is the director of public information at the Centers for Disease Control and Prevention, Atlanta. Mr. Howard has presented health communications workshops at the Illinois Public Health Leadership Institute twice. Mr. Howard brings a wealth of experience to his presentations about effective health communications. Prior to joining CDC, he was a career Navy officer assigned to public and media relations in a variety of settings. This interview took place immediately following a workshop conducted by Mr. Howard in September 1995.

"Communications" and "marketing" are words that frequently are used interchangeably. What is the difference between health communications and health marketing?

I think that health communications and marketing are almost interchangeable. Marketing is a management tool whereby you determine exactly what your market is, who the message is directed toward, who the audience is, who the communication is to go to. First, identify what your communication point is . . . your single overriding communication objective . . . your SOCO. Then go back and carefully examine who you are delivering this message to; who you are marketing this information to . . . what works with this audience . . . what works with this market. Then, decide how to deliver the health message to the audience to which it is directed. I think, to a great extent, "communications" and "marketing" are interchangeable. They cannot be separated. You cannot have good marketing without having good communication . . . and vice-versa. If you come up with a health message, you really do have to think about who you are communicating this message to. So, I think to a great extent the two terms are interchangeable.

Many public health practitioners have never had training or developed skills relative to working with the media. Can you speak to how the "average Jane and the average Joe," working day to day in a local health department, can improve their media relations skills?

The very first thing you have to do is you have to know *who* your local media representatives are. I think that as the local health officer or health administrator, it is important for you to get out and know these people. If you haven't already done it, you need to visit with your local media folks and introduce yourself. You need to find out who they are; they need to know who you are. It's important to know the individuals on the editorial boards of the local newspapers. You should also know the local assignment editor at the newspaper and the local television station and the news directors of the local radio stations. Let them know what use you can be to them and when they can call you. Let them know who they should call at the health department if there is an issue dealing with public health. Let them know what resources are available to them within public health. You do that by going around and getting to meet these people. There is nothing wrong with calling a reporter who covers a health beat consistently and does it very well and saying,

"You did a really great job covering that story. We really appreciate your effort." Everybody likes an occasional stroke, and it's important to say, "You did a super job on that story." At the same time, if a reporter gets something wrong, gently help that reporter get it right! Understand, the newspapers and radio stations are a medium through which you can market your communication message. It's important that you develop a relationship with them. The most important thing that a local public health official can do is to establish that base relationship with his or her media. Get to know them and discern and understand what works. Understand how you can best deliver your information locally. Public health workers at the local level are truly the core of public health practice. You are where the rubber meets the road. You are out there on a day-to-day basis dealing with issues locally. You are the ones that Dr. David Satcher, director of the Centers for Disease Control and Prevention, has been pointing to and saying, "We need your help to get a better understanding of the issues and problems that face local public health."

Many of the local health departments in Illinois, as well as in the nation, have small staffs and do not have a media expert or a public relations expert. Do you think that it is important to have one person in the agency designated as the media contact?

I think that it is very important for the media to have a single number that they can call or a single person they can contact if they have questions. There ought to be a single or central clearinghouse or clearing point that the media can go to. It is very important that you, in your agency or office, have a policy that tells the staff this is the procedure that you need to follow in responding to media inquiries. If you don't have a plan or a policy in place, develop one quickly to establish what should happen if you're not available. Designate the person who should respond to media inquiries in your absence. Your staff won't know what to do if there is not a policy. You need to develop a policy that works, that is unique to your specific area and your specific situation . . . develop that policy; identify that person. And, most important, make sure that everybody in the agency understands what the policy is. Go over it occasionally; share it and make sure that people don't violate it.

How can public health practitioners who use public health "lingo" on a daily basis translate our "language" in order to better "sell" our products to the media and the community?

I found that what works best at CDC is that the decisions about developing appropriate health messages are best not made in a vacuum. You need to put together a team of people in your office. Even if you have only four or five people on your staff, you will usually have one or two people who are pretty good at communication. It might be a nurse practitioner or somebody who is out there on a daily basis dealing with the public and who understands the best way to communicate with them. The public is not going to understand "risk" or "needs assessment." They're not going to understand "acute" and "chronic," or they're not going to understand "immunization schedules." Look to get your people who are working with the public to be a part of your communications team. Develop a team concept. Use the team to develop messages that the public will understand. These decisions cannot be made and communications messages cannot be developed in a vacuum by one person. It has to be a team approach.

What are the most important factors to keep in mind when preparing for an interview with someone from the media?

First, any time you give an interview, you ought to know *why* you are doing the interview, and you ought to know *exactly* who your target *audience* is. You ought to remember to tell yourself, "These are the people who brought me to this dance. These are the folks I'm representing, and I need to direct my message to them. I need to remember that they are the reason why I'm here, and I'm representing this agency or this office." You need to develop that communication point . . . your SOCO . . . your single, overriding communication message. What is the "take home" message for people when your public turns off the television that night? What is the "take home" message . . . the thing that you want them to remember from having seen your message? You can only develop that message if you sit down ahead of time and plan. You can't get from Chicago to Indianapolis without knowing the route; you have to plan your trip and plan your route; and you do that by sitting down with a map and thinking about how you're going to get there. You do the same thing when you're trying to market or communicate a message.

Sometimes media interviews become somewhat hostile. Is there any way to prepare for that? How do you deal with a hostile reporter?

If a reporter becomes hostile, I take that opportunity to absolutely "stay within my zone" as much as I can. You really do need to remember that if a media person becomes hostile, it does not mean that you have to become hostile. As soon as you become angry, remember that you're the person being quoted . . . you're the person being seen on camera. If you lose your cool, if you fall off the beam, that is all that will be seen . . . not the fact that the reporter became hostile. It is really important that you keep your focus and that you remember that your body language, your image, what you project, is going to be seen by people. If you are seen as hostile, that is what is going to be portrayed; so just stay within your zone. If a reporter asks you a hostile question or creates a hostile situation, don't buy into it. *Keep your cool!* If the question is inappropriate or improper, just say, "I'm not the person to address that issue" or "I don't share your feelings on that one" or "That's not what this agency represents." *Keep your cool!* Don't terminate an interview. Don't rip off a microphone and throw it down or storm out of the room. There is no quicker way to guarantee that you will see yourself on television than to do one of those things. The moment that you lose your cool, the moment that you lose control, is the moment I can guarantee that you will be quoted.

Is there any way to anticipate all or a majority of the questions that you might be asked to address during an interview?

No. You cannot anticipate all of the questions, but you *can* anticipate many of them by knowing local issues, by knowing local sensitivities, and by sitting down ahead of time with that communications team and developing some questions and answers and thinking about where the interview might go. For instance, what does the community really think about this issue? What are some of the sideline issues that might impact on this? You can't think of *every* question but you can sure think of *most* of them. There will be an occasional surprise question. Occasionally a reporter will surprise you, but you need to handle surprises as best you can. I find that generally you can predict around 80 percent of the questions you are going to get. Generally, the ones that you don't predict are relatively simple questions. If a reporter is coming to your shop to do an interview, there is probably some local tie-in or local issue to be explored. Try to keep your focus local. Try not to look at everything from a global or national perspective. Remember, once again, who brought you to the dance . . . who am I directing this interview to? Am I talking to doctors? Am I talking to nurses? Am I talking to teachers or to public health practitioners? Am I talking to the Hispanic community? Who is my audience? Factor your audience into all of your answers.

What should you do when the reporter keeps asking you the same question(s) over and over or tries to lead you down a path that you really don't want to go?

That is a frequent technique used by reporters. The most important thing to remember is the right answer is the right answer the first time and it's the right answer the tenth time. Don't change your answer just because you are asked the question again or asked the same question a little differently. If the reporter keeps doing it and becomes incessant, there is nothing wrong with saying, "I've already answered that question, but I'll be happy to answer it for you again." Then, if it gets to be too much, say, "I would really ask that we move on to something else. I've answered that question and I think I've answered it fairly, and I would like to move on to something else." But, *don't lose your cool!*

What should you do if the reporter won't accept that answer. Do you just repeat, "I've answered that question . . . we've talked about this issue . . . we need to move on"?

That's exactly what you do. It doesn't matter if you're asked that question 20 times. And, finally, when you've reached the allotted time you have established in advance for the interview, you say something like, "If you don't have any other questions, I have another appointment. I have something else I really have to get on to and it is time for me to go now, and I *have* answered your questions." When you agree to an interview, you should establish the parameters, including the amount of time you have available, where the interview is to be held, what the background is going to be, what subject(s) will be discussed, and the area(s) of questions. You establish those parameters at the beginning of the interview. You get the reporter to buy in to that. You say, "I have about 30 to 45 minutes to spend with you; is that all right?" When you reach the time period you have established, it's okay to say, "I really do have something else I need to attend to."

What can or should a public health practitioner do if a media representative just shows up on the doorstep to do an interview? Something is happening in the community, and a reporter is sent to the public health department to "get a story" or a statement and says, "This is the situation . . . do you have a comment?" Is it better to go ahead and "get it over with," even if you're not prepared, or are there other strategies that are effective in such situations?

If a reporter just shows up, the very first thing you need to do is to make sure you are the right person to talk to the reporter on the subject she or he wishes to discuss. First, have a policy in place as to who will comment on issues as they arise. Get in touch with that person, make sure the person is briefed on the situation, get a handle on what's going on locally that would cause that reporter to show up on your doorstep. Why is this reporter here unannounced? What has brought the reporter here? Sit down with that reporter and make a determination about what it is the reporter wants to talk about. Buy yourself as much time as you possibly can to think about your comments before you go on camera or begin a taped interview. If the cameras are already rolling, if they catch you and "ambush" you, then it's very important for you to say, "The public health concerns of this issue are of great importance to us . . . it's important to us that we get the right message and the right information to people. You have just 'shown up on our doorstep' and I have not had an opportunity to take a look at this issue yet. We're going to do that, and as soon as I find out what the situation is, we will get back to you immediately."

What should you do if the media tries to "pit" you against other levels of government, such as a local health official against a state health official, or a state health official against a federal health official, or vice-versa?

Remember that you should only address issues that are appropriate for you to address and that you ought to be addressing. It is appropriate to say, "I don't have those specifics in front of me and I cannot address a subject for which I do not have the specifics. I didn't know we would be doing this interview." Don't hesitate, particularly in a live situation, to let the public know you have been blind-sided and to let the people on the other end of the camera or microphone know that this is the first time you have seen or heard this information. Let the public know that this is not a prepared interview. Don't hesitate to say, "You caught me without my information available. I didn't know we would be chatting today. I would like very much to address this issue or get you to the right person to get this issue addressed."

If you had to write the three top rules to follow when preparing for an interview, what would they be?

The very first thing to do is to establish a team within your public health department. You need to have a communications team—people who will sit together and discuss and review the issues prior to the interview. It's the difference between fire prevention and firefighting. Everything should not be a firefighting situation. You shouldn't have to break out the hoses every time something goes wrong. It's a lot better to have that smoke detector in place. It's what your communication team is . . . it's your smoke detector. It's your team that smells the smoke and gets together to determine what you're going to do. Have a communications team in place. Make sure everyone knows what to do when something goes bad.

Number two: on any given issue, develop your communication point . . . your SOCO . . . your single overriding communication objective. Sit down, communicate, identify who your market or media segment is, who you are delivering this message to within the population. Share this information within your agency. Make sure that everybody understands within your office what the SOCO, the single overriding communication objective, is. Finally, write that down and take it with you when you do the interview. I mean *take it with you physically and mentally*. Be thinking about the SOCO during the interview. Think about delivering that message over and over. And always, particularly when you're dealing with broadcast media, think visually. What can we do to best communicate this through the visual media? What can we best do to communicate this in the way of background video or how can we portray this best, either in a picture or on camera? Try to think, what do the broadcasters want? Try to think that this is what they're going to want . . . they'll want a laboratory shot or they'll want an immunization shot. Then make sure that your people in those clinics or in those areas look appropriate and appear appropriate and they know about the SOCO and the press visit. It's all part of that process of your communications team sharing that information internally and externally.

Finally, deliver your message. That always sounds so simple, but on more occasions than I can count I have seen people prepare for interviews, write the SOCO down, take the SOCO with them, and go to the interview. But because they get so caught up in the excitement or the nervousness of the interview, they fail to deliver the message. They never take the opportunity to grab hold of that interview and say, "I'm here today to say . . ." It is really good to frame your answers with those kinds of attention-grabbing devices. And, most importantly, use what works for you. Everyone is an individual, not everything works for everybody.

Finally, **practice, practice, practice!** You only get good at these things by practicing. **Good communication does not come naturally to anybody.** You get good at communicating because you work at it and you do it a lot. You need to practice.

Case Study 9–C

HIV Prevention: Communications Success, Marketing Failure

Fred Kroger

"America Responds to AIDS" is the campaign banner for the federal government's campaign to inform the American public about HIV and AIDS. Campaign planners have employed marketing techniques which have resulted in its messages being seen or heard by more Americans and with greater frequency (e.g., more than 7 billion audience impressions estimated for 1993) than for any government-sponsored public service health campaign to date. Yet, its CDC sponsors consider it more a health communications program than a social marketing effort.

In 1993, a panel of health communications experts external to the CDC was asked to assess its national efforts to promote HIV prevention and to recommend strategies for improvement. The principal elements of the effort have been a national media campaign, national toll-free hotline services, a national clearing-house for distributing materials and managing databases on HIV services and programs, grant programs for national partnership development, grant programs to support state and local information activities, and communications research and evaluation.

The panel gave favorable marks for the program's marketing efforts to media gatekeepers and for its success in nurturing effective collaborations among its many and diverse national partnerships. Aggressive, sustained interaction with national and local public service directors helped place HIV prevention high on their list of concerns. The national partners advised CDC on its "product" development processes but also became its sales force in delivering materials and programs to constituencies at organizational and community levels. The communications program was recognized as an integrated system that allows information to flow bidirectionally, and that had mass, institutional, community, and individual elements to it.

Its shortcomings, however, fell within two dimensions that most social marketing practitioners consider essential—audience segmentation and product definition. Undergirding these two deficiencies, the fifth "p" of government-based marketing programs, "politics," was described as the major impediment to effective marketing in HIV prevention.

AUDIENCE SEGMENTATION

Congress had been clear in designating the general public as the primary audience for CDC's mass communication efforts on AIDS. An informed and supportive population is recognized by behavioral scientists to be an important ingredient for causing healthy behaviors to be initiated and sustained. The "America Responds to AIDS Campaign" was criticized by the AIDS Action Council, the Gay Men's Health Crisis in New York City, by other AIDS advocacy groups, and by the review panel for not meeting the needs of high-risk audiences, such as gay men, by not providing sexually explicit behavioral messages.

PRODUCT

"American Responds to AIDS," though viewed by some as a public service advertising and pamphlet distribution campaign, was designed to be a sophisticated communications system that includes on-line computer databases; toll-free, live telephone hotline services; and a network of national organizations to mediate and deliver education programs and materials. The product was seen by campaign planners as value-free, technically accurate information. AIDS activists called for condoms promotion as the principal product. Congress and media critics expected proof of prevention effects. In assessing this confusion over product specificity, the review panel called for a more behaviorally focused product—for example, "health information with an attitude." Disease preventing behaviors, including condom use, should be aggressively promoted.

Evaluation efforts have been undertaken to position the HIV prevention "product" in more consumer relevant terms. Just as athletic footwear is sold as aids to "soar through the air, slam dunk, in your face" feats of athleticism rather than as canvas covers for the feet, such prevention products as condoms, monogamy, or abstinence still lack similar consumer-oriented positioning.

The awareness task has been judged by experts to be complete. It has been accomplished primarily through communication tools. Can the adoption of risk-reducing behaviors now be sold to persons at highest risk and will the body politic be supportive? This more challenging goal will require better application of core marketing principles. Will the second decade of HIV prevention marketing improve upon the first? Stay tuned.

REFERENCES

1. S.P. Robbins and M. Coulter, *Management,* 5th ed. (Upper Saddle River, NJ: Prentice Hall, 1996).
2. R.B. Adler and J.M. Elmhorst, *Communicating at Work,* 5th ed. (New York: McGraw-Hill, 1996).
3. Adler and Elmhorst, *Communicating at Work.*
4. J.G. Liebler et al., *Management Principles for Health Professionals,* 2d ed. (Gaithersburg, MD: Aspen Publishers, 1992).
5. D. Walton, *Are You Communicating?* (New York: McGraw-Hill, 1989).
6. D. Tannen, *That's Not What I Meant* (New York: Ballantine, 1986).
7. R. Bolton, *People Skills* (New York: Simon & Schuster, 1979).
8. J.E. Hulett Jr., "A Symbolic Interactionist Model of Human Communication. Part 1: The General Model of Social Behavior; the Message Generating Process," *AV Communication Review* 14, no. 1 (1966): 5–33.
9. J.E. Hulett Jr., "A Symbolic Interactionist Model of Human Communication. Part 2: The Receiver's Function; Pathology of Communication; Non-Communication," *AV Communication Review* 14, no. 2 (1966): 203–220.
10. R.R. Sears, "A Theoretical Framework for Personality and Social Behavior," *American Psychologist* 6 (1951): 476–482.
11. N.L. Frigon Sr. and H.K. Jackson Jr., *The Leader* (New York: AMACON [American Management Association], 1996).
12. Robbins and Coulter, *Management,* 5th ed.
13. Tannen, *That's Not What I Meant.*
14. D. Tannen, *The Argument Culture* (New York: Random House, 1998).
15. Bolton, *People Skills.*
16. Adler and Elmhorst, *Communicating at Work.*
17. Adler and Elmhorst, *Communicating at Work.*
18. R. Pitino, *Success Is a Choice* (New York: Broadway Books, 1997).
19. Robbins and Coulter, *Management,* 5th ed.
20. Robbins and Coulter, *Management,* 5th ed.
21. Adler and Elmhorst, *Communicating at Work.*
22. T. Alessandra and P. Hunsaker, *Communicating at Work* (New York: Simon & Schuster, 1993).
23. P.R. Scholtes, *The Leader's Handbook* (New York: McGraw Hill, 1998).
24. Alessandra and Hunsaker, *Communicating at Work.*
25. D. Walton, *Are You Communicating?* (New York: McGraw Hill, 1989).
26. Adler and Elmhorst, *Communicating at Work.*
27. Adler and Elmhorst, *Communicating at Work.*
28. D. Walton, *Are You Communicating?*
29. Alessandra and Hunsaker, *Communicating at Work.*
30. Liebler et al., *Management Principles for Health Professionals.*
31. Liebler et al., *Management Principles for Health Professionals.*
32. B.D. Smart, *The Smart Interviewer* (New York: Wiley, 1989).
33. Smart, *The Smart Interviewer.*
34. J. Carver, *Boards That Make a Difference,* 2d ed. (San Francisco: Jossey-Bass, 1997).
35. Robbins and Coulter, *Management,* 5th ed.
36. J. Wycoff, *Mindmapping: Your Personal Guide to Exploring Creativity and Problem-Solving* (New York: Berkeley Books, 1995).
37. Adler and Elmhorst, *Communicating at Work.*
38. B. Nelson and P. Economy, *Managing for Dummies* (Foster City, CA: IDG Books Worldwide, Inc., 1996).
39. Robbins and Coulter, *Management,* 5th ed.
40. Walton, *Are You Communicating?*
41. S.M. Shortell et al., *Remaking Health Care in America* (San Francisco: Jossey-Bass, 1996).
42. L. Wallack and L. Dorfman, "Media Advocacy: A Strategy for Advancing Policy and Promoting Health," *Health Education Quarterly* 23, no. 3 (1996): 293–317.
43. L.B. Winet and L. Wallack, "Advancing Public Health Goals through the Mass Media," *Journal of Health Communications* 1 (1996): 173–196.
44. S. Iyengar, *Is Anyone Responsible? How Television Frames Political Issues* (Chicago: University of Chicago Press, 1989).
45. M. Siegel and L. Doner, *Marketing Public Health* (Gaithersburg, MD: Aspen Publishers, 1998).
46. Wallack and Dorfman, "Media Advocacy."

47. Wallack and Dorfman, "Media Advocacy."
48. J. Fallows, *Breaking the News* (New York: Pantheon Books, 1996).
49. M.R. Lum and T.L. Tinker, eds., *A Primer on Health Risk Communication: Principles and Practices* (Washington, DC: U.S. Department of Health and Human Services (Public Health Service, 1994).
50. S.P. Robbins and M. Coulter, *Management*, 6th ed. (Upper Saddle River, NJ: Prentice Hall, 1999).
51. Adler and Elmhorst, *Communicating at Work.*
52. S. Helgesen, *The Web of Inclusion* (New York: Doubleday, 1995).
53. D.J. Breckon, *Managing Health Promotion Programs* (Gaithersburg, MD: Aspen Publishers, 1997).
54. D. Tannen, *The Argument Culture* (New York: Random House, 1998).
55. A.J. DuBrin, *The Complete Idiot's Guide to Leadership* (New York: Alpha Books [MacMillan Reference USA], 1998).
56. A.J. DuBrin, *The Complete Idiot's Guide to Leadership.*
57. L.M. Harris, "Differences That Make a Difference," in *Health and the New Media*, ed. L.M. Harris (Mahwah, NJ: Lawrence Erlbaum Associates, 1995).
58. Robbins and Coulter, *Management*, 5th ed.
59. Liebler et al., *Management Principles for Health Professionals.*
60. P.R. Scholtes, *The Leader's Handbook* (New York: McGraw-Hill, 1998).
61. Alessandra and Hunsaker, *Communicating at Work.*
62. Hulett, "A Symbolic Interactionist Model of Human Communication. Part 1: The General Model of Social Behavior; the Message Generating Process."
63. Robbins and Coulter, *Management*, 5th ed.
64. Robbins and Coulter, *Management*, 6th ed.
65. M. DePree, *Leading without Power* (San Francisco: Jossey-Bass, 1997).
66. C.L. Brown, *Techniques of Successful Delegation* (Shawnee Mission, KS: National Press Publications, 1988).
67. C. Handy, *Understanding Organizations* (New York: Oxford University Press, 1993).
68. P. Hersey et al., *Management of Organizational Behavior*, 7th ed. (Upper Saddle River, NJ: Prentice Hall, 1996).
69. DuBrin, *The Complete Idiot's Guide to Leadership.*
70. J.A. Barker, *Future Edge* (New York: Morrow, 1992).
71. E. Goffman, *Frame Analysis* (Cambridge, MA: Harvard University Press, 1974).
72. D. Tannen, *Talking from 9 to 5* (New York: Morrow, 1994).
73. L.G. Bolman and T.E. Deal, *Reframing Organizations*, 2d ed. (San Francisco: Jossey-Bass, 1997).
74. D.K. Hurst, *Crisis and Renewal* (Boston: Harvard Business School Press, 1995).
75. G.T. Fairhurst and R.A. Sarr, *The Art of Framing* (San Francisco: Jossey-Bass, 1996).
76. D. Bohm et al., *Dialogue—A Proposal* (Gloucester, England: Dialogue, 1991).
77. L. Ellinor and G. Gerard, eds., *Dialogue* (New York: Wiley, 1998).
78. D. Bohm, *On Dialogue* (Ojal, CA: David Bohm Seminars, 1989).
79. J.C. Lammers, "Building Learning Communities To Expand Public Health Resources and Effectiveness" (paper presented at Association of State and Territorial Directors of Health, Promotion and Public Health Annual Meeting, Washington, DC, 27 April 1996).
80. M.R. Weisbord and S. Janoff, *Future Search* (San Francisco: Jossey-Bass, 1995).
81. Bohm, *On Dialogue.*
82. Tannen, *The Argument Culture.*
83. M. Doyle and D. Straus, *How To Make Meetings Work* (New York: Jove Publications, 1982).
84. Nelson and Economy, *Managing for Dummies.*
85. S. Randolph, "A Leadership Interview with Robert Howard," *Leadership in Public Health* 3, no. 4 (1995): 7–11.
86. K.S. Lord, "Issues in Health Communications," *Leadership in Public Health* 3, no. 4 (1995): 1–4.
87. Lord, "Issues in Health Communications."
88. A.R. Andreasen, *Marketing Social Change* (San Francisco: Jossey-Bass, 1995).
89. Winett and Wallack, "Advancing Public Health Goals through the Mass Media."
90. Winett and Wallack, "Advancing Public Health Goals through the Mass Media."
91. Winett and Wallack, "Advancing Public Health Goals through the Mass Media."
92. P. Kotler and E.L. Roberto, *Social Marketing* (New York: The Free Press, 1989).
93. Siegel and Doner, *Marketing Public Health.*

Chapter 10

Leadership and the Planning Process

We live in a world where no one is "in charge." No one organization, or institution has the legitimacy, power, authority, or intelligence to act alone on important public issues and still make substantial headway against the problems that threaten us all.

J.M. Bryson and B.C. Crosby, *Leadership for the Common Good*

No matter what changes occur in the world of public health, planning activities will continue to occupy much of the work time of public health leaders. Because preparing for the future is part of their mandate, public health leaders must devote substantial energy to strategic thinking, which is basically thinking devoted to the resolution of problems and the achievement of desired goals. Strategic thinking is essential for all varieties of planning, including working out the details of a total quality management (TQM) program, a re-engineering project, or a community partnership scheme. This chapter covers the skills that public health leaders need in order to do the full range of planning that they will be responsible for over the next few decades.

COMMUNITY HEALTH PLANNING

As noted, public health leaders work at many different levels, including the community level. Community health planning involves the development of public health goals and objectives and the ordering of the actions necessary to accomplish these. In this type of planning, it is important, first, to use an approach that is able to generate innovative public health strategies and, second, to keep in mind the core functions, organizational practices, and essential services of public health for guidance.

Planning is a form of rational decision making.[1] The first step in the process is to decide on goals and objectives. The next step is to determine the constraints on the planning process and the likely changes in the environment that may affect how easy the goals and objectives are to achieve. The third step is to figure out what actions, policies, and programs to implement. A good strategy at this stage is to develop a series of outcome scenarios so that those engaged in the planning have several options to choose from.[2] Note that even if a plan is a good one—that is, its implementation will lead to the achievement of the desired goals and objectives—leaders must remain constantly aware of factors that may undermine the implementation process and sometime will have to modify their activities as a result of unexpected happenings.

Planning is often viewed as a routine task and something that managers do rather than leaders. It has routine aspects to it, but planning, especially strategic planning, must ultimately be driven by the big picture—the leaders' vision of the future. Therefore, leaders need to remain intimately involved in the planning process.

The planning process can be formal or informal. Formal planning leaves a paper trail, for all critical decisions are documented, whereas informal planning is less organized and more guided by social interaction.

Planning, although time consuming, is almost never a waste of time. It gives structure to the activities that are directed toward achieving desired goals and may also save money by encouraging the monitoring of these activities. Planning does not eliminate change but rather fosters change. It can also foster flexibility in the implementation process, although it has the potential, if done poorly, to act in the opposite way and hinder flexibility.

In public health, planning was not common until the 1920s.[3] The increase in the funds devoted to public health over the years has created a need to plan for and be accountable for the expenditure of the funds. In the mid-1960s, Congress passed a comprehensive health planning act (P.L. 89–749), which required states and local areas to be involved in planning activities. The reasoning was that public health is the responsibility of state and local entities. The act did not work as well as expected. The development of health service agencies (HSAs) led to a duplication of activity. Many local health department leaders, even those involved in HSA activities, believed that the local public health agency should be doing the health planning. With the end of federal funding for HSAs in the 1980s, state and local public health agencies reabsorbed planning into their program portfolios.

Community health planning is key to the promotion of public health services.[4] Planning activities should use epidemiologic data and be community based in the sense that they integrate public and private interests for the benefit of the residents. Public health leaders should include community partners in the planning process, and the plans developed should encompass all segments of the community.

Roher describes three planning models that are typically used in the field of public health.[5] The rational planning model encompasses "fact finding, problem definition, goal setting, implementation, monitoring, feedback, and evaluation." This model is generally applied to planning directed toward reforming the internal operations of an agency. The community development model is empowerment oriented and promotes local citizen participation in planning activities. Decisions are reached by consensus. The activist model is applicable when community groups threatened by a particular public health danger become mobilized. These models are limited in value. The strategic-planning approach discussed in the next section has the advantage that it applies to both organizational reform and community health planning.

As discussed in Chapter 6, assessment is a prerequisite for planning, although assessment and planning activities are typically ongoing. The gathering of assessment data informs public health leaders about community needs that should be addressed immediately, and they can thus direct their planning activities at developing policies and programs to respond to these needs. Once the programs and policies are in place, their effectiveness should be evaluated, and if they are found to be less effective than expected, the leaders could then engage in further planning in order to improve them (Figure 10–1).

Public health leaders must

- use the core functions, organizational practices, and essential services of public health as a foundation for community health planning
- learn how to use the different planning methodologies and how to choose the appropriate model for a given initiative
- determine the actions necessary to achieve desired community health goals and objectives
- use premising and scenario building to discover innovative public health strategies
- be involved in formal planning activities
- create community partnerships to carry out planning activities

STRATEGIC PLANNING

The relationship between strategies and tactics is similar to that between goals and objectives. Both goals and objectives are ends or desired states of affairs. One difference is that goals tend to be broad in scope and objectives relatively less so. Another is that objectives are ends that are sought largely because they lead to the achievement of goals. Improving the level of health in a community is a good example of a goal. Relative to this goal, testing the community's water supply

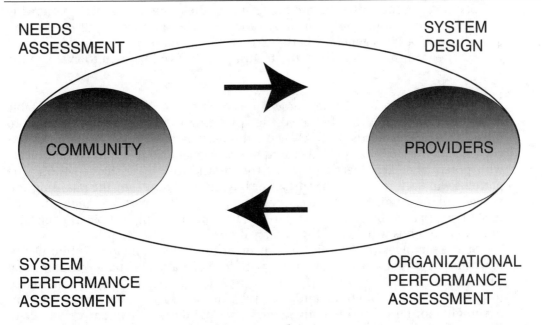

NEEDS ASSESSMENT

SYSTEM DESIGN

COMMUNITY

PROVIDERS

SYSTEM PERFORMANCE ASSESSMENT

ORGANIZATIONAL PERFORMANCE ASSESSMENT

Figure 10–1 Community-oriented health systems planning.

might be one objective. Note that it is relatively narrower in scope and would be one step on the way to achieving the goal.

Strategies are plans or methods that are relatively broad in scope, are often long term in nature, and often involve a significant expenditure of resources. Tactics are methods that are relatively narrow in scope and use relatively few resources. Roughly speaking, strategies are likely to be used in attaining goals, whereas tactics are likely to be used in attaining objectives. (Be warned that there is some looseness in the use of these terms and that many people employ *goal* and *objective* as synonyms and *strategy* and *tactic* as near synonyms.)

Strategic planning is planning directed at the achievement of goals—significant or even ultimate ends. As such, it is an extremely important task and falls largely on the shoulders of the leadership. Below is a list of strategic-planning guidelines and a 10-step strategic-planning model. As in the case of any major task, those responsible for completing the task should remain upbeat in order to motivate others involved to do their share. First, the guidelines:

1. Strategic planning is a team process in which the team members need to share the leader's vision. The team members also need to be carefully selected and represent all parts of the organization. The leader needs to be clear about the responsibilities of the team and may want to convene a community advisory board to discuss how the plan meets the health needs of the community.
2. The team needs to set a timeline for the planning process. The process should be short enough to devise a plan and implement it before events have rendered it irrelevant.
3. The team needs to consider how to get the plan accepted after the planning process.
4. The team needs to create a schedule for the planning process.
5. The team must disseminate the results of the process—the plan—following its completion. The team must carefully determine what will be disseminated, but it is generally better to disseminate more rather than less.
6. The team must decide on the techniques that will be used to evaluate the process.[6]

Bryson developed a 10-step procedure for strategic planning (see also Table 10–1).[7] The first step could be called the "planning to plan" stage.[8] According to Bryson, the leader needs to be clear on the reasons that strategic planning was chosen rather than some other technique. The leader also needs to communicate with potential stakeholders and to lay the groundwork for a shared vision. The partners will want to know what they are "buying" and how long the planning and implementation process will take. Bryson suggested that partners might do well to start the process by going on a retreat. Strategic planning can be an expensive process, and funds will be needed to carry it out.

Step 2 involves the clarification of organizational mandates. Public health practitioners are constantly bombarded with formal mandates that take substantial time to abide by. Not only that, public health agencies are legally mandated to perform certain functions and are given funds to carry these functions out but might not be funded to implement other public health initiatives closer to the mission of public health as defined by the local health department and the

Table 10–1 Bryson Strategic Planning Model Applied to Public Health

Bryson Model	Public Health Core Functions	Organizational Practices	Essential Services	System Activities
Initiation and agreement on a strategic-planning process	Policy development	Constituency building	Mobilization of community partnerships to identify and solve health problems	Coalition building and values clarification
Identification and clarification of the nature/ meaning of externally imposed formal and informal mandates	Policy development and assurance	Evaluation of programs in accordance with plans and policies	Enforcement of laws and regulations that protect health and ensure safety	Values clarification
Clarification of organizational mission and values	Policy development	Not applicable	Not applicable	Values clarification and mission and vision development
Assessment of the organization's external and internal environments to identify strengths, weaknesses, opportunities, and threats	Assessment	Assessment of health needs of the community Investigation of the occurrence of health effects and health hazards	Monitoring of health status to identify community health problems Diagnosis and investigation of health problems and health hazards in the community	Vision and goals and objectives development (based on assessment data)
Identification of the strategic issues facing the organization	Policy development and assessment	Analysis of the determinants of identified health needs Setting of priorities among health needs	Development of policies and plans that support individual and community health efforts	Development of goals and objectives and action plans
Formulation of strategies to manage these issues	Policy development	Development of plans and policies to address priority health needs	Development of policies and plans that support individual and community health efforts	Action planning

continues

Table 10–1 continued

Bryson Model	Public Health Core Functions	Organizational Practices	Essential Services	System Activities
Review and adoption of the strategic plan or plans	Policy development	Management of resources and development of organizational structure	Not applicable	Action planning
Establishment of an effective organizational vision	Policy development	Not applicable	Not applicable	Vision development
Development of an effective implementation process	Assurance	Management of resources and development of organizational structure Education of the public	Linkage of people to needed personal health services and assurance of the provision of health care when otherwise unavailable	Action plan development and implementation
Reassessment of strategies and the strategic-planning process	Assessment, policy development, and assurance	Evaluation of programs and performance of quality assurance activities	Evaluation of the effectiveness, accessibility, and quality of personal and population-based health services Research on new insights and innovative solutions to health problems	Evaluation using the systems perspective

community stakeholders. Stakeholders are persons or organizations that have an interest in public health programs and how they are implemented. They include concerned citizens, government representatives, other health and social service representatives, governing board members, church representatives, and members of professional associations.

It is critical to include the appropriate stakeholders in strategic planning. For example, major community employers, unions, regulatory or licensing agencies, bankers, and neighbors of the agency are often excluded from community coalitions despite the fact that they can prevent decisions from being implemented.[9] In general, stakeholders expect the agency and its leadership to be responsive to their needs and can even issue what might be called informal mandates. If the agency does not respond to these informal mandates, the stakeholders will look elsewhere for support. The local public health agency must determine whether the formal mandates prevent addressing the informal mandates. Several local public health administrators interviewed by the author said that responding to the formal mandates in their state took almost 90 percent of their agency's time. Creating innovative programs became virtually impossible because of the lack of time.

In step 3, agency leaders begin to investigate the values that will govern the agency and the agency's community relationships. The agency's mission should refer to its role in the community. By going through the values clarification process and developing a mission, the agency will be in a better position to monitor the strategic-planning process. This step might include the performance of a stakeholder analysis, which will clarify who the stakeholders are, what their values are, what their goals and objectives are, what issues are likely to affect them, and what their degree of commitment is to the status quo.

The fourth step involves the assessment of the internal and external environments in order to identify the opportunities and the challenges arising from the change process.[10] This has been referred to as a SWOT analysis, for it focuses on strengths, weaknesses, opportunities, and threats. The external assessment looks at forces that may impact agency programs, whether at the local, state, federal, or even global level. For example, diseases or disease-causing agents that originate in one portion of the globe may eventually spread to all other parts, as did the human immunodeficiency virus.[11] The analysis should include key stakeholders who have an agenda that they wish to see implemented and major competitors, such as local managed care organizations (who may want to take over public health roles and responsibilities). Assessing external forces should be an ongoing activity and not be limited to one step in the strategic-planning process.[12]

The internal assessment looks at the agency's resources, the process of carrying out the agency activities, and the performance outputs. Part 1 of the Assessment Protocol for Excellence in Public Health, described in Chapter 6, is an assessment of an organization's internal capacity.

The collection of information, the clarification of values, the development of a mission, and the assessment of the agency and its environment provide the foundation for the rest of the strategic-planning process. Step 5 is the identification of the issues to be addressed by the plan. In this stage, the stakeholders typically come together to define the issues utilizing a group process approach. The stakeholders need not only to identify the critical issues but also to explain why these issues are critical and to describe what the consequences of not addressing these issues will be.

Another approach to completing this step is to begin by defining goals and objectives and then develop issues based on the goals and objectives. Still another approach is for the partners in the strategic-planning process to devise ideal scenarios (descriptions of the way they would like the world to be) and present them to each other and try to come to a consensus. One problem with scenario building is that it is a complex process and requires the participants to be trained in how to create scenarios.[13] Without proper training, the participants may not be able to get results that are valid. In a fourth approach, the strategic-planning team tries to facilitate the formulation of issues by slowly guiding the stakeholders through the process.

Step 6 involves the development of strategies to address the issues delineated in step 5. In short, it is during this step that the strategic plan is actually devised.

Possible strategies include the setting of new policies or new rules and regulations, the development of new programs and services, and changes in the allocation of resources. The stakeholders need to determine how the chosen strategies interrelate and thus how the whole system works. Some strategies might involve both the agency and the community, some might involve just the agency or just agency subdivisions, and some might involve agency programs and services.

In step 7, the stakeholders review, modify, and adopt the strategic plan developed in step 6. Here, as in steps 5 and 6, they must consider the actions that will be necessary to carry out the plan. The plan in a sense consists of actions that are intended to achieve the goals and objectives identified by the stakeholders early in the planning process.

Step 8 is the creation or revision of the organizational vision. Strategic planning may lead to changes that impact the vision, and thus visioning is tied to each step of the strategic-planning process. In point of fact, the vision need not be fully determined early on but can be left to evolve during several cycles of this process.[14] The vision should grow out of an integration of past accomplishments and perceptions of the future. The vision also needs to provide inspiration to other stakeholders. However, the agency's mission tends to drive the strategic-planning process more than does the vision.[15]

Step 9 is the implementation of the plan. In prior steps, while developing the plan, the stakeholders need to define their roles in the implementation process. They also should try to ensure that accomplishments, even if small ones, will occur early in the process. Success tends to foster success, for the stakeholders will remain motivated and undiscouraged if they see progress. The stakeholders need to allocate the necessary resources before the implementation process begins. As changes are made, the agency and the other stakeholders need to adjust accordingly and monitor the effects of the changes over time.

Step 10 involves monitoring the implementation and making necessary mid-course corrections.

Each of the 10 steps of the Bryson model is related to one of the three core public health functions (assessment, policy development, and assurance). The model is in fact compatible with the systems approach to public health leadership shown in Figure 5–3, and all of the activities in this approach, which is based on the core functions of public health, are included in the Bryson model. The relationships between the model and the organizational practices and essential services of public health are more tenuous. For example, visioning is not included in typical lists of such practices and services.

As regards strategic planning, public health leaders must

- learn the benefits of such planning
- perform a stakeholder analysis
- expand the strategic-planning process to include stakeholders in the community
- remain optimistic during the strategic-planning process as a means of motivating other participants
- do the necessary homework to prepare for each successive step of the strategic-planning process
- be realistic about what is possible
- perform an assessment of organizational capacity

Exercise 10–1 is intended to give students a chance to use or develop their strategic-planning skills. The task is to use strategic thinking in the planning of a community education program designed to inform the public of the advantages of empowerment and community coalitions. An additional perspective can be seen in Case Study 10–A which explores the issues raised in border health disputes when strategic processes vary in two different countries.

CONTINUOUS QUALITY IMPROVEMENT

Whereas strategic planning is a process that can be analyzed into a number of specific steps, continuous quality improvement (CQI) involves accepting a whole new philosophy of doing business or providing services. Public health organizations have been slow to adopt CQI methods, and where they have done so, they have not had great success.[16] Part of the explanation for the lack of success is that public health leaders have not kept up with the developments in the field of CQI. In studying public health clinics in California, Scutchfield and his colleagues found that less than 20 percent of the agencies performed CQI activities.[17] They also found that public health leaders were often unclear when it was appropriate to use specific tools.

Public health agencies have a reputation for providing mediocre service. One problem obstructing the improvement of service is that federal and state funding for new public health programs has been shrinking. Another is that government rules and regulations, as well as union rules, put obstacles in the way of delivering services in a timely fashion. A third problem is that public health leaders often misinterpret quality assurance as a type of CQI. *Improving* quality is more than an assurance issue, and it depends on viewing the public health consumer as entitled to the best that public health professionals have to offer. It requires, in other words, a whole change in philosophy.

The focus of CQI activities in a public health agency is on improving service provision and enhancing relationships with external stakeholders.[18] These activities are based on information about the public health issues to be addressed, the strengths and weaknesses of the public health agency, and stakeholder concerns.

To improve service provision, public health leaders need to utilize a systems perspective, promote a client orientation,[19] and engage in strategic thinking. Some public health leaders have found that they can integrate strategic-planning approaches and CQI, especially if one of the strategic goals of the agency is to improve the quality of service.

CQI is closely related to another management methodology called *total quality management (TQM)*, and in fact the terms *continuous quality improvement* and *total quality management* are often used interchangeably.[20] They will be treated as synonymous here, and the term that appears in each instance below will be the term used by the particular author (or authors) under discussion.

TQM is based on the philosophy of total quality control, first promoted by Feigenbaum.[21] According to Sashkin and Kiser, TQM uses an evolving methodologic toolkit that includes all sorts of ways of measuring quality. The two main principles are that the focus of the organization must be on the customer and that everybody in the organization, not just the leadership, must be committed to quality. In their words, "TQM means that the organization's culture is defined by and supports the constant attainment of customer satisfaction through an integrated system of tools, techniques, and training. This involves the continuous improvement of organizational processes, resulting in high quality products and services."[22(p.39)]

CQI Models

Five names are tied to the CQI movement: Shewhart, Deming, Crosby, Juran, and Feigenbaum. Shewhart demonstrated that statistical control is critical in CQI activities.[23] Deming, the best known of the CQI theorists, in the 1950s had to go to Japan to test his ideas about quality. To publicize his ideas, he devised a 14-point set of principles (Exhibit 10–1). The focus of these principles is on training the work force and fostering a total commitment to quality. As Deming was aware, each customer wants high-quality products and services and evaluates the quality

---

Exhibit 10–1 Deming's 14 Points

1. Create constancy of purpose toward improvement of product and service with the aim to become competitive and to stay in business and to provide jobs.
2. Adopt the new philosophy. We are in a new economic age. Western management must awaken to the challenge, must learn their responsibilities, and take on leadership for change.
3. Cease dependence on inspection to achieve quality. Eliminate the need for inspection on a mass basis by building quality into the product or service in the first place.
4. End the practice of awarding business on the basis of price tag. Instead minimize total costs. Move toward a single supplier for any one item on a long-term relationship of loyalty and trust.
5. Improve constantly and forever the system of production and service to improve quality and productivity and thus decrease costs.
6. Institute training on the job.
7. Institute leadership. The aim of leadership should be to help people and machines and gadgets to do a better job. Leadership of management is in need of overhaul as well as leadership of production workers.
8. Drive out fear so that everyone may work effectively for the company.
9. Break down barriers between departments. People in research, design, sales, and production must work as a team to foresee problems of production and use that may be encountered with the product or service.
10. Eliminate slogans, exhortations, and targets for the work force asking for zero defects and new levels of production.
11. Eliminate work standards (quotas) in the organization. Eliminate management by objectives. Eliminate management by numbers, numeric goals. Substitute leadership.
12. Remove barriers that rob the hourly worker of rights to pride of workmanship. The responsibility of supervisors must be changed from sheer numbers to quality. Remove barriers that rob people in management and engineering of their right to pride of workmanship. Abolish annual or merit rating and M.B.O.
13. Institute a vigorous program of education and self-improvement.
14. Put everybody to work to accomplish the transformation.

of products and services received. Deming also developed the PDCA (planning, doing, checking, acting) cycle.[24]

Crosby argued that the only way to improve quality is to demand zero defects and refuse to accept anything less.[25] After all, customers define quality, and, in the business world, dissatisfied consumers will stop buying defective products. The public health customer, however, has limited service choices and will grudgingly accept less than the best, so it is up to public health leaders to empower their communities and make sure that high-quality standards are maintained. Public health leaders also need to gain support for the CQI approach from both internal and external stakeholders and must be prepared to cope with resistance.

CQI requires total commitment and involvement.[26] Crosby outlined a 14-step process for implementing TQM in organizations.[27,28] The process starts with a commitment by the leadership to the pursuit of quality and all that this entails. Most of the steps involve the core functions of policy development and assurance. There is only one step in which assessment plays the major role.

The Crosby model applies to intraorganizational change, whereas the kind of assessment public health agencies must perform encompasses both internal operations and community needs. The focus on intraorganizational change is a characteristic of the Deming model as well (Exhibit 10–1). Note, however, that, in the case of a public health agency, an assessment of community needs provides critical data for determining what intraorganizational changes are required and for integrating complex systems of health care in order to provide high-quality programming.

The fourth theoretician in the quality revolution is Joseph M. Juran. Juran pointed out that quality does not occur by chance.[29] It requires a planned process that encompasses planning, quality control, and quality improvement (known as the Juran trilogy). Juran also believed that leaders need to organize information for the purpose of monitoring the process. Finally, Feigenbaum held that quality is involved in every activity of an organization, from direct service activities to marketing and finance, and that an organization must determine the cost of quality improvement programs before embarking on them.[30]

Building on the work of the founders of the TQM approach, Creech identified what he called the five pillars of TQM: product (service), process, organization, leadership, and commitment.[31] According to Creech, TQM has been more effective in Japan than in the United States because Japanese businesses seem to accept the concept of quality more readily than American businesses do. Creech has further pointed out that TQM is an organizational philosophy and cannot deliver full benefits without complete organizational acceptance. In order to put the five pillars into perspective, Creech formulated 16 guidelines for the TQM process (Exhibit 10–2).

Figure 10–2 shows that organization is the central pillar of the five. How the organization is perceived and what its cultural orientation is will have an impact on the implementation and consequences of TQM. Also, whereas centralization has been the traditional management approach, decentralization appears to be better suited to TQM. Consequently, multidisciplinary teams play an important role. As Figure 10–2 shows, one of the pillars is leadership. As indicated by the comment about decentralization, the leaders of the organization must be willing to share their power.

Exhibit 10–2 Creech Guidelines for Five-Pillars TQM

1. Build your TQM approach, and its principles, on five system pillars.
2. Firmly establish the character and culture of your organization.
3. Use a decentralized, interactive system that integrates all levels.
4. Organization is the central pillar—it influences everything else.
5. Base the structural building blocks on small teams and not big functions.
6. Orient employees' focus and activity to their product, not their job.
7. Place the prime leadership focus on the outputs, not the inputs.
8. Keep score, assess, and provide timely feedback to one and all.
9. Know your marketplace inside out and create strong customer linkage.
10. Provide a climate of quality that promotes pride and professionalism.
11. Base any and all decisions on the inseparability of cost and value.
12. Provide detailed, focused training to employees at every level.
13. Give high priority and pay great attention to the communication flow.
14. Work unceasingly to instill common purpose from the bottom to the top.
15. Build the commitment through genuine ownership and shared success.
16. Build your TQM on all five pillars.

Organizational commitment to quality needs to occur at the border between the organization and its environment. If the frontline workers do not buy the quality message, TQM will be doomed to failure. In fact, everyone in the organization needs to make a commitment to quality.

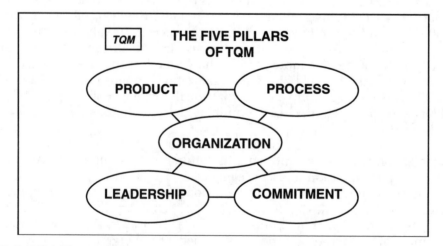

Figure 10–2 TQM: The need, the issues, the shape it must take.

The CQI Toolkit

CQI makes use of a number of tools, including various kinds of charts and diagrams. Traditional tools include

- control charts (for showing the results of statistical process activities)
- Pareto charts (for graphically showing defects or problems over time)
- fishbone diagrams (for tracing cause-and-effect relationships)
- run charts (for displaying trends over time)
- histograms (for showing service patterns at given time periods)
- scatter diagrams (for showing relationships between two factors)
- flowcharts (for showing input-output relationships)[32]

Seven new tools of use in CQI are shown in Figure 10–3 and described below.[33] The first is the affinity diagram, which allows a team to organize ideas and problems into general categories. The team would first sort the items into categories, then list the items in each category in a separate column. Affinity diagrams could be used for clarifying values; for constructing the organization's vision, the mission, and the goals and objectives; and for action and strategic planning. The affinity diagram process, like any group process, is affected by how well the team members get along.

The interrelationship digraph shows the interconnection between ideas, problems, actions, or other types of items. The arrows between the items show the direction of their relationship (e.g., cause to effect). Once a digraph is developed, it can be reworked to show new ways to relate the items. The team will want to simplify the digraph by looking for converging or diverging clusters of arrows. Constructing a digraph is especially useful for deciding on goals and objectives and during the action planning phase.

The third tool, the tree diagram, can be used in many leadership activities. For instance, a tree diagram could be used by the leadership team of a public health agency to map out how the agency's mission is to be fulfilled. The team might start by stating the mission, which, say, is to promote the health of the public and prevent disease. The next step would be to determine the goals and objectives needed to fulfill this mission, and the third step would be to decide on the tasks that must be performed to achieve the chosen goals and objectives. In CQI, the leadership team might use tree diagrams in developing quality improvement plans. In general, the process of creating a tree diagram begins with stating an overall goal (e.g., the agency's mission or an important subsidiary goal) and then breaking the process of achieving the goal into individual steps or tasks.

Prioritization matrices allow the leadership team to prioritize tasks, service activities, community activities, and so on. A prioritization matrix can be used in conjunction with a tree diagram to rank the tasks and responsibilities identified during the tree diagram process. If six activities are projected, the diagram allows the team to see what will happen if any two activities occur together. The team is able to calculate a score for each cell, and where the score falls in relation to the other scores determines the degree of importance of the conjunction of activities.

Brassard suggested that the prioritization process should encompass three steps.[34] The first step is to list and then rank the *criteria* that will be used in

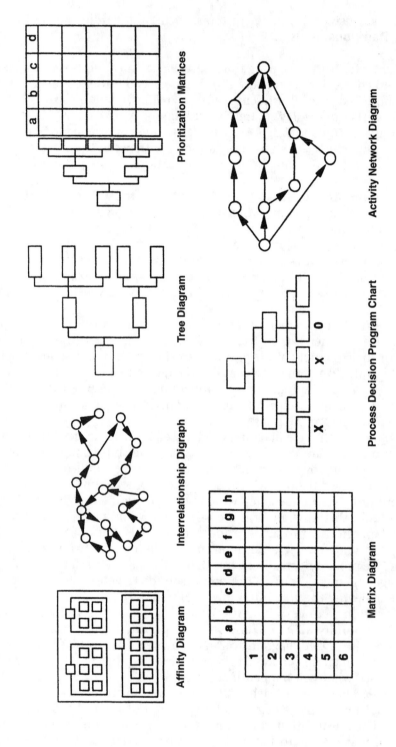

Figure 10–3 Seven Management and Planning Tools.

prioritizing the items (e.g., activities). Such criteria might include the speed of possible implementation, the likely degree of acceptance by staff, the impact on other parts of the agency, the cost, and the technology needed. Once the criteria are chosen, each should be assigned a percentage that reflects its perceived importance (the total of percentages should of course equal 100 percent). In step 2, each item is given a score in relation to each criterion. Finally, the total scores for all the items are calculated, and the results determine the priority ranking of the items.

The fifth tool is the matrix diagram, which allows the leadership team to compare two or more sets of items and explore the strength of the relationship between them.

Process decision program charts allow the leadership team to show probable events and contingencies that might occur as the action plan is implemented. For example, suppose the public health agency director wants to plan how the community will perform health assessment activities. The director might create a chart that shows how the community advisory board is to be selected, when the various activities will occur and how much time they will take, and how they will be carried out. Process decision program charts, like the other tools described here, can also be used to explore options.

The last tool, the activity network diagram, exhibits the schedule for the completion of tasks. This tool is also known as an arrow diagram. Exercise 10–2 provides an opportunity to practice applying the seven CQI tools just described.

CQI requires a total commitment by public health leaders and all their constituencies if it is to be successful. The professional staff of the public health agency must buy into the total quality approach. In order to get staff to do this, public health leaders must

- develop a commitment to quality and best practices
- become educated about CQI
- master the seven CQI tools
- educate the public about CQI
- inspire staff and others to see the value of the CQI approach
- train the public health work force
- integrate strategic-planning techniques and CQI techniques

RE-ENGINEERING

Sometimes an organization cannot be fixed in its present form. If this is the case, the organization must be restructured so that it can make use of new approaches to problem solving and decision making. The restructuring of an organization is often referred to as re-engineering. Manganelli and Klein defined re-engineering as "the rapid and radical redesign of strategic, value-added business processes—and the systems, policies, and organizational structures that support them—to optimize the work flows and productivity in an organization."[35(pp.7–8)]

Imagine a public health agency wants to incorporate bioterrorism interventions into the range of services it is capable of providing. If no new funding is presently available for the project, the agency leadership will look for methods to reorganize the agency and reassign staff to carry out the project. The leaders might not only phase out programs of less relevance but also re-educate the staff to work in different organizational units. This is not as easy a task as it might seem. Barriers to public health re-engineering include objections to the changes by a public employee union or by the board of health.

As Drucker pointed out, knowledge-intensive organizations require continual re-engineering.[36] Therefore, since the 21st century, like the 20th, will undoubtedly be a century of technological advances and new public health concerns, public health agencies will have to redefine and re-engineer themselves on an ongoing basis. Public health leaders will play an essential role in re-engineering projects, for, as pointed out repeatedly, they define their organization's vision and motivate others to share the vision.

To get stakeholders, including governing board members, involved in and committed to re-engineering, leaders must win their trust. Staff members are often wedded to the status quo and will have to be reassured that they will not lose their jobs as a result of the reorganization.[37] Another way to build trust is to include people from all parts of the organization on the re-engineering team. In the case of a local health department, the leaders might recruit community leaders and members of the local board of health to be on the team.

Several additional guidelines should be kept in mind when considering embarking on a re-engineering project. First, the leaders of an agency need to determine the agency's mission and how the re-engineering will increase its chances of fulfilling its mission.[38] If a local public health department is committed to the promotion of health but its activities are hindered by a cumbersome bureaucracy, it should explore re-engineering. Again, unless the legislature, city council, and board of health buy into the process, it will likely be unsuccessful.

Second, the leaders must recognize that the re-engineering process changes the culture as well as the job responsibilities of the staff. Third, they will need to develop new measures to evaluate staff performance and monitor the change process. Fourth, they should mobilize the staff for change and provide staff members with the tools they will need to carry out their re-engineering responsibilities. Fifth, they should define the goals and objectives of re-engineering. Sixth, they should ensure that communication channels exist between all those involved in the re-engineering process.

The leaders who are best qualified to oversee re-engineering projects tend to have a process orientation and a holistic perspective (Exhibit 10–3) and to be comfortable with strategic thinking. They are also creative, find the status quo boring, tend to be enthusiastic and able to motivate others, are persistent and tactful, and are excellent communicators who support teamwork and good interpersonal relations.

In reviewing the best practices of organizations that underwent re-engineering, Carr and Johansson searched for the lessons to be learned.[39] The rules they discovered are listed in Exhibit 10–4.

Manganelli and Klein presented a five-stage model for rapid re-engineering (Figure 10–4).[40] In the first stage, the leaders recognize there is a need for organizational change, foster a consensus among staff that such a need exists, clarify the mission of the organization, select and train a re-engineering team, and develop a plan to guide the re-engineering process (action plan). In stage 2, the leaders create a consumer-focused model for the organization, determine who the stakeholders are, and involve them in the re-engineering process. In stage 3, the leaders develop

Exhibit 10–3 Characteristics of a Reengineering Leader

- A process oriented and holistic cognitive style: a facility for seeing the big picture, for distinguishing trees from forests, for understanding how tasks fit together to form a process and how process designs and organizational designs fit together to form a business.
- Design skills: the facility both to envision a new way of doing things and then to flesh it out, turning it from a concept into something that can actually be implemented.
- An inclination toward change that borders on restlessness: a congenital inability to accept things as they are, and a determination to find what lies over the rainbow.
- Enthusiasm and optimism: the internal fortitude to keep going despite the slings and arrows of outraged constituencies and despite the fact that it often seems as though the light at the end of the tunnel is an oncoming train.
- Persistence and tact: the ability to keep pushing despite the fact that people are pushing back at you and eventually to wear them down and convert them to your point of view.
- Interpersonal, teamwork, and communication skills: the ability to work as part of a tightly woven team, the patience to listen to the needs, fears, and concerns of everyone who will be affected by reengineering, and the talent to craft messages that will induce them to accept unpalatable truths and their consequences.

a realistic vision based on current process performance activities and on projections of where the organization is headed.

In stage 4, a re-engineering plan tied to the vision is developed. Technical design issues are addressed in the first part (stage 4A), and social design issues are addressed in the second (stage 4B). Finally, the implementation of the new organizational model occurs during stage 5.

Public health leaders must be committed to restructuring the agency if substantial changes are necessary for it to carry out its mission. They must, therefore,

- learn to distinguish between re-engineering, strategic planning, and continuous quality improvement
- master new approaches to organizational improvement
- improve relationships with key stakeholders
- work closely with the re-engineering team
- master the five-stage rapid re-engineering model

REINVENTING GOVERNMENT

The last few years have seen an increase in public discussions about the structure and function of government. Some have argued that the old ways of governing do not work any longer[41] and that the public sector must keep open the option of employing entrepreneurial techniques from the business sector. *Reinvention* is the term used to describe the use of entrepreneurial techniques by those in the public sector. Osborne and Plastrik defined reinvention as "the fundamental transformation of public systems and organizations to create dramatic increases in their effectiveness, efficiency, adaptability, and capacity to innovate. This transformation is accomplished by changing their purpose, incentives, accountability, power structure, and culture."[42(pp.13–14)]

Exhibit 10–4 Re-engineering Principles

1. Recognize and articulate an "extremely compelling" need to change.
2. Start with and maintain executive-level support.
3. Understand the organization's "readiness to change."
4. Communicate effectively to create buy-in. Then communicate more.
5. Instill in the organization a "readiness and commitment" to sustained change.
6. Stay actively involved.
7. Create top-notch teams.
8. Use a structure framework.
9. Use consultants effectively.
10. Pay attention to what has worked.
11. Link goals to corporate strategy.
12. Listen to the "voice of the customer."
13. Select the right processes for re-engineering.
14. Maintain focus: Don't try to reengineer too many processes.
15. Create an explicit vision of each process to be re-engineered.
16. Maintain teams as the key vehicle for change.
17. Quickly come to an as-is understanding of the processes to be re-engineered.
18. Choose and use the right metrics.
19. Create an environment conducive to creativity and innovation.
20. Take advantage of modeling and simulation tools.
21. Understand the risks and develop contingency plans.
22. Have plans for continuous improvement.
23. Align the infrastructure.
24. Position IT as an enabler, even if the extent of the IT change necessary is great.

Reinvention of government became more common during the 1990s and was seen as less radical than originally believed.[43] It involves strategies such as tying rewards to performance, listening to and being accountable to community consumers, making organizations less hierarchical and more decentralized, and empowering staff to make decisions and influence work processes.

For reinvention to work, it needs to be seen as more than a patching operation. It must involve a significant restructuring of organizations, a rethinking of the activities and mission of the organization, and an abandonment of old models that no longer work. Also necessary is the reformation of the relationship between government entities and community-based organizations.[44] For one thing, bureaucracy seems to get in the way of reinvention activities.

As for reinvention in the public health arena, it has been predicted that, during the next decade, the urgency of dealing with public health issues, including community violence, will force public health agencies to develop innovative programs capable of being funded.[45] Funding itself is an issue that may motivate reinvention efforts. The decrease in money available for local public health agencies means that the agencies have to become more efficient. Public health agencies also seem to be struggling with their identity. The general public and many public health professionals think that public health programs are only for the poor, and traditional public health activities are being taken over by the private managed care sector.

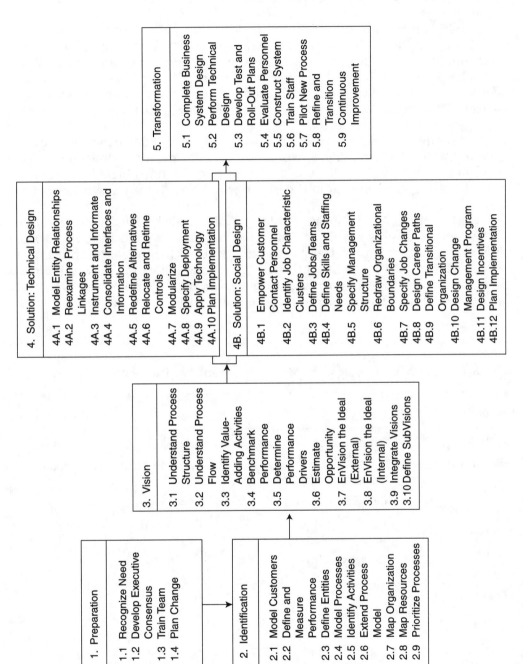

Figure 10-4 Stages and tasks.

Other traditional public health activities are being transferred to other types of agencies. Despite this, public health leaders seem reticent to lobby for the public health agenda.

Public health leaders must act as advocates for public health in the debate over the appropriate roles for government agencies. They have the responsibility to ensure that public health is practiced in schools, managed care organizations, and other venues in the public and private sectors. The real goal of public health re-engineering should be to create in each community an integrated health care system that increases access to health-related services so that no one is prevented from getting needed services.

According to Bacon, reinvention of government should encompass capacity building, work force training, performance monitoring, and public and private collaboration.[46] Exhibit 10–5 contains lists of recommended ingredients for reinvented government culled from three sources (the fourth list is a synthesis of the other three lists).

During the early 1990s, Vice President Gore headed a national performance review whose mission was to find out how to make government agencies more effective and less expensive. Every office and agency of the federal government was examined. Exhibit 10–6 presents the principles that guided the review. The goals were to cut spending while serving customers better and empowering employees and communities. The means to achieve these goals, listed in the second part

Exhibit 10–5 Recommended Ingredients for More Effective and Efficient Government

Osborne / Gaebler[1]	NCSLPS[2]	Thompson[3]	Synthesis
Catalytic	Strong executive leadership	Leadership	Capacity building
Community-owned		Productive work force	High performance
Competitive	Lean, responsive		Leadership
Mission-driven	High-performance work force	Information management	Public / private cooperation
Results-oriented		Public / private networks	Fiscal stability
Enterprising	Citizen involvement		
Anticipatory	Fiscal stability	Fiscal reform	
Decentralized			
Market-oriented			

[1]D. Osborne and T. Gaebler, *Reinventing Government: How the Entrepreneurial Spirit Is Transforming the Public Sector* (Reading, MA: Addison-Wesley, 1992).

[2]The National Commission on the State and Local Public Service, *Hard Truths/Tough Choices: An Agenda for State and Local Reform* (Albany, NY: Nelson A. Rockefeller Institute of Government, 1993).

[3]F.J. Thompson, ed., *Revitalizing State and Local Public Service: Strengthening Performance, Accountability and Citizen Confidence* (San Francisco: Jossey-Bass, 1993).

Exhibit 10–6 Principles of the National Performance Review

We will invent a government that puts people first, by:

- Cutting unnecessary spending
- Serving its customers
- Empowering its employees
- Helping communities solve their own problems
- Fostering excellence

Here's how. We will:

- Create a clear sense of mission
- Steer more, row less
- Delegate authority and responsibility
- Replace regulations with incentives
- Develop budgets based on outcomes
- Expose federal operations to competition
- Search for market, not administrative, solutions
- Measure our success by customer satisfaction

of the exhibit, include creating a clear sense of mission, delegating authority and responsibility, replacing regulations with incentives, and fostering competition. Exhibit 10–7 contains National Performance Review recommendations for the Health Care Financing Administration, Department of Health and Human Services.

Despite the findings of the National Performance Review, Congress has not passed enabling legislation to help implement the recommendations.[47] Bureaucracy, including the civil service system and the federal budgeting system, has to be streamlined, and by means of appropriate legislation this goal can be achieved. For instance, the Health Care Financing Administration has seen a tremendous increase in its health care responsibilities over the last four decades, yet the organization as a whole has not grown substantially. This proves that government agencies can become more effective without major staff increases.

Local public health departments, too, need to be creative in their utilization of resources. For example, some local agencies, required to perform state nursing home inspections, have been burdened with additional responsibilities. A reinvention process could address the drain on resources caused by inspections through innovative techniques and collaboration between agencies.

Reinvention should not be confused with internal reform or downsizing.[48] Its goal is change in the social and organizational fabric of a community, and its methods are entrepreneurial and self-renewing. Osborne and Plastrik likened the changes brought about by reinvention to changes in the DNA of government. They suggested there were five key strategies to reinventing government, the five C's, as they called them: the core strategy, the consequences strategy, the customer

Exhibit 10–7 National Performance Review Standards for the Health Care Financing Administration

Health Care Financing Administration manages the Medicare and Medicaid programs.

Written responses:

- We will answer your written inquiries within 30 days of receipt. If getting you an accurate answer will take longer, we will keep you informed.

Telephone standards:

- We will respond to your telephone inquiries in a pleasant and helpful manner. We will provide an immediate answer whenever possible. If we cannot provide an immediate answer, we will give you a firm commitment as to when an answer can be provided.
- Nobody likes to be put on hold. Our standard is that callers will be "on hold" for no more than two minutes.
- Calls made in off hours will be returned the next business day.

Information needs:

- We are asking our customers to help us improve all of our publications and notices so they can be understood by our customers. We will begin using new publications and notices beginning early next year.

Claims processing (Medicare):

- We are currently working hard to simplify our claims processing system to provide you with more consistent determinations.
- We will process your claims for service accurately and within the times provided for in the law.
- If you are not satisfied with the action we take on your claim, you can appeal and we will process your appeal fairly, accurately, and within established time frames. We are working to reduce the paperwork burden associated with appeals.

Customer satisfaction:

- We will measure your satisfaction with Medicare and Medicaid through the use of customer surveys, focus groups, public comments, and meetings with customer representatives.
- We are setting up groups of customers who volunteer to give us assistance in setting standards and evaluating our performance.
- We will identify customers who have special needs related to vision, hearing, mobility, health status, literacy, language, and other factors. We will make a special effort to help these customers with access to services and information.

Health care choices:

- We will provide clear, understandable information about the options our customers have in choosing a managed health care plan, including information about individual plans, to assist them in making health care decisions.

continues

Exhibit 10–7 continued

Medicaid special standard:

- We will encourage all states to establish customer service standards for Medicaid, and we will work with them to assure a goal of continuous improvement in customer service and program administration.

Health care quality:

- We will provide doctors and hospitals with information they can use to give better care to our beneficiaries, and we will monitor the effect of those activities.
- We will expedite our investigative and case review process as much as the law will permit when a complaint involves quality issues.
- We will respond to verbal or written complaints from beneficiaries or their representatives by mailing a complaint form to them within two working days of the telephone contact or responding in writing to written beneficiary complaints within 10 working days.

Program administration:

- We will fully investigate all leads about potential program fraud and abuse in order to protect against unnecessary expenditures.
- We will work with our partners, our agents, states, other interested parties, and our customers to identify and implement creative and effective approaches to improving our programs and our performance.

strategy, the control strategy, and the culture strategy (Table 10–2). Note that a cookbook approach to reinvention is not really possible, since each community and each government agency is different.

It is increasingly clear that traditional concepts of community are no longer relevant. As a consequence, community must be reinvented. In any actual community, community values must be clarified and redefined, key community stakeholders must be identified and empowered, and social structures and organizations that are consistent with the new values must be put into place. Once a community knows its values and its assets, it can tackle its problems, and thus a community assessment directed toward documenting community assets is another essential element of the reinvention process.

Public health agencies are not the only organizations that will address the public health needs of the community. Community reinvention should include creation of a partnership between all health care and public health stakeholders—a partnership in which all players are equal. In addition, the partners must work with other community stakeholders to ensure public health needs are met. Thus, reinvention demands strategy and communication at many levels if it is to work.

Reinvention calls for new concepts of leadership. First, leadership must be shared among members of community teams. Secondly, community stakeholders must be empowered. With empowerment, people become free to influence their own future. Yet, for empowerment to occur, people need to be informed about their options and be provided with the skills needed to exercise these options. In

Table 10–2 The Five C's: Changing Government's DNA

Lever	Strategy	Approaches
Purpose	Core strategy	Clarity of purpose Clarity of role Clarity of direction
Incentives	Consequences strategy	Managed competition Enterprise management Performance management
Accountability	Customer strategy	Customer choice Competitive choice Customer quality assurance
Power	Control strategy	Organizational empowerment Employee empowerment Community empowerment
Culture	Culture strategy	Breaking habits Touching hearts Winning minds

particular, community stakeholders need to be educated about public health and have their leadership skills developed through continuous learning opportunities.

There is more to reinventing community and government than meets the eye. Reinvention provides an opportunity to make constructive changes. The danger is that it can be used to justify funding cuts and downsizing rather than as means of strengthening the community and the public health system. Strategic planning and CQI methods can be combined with reinvention techniques as a way of improving the reinvention process and increasing the chance of success. In a sense, reinvention is a form of strategy, for it involves major medium- and long-term changes in the structure of the community for the improvement of community life.

Public health leaders must

- be prepared to move from a traditional hierarchical organizational structure to an entrepreneurial one (which may still be hierarchical in form)
- use public funds and grants in new ways that increase productivity and efficiency
- create coalitions that support change
- understand the realities of the information age and how they can affect organizational change
- utilize reinvention techniques not only for organizational change but for system change as well
- see reinvention as necessary at the local, state, and federal levels
- empower staff and community partners to share leadership and responsibility for changes that occur
- practice the five C's strategy

PUBLIC-PRIVATE PARTNERSHIPS

A public health agency, although it must lead the way, cannot carry out all the public health activities needed to protect and improve the health of a community. Consequently, it must foster new types of alliances and partnerships, including joint ventures, research sharing, community-based projects and programs, and semi-structured alliances.[49] For example, a local public health agency might contract with a local HMO to provide childhood immunizations at a price that the health maintenance organization (HMO) cannot match—an interesting example of what the business community calls outsourcing.

Because trust is a critical component of any partnership, the public health agency must know both its agenda and the agendas of its partners, whether from the public or private sector. Possible partners include businesses, hospitals and managed care organizations, private health care providers, local community organizations, local community clubs, churches and synagogues, schools, and police and firefighter groups, among others.

A local health leader told the author that a good way to involve the private sector in public health is for public health leaders to become involved in local organizations, such as the Kiwanis or the local chamber of commerce, which will create opportunities for them to network with other leaders on community issues. Public health leaders need to become known in the community if they are to gain credibility. Their goal should be to create an integrated system of care that will provide every resident of the community with the care they need and at the same time to promote a healthy life style among the residents in order to prevent disease.

Public health leaders must

- develop public and private relationships to improve the local community public health system
- share power and responsibility with other community members who have an interest in improving the community's health
- become involved in the activities of the community
- join local community groups and organizations
- act to gain the trust of the community

SUMMARY

The needs of the public are constantly changing, and public health agencies need to respond to the changes. The first step in responding adequately is to develop a plan of action, which is the subject of this chapter.

Leaders learn that creating a vision is not enough; the vision will remain just that without a strategy for making it a reality. Strategic planning, continuous quality improvement, re-engineering, and reinventing government are all useful, individually or jointly, for turning a vision into programs and services. For example, the tools of CQI can be used to monitor the strategic-planning process, and the CQI goal of improved customer service could be a guiding principle. Also, since the methods overlap, public health leaders can create a customized planning methodology that includes pieces from all of them.

Public and private alliances and partnerships are needed at the planning stage as well as at the implementation stage. Developing and maintaining collaborative relationships require leadership skills, and public health leaders must master these skills and the planning skills necessary to formulate strategies for improving the community's health.

Discussion Questions

1. What is strategic planning?
2. What is the relationship between strategies and tactics?
3. What is the relationship between strategies and goals?
4. What roles do an organization's mission and vision play in strategic planning?
5. What are the five pillars of total quality management?
6. What steps are necessary for implementing a continuous quality improvement process in a local health agency?
7. What are some of the tools used in total quality management?
8. What distinguishes re-engineering from other forms of organizational reform?
9. What are the principles of reinventing government?
10. What are some ways to open the door to public-private partnerships?

Exercise 10–1

TRAINING COURSE DEVELOPMENT

Purpose: to use strategic thinking in developing a community education program and in creating a conducive environment for putting together a public health coalition

Key concepts: coalition building, community education plan, empowerment, leadership style, strategic thinking

Procedure: As a homework assignment, each student is given the task of devising a 10-step plan for implementing a community education program. The student is to imagine that he or she has been hired as a consultant by the Burchfield County Health Department. The health department has struggled unsuccessfully to create a coalition to promote public health in the county, which has few residents but many health-related problems. The head of the department, Dr. Hanson, has hired the consultant to devise a 10-step plan for implementing a program intended to educate the public on the advantages of community coalitions and empowerment.

All the students bring in the homework assignment on a designated day. The class is divided into groups of 8–10 members. One group member is assigned the role of the consultant; another, the role of Dr. Hanson, director of the county health department; a third, the role of Professor Alexander, a faculty member at the local university who has applied for a grant to train county residents in the techniques of empowerment; and a fourth, the role of Dr. Cassidy, prospective head of a wellness institute with a strong community education component that Western Health Alliance, an HMO servicing the county, plans to locate in the county. Dr. Hanson invites the consultant, Professor Alexander, and Dr. Cassidy to a 30-minute staff meeting to present and defend the community education plan the consultant has developed. The students playing Dr. Hanson, Professor Alexander, and Dr. Cassidy, since they have all created their own 10-step plans, should be able to offer insightful criticisms of the consultant's plan or make helpful recommendations to improve it. Following the review of the plan, the group should then discuss strategic thinking and its role in devising the plan.

Exercise 10–2

PLANNING TOOLS IN ACTION

Purpose: to explore ways to combine strategic planning tools and continuous quality improvement tools

Key concepts: activity network diagram, affinity diagram, continuous quality improvement, interrelationship diagraph, matrix diagram, prioritization matrix, process decision, progress chart, strategic planning, tree diagram

Procedure: Each team should re-examine the community action plan developed in Exercise 10–1, identifying areas where one or more of the seven planning tools discussed in this chapter could be used to enhance the plan and its acceptance by the community. Discuss the relative advantages and disadvantages of using each planning tool in the creation of the plan. After 30 minutes of discussion, each team should reach consensus on the specific tools to be used in improving the plan and on how these tools are to be applied. A representative from each team should present the rationale and conclusions reached to the full class.

Case Study 10–A

Health Issues at the United States–Cannico Republic Border

Bailus Walker

INTRODUCTION

One of the tasks of public health is to ensure that services necessary to achieve agreed-upon goals are provided. The assurance function does not always entail the direct supervision of needed services but rather their identification and development, their coordination, and oversight of their accessibility and quality.

As the governmental presence in health, public health has the responsibility for ensuring (1) that every community is adequately served by an emergency health services system, by adequate hospitals with prenatal care, and by appropriate environmental health services and (2) that community residents are properly immunized and are provided with services designed to prevent the transmission of infectious diseases and the occurrence or progression of noninfectious diseases and dysfunction as well.

The assurance function today requires that state and local health agencies not only merge the pursuit of comprehensive health services with social and economic goals within state or local boundaries but also recognize the transboundary dimensions of public health challenges and opportunities. Massive amounts of goods, services, and capital and large numbers of people flow across international boundaries each day. At the same time, certain human activities continuously increase the risk of disease, dysfunction, and premature death as well as create unprecedented demands on the health services system.

For example, along the 2,000-mile border between the United States and Cannico, U.S. hospitals report that a third of the emergency admissions are Cannico nationals who cannot afford treatment or other personal health services. The health, social, and economic conditions in one border community raise critical issues for policy makers and health service specialists, administrators, and program managers dedicated to making sure their community is adequately served by a comprehensive public health service system.

BINGO COUNTY

Bingo County is in the southwest section of the state of Pennsylcola. It is on the United States–Cannico border. Bingo City has been the county seat since 1871. The chief employment opportunity in the county is manufacturing. Farm production, timbering, tourism, and military installation are major sources of employment.

Bingo County, which is larger than Massachusetts and Rhode Island combined, covers 9.266 square miles, of which 25 percent are rural. The county includes a population estimated in a special 1990 census to be 1.2 million. Within the county are five incorporated cities: Bingo City (population 669,000), Randolph (101,000), Pickett (94,000), Thompson (78,000), and Edgar (67,000). There are 14 other incorporated towns of less size (with populations ranging from 2,000 to 20,000) and 163,000 people living in unincorporated areas of the county. In the 1990 census, 93.4 percent of the residents were considered urban.

According to the same census, 80.9 percent of the county's population was white, 14.6 percent Hispanic, 3.4 percent black, and 1.1 percent Native American.

Estimates furnished by the Pennsylcola Department of Economic Security in 1990 placed the median family income at approximately $12,100, with 15.8 percent of the population falling below the poverty line. Of the population over age 25, 49.7 percent had completed high school. In December 1990, 9.3 percent of the work force was unemployed.

CANNICO

Within the last five years, the country of Cannico restructured its government, moving from a communist system toward democratization of all aspects of its society, including more liberal migration policies. In the process of this change, Cannico experienced severe social and economic problems. Prices rose and wages fell because the industries no longer received huge allotments of cash from the government for their payroll. Food shortages were pervasive and health services were described by some analysts as "substandard" by U.S. criteria.

There is very little information on demographics and health resources of Cannico because during the upheaval that led to the change in government many valuable records and databases were destroyed. What is clear is that the border with Bingo County has become a favored place of entry for Cannico nationals desiring to get into the United States. This development has been fueled by growth in Cannico's population and shifts in the country's economy.

BINGO COUNTY HEALTH RESOURCES AND SERVICES

There is an estimated 900 primary physicians in Bingo County, and several health maintenance organizations (HMOs) serve the county. The state of Pennsylcola has 8 programs for Medicaid enrollment, each with its own criteria for eligibility. There are 10 privately owned acute-care hospitals with a combined bed capacity of 3,228. Several of the hospitals in the area provide extensive outpatient services, drawing clientele from the entire region. Five hospitals are tertiary care centers.

The mission of the Bingo County Department of Public Health reads as follows: "To provide for the health care of the people and to protect and promote the health of all persons in the county in a professional and effective manner."

The Bingo County Department of Public Health provides a range of services, including disease control, sanitation, food inspection and licensure, screening, and health education. The department provides direct personal health services, including maternal and child health services; nutrition services, including a Women, Infants and Children (WIC) supplemental feeding program; and categorical programs to cope with alcohol and drug abuse. All of the varied activities of the agency are ultimately accountable to the Bingo County health officer, who has statutory responsibility for leadership of the department.

THE COUNTY GOVERNMENT

Bingo County operates under an executive-commission nonpartisan form of government. The executive is entrusted with broad powers and appoints most of the administrative officials and department heads, including the head of the local board of health and the county director of public health.

In the state of Pennsylcola, the local health department operates with decentralized authority in relation to the state department of health. The state's guidance and support are regarded as "moderate."

It is the view of the state policy makers that the Bingo County Department of Public Health has three responsibilities: (1) promotion of personal and community health, (2) maintenance of a healthful environment, and (3) prevention of disease and disability.

BINGO COUNTY DEPARTMENT OF PUBLIC HEALTH PERSONNEL AND SERVICES

In 1990, the Bingo County Department of Public Health had a staff of approximately 1,000 people who provided medical care, social services, environmental health services, and nursing, among other services. Of the 20.5 full-time equivalent (FTE) physician employees, 10 were full-time. Three of these employees had administrative positions. The other 10.5 FTE physicians were part-time physicians engaged in private practice.

The majority of personal health services are delivered through the department's family primary health care program, which operates three health centers. These clinics provide the following services for all age groups:

- promotion and maintenance of health
- prevention of illness and disability
- basic care during acute and chronic phases of illness
- guidance and counseling of individuals and families
- referral to other health care providers and community resources

The department also provides *dental services*. The head of dental services for the Bingo County Department of Public Health, Dr. Bush, DDS, told the Centers for Disease Control (CDC), "By definition our department is the provider of last resort in dental care."

Limited laboratory services are provided for water and food analysis and to support efforts in infection control.

Environmental health services include regulatory services in food sanitation, sanitary nuisances, water quality monitoring, housing and recreational sanitation (e.g., swimming pools and air pollution monitoring). The department also participates in land use planning, including the approval of community development (e.g., housing construction).

The department makes modest use of nurse practitioners; they are classified as public health nurse clinicians. Other personnel include family planning specialists, laboratorians, dentists, environmental health specialists, and veterinarians.

The Bingo County Department of Public Health employs approximately 15 community health services assistants. These workers are from disadvantaged backgrounds, lack formal education, and serve as patient advocates, helping consumers interact with other agencies (e.g., social services) and enroll in appropriate programs (e.g., food stamps).

Because the department has a number of categorical programs, staff members are generally employed by specific programs. This practice constrains, to some extent, staff mobility and departmental flexibility.

Encounter data for a number of the department's major activities are shown in Table 10–A–1.

The total budget for fiscal year 1989 was $26,652,351 (Exhibit 10–A–1). The budget is made up of 12 different state contributions or allocations (each representing separate state laws), federal grant programs, numerous fees, and different local actions. From the revenue of $21,283,954 Bingo budgeted a wide variety of services shown under public health control and regulatory programs.

OTHER ECONOMIC CONSIDERATIONS

The undocumented immigrant population (from Cannico) of Bingo County costs nearly $172 million a year in local government services.

A two-year study conducted by private consultants for the Pennsylcola state auditor general examined the impact of the city's 200,000 illegal immigrants on

Table 10–A–1 Service Encounters (1989–1990)

Program	Number of Encounters
Communicable Disease	52,172
Immunizations	10,966
Venereal Disease	15,229
Chronic Disease	2,000
Multiphasic Screening	1,109
Well-Child Conference	5,063
Prenatal Classes Attended	6,784
Family Planning	21,000
Environmental Health Inspection	19,000

Exhibit 10–A–1 Bingo County Department of Public Health Budget

General Revenue Funds (State)

General	$6,330,294
AIDS Patient Care	379,000
School Health	205,198
Improved Pregnancy Outcome	667,513

Federal Funds

Family Planning	$240,136
Child Health	33,610
AIDS	129,199
Hypertension	37,041
Nutrition Program Administration	250,000
EPA Grants	128,300
Child Health Improvement Program	50,000
Sterilization	11,337
AIDS Testing and Counseling	31,891

Fees

For Enforcement	$361,784
Personal Fees	87,280
For Primary Medical Care	623,475

Other Sources

Interest on Trust Fund	$100,000
Primary Care	3,000,000
Sexually Transmitted Diseases	198,675
State Lab Revenue	561,459
Tuberculosis Control	95,851
Immunizations	48,947
Supplemental Food Supplies	1,763,703
Pharmacy	452,929

County Support

General Appropriation	$5,611,055
Fees	1,618,556
Building Rental	1,595,148
Maintenance of Buildings	481,134
School Board	55,000
County Air Pollution	398,308
County Toxic Substance Control	83,102
Epilepsy Foundation	18,000
Primary Care Grant	716,898
Headstart Dental Program	1,700
Sabal Palm (Private Grant)	27,398
Robert Wood Johnson (Grant)	87,879
Communications	170,551
Total	$26,652,351

Exhibit 10–A–1 continued

Expenditures
Control and Regulatory Programs

Immunizations	$536,163
Sexually Transmitted Diseases	353,082
AIDS	111,156
Tuberculosis Control	405,393
Communicable Diseases Control	287,697
Private Water Systems	32,693
Public Water Systems	379,237
Bottled Water	26,154
Swimming Pools	307,313
Individual Sewage Disposal	496,931
Public Sewage System	235,388
Solid Waste Disposal	170,003
Water Pollution Control	268,081
Food Hygiene	1,013,478
Group Care Facilities	379,237
Migrant Labor Camps	104,617
Housing Safety and Sanitation	130,771
Mobile Home Parks	32,693
Occupational Health	26,154
Consumer Product Safety	26,154
Sanitary Nuisances	241,927
Air Pollution Control	536,163
Radiologic Health	19,616
Toxic Substances	111,156
Rabies Control	13,077
Arbovirus Surveillance	13,077
Emergency Medical Services	13,077
Vital Records	268,081

Personal Health Services

Chronic Disease Services	$286,327
Nutrition Services	805,293
Family Planning	702,313
Improved Pregnancy Outcome	3,684,791
School Health	2,113,801
Dental Health Services	1,355,180
Comprehensive Child Health	2,765,493
Comprehensive Adult Health	3,032,187
Total	$21,283,954

schools, law enforcement, health care, and social services. Some groups have criticized the report. They suggest that any discussion of the impact of immigrants must include the fact that this population provides a cheap, flexible labor pool that stimulates the creation of new businesses and helps preserve labor-intensive ones in Bingo County and the surrounding region.

The findings also indicate that HIV-related health care provided through the Pennsylcola Medicaid Program costs about $2,800 per month per person. The data used to calculate this statistic were from a fixed period and included many persons who were still in the early stages of infection at the end of the data collection period.

Although in theory Cannico has a national health system, in fact, there are major gaps in access and quality. Persons with a large income have access to private facilities and practitioners at home and abroad. The middle class, which includes government workers and residents of certain agricultural communities, generally have access only to government clinics and hospitals.

Utilization by Canniconians of health services in the United States takes place on the following levels. First, there are the wealthy, who pay in full or on a fee-for-service basis for their physician and hospital care. Second, there are those who seek care in the United States because of their desire to have a child who is a U.S. citizen, because they hope to find adequate services, or because they are responding to an emergency. In urban areas of Cannico, the Health and Welfare Ministry maintains health clinics and hospitals often staffed by recent medical school graduates. Rural areas of Cannico are likely to be served only by a nurse. Hospital access for those who are poor and not covered by the Health and Welfare Ministry programs is often limited to civil hospitals, which are not well staffed or funded.

COMMUNITY HEALTH ASSESSMENT

In November 1989, Frank Daly was appointed county executive. When the county health officer retired soon afterward, Daly appointed James Verdon Reed, MD, MPH, to fill the position. Concerned about the health problems of Bingo County, Dr. Reed asked the CDC to conduct a community health assessment.

This community health analysis provided indicators of how citizens, activities, and services on one side of the border relate to and influence those of the other side and ultimately both nations. The CDC report suggests that it is unlikely that any other bi-national border has such variety in health status and health care utilization. What follows are relevant findings of the CDC analysis.

General

While most residents of Bingo are eligible for public assistance, relatively few physicians are willing to accept Medicaid payment and the tangle of paperwork that goes with it. People seeking Medicaid assistance in Bingo County also must go through a complicated set of procedures. The state of Pennsylcola has 8 programs for Medicaid enrollment, each with its own eligibility criteria. An indigent, mentally disabled person must negotiate up to 13 different application procedures for federal and state benefits. Many of these programs, the CDC team reports, have periodic review procedures with provisions for termination of benefits for those who do not complete the necessary paperwork. It is not uncommon for persons who are functioning marginally and miss filing deadlines for review of their disability benefits to learn that their benefits have been terminated.

In the county, an estimated 13,000 women are eligible for Medicaid maternity benefits, but only 50 doctors are willing to treat them under the state aid program—a patient:doctor ratio that CDC representatives call far too high.

In Bingo County, there are 9 nonprofit community health centers, which charge fees based on the patients' ability to pay. The centers served approximately 8,000 patients in 1989, 44 percent of them children. But many more were turned away because of excessive patient loads. As many as 3,000 people, both from Bingo County and Cannico, are typically on waiting lists for the tight-budgeted health centers. In Bingo County, last winter, amid a heavy viral respiratory outbreak, there were waiting periods up to 36 hours for pediatric care.

The effects of the lack of care are various, according to the CDC report. Pregnant women who have received no prenatal care often suffer severe complications, and many babies are born underweight, contributing to the infant mortality rate of 19 per 1,000 live births (for the past three years) in Bingo County. A separate CDC study of five counties in Pennsylcola, including Bingo County, showed that the chance of a bad pregnancy outcome was 35 percent greater for women without health insurance, even when income, race, and other factors were controlled for. A study prepared by the Bingo Chamber of Commerce reported that, in 1989, 19.9 percent of the city's residents had no insurance coverage, largely because their employers did not provide it and their wages were so low that they could not buy a policy. The results of the lack of insurance can be seen every day in hospitals along the Bingo-Cannico border where patients whose medical problems might have been prevented or easily treated in the early stages have waited until they have become acute.

The CDC reports that childbirth itself is an issue in Bingo County. Many pregnant Cannico women show up at hospital emergency rooms in Bingo County at the last minute, so far along in labor that they cannot be turned away. The children they bear are American citizens eligible for immediate medical and nutritional aid as well as other long-term benefits.

According to the CDC analysis, the Lamplight Medical Center, a private hospital, receives the largest share of what is known as "disproportionate funds" from the state to help compensate for care given to patients from both sides of the United States–Cannico border.

In one lower socioeconomic section of Bingo County, there is only one pediatrician for a population of 170,000 people, and only 6 physicians in the area accept Medicaid. Of the 900 physicians in the county, only 20 have offices or clinics south of Burlington Highway, the line of demarcation between the poor and middle-class neighborhoods and the entry point for most Canniconians.

These health service problems are developing at a time when rapid population growth shifts have severely taxed the infrastructure of Bingo County. Lured by the possibility of jobs in the United States, hundreds of impoverished Canniconians from the interior of the country have made their way to the border neighborhoods near Bingo.

During the last several years, as the Cannico economy has weakened, the border population has ballooned from 36,000 to more than 500,000, and most of the growth has occurred in the last two years. Shantytowns, without sewers or running water, have become part of the border landscape.

Cholera

The CDC report indicates that the Pennsylcola-Cannico border is an ideal setting for an outbreak of cholera that has taken an estimated 5,000 lives in 14 states of Cannico. At least one cholera case has been confirmed recently in Bingo County. A woman contracted the disease from eating contaminated shrimp while on a trip to Borisville, the southernmost city of Cannico.

Rubella

From January through June 1989, an outbreak of rubella occurred among Bingo County residents. It was part of a widespread outbreak reported among lower socioeconomic groups in three states in Cannico and the state of Pennsylcola on the U.S. side.

The Bingo County Department of Public Health, in cooperation with the CDC, conducted an investigation to document cases of rubella among pregnant women in Bingo County.

The health department and the CDC identified 89 women from Bingo County and Cannico as having rubella-like illness during pregnancy. Vaccination histories were available for 25 of these women. One (from Bingo County) had a history of prior rubella vaccination. Of the 89 women, 18 (20 percent) had laboratory-confirmed acute rubella; 31 specimens were insufficient for analysis, and no specimens were obtained from the remaining 40.

Based on the findings for a five-month study period, the rate of congenital rubella infection was 83 per 1,000 live births in the lower socioeconomic groups of Bingo County. The CDC notes that the risk of congenital rubella syndrome is greatest when maternal infection occurs early in pregnancy. When infection occurs during the first trimester, congenital rubella syndrome occurs in up to 85 percent of births.

Dengue Fever

Another problem on the Pennsylcola-Cannico border is dengue fever. Indigenous dengue transmission was documented in Southern Cannico in the 1980s, where of 63 reported cases at least 27 cases were identified in patients who had traveled outside that country before the onset of the disease. In Bingo County, 10 cases were reported as imported cases. Persistent large-scale outbreaks of dengue fever in Cannico makes this area more at risk, but a widespread outbreak could occur in the United States, because the *Aedes aegypti* mosquito is now in the Bingo County region and on the Pennsylcola-Cannico border. There is no eradication program at this time.

Tuberculosis and AIDS

A review of 2,205 clinical charts for 1985–1989 at the four largest hospitals in Bingo County for patients who had *Mycobacterium* tuberculosis isolated from spinal fluid revealed that 455 patients (21 percent) also had an HIV infection. Of the 37 HIV-infected patients with tuberculosis meningitis for whom records were available, 24 (65 percent) had clinical radiological evidence of extrameningeal tuberculosis at the time of admission.

Local officials believe that in recent years men from Cannico have brought AIDS to Bingo County. Doctors and epidemiologists report that official statistics on AIDS in Cannico describe only the tip of the phenomenon, which remains submerged in denial and social taboos.

The nurse in charge of AIDS treatment at a Cannico hospital, having carefully traced the sexual partners of her patients, concludes that a score of local people in Cannico are probably infected. Few of them wanted to be tested for the virus. National health officials in Cannico emphasize that, even when suspicious cases are added to those in which AIDS infection can be clearly traced to the victim's migration to Bingo County, the connection still accounts for only a small fraction of the 9,000 cases of the disease reported in Cannico.

Given the hundreds of Canniconians who cross legally and illegally into Bingo County each year, the number of those who come to Bingo County with AIDS and those who return to Cannico with AIDS appears to be small. But as the epidemic in Cannico has begun to level off among homosexual men and victims of a blood supply that was still poorly screened and badly contaminated less than five years ago, the spread of AIDS among migrants has become a growing concern on both sides of the border.

The concern is fueled by the difficult lives of undocumented workers from Cannico and the different sexual mores of two neighboring societies. While Cannico migration patterns have more women and families joining the flow of male job seekers, it is the archetypal lonely young men who are at highest risk. Almost everywhere these young men land, activities that put them at risk of infection tend to be more available than affordable health care, AIDS prevention programs, or information in the Canniconian language. Moreover, sexually transmitted disease on the border has long been a problem, not only because of the cross-border use of red light districts but also because contact tracing is much more difficult.

Measles

During the past three years measles cases and deaths have risen sharply in Bingo County. In 1989, more than 500 cases and 9 deaths were reported, the largest number of deaths in two decades. The epidemic intensified during 1990, with more than 700 cases and more than 11 deaths. The principal cause of the measles epidemic was failure to provide vaccine to children at the recommended age.

According to the CDC, many families in Bingo County have no ongoing relationship with a health care provider. The low immunization rate reflects, in part, inadequate access to health services. The CDC's analysis also showed that many opportunities to provide the needed vaccines were missed. Two types of missed opportunities were particularly noticeable in Bingo County: (1) a child brought to a center for immunization is not vaccinated because of inappropriate contraindications, such as minor illness, or only one of two vaccines is given when, in fact, others are also needed and should be given, and (2) a child in need of vaccination has contact with a health care provider for other reasons but his or her immunization status is not assessed and immunizations are not offered.

Reproductive and Developmental Problems

From 1986 to 1989, 102 women in Bingo County gave birth to babies without brains. The rate occurrence in the county of this rare congenital defect, known as anencephaly, is 10 times the national average. No cause has been identified, but some longtime residents of Bingo County suspect toxic emissions from factories above the border in Cannico. Other residents suspect the nuclear power plant accident that occurred inside Cannico several years ago.

On the Cannico side of the border, the infant mortality rate is significantly higher than in Bingo County and in the United States as a whole, although it is beginning to decline. In Cannico, the infant mortality rate has declined from an estimated 59 deaths per 1,000 live births during 1967–1971 to 47 during 1982–1987.

In Bingo County, the infant mortality rate for the period between 1982 and 1987 was 18 per 1,000 live births. Bronchitis and pneumonia, noninfectious gastroenteritis, and intestinal infection disease accounted for 220 deaths in the postneonatal period in Bingo County from 1982 to 1989.

Chronic Disease

In 1989, the overall mortality rate for coronary heart disease, stroke, lung cancer, cervical cancer, cirrhosis, and diabetes in Bingo County (age adjusted) was 75.8 per 100,000 population. Of the five risk factors examined—cigarette smoking, hypertension, obesity, alcohol consumption, and "never use Pap screening"—cigarette smoking made the largest contribution to deaths from the six diseases (30 percent). Examined one at a time, other risk factors also contributed to deaths from these diseases: obesity (25 percent), high cholesterol level (15 percent), hypertension (15 percent), and diabetes (10 percent).

Environmental Health

Sanitation in Cannico (i.e., water supply, waste water disposal, and solid waste collection and disposal) is far below U.S. standards. There is no evidence of regulatory control of environmental quality—broadly defined—in Cannico. Daily, 12 million gallons of raw sewage flow into the Kopa River, which flows into the Bingo County area from Cannico. Users of well water in the rural areas in Bingo County have noted increased contamination.

Air pollution in the Bingo-Cannico area has been a continuing problem, and discharges from the smelters on the Bingo side have been cited as a cause of high blood lead levels in both Cannico and Bingo County. More recently, Bingo County has exceeded EPA's ozone and carbon monoxide standards, largely because of older vehicular fleets in Cannico, the lack of emission controls, and the poor quality of gasoline used. Depending on wind speed and wind direction, air pollutants discharged in Cannico can add to the pollution load in Bingo County. Emissions in Bingo County may also impact atmospheric conditions in Cannico.

REFERENCES

1. B.J. Turnock, *Public Health: What It Is and How It Works* (Gaithersburg, MD: Aspen Publishers, 1997).
2. J.M. Bryson and B.C. Crosby, *Leadership for the Common Good* (San Francisco: Jossey-Bass, 1992).
3. G. Pickett and J.J. Hanlon, *Public Health: Administration and Practice,* 9th ed. (St. Louis: Times Mirror and Mosby College Publishing, 1990).
4. J.E. Rohrer, *Planning for Community-oriented Health Systems* (Washington, DC: American Public Health Association, 1996).
5. Rohrer, *Planning for Community-oriented Health Systems.*
6. A. Ross, *Cornerstones of Leadership for Health Services Executives* (Ann Arbor, MI: American College of Healthcare Executives, 1992).
7. J.M. Bryson, *Strategic Planning for Public and Nonprofit Organizations,* rev. ed. (San Francisco: Jossey-Bass, 1995).
8. L. Goodstein et al., *Applied Strategic Planning: A Comprehensive Guide* (New York: McGraw-Hill, 1993).
9. P.R. Scholtes, *The Leader's Handbook* (New York: McGraw-Hill, 1998).
10. Bryson, *Strategic Planning for Public and Nonprofit Organizations.*
11. Bryson, *Strategic Planning for Public and Nonprofit Organizations.*
12. Goodstein et al., *Applied Strategic Planning.*
13. H. Mintzberg, *The Rise and Fall of Strategic Planning* (New York: The Free Press, 1994).
14. Bryson, *Strategic Planning for Public and Nonprofit Organizations.*
15. Goodstein et al., *Applied Strategic Planning.*
16. F.A. Scutchfield et al., "The Presence of Total Quality Management and Continuous Quality Improvement Processes in California Public Health Clinics," *Journal of Public Health Management and Practice* 3, no. 3 (1997): 57–60.
17. Scutchfield et al., "The Presence of Total Quality Management and Continuous Quality Improvement Processes in California Public Health Clinics."
18. G.P. Mays et al., "CQI in Public Health Organizations," in *Continuous Quality Improvement in Health Care,* eds. C.P. McLaughlin and A.D. Kaluzny, 2d ed. (Gaithersburg, MD: Aspen Publishers, 1999).
19. C.P. McLaughlin and A.D. Kaluzny, "Defining Quality Improvement: Past, Present, and Future," in *Continuous Quality Improvement in Health Care,* eds. C.P. McLaughlin and A.D. Kaluzny, 2d ed. (Gaithersburg, MD: Aspen Publishers, 1999).
20. McLaughlin and Kaluzny, "Defining Quality Improvement."
21. A.V. Feigenbaum, *Total Quality Control* (New York: McGraw-Hill, 1961).
22. M. Sashkin and K.J. Kiser, *Putting Total Quality Management to Work* (San Francisco: Berrett-Koehler Publishers, 1993).
23. W.A. Shewhart, *Statistical Method from the Viewpoint of Quality Control* (Mineola, NY: Dover, 1986).
24. M. Walton, *Deming Management at Work* (New York: Pedigree Books, 1991).
25. P.B. Crosby, *Quality without Tears* (New York: Penguin Plume, 1984).
26. P.B. Crosby, *Completeness* (New York: Penguin Dutton, 1992).
27. P.B. Crosby, *Quality Is Free* (New York: McGraw-Hill, 1989).
28. P.B. Crosby, *Let's Talk Quality* (New York: Penguin Plume, 1990).
29. J.M. Juran, *Juran on Leadership for Quality: An Executive Handbook* (New York: The Free Press, 1989).
30. A.V. Feigenbaum, *Total Quality Control* (New York: McGraw-Hill, 1961).
31. B. Creech, *The Five Pillars of TQM* (New York: Truman Talley Books and Dutton, 1994).

32. Sashkin and Kiser, *Putting Total Quality Management to Work*.

33. M. Brassard, *The Memory Jogger+* (Methuen, MA: Goal and QPC, 1989).

34. Brassard, *The Memory Jogger+*.

35. R.L. Manganelli and M.M. Klein, *The Reengineering Handbook* (New York: AMACOM [American Management Association], 1994).

36. P.F. Drucker, "Really Reinventing Government," *Atlantic Monthly* 275, no. 2 (1995a): 49–61.

37. S.P. Robbins and M. Coulter, *Management*, 6th ed. (Upper Saddle River, NJ: Prentice-Hall, 1999).

38. J. Champy, *Reengineering Management* (New York: Harper Business, 1995).

39. D.K. Carr and H.J. Johansson, *Best Practices in Reengineering* (New York: McGraw-Hill, 1995).

40. Manganelli and Klein, *The Reengineering Handbook*.

41. D. Osborne and T. Gaebler, *Reinventing Government: How the Entrepreneurial Spirit Is Transforming the Public Sector* (Reading, MA: Addison-Wesley, 1992).

42. D. Osborne and P. Plastrik, *Banishing Bureaucracy* (Reading, MA: Addison-Wesley, 1997).

43. D. Osborne, "The State of the Revolution: An Interview," *Leader to Leader* 6 (1997): 43–49.

44. Osborne, "The State of the Revolution."

45. J.M. Bacon, "Reinventing Government for Public Health Improvement," *Leadership in Public Health* 3, no. 3 (1994): 1–5.

46. Bacon, "Reinventing Government for Public Health Improvement."

47. Osborne, "The State of the Revolution."

48. Osborne and Plastrik, *Banishing Bureaucracy*.

49. P.F. Drucker, *Managing in a Time of Great Change* (New York: Truman Talley Books and Dutton, 1995).

Chapter 11

Leadership, Decision Making, Conflict, and Negotiation

Once a decision was made, I did not worry about it afterward.

Harry S. Truman, *Memoirs*

Leading involves decision making, and decision making involves taking risks. Public health leaders often confront disagreement or discontent with their decisions. They need to be aware of this possibility and that leadership and risk go together.[1] Risk taking is prerequisite for "challenging the process" and being innovative.[2] As part of the decision-making process, public health leaders need to evaluate the costs and benefits of their decisions—the expenditures necessary to carry out their decisions and the consequences, good and bad, for the functioning of the public health agency—and also consider the ethical implications of their decisions.

Public health leaders, like all decision makers, will make mistakes and will hopefully learn from their mistakes.[3] Taking risks, after all, means opening oneself to the possibility of making mistakes. One way public health leaders can reduce the burden of the bad consequences of their decisions is to develop power-sharing arrangements with community partners. If different partners take responsibility for different pieces of a project, for example, the costs associated with problems that occur (or even the failure of the project) will be borne by more than one entity.

Consequently, leaders will need to develop, in addition to decision-making skills, conflict resolution skills and negotiation skills. This chapter discusses what can be done when decision making gets complicated by conflict. As should be obvious, in decision making, conflict resolution, and negotiation, communication skills are absolutely essential (see Chapter 9).

DECISION MAKING

Any organization's vision and mission need to be tied to the real world.[4] A vision without substance is pointless. The challenge for the leaders of an organization is to figure out what strategies will be most effective in realizing its vision, make the hard decisions required to implement these strategies, and get others in the organization to accept the decisions and commit themselves to carrying out the strategies.[5] Leaders need to be aware that a decision itself does not change an organization; rather the actions resulting from the decision are what bring about change.[6]

Decision making is an essential step in problem solving. Leaders need to address problems as they arise and modify operations in light of the factors introduced by the problems. One strategy is to appoint a task force to develop potential solutions to a problem and then decide what to do based on recommendations of the task force or the information provided by it. For example, a public health administrator in a suburb adjoining an urban neighborhood with a high crime rate might appoint a community task force consisting of professionals from the health department and the police department to determine how the community could prevent gang violence.

Problem solving can sometimes assume a cyclic form.[7] Suppose the leaders of an organization discover a serious problem that demands action. They determine the nature of the problem, come up with solutions, and begin to implement them. The problem, as it begins to be addressed, becomes less serious and of less concern to the leaders and others in the organization. One result might well be that the implementation of the solutions is not carried through to its conclusion, allowing the problem to intensify again and eventually causing the leaders to restart the problem-solving process. Organizations that concentrate on putting out fires do not advance much but instead struggle constantly with maintaining the status quo.

Leadership style, leadership practices, and governing paradigms affect the process of making decisions and the outcomes of the decisions. Also impacting the process and outcomes are the kind and quality of the information that is available. In particular, public health leaders depend on epidemiologic assessment data, among other types of information, for making decisions about community health programs.

Decision-making Roles and Styles

Mintzberg identified four decisional roles that leaders assume.[8] First, leaders take on an entrepreneurial role when making decisions that expand the parameters of the organization. As pointed out previously, leaders of public health agencies need to look for resources from the private and public sectors if they want to fulfill the overall public health mission—improving health and preventing disease.[9] Approaching businesses for funds to support public health programs is a form of entrepreneurism.

Second, leaders are occasionally confronted with work disturbances that require administrative decisions for their resolution.[10] Third, leaders must act as resource allocators and determine where the limited human and financial resources of the agency could best be applied to implement or operate agency programs. Finally, leaders must occasionally act as negotiators.

Robbins and Coulter identified three decision-making styles.[11] First, some leaders avoid finding out that problems exist so they don't have to make decisions. This strategy protects the status quo and shows a lack of commitment to organizational change. Other leaders are natural problem solvers. They are interested in solving problems immediately by combining the problem-solving and decision-making processes. The third type of leader is the problem seeker. Problem seekers search out potential problems in order to solve them early and integrate the solutions with the organizational vision. These leaders are always looking for new opportunities for improvement and growth.

Fear of risk is one of the main barriers to the making of rational decisions. Effective leaders constantly take risks and do not avoid them. A strategy of incremental change will weaken an organization if substantial reforms are necessary. By giving into caution, leaders pass up the chance of being creative. Such leaders also tend to ignore negative feedback, which can lead to disaster.

Decision making can be rational or intuitive, and it can also exhibit a high or low degree of tolerance for ambiguity.[12,13] As shown in Figure 11–1, an analytic style of decision making is rational and exhibits a high degree of tolerance for ambiguity. Analytic decision makers base their decisions on information. A directive style is characterized by a high degree of rationality but a low degree of tolerance for ambiguity. Directive decision makers are logical and tend to make decisions quickly and for the short term. Directive decision making is a style favored by managers. Conceptual decision making is intuitive and exhibits a low degree of tolerance for ambiguity. Conceptual decision makers tend to concentrate on the future and its possibilities, and they also tend to be very creative. The behavioral style of decision making is intuitive and shows a low degree of tolerance for ambiguity. Decision makers who use this style concentrate on people relationships and tend to accept information from other staff before making a decision.

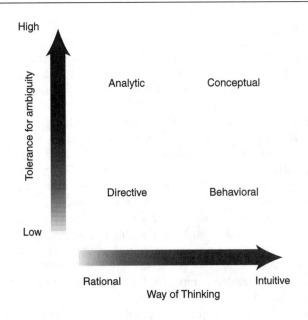

Figure 11–1 Decision-making styles.

Decisions require implementation, and the implementation process is often complex and hard to complete.[14] Leaders must determine the sequence of implementation steps and the interactions that are likely to occur at each step. Further, they must understand that the implementation process has important decision points—places where critical decisions must be made. At these decision points, the leaders review the implementation process in order to determine if modifications are necessary and if the objectives of the implementation are being achieved.

Shared Decision Making

Decision making may be a shared activity. Much public health work occurs in teams, coalitions, and other groups, and if power is shared, decision making would likely be shared as well. There are at least four advantages to shared decision making.[15] First, each party brings to the group new information, a diversity of experience, different professional credentials, and a different perspective. Second, a group is likely to come up with more options than an individual. Third, there is likely to be more acceptance of a decision if more people are involved in making the decision. A group-made decision is a decision with a ready-made consensus. Finally, the involvement of others increases the legitimacy of the decision.

There are also four disadvantages to shared decision making, whether in a team, coalition, or other group.[16] First, the process can consume a great amount of time. In decision making, reaching a quick decision is often critical, and delays can prevent a solution from being fully effective. Second, a strong minority will sometimes try to dominate the whole process—and will sometimes succeed. Third, the appearance of agreement or consensus may disguise the fact that there really is no agreement. Finally, shared decision making and the shared sense of responsibility that goes with it can lead to a situation where no one feels responsible for negative outcomes related to the decisions.

Decision-making Models

Exhibit 11–1 presents an outline of three decision-making models. As can be seen, the basic decision-making process is similar in all three. They each start with a problem, utilize information to evaluate the problem, and eventually lead to a decision.

In the first model, designed by Liebler and colleagues, the first step is to set an agenda, which includes recognizing that a problem or challenge to the status quo has arisen and collecting information to validate the problem or challenge.[17] Searching for alternative solutions is the second step. The leaders need to be objective and to listen to possible scenarios presented by their colleagues. The third step is the evaluation of the alternative solutions to determine which one is the most promising. The task in the fourth stage is get a commitment to the chosen solution from participants in the decision-making process. The solution is then pilot tested, and if the results are positive, the leaders devise an implementation plan. The final step involves assessing the results of the chosen solution during the implementation, including the results of decisions made as part of the implementation process.

The second model, designed by Robbins and Coulter, begins with roughly the same first step as the model described above, that is, problem identification.[18]

Exhibit 11–1 Three Contrasting Approaches to Decision Making

Liebler et al.[1]	*Robbins and Coulter*[2]	*Systems Approach*
Build agenda.	Identify problems.	Set goals and objectives.
Search for alternatives.	Identify decision criteria.	Engage in action planning.
Evaluate alternatives.	Allocate weights to criteria.	Implement action plans.
Commit to chosen alterna-	Develop alternatives.	Evaluate implementation of
tives.	Analyze alternatives.	plans.
Continually assess decisions.	Select alternative.	
	Implement alternative.	
	Evaluate effectiveness of	
	implementation.	

[1]J.A. Liebler, R.E. Levine, and J. Rothman, *Management Principles for Health Professionals*, 2d ed. (Gaithersburg, MD: Aspen Publishers, 1992).
[2]S.P. Robbins and M. Coulter, *Management*, 6th ed. (New York: Prentice Hall, 1999).

The problem identified might be related to legal mandates, budget restrictions, lack of information, or lack of support from the local board or from community constituencies. The next two steps are to identify decision criteria and attach weights to them (so that relatively unimportant criteria do not influence the decision to the same degree as important criteria). Then alternative solutions are developed and analyzed. The best solution (or the one that seems the best) is chosen and implemented. Finally, as in the preceding model, the results of the implementation are evaluated.

In the third model, the first step is to identify goals and objectives based on the organization's mission and vision. The next step is to embark on the task of devising action plans to achieve the goals and objectives. The plans are then implemented and the implementation process is evaluated, as in the other two models.

To be effective decision makers, public health leaders must

- learn that making decisions involves risk taking
- learn the differences between problem solving and decision making
- build decision-making strategies into implementation plans
- empower employees and community partners to take an active role in decision making
- identify their style of leadership and understand how to use it in decision making
- tie decisions to the goals and objectives of the organization

CONFLICT RESOLUTION

The Dangers of Conflict

Life and leadership are full of twists and turns, and there are always individuals who disagree with any position taken on an issue. This is partially explained by the multicultural nature of our society and partially by the wide spectrum of political positions held by policy makers.

Conflict over a decision needs to be resolved if the decision is to be effective. As pointed out above, decision making does not occur in a vacuum and is usually a group process. Even when conflict appears to be absent or to have been resolved, there is no guarantee of full acceptance of the solution.[19] Moreover, the main disagreement may be, not over the solution, but over how to implement the solution.[20]

Conflict, although based in the facts of a given situation, is often partly the result of differences in ideology,[21] and there are typically mythologies that support the positions of the partners to a conflict. Ideology, information, and key players change over time, and thus the techniques needed to resolve conflicts also change.

Conflict is the reverse of cooperation.[22] When it permeates an entire organization, it needs to be addressed immediately. Conflict entails negativity and opposition to decisions.[23] In addition, people fear conflict and suffer stress as a result of conflict, another serious consequence of a situation in which conflict remains rampant.[24]

Yet, life without conflict is not a possibility, especially in our complex society.[25,26] In fact, conflict will, if anything, become more prevalent in the 21st century. Therefore, leaders must learn how to handle conflict. Exercise 11–1 allows students to explore the meaning of conflict and to experience ways in which conflict may be resolved.

Conflict within an organization can have diverse causes, including the culture and atmosphere of the organization, its structure, the needs of the leadership and the organization, and the solutions to past conflict.[27] Major sources of conflict and obstacles to conflict resolution include these:[28]

- Conflict arises when different leaders assert their authority and engage in a power struggle. In the U.S. Congress, power struggles are common causes of gridlock (the inability to pass major legislation).
- The assignment of the wrong people to a team or task force can lead to conflict. It is unfortunately common to see an executive appointed to a major task force either not attend most of the meetings or send as a proxy someone without the power to make decisions.
- Conflict will naturally arise in a meeting run by someone who lacks respect for the attendees, communicates poorly, or hides the reason for the meeting.
- Having a clear mission and vision and basing the discussion of issues on these is essential for conflict avoidance. Conflict will inevitably occur in a team, for example, if the members are unclear as to the team's mission.
- It is important not to spend time revisiting conflicts that have been resolved unless the solutions did not win real agreement. Some groups continually return to conflicts that have already been worked out, thereby wasting time and often generating frustration.
- Conflict resolution by a group requires that the group be given full authority to resolve the conflict. If the group doesn't have adequate authority, it will spend fruitless hours discussing issues that are beyond its power to do anything about.

Conflicts use up much of the leader's time. For example, if a public health leader is spending 20 percent of the workday resolving conflicts, he or she should look at ways to reduce that amount. And time is not the only issue. As noted above, conflict creates stress, and the leader must not allow his or her personal health to be jeopardized as a result of managing conflict.

A third danger is the potential for sabotage by employees who have become disaffected because of the prevalence of conflict.[29] Conflict can also increase workplace violence. For example, if employees who are members of a union come in conflict with employees who are not, the difference in perspective between these two groups could lead to a buildup of tension and eventually to actual violence.

Dealing with Conflict

A preliminary step in resolving conflict is to select an appropriate strategy or style. Which conflict resolution style is best will depend on the nature of the conflict and the situation in which the conflict occurs.[30] Rahim defined five styles that a leader might use to deal with conflict between him- or herself and other parties.[31] Figure 11–2 shows them in arrangement based on the degree of concern for self and degree of concern for others exhibited by the leader. The integrating style, which involves collecting pertinent facts as part of the conflict resolution process, is oriented toward finding an innovative solution that satisfies both parties. The leader who uses this style exhibits a concern both for self and others.

An obliging style would be typical of a leader who showed great concern for others but little concern for self. The leader would tend to go along with whatever the other party to the conflict wanted, perhaps out of a worry that he or she lacked the expertise necessary to resolve the conflict in any other way. This style is diametrically opposite to the dominating style, in which the leader exhibits great concern for self but little for others. The leader acts in an authoritarian manner and basically lays down what the resolution is going to be.

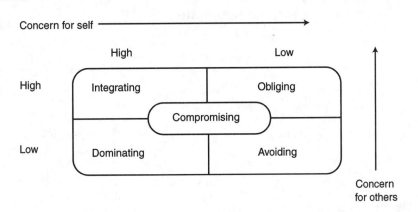

Figure 11–2 Five conflict management styles.

One way to deal with conflict is to avoid it, and the avoiding style is often used by leaders who exhibit a low degree of concern for self and for others. The goal is to protect the status quo, and the conflict-avoiding leader stays in the background and lets others deal with the conflict and its ramifications.

The compromising style is the middle-of-the-road style, and the compromising leader shows average concern for self and others. Compromise involves reciprocity, which means that each party to the conflict gets something. This style is very useful for resolving conflict between individuals engaged in a partnership, for the partners are treated as they expect to be—with equal respect.

Conflict may be planned or unplanned (Figure 11–3). Conflict stimulation is sometimes needed if change is to occur. It can be a method of ending gridlock and breaking through barriers protecting the status quo. Leaders need to know not only when to stimulate conflict for the good of the organization but also how to deal with it once it occurs.

Robbins and Coulter make a distinction between functional and dysfunctional conflicts.[32] Functional conflicts contribute to the attainment of goals and objectives, whereas dysfunctional conflicts hinder their achievement. The former, of course, are conflicts of the kind that leaders would want to stimulate if they were not occurring in the natural order of things.

The end result of all these activities is a regimen of activities that leads to the favorable or unfavorable resolution of the conflict. The resolution of the conflict is not sufficient. The leader still needs to make a decision and put the solution into action.

A Conflict Resolution Process

Weeks devised a process for dealing with conflict.[33] The steps are as follows:

1. Create an effective atmosphere.
2. Clarify perceptions.
3. Focus on individual and shared needs.
4. Build shared positive power.
5. Lead to the future, then learn from the past.
6. Generate options.
7. Develop doables.
8. Make mutually beneficial agreements.

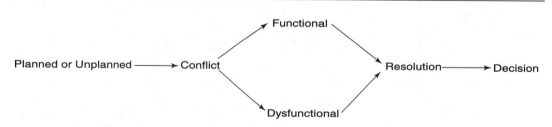

Figure 11–3 Elements of resolution of conflict.

There are at least two sides to every conflict. Each party enters the conflict situation with an agenda based on personal, organizational, or community concerns and values and possibly goals and objectives. Emotions get involved. Out of this mix a consensus of some kind needs to be forged.

To achieve a consensus, the leader needs to create an environment conducive to working on a resolution to the conflict (step 1 in the conflict resolution process outlined above). For instance, the leader must try to create the right atmosphere for meetings between the parties and make sure that the times and locations of meetings are agreeable to everyone. A neutral meeting place is often the best choice. The leader, in preparation for the first meeting, might develop several possible scenarios for starting the conflict resolution process. The choice of the right scenario might have to happen at a moment's notice.

People's perceptions are affected by many factors, including past experiences as well as present realities. In step 2, the leader needs to determine whether the conflict is tied to personal, organizational, community, or professional concerns. Is the conflict related to values or needs? Are goals and objectives driving the process? Finally, the leader must examine the components of the conflict and develop strategies based on his or her analysis.

In step 3, each party to the conflict identifies his or her personal needs. The leader then helps the parties to identify needs that they share. The process of looking at their needs often helps the parties to discover needs, values, and perceptions they unknowingly possess.

The goal in step 4 is to develop the power (means) to resolve the conflict and get the parties to share in this power. For power sharing to occur, the parties must come to share a clear mission and vision, be willing to settle for realistic goals and objectives, and view resolution of the conflict as in everyone's best interest.

Step 5 requires the leader to evaluate how past decisions influence the present conflict and prepare the way for a less conflictive future. The parties need to be careful not to let past experiences keep them from building a better future.

In step 6, the parties identify and explore options for resolving the conflict. These options can help the parties to see the issues more clearly and be less governed by previous perspectives. This step requires the parties to be creative and to use imaging techniques to examine the likely consequences of the various options. The use of the dialogue technique described in Chapter 9 might be beneficial here. Dialogue allows each party to present his or her position and possible solutions to the conflict without interruption and comment. When the parties move into the discussion phase, the agenda of each party will be helpfully on the table.

In step 7, the parties need to develop a set of "doables," which are small actions that are easy to complete and that will improve the relationship between the parties.

As their relationship improves, they will be better able, in step 8, to agree on a final resolution to the conflict. This resolution, like the doables, must be realistic and mutually beneficial. Otherwise the process will fail.

Conflict resolution is best achieved through a fairly flexible series of activities that are modified to address the unique issues associated with the particular conflict. The model presented above allows flexibility in each of the eight steps so that the different perspectives of the parties can be accommodated. Guidelines for conflict resolution are listed below. To reduce the number and intensity of conflicts and resolve them when they occur, public health leaders must

- utilize conflict resolution techniques to define disagreements between colleagues or external partners
- define whether a conflict enhances or hinders the ability of the organization to fulfill its mission, vision, goals, and objectives
- monitor power struggles between colleagues or external partners
- decrease (if possible) the percentage of time allocated to conflict resolution
- select the best method of conflict resolution to use based on their personal leadership styles and the core functions of public health
- implement a protocol that colleagues or partners agree upon in order to resolve conflicts
- put solutions to conflict into action as fast as possible
- identify the mutual benefits to be obtained by conflict resolution

NEGOTIATION

Conflict can be resolved through coercion (the threat or exercise of physical force), adjudication (legal proceedings), mediation, arbitration, or negotiation.[34] Negotiation, the topic of this section, is also used in bargaining (e.g., when two parties are engaged in working out an exchange of goods and services) and in forming partnerships and other types of alliances.

In negotiation, two or more parties are involved in trying to reach an agreement (or resolve a conflict); each is represented by a negotiator, whose role is to help make the agreement satisfactory to all parties. Mediation occurs when a neutral third party takes on the role of honest broker and tries to get the interested parties to reach an agreement. Both negotiation and mediation are covered in this section.

Every person is continually involved in informal negotiations throughout life.[35] Negotiation skills can be used to resolve personal, organizational, community, and professional issues and problems. Most people use what might be called soft negotiation techniques. In soft negotiation, each party wants a decision reached or a problem resolved with as little fuss as possible and without antagonizing the other parties. Hard negotiation is favored by those who love the challenge of the negotiation game and tend to shoot for more than they can easily get.

Principled negotiation occurs when the parties attempt to resolve a conflict based on merit rather than on their personal agendas.[36] In a sense, the relationship between the parties becomes more important than the conflict. In some cases, this type of negotiation is not applicable, for objective criteria needed to reach a "fair" or defensible resolution may be lacking. Each party simply possesses a given agenda, the agendas are inconsistent with each other, and there is no right or wrong conclusion to the process.

Exhibit 11–2 lists 16 skills and abilities that a leader-negotiator (or leader-mediator) needs in order to be successful. Negotiation skills are applicable to a range of types of negotiation, from union negotiations to bargaining over salary and position title to negotiations with the local health board regarding the distribution of funds for specific activities.

Exhibit 11–2 Interpersonal Skills for the Negotiator

1. Being in control of oneself.
2. The ability to elicit the needs, interests, and goals of those on whose behalf the negotiator is acting.
3. The ability to properly counsel those persons regarding the realities of the situation.
4. Obtaining clear authority from the appropriate decision maker.
5. Understanding and being able to utilize the full range of effective strategies and tactics.
6. Planning efficiently.
7. Being credible.
8. Perceptively analyzing the other party and its negotiator.
9. Being able to tolerate conflict and ambiguity.
10. Knowing or learning the relevant market factors.
11. Disclosing information selectively and persuasively.
12. Obtaining necessary information.
13. Listening to and perceiving the real information being conveyed.
14. Making changes in strategy and tactics or counseling those for whom the negotiator is acting regarding terms, as appropriate during the negotiation.
15. Being both patient and tireless.
16. Knowing when and how to either close the negotiation with an agreement or to terminate it because a desirable agreement cannot be reached.

Negotiation is both an art and a science.[37] It is a science inasmuch as negotiation models exist that lay out procedures for reaching agreements and resolving conflicts. It is an art inasmuch as effective negotiations require flexibility and an intuitive ability to choose the appropriate skills and apply them expertly and at the right time.

Prenegotiation

Negotiators must deal with a number of issues before the actual negotiations begin.[38] First, they must determine how many individuals or group representatives will be involved in the process. The more might not be the merrier. They must also consider whether the organizations being represented are monolithic or made up of diverse components each with its own perspective. In a complex, multiperspective organization, an agreement reached through the efforts of a single representative might not be perceived as acceptable by certain components within the organization.

The negotiator for each organization should find out if the other organizations involved in the negotiations spend large amounts of time in bargaining situations. If they do, the process may become more important than the outcome, and the negotiator should be forewarned of this possibility.

Another issue is whether there is a connection between the outcome of the negotiations at hand and the outcomes of other negotiations. If there is, this will complicate the current negotiations. Other issues include whether an agreement must be reached, whether ratification is required, and whether agreement between the parties creates a binding contract. The negotiators need to know if there are any internal or external threats to the negotiation process. They also need to determine whether the negotiations are to be open or closed.

Negotiation Barriers

Negotiations, like any human activity, face many obstacles in the way of their completion.[39] First, the process might become more expensive, in time and money, than expected. Second, people are often resistant to change and will fight for maintenance of the status quo. Third, negotiators sometimes view the issues at stake in the negotiations as making up a "fixed pie" and assume that their role is to ensure that their slice is as big as or bigger than it was before. They seem not to realize that negotiations can result in a bigger piece of pie for everyone.

Another obstacle is that negotiators occasionally hold onto old opinions or keep bringing up issues that were settled early in the negotiations. In addition, they may present information to the other negotiators in a way that leads to the disintegration of the whole process. A sixth obstacle is that important information is sometimes unavailable, and an agreement reached on the basis of partial information may not be the best agreement for one or more of the parties.

There is also the "winner's curse."[40] The "winner" in a negotiation may wish the process would continue and may be depressed about its closure. Further, the negotiators must not allow overconfidence to thwart the process, nor should they make the mistake of treating disagreement among the parties as more important than the relationship that is being forged between them.[41]

Negotiation has unique characteristics that differentiate it from other types of conflict resolution. Two processes, with feedback loops connecting them, are going on at the same time: the planning process and the actual negotiations. Public health leaders in negotiations receive feedback from the community, they receive feedback from colleagues in the public health agency, and they and the other negotiating parties give and receive feedback from each other.

Getting to Yes

There are many approaches to prenegotiation and negotiation activities. We will look at two of them. First, Fisher and colleagues developed the "Getting to Yes" model.[42] This model, which is intended to be user friendly, allows great flexibility. The steps are as follows:

1. Determine interests.
2. Identify options.
3. Determine alternatives.
4. Review the legitimacy of the process.
5. Choose appropriate communication strategies.
6. Strengthen relationships.
7. Promote commitment.

The first step is to determine the interests of the parties to the negotiation. These interests are more important than the official position held by each party. The negotiators must try to clarify the issues involved. The second step is to identify options for resolving the conflict. The parties should be aware that they all could gain from the resolution of the conflict although no party is likely to get everything desired.[43] The third step is to determine alternatives. The fourth step is to review the legitimacy of the process. Since complete agreement between the parties is not likely to occur, they must accept the legitimacy of the process and of its outcome. The fifth step is to choose an appropriate communication strategy. Two-way communication is essential if the negotiations are to proceed smoothly. For one thing, the reframing of issues may be a continuous activity. In step 6, the negotiators try to strengthen their relationship. It is important in this step to separate substance from relationship. The promotion of commitment to the agreed solution occurs in the final step. This commitment is critical to the success of the whole process.

The "Getting to Yes" model has been criticized as unrealistic.[44] Nonetheless, the model seems to work and has been used successfully in teacher–college administration contract negotiations. Public health leaders may find the model easier to use if the proper coalition development has occurred, for then the parties to the negotiations will have already established a working relationship.

The Schoenfield and Schoenfield Negotiation Model

Schoenfield and Schoenfield developed a 14-step model that incorporates major steps from other negotiation models.[45] The model comprises both prenegotiation and negotiation steps:

- prenegotiation
  1. prenegotiation information gathering
  2. determining goals
  3. identifying issues
  4. analyzing the market
  5. assessing strengths and weaknesses
  6. estimating the other party's bottom line and opening position
  7. considering win-win outcomes
- negotiation
  8. setting the opening position
  9. setting the bottom line
  10. choosing strategies and tactics
  11. considering concessions and trade-offs
  12. determining an agenda
  13. analyzing timing
  14. choosing the modes of communication

The first seven steps of this model overlap the steps of the "Getting to Yes" model, although the Schoenfield and Schoenfield model is more specific. Its higher degree of specificity can be both an advantage (because it provides detailed guidance) and a disadvantage (because it decreases flexibility and increases the burden placed on the negotiators). One of its faults is that it does not take into account the feedback loops that need to exist if the negotiations are to be as effective as possible and lead to agreements that the parties can commit to.

In the first step, each negotiator collects needed data. For public health issues, data from community assessments will have to be gathered. The parties should identify information gaps and make plans to search for the missing data or knowingly proceed with the negotiations under the current data limitations. (Note that public health negotiations often involve more than two parties,[46] but for ease of exposition this account of the model assumes there are just two parties.)

Step two involves setting goals for the planning process. These goals will include short- and long-term goals and also essential and merely desirable goals. The last task in this step is to prioritize the goals.

In step 3, the parties identify the issues that will be the focus of the negotiations and begin to discuss concessions and trade-offs.

The purpose of step 4 is to look at the market (or the community, in the case of public health) and identify the market factors that might influence the negotiations. Public health leaders, in their negotiations, must keep in mind that the public might have an agenda that diverges from the agenda of each negotiating party. They should also review the culture and norms of the specific population that will be directly affected by the outcome of the negotiations. In general, they have an obligation to look after the needs of the community during the negotiation process.

In planning step 5, each party looks at its own strengths and weaknesses and, to the extent possible, those of the other party. The problem here is that each party assesses strengths and weaknesses based on its own world view. During this step, each party also considers settlement alternatives and determines what, in its view, would be the "best alternative to a negotiated agreement"(BATNA).[47]

In step 6, each party estimates the other party's bottom line and likely opening position. This step aids in identifying areas of agreement as well as difference. The negotiators also need to determine if personal values could interfere with the process.

The final step in the prenegotiation phase is the consideration of win-win scenarios—outcomes that represent net gains for each of the negotiating parties. This step is essential, for win-win outcomes are the ones that both parties are liable to accept eventually. Each party should understand going into the negotiations that it is not going to get everything it wants but can get some of what it wants if it is willing to compromise and allow the other party to win something as well.

The eighth step is the opening step in the negotiations themselves. Here the parties put forth their opening positions. In the ninth step, each party sets the bottom line—the minimum it will accept. In other words, each party lets the other know what its particular BATNA is. The discussion in this step helps to determine if a negotiated agreement is possible or not.

At any stage in the negotiation process, one or both parties may return to an earlier step and redo it in the interests of arriving at a better outcome. For example, the negotiators may want to re-evaluate information collected earlier in order to determine whether their current bottom line is justified or needs to be revised.

Negotiation strategies and tactics are chosen in step 10. The negotiators might use the strategy of expressing upfront their desire to achieve a win-win outcome and or they might take a no-concessions stance. Each strategy has several tactics associated with it. Examples of tactics include the setting of deadlines and methods for dealing with a deadlock.

In step 11, the negotiators consider concessions and possible trade-offs. Planned concessions and tradeoffs are needed for a successful outcome.[48] Negotiations in which there are more than two parties provide extra opportunities for trade-offs, for deals can be struck between some of the parties but not all. During this step especially, the parties need to make an effort to act respectfully toward each other and build trust among themselves. The best strategy is to focus on the issues at the heart of the negotiations and not on the personalities of the people at the table.

Also, the beginning positions set forth by the negotiators need to be open to revision. If they are not, the result will be inaction and a breakdown in the negotiations. The best strategy is to focus on the interests that lie behind the stated positions rather than the positions themselves. In addition, the development of options should be separated from the decision making, and objective criteria should be used in the decision-making process, for they provide the parties with a template for action and make concessions and trade-offs easier to navigate.

Agenda setting occurs in step 12. The main task is to determine the actions that are going to have to be completed, such as the identification of issues and the making of concessions. The parties need to agree on the agenda, and if they are unable to reach an agreement, they may have to return to an earlier step and work through the process again.

The agenda identifies the actions; the schedule, to be devised in step 13, lays down time frames in which the actions are to occur. The task of creating a schedule is complicated by the fact that the parties to a negotiation often have hidden agendas (and even hidden deadlines) that only become apparent over time.

The model's final step is to choose the modes of communication that are most appropriate to the situation (see Chapter 9 for a discussion of communication skills and strategies). Of course, resolution of the negotiation issues and obtainment of an agreement are yet to come, and they might be considered to compose the fifteenth step.

Negotiation Strategies

The two models of negotiation described above cover the major steps that parties to a negotiation need to go through. A separate issue is the strategies that are available for use during these steps. Below is a list of strategies that negotiators can use to reach an outcome satisfactory to them (strategies 1–9 are described in Fuller[49] and 10–16 are described in Schoenfield and Schoenfield):[50]

1. win-win
2. stonewalling
3. good Samaritan
4. finessing the process
5. splitting the difference
6. nickel and dime tactics
7. controlling the action
8. ambiguity
9. defensive techniques
10. no concessions
11. deadlock-breaking techniques
12. high realistic expectations with small systematic concessions
13. concede first
14. problem solving
15. extraneous goals
16. closure strategies

Several of these strategies can undermine the negotiation process. Therefore, they must be used cautiously. Also, note that for every strategy, there is a counter strategy.

As pointed out, each party to a negotiation wants to gain something as a result of the negotiation. A commitment to try to win and let the other party win too—the essence of a win-win strategy—increases the chances that the negotiation will continue until a final agreement is reached. A win-win strategy, although it seems to make good sense, is not always easy to follow, for negotiators tend to be protective of their interests and do not want to lose anything. For some negotiators, the goal is to prevent losses rather than accumulate gains, and this goal is usually inconsistent with a win-win strategy, for it is rare that both parties can win without cost.

Stonewalling is used to slow down the negotiation process. Some negotiators look for bargain solutions and practice stonewalling to wait for the bargains to appear. Negotiators need to learn how to break through stone walls and get the negotiation process moving again. One useful tactic is to set deadlines for decisions.

Some negotiators present themselves as good Samaritans and try to convince the other parties of their beneficent motives. This kind of behavior should send up a warning signal. Most "good Samaritan" negotiators are dishonest and their protestations of good intentions are a sham. To counteract this strategy, the other parties need to refocus on the facts and get away from considering motives.

A good example of finessing the process is to engage in a form of brinkmanship and confront the other parties with a stark choice: accept the terms of agreement currently on offer or watch the negotiation process disintegrate. This strategy can sometime scare parties into accepting terms they otherwise wouldn't have agreed to, but it runs the risk of causing a lose-lose situation—that is, if the negotiations really end without an agreement.

Some negotiators and partners are committed to compromise and are willing to split the differences in order to come to a solution. The negative side of this strategy may be a half win-win situation with losses involved for all partners. The selection of this strategy must be weighed carefully to determine its relevance to a specific set of negotiations.

There are also strategies that micromanage the process and are so detail-based that very little seems to be done. The nickel and dime strategy is a very slow one where each element is evaluated piece by piece. The advantage of this strategy is that it lessens the disagreements of the parties to the negotiation. On the negative side, it often seems that a final agreement is not reached.

Most people feel more secure on their own turf, and negotiators who demand that the negotiation talks take place in their work environment are trying to control the action. If any of the negotiators feel uncomfortable with a potential meeting location, neutral territory should be found.

Language is not a perfect tool, and there is likely to be some unclarity of meaning and some vagueness to any agreement no matter how long and carefully the negotiators work on it. What have to be watched out for are cases of intentional ambiguity, where one of the negotiators tries to keep the language so loose that the agreement doesn't adequately resolve the pertinent issues but merely seems to. Of course, the negotiators may allow some loose ends to remain untied in order to permit flexibility in the interpretation of the agreement, but they should do this with their eyes open and not be fooled into doing it.

Because some negotiating strategies are deceitful, negotiators need to learn defensive techniques to combat these strategies. Public health leaders acting as negotiators must thoroughly understand the negotiation process and the major impediments to a successful completion of the process.

Sometimes a negotiator will decide that a point in the negotiations has been reached beyond which no further concessions will even be entertained.[51] Though dangerous, for it can cause the negotiations to break down entirely, this strategy has the potential to force the parties to come to some kind of agreement.

Some strategies, including stonewalling and the no-concessions strategy just mentioned, can cause negotiations to become deadlocked. Since a deadlock is an impasse, negotiators should have on hand strategies to break deadlocks. One strategy is a return to one of the prenegotiation steps in order to clarify issues and goals and thereby get the negotiations back on track.

The 12th strategy listed is abbreviated as HRESSC (high realistic expectations with small systematic concessions).[52] Negotiators who use this strategy maintain expectations that are high but can be met. They also realize they will have to make some concessions in order to keep the negotiation process headed toward completion. Since the expectations are high, the concessions and trade-offs tend to be small.

Some negotiators start the negotiating process by making concessions immediately. This strategy can disarm the other party and actually lead to a better outcome for the party using the strategy. It is best employed from a position of strength. If the party doing the conceding is perceived as weak, the other party will view the strategy as a further sign of weakness and may try to push its own agenda as far as it can, defeating the purpose of the strategy.

The next strategy involves a focus on problem solving. The strategy demonstrates that there is confusion between conflict resolution strategies that are oriented to the long-term and problem-solving that tends to be more short-term in effect. Many factors and interests enter into negotiation.

One delaying tactic used by negotiators is to direct attention to goals or issues that are peripheral to the main goals or issues. This may seem to be a counterproductive strategy, but in some situations it can in fact clarify the major interests involved, prevent a breakdown in the negotiation process, allow important information to be discovered, and influence the other parties to come to a resolution more quickly.

Finally, negotiators make use of closure strategies to get an agreement written and accepted by all parties. Once this is done, closure can occur. However, a decision may be made to review progress in a specified period of time.

Every negotiation is unique, and negotiators often combine standard strategies or create new ones to deal with the specifics of the individual case. Exercise 11–2, adapted from a case study by Jurkowski and Neuberger,[53] presents a scenario in which the students have the opportunity to carry out a negotiation regarding a critical public health problem. The students can either use some of the strategies described above or create their own strategies.

Negotiation is a complex type of process that has many potential pitfalls. It is related to the other types of process described in this chapter, and indeed decision making, problem solving, and conflict resolution can all play a role in typical negotiations. Public health leaders must

- learn to resolve conflict through negotiation, adjudication, mediation, and arbitration
- learn various methods for carrying out negotiations
- use well-trained and experienced negotiators for negotiating with other parties
- make sure that the negotiators have skills and abilities described in this section
- learn to use the "Getting to Yes" and the Schoenfield and Schoenfield negotiation models
- master the steps of the negotiation process
- learn the standard negotiation strategies and tactics

SUMMARY

This chapter has presented new tools to add to the public health leadership toolkit. Public health leadership, like other kinds of leadership, encompasses the essential activities of decision making, conflict resolution, and negotiation. Public health leaders who lack the skills needed to perform these activities will fail, at least partially, to live up to their responsibility as leaders. Further, to develop these skills, they must open up the public health leadership toolkit and work with the tools, even if they are less adept at using them than more experienced colleagues. Learning new skills is difficult and requires dedication and a willingness to take risks. Leaders who put in the time and effort, however, will soon master the skills and become expert at making decisions, resolving conflicts, and negotiating agreements that are beneficial to their organizations.

Discussion Questions

1. Why is risk taking an important part of public health leadership?
2. What are three examples in which you have taken a leadership risk during the last year?
3. What are the differences and similarities between decision making and problem solving?
4. What are some effective conflict resolution strategies?
5. Is intraorganizational conflict always to be avoided? Explain.
6. What are some usual obstacles to successful negotiation?
7. What is the difference between mediation and negotiation?
8. What are the key elements in the prenegotiation phase and the negotiation phase?
9. What are some common negotiation strategies?

Exercise 11–1

THE MEANING OF CONFLICT

Purpose: to recognize the causes of conflict and how to resolve conflict

Key concepts: conflict, conflict resolution

Procedure: The class should break into groups of 8–10 members. First, each group member offers one word in reaction to the term *conflict*. The words are put on a large sheet of paper and discussed by the group. The group then divides into two subgroups, one of which assumes the role of a team from the local health department, the second of which assumes the role of a management team from a local HMO. The HMO wants to build a major new medical center on land owned by the city, but the public health department wants the land for a new substance abuse clinic. Each team explains its position, and together they try to resolve the conflict between them.

Exercise 11–2

NEGOTIATION AND HIV PREVENTION CASE

Purpose: to explore the use of negotiation techniques to address a major community health problem

Key concepts: coalition building, negotiation, prenegotiation, win-win strategy

Scenario: The Benton County HIV Prevention Council has experienced internal disagreements about how to allocate federal funds for HIV/AIDS community programs. Some members of the council adamantly reject needle exchange programs whereas others are strongly in favor of them. Since the conflict between the council representatives has lasted more than two years, the council has agreed to implement a negotiation process to build an agenda and protocol to guide the allocation of financial resources for HIV/AIDS prevention and treatment. The key players include a variety of stakeholders and constituency groups from the local department of health (located in Hamilton, the largest city in the county), the Benton County Health Department, and the community at large. Substance abuse is a major problem in Hamilton, and the number of reported HIV/AIDS cases has doubled in the last five years. HIV/AIDS cases are also increasing in the rural areas of the county. The Benton County Board of Health has hired a professional negotiator to work with the Benton County HIV Prevention Council. The county has also been informed that it will receive a million dollars from the federal government to fund the protocol that is developed.

Procedure: The class should divide into groups of eight. Seven of the group act as members of the Benton County HIV/AIDS Prevention Council and the other person becomes the negotiator. The group should spend an hour negotiating an end to the conflict using the Fisher et al. model and another hour using the 14 steps of the Schoenfield and Schoenfield model, if possible. If both models are used, the group should discuss the similarities and differences between the two models. Once all groups have completed their comparison of the two models, a representative from each group should present a five-minute talk to other groups about the negotiation process, and then all groups should engage in a discussion about the negotiation strategies that were used.

REFERENCES

1. M. DePree, "The Leaders Legacy," in *Leader to Leader*, eds. F. Hesselbein and P.M. Cohen (San Francisco: Jossey-Bass, 1999).
2. J.M. Kouzes and B.Z. Posner, *The Leadership Challenge*, 2d ed. (San Francisco: Jossey-Bass, 1995).
3. N.L. Frigon and J.K. Jackson Jr., *The Leader* (New York: AMACOM [American Management Association, 1996).
4. R. Fritz, *Corporate Tides* (San Francisco: Berrett-Koehler, 1996).
5. P. Hersey et al., *Management of Organizational Behavior*, 7th ed. (Upper Saddle River, NJ: Prentice Hall, 1996).
6. J. Pfeffer, *Managing with Power* (Boston: Harvard Business School Press, 1992).
7. Fritz, *Corporate Tides*.
8. H. Mintzberg, *Mintzberg on Management* (New York: The Free Press, 1989).
9. D. Osborne and T. Gaebler, *Reinventing Government: How the Entrepreneurial Spirit Is Transforming the Public Sector* (Reading, MA: Addison-Wesley, 1992).
10. Mintzberg, *Mintzberg on Management*.
11. S.P. Robbins and M. Coulter, *Management*, 6th ed. (Upper Saddle River, NJ: Prentice Hall, 1999).
12. S.P. Robbins, *Supervision Today* (Englewood, NJ: Prentice Hall, 1995).
13. Robbins and Coulter, *Management*, 6th ed.
14. J.L. Pressman and A. Wildavsky, *Implementation*, 3d ed. (Berkeley, CA: University of California Press, 1984).
15. Robbins and Coulter, *Management*, 6th ed.
16. S.P. Robbins and M. Coulter, *Management*, 5th ed. (Upper Saddle River, NJ: Prentice Hall, 1996).
17. J.G. Liebler et al., *Management Principles for Health Professionals*, 2d ed. (Gaithersburg, MD: Aspen Publishers, 1992).
18. Robbins and Coulter, *Management*, 6th ed.
19. B. Wall et al., *The Visionary Leader* (Rocklin, CA: Prima Publishing & Communication, 1992).
20. A.J. DuBrin, *The Complete Idiot's Guide to Leadership* (New York: Alpha Books, 1998).
21. J.A. Schellenberg, *Conflict Resolution: Theory, Research, and Practice* (Albany, NY: State University of New York Press, 1996).
22. Liebler et al., *Management Principles for Health Professionals*.
23. Robbins and Coulter, *Management*, 6th ed.
24. P.C. Nutt, *Making Tough Choices* (San Francisco: Jossey-Bass, 1989).
25. W. Hendricks, *How To Manage Conflict* (Shawnee Mission, KS: National Press Publications, 1991).
26. D. Weeks, *The Eight Essential Steps to Conflict Resolution* (New York: Jeremy P. Tarcher and Putnam Books, 1994).
27. Liebler et al., *Management Principles for Health Professionals*.
28. M. Winer and K. Ray, *Collaboration Handbook* (St. Paul, MN: Amherst H. Wilder Foundation, 1994).
29. DuBrin, *The Complete Idiot's Guide to Leadership*.
30. Robbins and Coulter, *Management*, 6th ed.
31. A. Rahim, *Organizational Conflict Inventories* (Palo Alto, CA: Consulting Psychologists Press, 1983).
32. Robbins and Coulter, *Management*, 6th ed.
33. Weeks, *The Eight Essential Steps to Conflict Resolution*.
34. Schellenberg, *Conflict Resolution*.
35. R. Fisher et al., *Getting to Yes*, 2d ed. (New York: Penguin Books, 1991).
36. F.E. Jandt, *Win-Win Negotiating* (New York: Wiley and Paul Gillett Books, 1985).
37. H. Raiffa, *The Art and Science of Negotiation* (Cambridge, MA: Harvard University Press, 1982).
38. Raiffa, *The Art and Science of Negotiation*.
39. Robbins and Coulter, *Management*, 5th ed.
40. Robbins and Coulter, *Management*, 5th ed.
41. Jandt, *Win-Win Negotiating*.
42. Fisher et al., *Getting to Yes*.
43. Jandt, *Win-Win Negotiating*.

44. Jandt, *Win-Win Negotiating.*
45. M.K. Schoenfield and R.M. Schoenfield, *The McGraw-Hill 36 Hour Negotiating Course* (New York: McGraw-Hill, 1991).
46. E. Jurkowski and B. Neuberger, *Negotiation Skills for Community Resource Planning* (Chicago: Illinois Public Health Leadership Institute, 1995).
47. R. Fisher and D. Ertel, *Getting Ready To Negotiate* (New York: Penguin Books, 1995).
48. Schoenfield and Schoenfield, *The McGraw-Hill 36 Hour Negotiating Course.*
49. G. Fuller, *The Negotiator's Handbook* (Paramus, NJ: Prentice Hall, 1991).
50. Schoenfield and Schoenfield, *The McGraw-Hill 36 Hour Negotiating Course.*
51. Schoenfield and Schoenfield, *The McGraw-Hill 36 Hour Negotiating Course.*
52. Schoenfield and Schoenfield, *The McGraw-Hill 36 Hour Negotiating Course.*
53. Jurkowski and Neuberger, *Negotiation Skills for Community Resource Planning.*

Chapter 12

Cultural Competency

Only by venturing into the unknown do we enable new ideas to take shape, and those shapes are different for each voyager.

Margaret Wheatley, *Leadership and the New Science*

By the year 2030, racial and ethnic minorities are expected to total 40 percent of the U.S. population (Figure 12–1), up from 30 percent at the start of the new century. As a result, the professions, like the general population, will include a steadily increasing percentage of minorities as members. The growth in minority representation will bring both challenge and promise.

A recent federal report on the public health work force in the 21st century stated that it would be in the best interests of the American public to be served by a work force that is ethnically and culturally diverse.[1] Furthermore, a study of middle-class Americans found that that these Americans generally support multiculturalism.[2] However, they also generally believe that all immigrants should learn English and become integrated into American society—a point of view referred to as "benign multiculturalism."[3] Many immigrants and native-born minorities think that the emphasis on integration into the mainstream is a form of disrespect toward and denigration of the cultural values of the diverse minority groups that make up a large portion of the U.S. population. In short, it seems as if recent attempts to value the full range of different minority groups have been a failure.[4] Some of these issues are explored in Case Study 12–A which explores the issue of racism in a small rural city undergoing demographic change.

Public health leaders, to function effectively in a more culturally diverse environment, will have to confront their personal prejudices and stereotypes and take measures to overcome them. They also should try to understand the nature of the challenges presented by increased cultural diversity at the organizational and community levels.[5] First, many people want to maintain things as they are because they feel comfortable with the familiar. Second, some people are prejudiced against certain racial or ethnic groups because of how they were raised. Third, organizations often use impersonal hiring methods and favor people who fit the

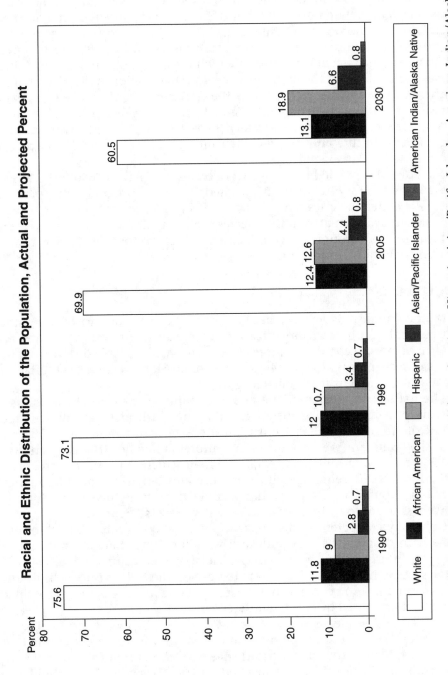

Figure 12–1 Diversity in the United States. Minority (African American, Hispanic, Asian/Pacific Islander, American Indian/Alaska Native) representation in the U.S. population is expected to exceed 30 percent within the decade and climb to nearly 40 percent by 2030.

organizational mode, which usually means people like those who are already organizational members.

Affirmative action programs were instituted to address the fact that the makeup of many organizations did not reflect the makeup of the general population. Their goal is not to obliterate differences but rather to create an environment in which cultural diversity becomes a strength. Having employees with a range of different backgrounds and cultural values can create synergy and lead to greater effectiveness. A synergistic system is not one in which individual differences are obliterated but rather one in which the parts work together harmoniously. Therefore, if public health leaders are to be successful in the 21st century, they need to deal with the issue of cultural diversity today and learn to appreciate the diversity that exists in our society.[6] In the past, leaders expected people to adjust to the existing organizational culture and suppress their unique characteristics. This expectation has ceased to be a reasonable one.

Moreover, no public health agency operates independently of other organizations, the community in which it is located, or, for that matter, other parts of the globe. Global health issues have a way of affecting local communities. Thus local public health leaders may find themselves dealing with an extremely diverse range of colleagues from around the world, one more reason for these leaders to work at becoming culturally competent.

MULTICULTURALISM

Multiculturalism is tied to what has been called the "politics of recognition."[7] Each cultural group in an organization, community, or country strives for acceptance. If not accepted, the group feels demeaned or looked down upon. The politics of recognition are not new in the United States. Different cultural groups have repeatedly fought for public recognition.

The nature and degree of the public's commitment to multiculturalism are not easy to determine.[8] For instance, public health leaders and others argue in support of "multiculturalism" but typically expect different cultural groups to accept the dominant Western European culture. Public health organizations need to review, restudy, rethink, and reorganize their structure in order to truly become multicultural.[9] Differences based on culture and language should enhance the profession of public health community rather than create divisions within it. Yet divisiveness seems to be increasing as we enter the 21st century.

Culturally competent leaders have the skills and attitudes needed to relate to people with different backgrounds and with different characteristics, including people of different races, genders, ages, sexual orientations, social classes, and lifestyles (see Exhibit 12–1).[10] One way to develop these skills is to walk around the workplace and talk to people regularly. Furthermore, talking directly to individuals defuses friction caused by cultural differences.

Public health leaders must get to know not only their work force but also their community. Getting out of the office and meeting with different cultural groups helps leaders define the public health needs of the community better and also presents the public health agency in a better light. The agency might hold an open house to allow the community to get a better sense of what a public health agency does. An agency leader might invite residents from a range of backgrounds to his or her home for a party. By eating at local ethnic restaurants, leaders can learn

Exhibit 12–1 Categories of Diversity

- Race
- Sex
- Religion
- Age (young, middle-aged, old)
- Ethnicity (country of origin)
- Education
- Job-relevant abilities
- Mental disabilities (attention deficit disorder)
- Physical disabilities (hearing impairment, wheelchair use)
- Values and motivation
- Sexual orientation (heterosexual, homosexual, bisexual)
- Marital status (married, single, cohabitating, widow, widower)
- Family status (children, no children, two-parent family, single parent, grandparent)
- Personality traits (introverted, extroverted, conscientious)
- Functional background (area of specialization)
- Technology interest (high-tech, low-tech, technophobe)
- Weight (average, obese, underweight, anorexic)
- Hair (full head of hair, bald, wild hair, tame hair, long hair, short hair)
- Tobacco use (smoker versus nonsmoker, chewer versus nonchewer)
- Gum use (chewer versus nonchewer)
- Styles of clothing and appearance (dress up, dress down, professional appearance, casual appearance)

about different cultural groups and reach out to those groups at the same time. Public health practitioners in general should be encouraged to learn languages, for being able to speak the native language of a community group will enhance the public health agency's credibility.

Although most cross-border alliances are business related, public health leaders may be involved in the creation of a cross-border alliance or partnership, in which case they need to engage in assessing and understanding the cultural differences that exist as one of the preliminary steps.[11] Further, they must continue to address cultural factors even when they seem to have become less important. Management of cultural differences should be a part of any cross-cultural relationship.

To increase their cultural competency and act with cultural sensitivity, leaders should follow these five guidelines:

1. They need to be aware of their own strengths and weaknesses as well as their own prejudices. Without this kind of self-awareness, they will not be able to address effectively the cultural issues that arise in their organization.
2. They need to be alert for opportunities to receive feedback. Feedback, in this area as well as others, is an important information source.
3. They need to become lifelong learners always on the lookout for new knowledge and skill development opportunities.
4. They need to integrate work life with personal life and to maintain a multicultural perspective in both.
5. They also need to learn to respect the differences between people. Out of existing differences can come strength.

Multicultural issues need to be addressed early in the formulation of a multi-cultural team, coalition, or partnership.[12] Exercise 12–1 was developed by Rosenthal to gauge the effectiveness of a group in addressing multicultural issues.

To deal with multicultural issues, public health leaders must

- learn how to analyze demographic data
- study social, economic, and political trends
- increase the number of minority public health staff so that the agency's makeup reflects the community's makeup
- consult with community leaders with different cultural backgrounds to guarantee that the programs developed fit the needs of the relevant cultural groups
- use feedback to monitor communication with cultural groups
- evaluate the workplace using the inclusivity checklist (see Exercise 12–1)

CULTURAL DIVERSITY

Cultural diversity programs are distinct from affirmative action programs. Affirmative action programs are generally intended to guarantee access to jobs by minority groups. Cultural diversity programs address the differences between people and try to ensure that people from different cultural backgrounds respect each other and are able to work together in harmony. They teach people to look beyond race, gender, and sexual orientation, for example, and treat each individual with the full respect due a human being. In Exercise 12–2, the students explore the cultural diversity that exists among themselves with the purpose of gaining greater cultural understanding.

It is imperative that leaders view multicultural differences from a positive perspective rather than a negative one. Negativism undermines the communication process and obstructs the positive effects of building community partnerships. It is worth pointing out here the essential role that communication plays in dealing with cultural diversity. Little progress can be made unless everyone understands each other. Note that communication encompasses vocal inflections, hand gestures, and other types of nonverbal communication.

Public health leaders must keep track of trends that have the potential to affect the extent and nature of the cultural diversity confronting them, such as the globalization of business, and the ways of dealing with cultural diversity, such as new types of programs.

Public health leaders must be devoted to promoting the health of everyone in the community, including members of diverse minority populations. The special health needs of these populations and their lack of access to programs and services must be addressed. Noncommonality of language is sometimes an obstacle in the way of residents' receiving needed services, and public health leaders need to ensure that individuals who do not speak English will still get the care or services they require.

A report of the President's Initiative on Race cited major health findings regarding culturally diverse populations.[13] For example, the infant mortality rate is two and a half times higher for African Americans and one and a half times higher for Native Americans than for whites. In 1995, the age-adjusted rate of death attributable to heart disease for African Americans was 147 deaths per 100,000 people, compared with 105 deaths per 100,000 for whites and 108 deaths per 100,000 overall. The number of new acquired immune deficiency syndrome cases among African Americans is now greater than the number of new cases among whites. The prevalence of diabetes is 70 percent higher among African Americans than among whites, and the prevalence among Hispanics is nearly double the prevalence among whites. As for national immunization rates, 79 percent of white children less than two years of age have the full series of vaccinations, whereas only 74 percent of African American youngsters and 71 percent of Hispanic youngsters do. There are inequities in access to health care as well. For example, minority mothers are less likely than white mothers to get prenatal care. Access seems to be directly related to income level, which partly explains why certain minority groups have low rates of service use. Another access-related issue is whether a cultural group favors using traditional healers rather than medical school–trained physicians.

Figure 12–2 presents an interactionist model showing how diversity influences the careers of leaders and the effectiveness of their organizations.[14] As can be seen in column one, cultural diversity can have an impact at the individual, team, and agency levels (and, as noted above, it can also influence relations between a public health agency and the community in which it is located). The next two columns list possible effects on the individual and the organization. To get a fix on the diversity climate in an agency or a community, agency leaders can answer the questions in Exhibit 12–2.

The road from merely managing diversity to creating a culturally competent organization has many steps.[15] First comes awareness and understanding of cultural diversity, then action plans are developed. Figure 12–3 presents one model for developing cultural competency. Note the importance given to integrating diversity issues into planning activities. As in any extended process, regular feedback is essential, and revisiting the issue of cultural awareness and understanding may be beneficial after the implementation of certain action steps.

Leaders must be sensitive to the needs of cultural groups in the community as well as in the agency. They should monitor these needs using epidemiologic data. To be fully culturally competent, public health leaders must

- directly address the issue of cultural diversity in the workplace
- concentrate on understanding the cultural values and norms of community partners
- learn to face personal stereotypes and prejudices in order to remove barriers due to cultural differences
- learn to be culturally sensitive and empathic to those they interact with
- evaluate the work environment to determine the positive and negative effects of a diverse work force
- learn epidemiologic techniques for analyzing the health needs of the community
- analyze diversity issues at each step in the leadership process
- develop a cultural diversity training program for all employees
- develop a workplace policy statement on cultural differences

Exercise 12–3 provides an opportunity to explore the way in which cultural diversity impacts public leadership activities.

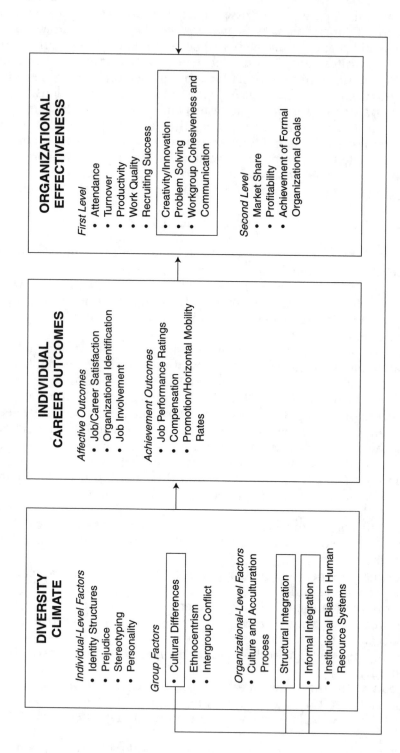

Figure 12–2 An interactional model of the impact of diversity on individual career outcomes and organizational effectiveness.

Exhibit 12–2 Diversity Climate Index

---

1. Identify personal stereotypes and prejudices.
2. Do these stereotypes affect my job performance?
3. Does the staff in my agency judge others by standards different from community standards?
4. How is intergroup conflict resolved?
5. Within the agency, does the composition of the work force reflect the community diversity?
6. Are culturally diverse people in the upper echelons of the organization?
7. How do the agency personnel interact with the community?
8. How does the community relate to the agency?
9. Does the agency address the key health issues of concern to the community?
10. Have community partnerships been developed?

CULTURAL COMPETENCY SKILLS

Cultural competency includes the willingness and ability to develop programs and services for people of different cultures. As the report of the President's Initiative on Race states, "By understanding, valuing and incorporating the cultural differences of America's diverse population and examining one's own health-related values and beliefs, health providers deliver more effective and cost-efficient care."[16(p.17)]

Further, public health leaders need to ensure that all agency staff act in a culturally sensitive way by setting and publicizing appropriate policies and procedures. A lack of concern for the needs of culturally diverse populations can have legal consequences. Case Study 12–B involves a discrimination complaint made to an Office for Civil Rights. (This case study was written by a team of public health leaders based on their personal experiences.)

It is through language that we express our culture and our personal needs. Words have power.[17] In American society, most people view English as the language of choice. The assumption that only English should be spoken in public venues, such as a health care clinic, constitutes a denigration of other languages and leads to a resistance to helping people who do not speak English or speak English peppered with words from their native language. Public health leaders and organizations have to address the issue of bilingualism in their community if they are to maintain credibility.

As pointed out above, it is necessary to go through a series of stages—awareness, understanding, and action—before cultural competency is attained.[18] Of course, this analysis of the process of achieving cultural competency is very general, and the process can be broken down further, as in the following model:[19]

1. Cultural destructiveness occurs when cultural groups are discriminated against.
2. If the public health system is biased and culturally incompetent, it will be unable to facilitate change in health behaviors of culturally diverse groups.

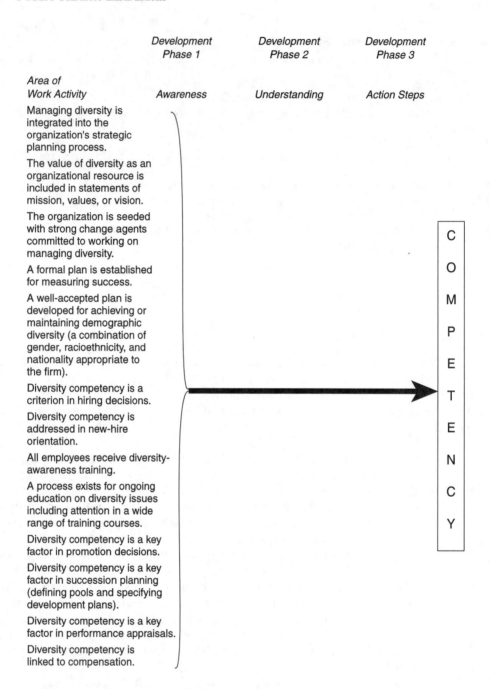

Figure 12–3 Diversity competency model for organizations.

3. Cultural incompetency may in part be a result of cultural blindness on the part of public health leaders, including a lack of awareness of the cultural factors in health and disease.

4. The fourth stage is reached when public health leaders and other practitioners begin to achieve cultural sensitivity. They become aware of cultural

differences and attempt to develop special programs to address the needs of different cultural groups.

5. Cultural competency is achieved when the leaders develop programs tied to different cultural groups.
6. If the programs are successful in meeting the special needs of different cultural groups, the public health leaders can be said to have become culturally proficient.

Exercise 12–4, based on Case Study 12–B, allows the students to develop an action plan based on the cultural competency models presented above.

Cultural competency must start at the individual level, but it also must be present at the organizational and community levels (Figure 12–4).[20] Each individual in an organization has the responsibility of becoming culturally competent, and the organization's leaders need to support cultural competency by developing a written policy on cultural competency and providing awareness training to staff. They themselves need to be trained in demographic analysis, at least to the extent of being able to understand the demographic changes in the community and in the health status of culturally diverse populations.[21] The achievement of organizationwide cultural competency will likely result in changes in recruitment programs, staff orientation, performance appraisals, compensation packages, and promotion rules.

It is important to reinforce culturally competent staff behavior[22] and to recognize the value of cultural competency and the value of protecting diverse viewpoints. Public health leaders need to celebrate diversity in the community by holding, for example, an annual diversity and health fair. Leaders should also honor individuals involved in innovative diversity programs and publicize the positive results of these programs.

Cultural competency confers many benefits (Figure 12–5). For one thing, community residents want to feel that the programs of the local public health

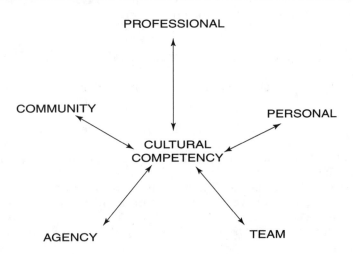

Figure 12–4 Multidimensional aspects of cultural competency.

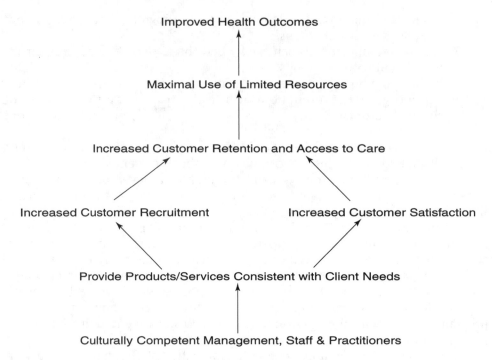

Figure 12–5 Benefits of cultural competence in health care.

agency are oriented toward them and will be more satisfied with programs that are culturally competent. Such programs will increase access to care by culturally diverse groups. Exhibit 12–3 lists five of the benefits of cultural competency that accrue to health agencies and the recipients of their services.

It is true that money is always an issue. Leaders will need to make choices as to how many resources to devote to creating a culturally competent organization. They will also need to ensure that the resources assigned to improving the level of cultural sensitivity are used as efficiently as possible.

Exhibit 12–3 Positive Effects of Cultural Competency in Health Agencies

- It allows the provider to obtain more specific and complete information to make a more appropriate diagnosis.
- It facilitates the development of treatment plans that are followed by the patient and supported by the family.
- It reduces delays in seeking care and allows for more use of health services.
- It enhances overall communication and the clinical interaction between provider and patient.
- It enhances the compatibility between Western health practices and traditional cultural health practices.

Public health leaders must

- lead the agency at all times with cultural diversity in mind
- monitor the appropriateness of programs and services for multicultural groups
- put cultural diversity policies into practice and live the policies
- develop cultural awareness programs and foster intercultural understanding
- understand the stages necessary to make cultural proficiency a reality
- evaluate agency progress toward cultural competency on an ongoing basis
- celebrate the accomplishments of others in the area of cultural competency
- develop diversity and health community fairs with community partners

SUMMARY

People do not feel that many social programs work. There is a critical need to concentrate on what works rather than what does not work. It is up to the public health system and its leadership to help find solutions for problems related to our cultural diversity. The task will not be easy and yet it is necessary. The trend toward greater cultural diversity will not stop. Public health leaders need to be at the forefront of attempts to get rid of our stereotypes, correct inaccurate cultural assumptions, build solid relationships with cultural neighbors, and empower all Americans.

Discussion Questions

1. How would you as a public health leader deal with the alleged ethnic discrimination described in Case Study 12–A?
2. How would you set about helping the local high school develop a cultural diversity training program?
3. What are the guidelines for dealing with cultural diversity in the community and in the public health agency work force?
4. What are the steps that someone needs to go through to reach cultural competency?
5. What are some strategies for creating a cultural competent staff?

Exercise 12–1

ROSENTHAL INCLUSIVITY CHECKLIST

Purpose: to learn how to build multicultural teams and coalitions and evaluate inclusivity issues

Key concepts: inclusivity, multiculturalism, team performance

Procedure: The class should divide into teams of 7 or 8 members. Each team then fills out the Rosenthal inclusivity checklist and discusses how the team might function in a multicultural environment. The discussion should focus on those items on the checklist that are not checked and the implications for team

Exhibit 12–1–A Inclusivity Checklist

Instructions:
Use this Inclusivity Checklist to measure how prepared your coalition is for multicultural work and to identify areas for improvement. Place a check mark in the box next to each statement that applies to your group. If you cannot put a check in the box, this may indicate an area for change.

☐ The leadership of our coalition is multiracial and multicultural.

☐ We make special efforts to cultivate new leaders, particularly women and people of color.

☐ Our mission, operations, and products reflect the contributions of diverse cultural and social groups.

☐ We are committed to fighting social oppression within the coalition and in our work with the community.

☐ Members of diverse cultural and social groups are full participants in all aspects of our coalition's work.

☐ Meetings are not dominated by speakers from any one group.

☐ All segments of our community are represented in decision making.

☐ There is sensitivity and awareness regarding different religious and cultural holidays, customs, recreational and food preferences.

☐ We communicate clearly, and people of different cultures feel comfortable sharing their opinions and participating in meetings.

☐ We prohibit the use of stereotypes and prejudicial comments.

☐ Ethnic, racial, and sexual slurs or jokes are not welcome.

---

functioning and performance. As part of the discussion, team members should also consider the types of environments in which the team would be likely to perform well and the types of environments in which the team would perform poorly. Representatives from each team should then summarize their results and conclusions for the class as a whole.

Exercise 12–2

CULTURAL UNDERSTANDING

Purpose: to explore the issue of diversity and the best means of increasing cultural understanding

Key concepts: cultural diversity, cultural understanding, personal characteristics

Procedure: Each student is given a "Quest for Diversity" form and, for each category, tries to find the person in the class who best represents that category. When the student succeeds in identifying a person for a category, the student then talks to that person about one of his or her personal characteristics. Students should be careful to avoid cultural stereotyping and similar barriers to understanding. Students who find representatives for the most categories and for the least

Exhibit 12–2–A Quest for diversity form

Diversity Categories	Found People	Personal Characteristics
professional woman/ homemaker		
oldest grandparent		
youngest parent		
Native-American background		
Asian-American background		
African-American background		
in public health at least 30 years		
parent was a migrant worker		
parent who was an immigrant		
largest number of siblings		
first in family with college degree		
Latino background		
Russian or Polish background		
an elected official		
most children		
man who is homemaker		
rural dweller		
world traveler		
person with a disability		
speaks five languages		

categories should be selected to present their findings to the class as a whole. The class should discuss the merits and limitations of each student's approach to diversity categorization.

Exercise 12-3

LEADERSHIP AND CULTURAL DIVERSITY

Purpose: to explore how diversity influences the way in which public health leaders carry out their responsibilities

Key concepts: cultural diversity, leadership system activities

Procedure: The class should divide into groups of 7 or 8 members. Each group explores the ways in which diversity affects team building; values clarification; the development of a mission, a vision, goals and objectives, and action plans; the implementation of program interventions; and the evaluation of programs. After the discussion, each group prepares a five-minute presentation based on the discussion and shares its findings with the other groups.

Exercise 12-4

CULTURAL COMPETENCY IN GOLD COUNTY

Purpose: to develop a personnel recruitment action plan to diversify the public health agency work force

Key concepts: action planning, cultural competency, cultural sensitivity, personnel recruitment

Procedure: Case Study 12–B presents the demographics for Gold County. An analysis of the ethnic and racial makeup of the county health department indicates that 80 percent of the staff are white, 15 percent are African American, and 5 percent are Hispanic. The class should divide into teams, and each team should discuss the action steps needed to ensure that the health department is culturally competent. One area of focus should be the development of a personnel recruitment plan to ensure that the health department's work force is capable of understanding and responding appropriately to cultural issues within the community it serves. An issue that needs to be decided is whether the best approach is to attempt to recruit a work force that mirrors the demographic composition of the community.

Case Study 12–A

Racism: A Mental Health Issue

D. Clemons, J.A. Janssen, K. Pakieser-Reed, J. Pitzer, and S. Strachniak

BACKGROUND

A Mexican-American male (father of two children, married, intact family) was accused of molesting a young "white" girl. The incident occurred in Harvest City. The allegation was publicized in the local paper. A group of Anglo males gathered outside the Mexican-American's home and stoned it. Two Anglos were arrested for ethnic intimidation. The charge against the Mexican-American male was dropped as a false charge, without publicity.

The local newspaper's editorial declared the incident was racist in nature and stated that the community cannot "sweep [it] under the carpet." Local church leaders offered (1) to facilitate the process of cultural awareness by the majority population of the minority population, (2) to increase awareness of racism in the community, and (3) to increase understanding between people.

The Harvest City Council established a human relations committee in the fall of 1991 and hired Mr. George as a consultant to help define the committee's role. As a result of George's actions, the city forwarded a survey to the local schools for distribution to all parents and high school seniors. The survey focused on identifying the perceived community needs as determined by the parents and seniors. The committee's actions would then be directed by the survey results. In the spring of 1992, tension continued to grow, and some fighting occurred between Anglos and Hispanics in the Harvest community.

The human relations committee sponsored "Fiesta Days" to increase cultural awareness in a fun atmosphere in the summer of 1992. The celebration was a success!

CASE STUDY CHRONOLOGY

Fall 1992

Tension increased between Anglo and Hispanic students at Harvest High School. The Harvest City Council Human Relations Committee met with the dean of students to discuss the problem. They determined that this was not a gang problem but did have some "ganglike" aspects. The school hired George to serve as a consultant and to develop plans to deflate the racial tension. The Harvest police chief said that the problems were the responsibility of the parents and that the parents needed to be involved in the solutions.

Fistfights broke out among the Anglo and Hispanic students at Harvest High School and Junior High School. Both Anglo and Hispanic students were suspended. School officials believed that the fights were racially motivated. (About 10 percent of the high school students were Hispanic.) Additional fights between Anglos and Hispanics were reported at various locations within the community.

The Temporary Farmers Association approached the Macmillian County Mental Health Board with a request for funding a mental health advocate position (Hispanic liaison) that would be "bilingual and bicultural and dedicated to improving the accessibility and quality of mental health and social services for the Hispanic residents of Macmillian County." The association stated that a growing number of residents in the county were Hispanic, spoke only Spanish, and were becoming an "at risk" population due to little or no access to services that would improve their lives. The board denied the request and recommended formation of a task force to study the issue.

In a separate request, the Temporary Farmers Association requested funding from the Macmillian County Mental Health Board for a six-month study of racism in the county and its effects on the mental health of Hispanic residents. This project was funded.

As a result of the Mental Health Board's recommendation, an Hispanic connection task force was developed, primarily through the efforts of the association. The task force represented almost all of the social service, law enforcement, and religious organizations within the county. In its first meeting, the task force discussed the difficulties of providing services to the Hispanic population. The task force concluded that each member organization would benefit from the services of a countywide Hispanic liaison. They also decided that a "needs assessment should be done to determine county resources and needs regarding Hispanics."

The task force met a second time to design the needs assessment survey and to identify who should receive it. The task force also discussed the Hispanic liaison position: what should be the focus, where would the position be "housed," and how would it be funded? The members agreed that the position should be within the Temporary Farmers Association because the association was the "only agency within the county that has an ongoing and committed relationship with the county's Hispanic population." They also agreed that it must be apparent that all of the task force's member agencies endorsed and supported the liaison role and that the task force would actively support and coach the person chosen as liaison.

In an unrelated action, the Harvest City Council Human Relations Committee requested from the Macmillian County Mental Health Board funding for and/or assistance with the creation of workplace cultural diversity training programs to build bridges between people (Anglos and Hispanics). The project was not funded because it did not directly relate to the provision of mental health services.

Winter 1992–1993

The Hispanic Connection Task Force forwarded a survey to social service and mental health agencies to "better assess available county resources and needs related to our Hispanic population".

A second survey, one for the Hispanic community, was developed by the Hispanic Connection Task Force and distributed to the population through member agencies of the task force. Survey results were slow coming in, partially due to the length of the survey. The task force extended the time for the survey to receive sufficient responses to make a conclusion.

After summarizing results from both needs assessments, the task force developed and forwarded a resolution to government and social service agencies countywide. The resolution acknowledged the value of ethnic and cultural diversity and showed the organizations' support of the Hispanic liaison position. Sixty organizations signed the resolution, including churches, libraries, and mental health and health organizations as well as the county board.

The Macmillian County Board voted 19-2 in support of the liaison position. However, some board members felt that all non-English-speaking residents should have liaison services available to them and that the position as proposed was providing Hispanics with special status. No funding decision was made with this vote.

Following the passing of the resolution, the Macmillian County Mental Health Board approved partial funding for a Hispanic liaison position as presented by the Temporary Farmers Association. They forwarded information about the position and a request for the second half of the salary (up to $20,000) to the Macmillian County Board Health and Human Services Committee. The mental health board felt that the liaison position would help the Hispanic population of 11,000 people to access mental health, school, social service, and government programs and enhance their functioning within the county as a whole. The mental health board felt that prevention and lessening of barriers would decrease the likelihood of more intensive (and expensive) mental health interventions in the future. The liaison would also be responsible for community coordination between Latino and non-Latino organizations.

Spring 1993

Two agencies that did not originally sign the resolution altered their positions to a more positive stance regarding the liaison position. The All Faith Church wrote a letter to the Macmillian County Mental Health Board in full support of the liaison position. Charitable Services signed the resolution with qualifications noted.

The Macmillian County Board and Human Services Committee voted in favor of funding the liaison position to "bridge the cultural gap between Hispanics and county officials in delivering services." Prior to the vote, one member of the committee raised the question of the appropriateness of mental health funds being allocated for a Hispanic liaison position that was developed in response to racist actions. Members of the committee who voted for the position felt that racism was a mental health issue. The committee forwarded the position and funding request to the Macmillian County Board Finance Committee for final recommendation to the county board.

A week after the health and human services committee voted in favor of the liaison position, Charitable Services stated that it had been providing liaison services for the past three and a half years in Harvest and Stone Lake. The county board chairperson, Ms. Ace, stated that she would investigate to see if the new liaison services were needed and would determine if it was appropriate for the county board to fund the position. The mental health board president, Mr. Jones, stated that the proposed liaison position was much broader in scope than the newly discovered social service position.

The county board chairperson decided to not recommend funding to the finance committee of the county board for the proposed liaison position until the Temporary Farmers Association and Charitable Services met, discussed the proposed position, and resolved funding issues. (By now, both groups wanted to be considered for the total of $40,000 salary funds.) The groups agreed to meet with the mental health board executive director, Mr. Jones, and come to a resolution.

Mr. Jones and Ms. Hope, Temporary Farmers Association director, kept a scheduled meeting with the Macmillian County Board Finance Committee to discuss the position. The committee then voted 4-3 against funding the position but agreed to discuss the position again in two months after further study.

The Charitable Services and Temporary Farmers Association directors met and clarified the roles of the two liaison positions. A letter was sent to the county board chairperson noting the clarification and joint support of the new position as proposed.

In the meantime, the mental health board voted to fund the proposed liaison position on a full-time basis for six months. The board felt that the issue was too important to wait for a final funding vote by the county board. The Temporary Farmers Association had to make a decision whether to take the risk and hire a full-time liaison or wait for the county board's funding decision.

The Temporary Farmers Association filled the position; Mr. George gave up his SASS position to become the liaison through November with the hope that additional funds would be approved by the county board.

Two months later, after a positive recommendation from Ms. Ace, the Macmillian County Board Finance Committee met again and unanimously recommended funding of the position through FY 93. The next month, the finance committee's recommendation for funding went to the full county board. The vote was 20-4 in favor of funding the position.

Since 1993, the position has continued to be funded jointly by the county board and the mental health board and has been responsible for the development of five community human relations councils and hundreds of interventions with the Latino and non-Latino communities on individual and organizational levels.

CONCLUSION

Racism is a topic that many people would rather not address, as evidenced by the population described at the beginning of the case study. When racism finally reaches a level that cannot easily be ignored, ownership of the resolution process can be difficult to determine.

Racism can be evidenced by property and personal damages. Wouldn't the proper "owner of the problem" be the legal and law enforcement authorities? When the symptoms lead to physical harm that requires medical attention, then wouldn't the "owner" be the health care institution? If the symptoms are acts of disregard for the human spirit, then isn't the rightful "owner" the church membership? What symptoms need to be exhibited for the problem of racism to fall under the ownership of mental health?

Using the core values of public health as a guideline, answers to these questions can be achieved, as well as a perspective on how racism becomes a public health problem falling within the purview of mental health.

Case Study 12–B

Gold County Health Department:
A Case of Discrimination Requiring Assessment, Policy
Development, and Assurance Practices

Nancy Bluhm, Valerie L. Webb, Ann Rodriguez, Robert Brewster, and Dale W. Galassie

INTRODUCTION

The Gold County Health Department received a discrimination complaint from the Office for Civil Rights necessitating identification (assessment practices), development of policies and plans (policy development practices), and management of organizational resources (assurance practices) to adequately address the complaint, which claimed a lack of adequate interpreter services. Approximately 46 percent of this large urban health department's budget was funded by grants or reimbursables now placed at risk due to the discrimination complaint.

The landmark document *Healthy People 2000: National Health Promotion and Disease Prevention Objectives* noted that by the year 2000 the racial and ethnic composition of the American population would differ significantly. Whites will decline in population from 76 to 72 percent of the population. The Hispanic population could rise from 8 to 11.3 percent. Blacks could increase their proportion from 12.4 to 13.1 percent. In addition, other groups are projected to increase from 3.4 to 4.3 percent. The coloring of the American work force is clearly evident by these statistics. That information further grounded the need for the Gold County Health Department to offer adequate interpreter services to meet the needs of its constituency.

STATEMENT OF FACTS

The Office for Civil Rights (OCR) received a complaint filed against the Gold County Health Department on October 8, 1992. The complainant, Mr. Peter Citizen, who filed on behalf of himself and non-English- and limited-English-speaking people, alleged a violation of Title VI of the Civil Rights Act of 1964 and its implementing regulation, 45 CRF Part 80. Specifically, the complainant alleged that the Gold County Health Department discriminated against non-English- and limited-English-speaking people on the basis of national origin by denying and delaying services, requiring them to provide their own interpreters, and treating them in a discriminatory manner, as evidenced by negative comments and a hostile attitude and by assigning them to Spanish-speaking clinics.

The behavior cited in the allegation would constitute a violation of Title VI and its implementing regulation. OCR has jurisdiction over complaints alleging discrimination on the basis of race, color, and national origin by recipients of federal financial assistance. The Gold County Health Department is a recipient of substantial federal financial assistance and is, therefore, subject to the provisions of Title VI, which prohibits such discrimination. The millions of federal dollars received by the agency are for the Alcohol, Drug Abuse, and Mental Health Block Grant, Medicare, and Medicaid programs.

A prompt investigation to determine whether a violation occurred was scheduled by OCR (within 30 days). During the course of the investigation, the OCR representatives advised they would investigate all allegations in the complaint, interview the complainant, contact and develop information from the Gold County Health Department, and interview any witnesses having information or material relevant to the alleged discrimination.

If a violation had occurred, OCR would attempt to bring the affected institution into voluntary compliance through negotiations. If such corrective action was not secured, OCR would initiate formal enforcement action and perhaps freeze future funding.

The OCR Office notified the Gold County Health Department of the following request prior to the investigation scheduled for November 20, 1992:

1. Copies of policies and procedures relating to the provision of translators for people who are non-English- or limited-English-speaking and how this information is disseminated to staff, persons seeking services, and relevant community organizations;
2. A description of staff training on how and when to offer and use a translator;
3. A list of bilingual staff (or other translators available to the recipient) showing:
   a. Name;
   b. Position, unit in which employed or name of outside organization, if appropriate, and telephone number;
   c. Language spoken and level of fluency;
   d. Hours of availability;
   e. For each outside organization used, a copy of any agreement or a description of the nature of the arrangement;
4. Copies of brochures, forms, and other information in each language in which they are available;
5. An explanation of how written information, policies, consents for treatments, etc., are provided to persons not fluent in English;
6. A copy of the complainant's job description;

7. Copies of the complainant's past and current work evaluations.

BACKGROUND

Racial, cultural, and linguistic minorities comprise a rapidly increasing percentage of the county population. The number of Hispanics, for example, increased by 83.1 percent since 1980 (Exhibit 12–B–1).

The Gold County Health Department, as a major provider of preventive and primary health and mental health services, experienced serious difficulties in meeting the needs of non-English-speaking clients. During 1992, for example, the ambulatory primary health care clinics alone delivered 23,649 patient visits. Hispanics now account for nearly 30 percent of the visits, with nearly half requiring assistance from bilingual staff.

Other linguistic minorities are also served. In Gold County, the number of major languages spoken at home is representative of the challenges faced by federally funded primary care providers throughout the country (Table 12–B–1).

Despite Gold County Health Department's having spent considerable resources to meet multicultural needs through the development of Hispanic clinics, bilingual brochures, and recruitment of minority staff, the OCR investigation directly advised the Gold County Health Department that, effective immediately, Hispanic clinics must be abolished and clients must be served in their primary language.

Exhibit 12–B–1 Gold County 1990 Census

	Total	Hispanic
County population	516,418	38,570
White	450,666	20,100
Black	34,771	1,035
Asian and Pacific Islander	12,588	453
American Indian	1,198	189
Other	17,195	16,793

Hispanic Population 1980–90 Change

1980	1990	Number	Percent
21,064	38,570	+17,506	+83.1%

Hispanic Origins (1990)

Mexican	27,220	5.3%
Puerto Rican	4,829	0.9%
Cuban	539	0.1%
Other Hispanics	5,976	1.2%
Hispanic origin	38,570	7.5% of county population

Table 12–B–1 Language Spoken at Home
(Gold County Census Data)

Language	Number of Persons
Spanish	30,759
German	5,000
Polish	3,348
Italian	3,041
French	2,599
Tagalog	2,402
Chinese	1,635
Indic	1,397
Korean	1,248
Slavic	1,050
Greek	1,028

OCR requested the Gold County Health Department to compile and forward the requested information to its office within 20 days of the date of the written request. These data would be retained by the reviewer as partial documentation of the findings.

The Gold County Health Department was in the midst of an administrative transition as well. The executive officer had resigned only two and a half months earlier, and the health board appointed an interim director. The recruitment process for the executive officer occurred at the same time as the complaint investigation.

The breadth of the discrimination complaint required that all clinic facilities countywide be audited for multicultural sensitivity and the ability to meet non-English-speaking clients' needs. In addition, the health board recently had approved a hiring freeze to be implemented on December 1, which would inhibit increasing the current staff to address the need for interpreters.

An on-site investigation was scheduled for November 20, 1992.

REFERENCES

1. Public Health Service, *Public Health Workforce: An Agenda for the 21st Century* (Washington, DC: U.S. Department of Health and Human Services, 1997).
2. A. Wolf, *One Nation after All* (New York: Viking Penguin Books, 1998).
3. Wolf, *One Nation after All*.
4. T. Wicker, *Tragic Failure* (New York: Morrow, 1996).
5. W.J. Paul and A.A. Schnidman, "Valuing Differences: The Challenges of Personal Prejudice and Organizational Preference," in *The Promise of Diversity*, eds. E.Y. Cross et al. (Burr Ridge, IL: Irwin Professional Publishing, 1994).
6. A.M. Schlesinger Jr., *The Disuniting of America* (New York: Norton, 1992).
7. C. Taylor, ed., *Multiculturalism* (Princeton, NJ: Princeton University Press, 1994).
8. R. Bernstein, *Dictatorship of Virtue* (New York: Knopf, 1994).

9. E.Y. Cross et al., eds., *The Promise of Diversity* (Burr Ridge, IL: Irwin Professional Publishing, 1994).
10. A.J. DuBrin, *The Complete Idiot's Guide to Leadership* (New York: Alpha Books, 1998).
11. L. Segil, "Managing Culture in Cross-Cultural Alliances," *Leader to Leader* 6 (Fall 1997): 12–14.
12. B. Rosenthal, "Inclusivity Checklist," in *From the Ground Up: A Workbook on Coalition-Building and Community Development*, eds. T. Wolff and G. Kaye (Amherst, MA: AHEC Community Partners, 1995).
13. President's Initiative on Race, *Health Care Rx: Access for All* (Washington, DC: U.S. Department of Health and Human Services, Health Resources and Services Administration, 1998).
14. T. Cox Jr., *Cultural Diversity in Organizations* (San Francisco: Berrett-Koehler, 1993).
15. T. Cox Jr. and R.L. Beale, *Developing Competency to Manage Diversity* (San Francisco: Berrett-Koehler, 1997).
16. President's Initiative on Race, *Health Care Rx: Access for All.*
17. C. Lemert, ed., *Social Theory: The Multicultural and Classic Readings* (Boulder, CO: Westview Press, 1993).
18. Cox and Beale, *Developing Competency to Manage Diversity.*
19. J.L. Rorie, et al., "Primary Care for Women: Cultural Competence in Primary Care Services," *Journal of Nurse Midwifery* 41, no. 2 (1996): 92–100.
20. Cox and Beale, *Developing Competency to Manage Diversity.*
21. T.H. Cox and S. Blake, "Managing Cultural Diversity: Implications for Organizational Competitiveness," *The Executive* 5, no. 3 (1991): 45–56.
22. S.P. Robbins and M. Coulter, *Management*, 6th ed. (Upper Saddle River, NJ: Prentice Hall, 1999).

Chapter 13

Mentoring and Training in Public Health

My experiences as a mentor were first rate. Just say yes, if you're asked to serve as a mentor.

S.F. Randolph, "The Mentoring Experience"

Mentoring is a critical leadership activity. Leadership development depends on experienced leaders acting as role models for novice leaders. Leader-mentors need to understand leadership and promote the development of leadership skills by others.[1] Mentoring novice leaders will become even more important in the new century, which will almost certainly experience a higher rate of change than the century past.

In general, mentoring is a form of one-to-one teaching, to be contrasted with training, which involves instructing more than one person. Public health leaders do engage in training as well, such as in team building.[2] A public health leader might facilitate the team-building process by presenting guidelines to the team as a whole and also act as a mentor for each team member. (Peer mentoring is also possible in a team situation.) Mentors generally do not give formal instruction but instead teach by example.[3] They understand how the organization works and can explain the written and unwritten laws to their mentees.[4]

Some authors use the term *coaching*[5] rather than *mentoring*, but the activity is essentially the same. The relationship between the mentor and the mentee (or the coach and the coached) is a true partnership, and each should gain something from it (in other words, it should be a win-win relationship). It should also be contractual, which means that the needs and expectations of both parties should be addressed when the relationship is first established. Note that in this chapter *mentor* and *mentoring* will be used instead of *coach* and *coaching*.

Mentors can help in the training of a team by guiding the learning of each team member in leadership. The challenge for the mentor in formal training situations is to help the team become a learning community. The mentor must be committed to the goals of the team and facilitate the learning process for the team members, including through direct one-on-one interaction related to the professional needs of a given member.

The remainder of this chapter explores the nature of mentoring and training and their role in leadership development.

MENTORING

The Benefits of Mentoring

Mentoring offers a number of benefits.[6] First, mentoring young professionals in a given field expands the network of professionals working in that field. This is especially important in public health, where practitioners come from many different disciplines. The mentees also gain the knowledge and tools needed to develop leadership skills. (Note that mentors give tools to their mentees, but the tools need to be translated into action for leadership skills to begin to evolve.) In addition, mentoring usually increases the mentees' chances for promotion.[7]

If a mentor is impressed by a mentee, the mentee may be assigned more challenging tasks. The mentor helps the mentee not only solve problems but make decisions as well. The mentee can acquire cutting-edge information that will aid the mentee in providing technical assistance to others in the future. The mentor can help the mentee navigate through tough choices. The mentee learns the ropes and will know, during his or her tenure as a leader, how to change the ropes as they fray.

For the mentor, the relationship can be extremely positive. Being a role model increases the self-esteem of the mentor and adds to the mentor's legacy.[8] To be looked upon as a person who has knowledge to impart also is important for the mentor. Mentors are usually among the senior members of an organization, and having the sense of being needed by younger members is a clear benefit for them.[9] In general, mentoring is a renewal process for mentors, who may feel rejuvenated. Case Study 13–A reports on the experiences of a mentor.

The organization also gains from mentoring.[10] Often both the mentor and the mentee become more productive as a result of their relationship. Working together, they are able to assess problems and find solutions better than when working solo. Since mentoring leads to leadership development, the mentee is soon able to take over leadership activities. The mentoring relationship may also lead to the discovery and nurturing of hidden talents possessed by the mentee and can help the mentee to hone his or her rough edges. Mentored professionals tend to stay in organizations for longer periods and also move up in the organizational hierarchy more easily.[11]

Mentoring can occur anywhere in the organization. What is needed is an organizational commitment to mentoring. As one author put it, professionals need "mentorcentives."[12]

Exhibit 13–1 lists qualities that mentors should possess and roles they should play. At various times in the mentoring process different qualities and roles will predominate, partly because the influence of the mentor decreases over time as the mentee begins to develop the skills that the relationship is intended to foster.[13] Indeed, mentoring needs to be time limited; it should not result in long-term dependency.

Exhibit 13–1 Mentor Qualities and Roles

- Role model
- Guide
- Willing to be a mentor
- Supporter
- Experienced
- Adviser

- Trusted counsellor
- Leader
- Friend
- Listener
- Knowledgeable
- Shares resources

- Observes confidentiality
- Interested
- Shows mutual respect
- Shows affection
- Accessible
- Networker

Professionals want mentors who will give advice, support, and assistance, such as with the task of setting career goals.[14] The mentee has a responsibility to allocate time and effort to improving skills and competence.[15] Since not all leaders are good mentors, mentees should be careful in choosing whom to establish a mentoring relationship with. Mentoring can be formal, with each new employee assigned to a mentor for a period of time, or informal, where professionals who want a mentor seek one who will understand their professional aspirations. In general, it is preferable for mentees to choose their own mentors.

Developing a Mentoring Relationship

Public health professionals may look for mentors outside of their agency. For example, a community leader or board of health member may help a public health professional better understand how the community works. It is possible to have more than one mentor at a given time, but the more usual scenario is to have several mentors sequentially. Exercise 13–1 allows students to explore their personal mentoring history.

As mentioned above, in some organizations mentees are assigned to mentors. Whether a mentor is assigned or freely chosen, there is no guarantee mentor and mentee will be right for each other. To increase the chance that they will be, a potential mentee can go through a selection process such as the one laid out in Exhibit 13–2. As can be seen, the mentee needs to determine the things that he

Exhibit 13–2 The 21 Steps To Choosing Your Mentor

1. Brainstorm desires.
2. Set goal.
3. Identify achievers.
4. Select top candidates.
5. Research backgrounds.
6. Set goals for meeting.
7. Write letter to mentor prospect.
8. Call to set appointment.
9. Prepare 10 questions.
10. Ask to hear life story.
11. State goals, ask questions.
12. Ask for suggestions.
13. End trial.
14. Send thank-you note, gift.
15. Evaluate information.
16. Take action on mentor suggestions.
17. Call mentor with activity results.
18. Evaluate prospect's response.
19. Request second appointment.
20. Propose a mentoring relationship.
21. Commit to the 16 Laws of Mentoring [Exhibit 13–4].

or she wants to accomplish and then select at least one goal to attain. The process is complex, for the mentee must first engage in personal values clarification and develop a personal vision as steps on the way toward developing personal goals, then determine if there is anyone in the organization who has accomplished similar goals. The best strategy is to identify several possible mentors and do research on them. See Exhibit 13–3 for a contrasting set of selection criteria.

After a mentor is selected, the mentor and mentee go through a series of steps as part of the development of the mentoring relationship. They need to set meeting goals, make appointments, and set an agenda. Early on, the mentor should tell his or her personal story, and together the mentor and mentee will discuss possible goals for the relationship and set a timetable for achieving the goals they choose. The deadlines should be flexible, however, and the timetable can be revised if both parties approve. During the entire relationship, mentor and mentee will need to negotiate with each other and discuss results on a regular basis. Another view of mentoring is provided by the 16 laws listed in Exhibit 13–4.[16]

For mentoring to be successful, whether within an agency or within a community, the environment must nurture the mentoring relationship. In addition, the focus should be on developing the mentee's character as well as on the sharing of information. Finally, the mentoring relationship should have as its ultimate goal independence for the mentee. Good mentoring will make the mentee feel so comfortable with change that his or her reliance on the mentor eventually disappears.

The mentee shares the responsibility for the relationship and its direction. The mentor and mentee are partners who together choose goals for the relationship,

---

Exhibit 13–3 Criteria for Selection of Mentors

1. Must be an accomplished, recognized leader in the health and public health arena.
2. Must be willing to work for one year as a mentor to five fellows, providing consultation and assistance as appropriate.
3. Must be able to participate in orientation/training, the three-day Institute, the two-day 6-month follow-up meeting, the one-day 12-month follow-up meeting, and four to six meetings with the assigned fellows' group.
4. Must have the skills to provide insights to fellows during discussion of case studies.
5. Must be able to facilitate small-group discussions and guide group to consider most important factors in case studies and readings.
6. Must be willing to provide ongoing support to fellows in their professional growth and implementation of successful leadership practices following the formal training program.
7. Must be supported by employer (i.e., time off from regular duties to serve as mentor).
8. Must have held a leadership position in public health for at least 10 years.
9. Should have national leadership credentials as well as state/local recognition.
10. Must have demonstrated skills in administering and directing the three core governmental functions: needs assessment, policy development, and assurance.
11. Must have considerable experience in working successfully with subordinates.

Exhibit 13–4 The 16 Laws of Mentoring

1. The law of positive environment	9. The law of small successes
2. The law of developing character	10. The law of direction
3. The law of independence	11. The law of risks
4. The law of limited responsibility	12. The law of mutual protection
5. The law of shared mistakes	13. The law of communication
6. The law of planned objectives	14. The law of extended commitment
7. The law of inspection	15. The law of life transition
8. The law of tough love	16. The law of fun

make plans to achieve the goals, and implement the plans. They will regularly study options and scenarios. If the mentee becomes overly dependent on the mentor, the latter may have to exhibit a little tough love. The mentoring process usually consists of a series of small changes that accumulate; massive sudden changes are rare. The relationship also carries with it some risk. A mentee can adversely affect the reputation of the mentor. In addition, the mentor's advice may not work in some situations. These caveats aside, the mentoring relationship tends to be mutually beneficial.

The mentoring relationship is mainly a working-hours relationship unless the two partners define it differently. The mentor guides the mentee in learning how to be effective on the job, not how to deal with his or her personal life. One secret of mentoring is that it should be fun as well as exciting. Another is that the best mentoring relationships are mismatches rather than pairings of similar individuals.

Mentoring and Cultural Diversity

As pointed out in the last chapter, cultural diversity issues may affect many relationships in an organization. Mentor and mentee should respect each other as human beings and not let race, ethnicity, or gender get in the way of the relationship. Currently, men often mentor women, partly because men still predominate in the higher levels of most organizations. Cross-sex mentoring must include rules for the relationship that preclude sexual involvement of any kind, coerced or not.[17] Whereas sex can be an issue in cross-sex mentoring, the dearth of women in some organizations can cause women at the top to feel threatened by women poised to move upward, and the feeling of threat can prevent same-sex mentoring relationships from being effective. Note that women make up a large proportion of the public health work force and that women in the upper echelons of public health often serve as mentors to both men and women.

Mentoring by women, according to one author, is "more about commitment than about chemistry. It's about personal growth and development rather than about promotions and plums. And it's more about learning than power."[18(p.188)] Many of the old approaches to mentoring have been revised by women. Female mentees tend to get mentoring from several different mentors on different issues.

Mentoring Guidelines

Figure 13–1 presents a mentoring model that includes mentoring functions and activities. The mentoring relationship is based on role modeling and nurturing. The purpose of the relationship is to get the mentee to put the lessons learned into action. Exhibit 13–5 presents a list of 10 rules that apply to mentoring.

Public health leaders should research mentoring and develop a mentoring program within their agencies. Guidance is needed if the core public health functions model, the organizational practices model, the essential services model, or some combination model is to be implemented successfully in a public health organization. Public health leaders must

- adopt a formal agency mentoring program
- devise "mentorcentives" to increase the number of mentoring relationships

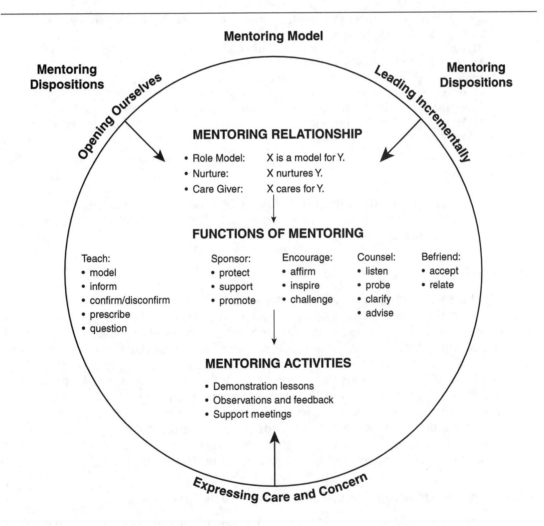

Figure 13–1 Anderson and Shannon mentoring model.

Exhibit 13–5 The Ten Commandments of Mentoring

1. Don't be afraid to be a mentor. Many people, especially women, underestimate the amount of knowledge that they have about…their organization, the contacts they have, and the avenues they can use to help someone else. A person does not have to be at the absolute top of his or her profession or discipline to be a mentor.
2. Remember that you don't have to fulfill every possible function of a mentor to be effective, but let your mentees know where you are willing to help and what kind of information or support you can give that you believe will be particularly helpful.
3. Clarify your expectations about how much time and guidance you are prepared to offer.
4. Let mentees know if they are asking for too much or too little of your time.
5. Be sure to give criticism, as well as praise, when warranted, but present it with specific suggestions for improvement. Do it in a private and nonthreatening context.
6. Where appropriate, "talk up" your mentees' accomplishments to others in your department and institution, as well as at conferences and other meetings.
7. Include mentees in informal activities whenever possible.
8. Teach mentees how to seek other career help whenever possible, such as money to attend workshops or release time for special projects.
9. Work within your institution to develop formal and informal mentoring programs and to encourage social networks as well.
10. Be willing to provide support for people different from yourself. "It is far easier for women than it is for many men to cross boundaries such as race, color, ethnicity, class and religion in working with others. But we all need to practice this skill and avoid the temptation to assist only those with whom we feel the most comfortable, those who are the closest to being clones of ourselves."

- develop a mentoring contract for use by mentors and mentees
- integrate leadership skills with core public health functions in the mentoring relationship

TRAINING

Business leaders have known for a long time that an educated work force will increase the effectiveness and efficiency of a company. They view the cost for training as low in comparison with the long-term benefits. In the government sector, on the other hand, training has been seen as a luxury that often cannot be justified. The result for public health has been a learning gap that has kept public health practitioners from promoting public health in their communities in an effective manner. There is increasing fear that public health agencies may not have a future. The challenge is to train public health leaders for the 21st century. Many public health leaders lack an adequate background in public health, have had limited exposure to academic public health content, are ignorant of advanced information technology, and have had limited leadership training.

A Strategy for Training the Public Health Work Force

In a report of the Public Health Functions Project of the U.S. Department of Health and Human Services (HHS), a five-pronged strategy was laid out for training the public health work force for the 21st century. The report also included a series of steps for achieving training-related goals.[19]

The first prong concerns the development of a national public health leadership (Exhibit 13–6). The suggested federal role is to provide standards and guidelines, promote and conduct research, disseminate the results, guarantee equity across states, and develop priorities for the nation every 10 years.

The second prong concerns leadership at the state and local levels (Exhibit 13–7). Each state is different, and public health leaders, in applying any public health model, need to be guided by the unique characteristics of their state or locality. Training should include leadership development initiatives created in partnership with academia. Local and state public health leaders need to let the national leadership know about the day-to-day realities of public health practice.

The training process includes monitoring the public health work force and acting to ensure that its composition reflects the ethnic and racial diversity of the society at large (Exhibit 13–8). The first step is to define the public health work force. The HHS report defined the work force as all professionals who are responsible for providing essential public health services regardless of the organization for which they work. One of the next steps is to classify and count the public health professionals, and the final step is to identify and implement plans to ensure that the work force is ethnically and culturally diverse.

The fourth prong of the strategy is to develop a curriculum based on the competencies needed for public health practice (Exhibits 13–9 and 13–10).[20] Public health leaders need to determine the skills, abilities, and knowledge bases that the public health work force will need in the 21st century. Included among these are the following: analytic skills, communication skills, policy and development and program planning skills, cultural competency, and basic public health sciences knowledge. Once public health leaders determine the appropriate competencies, they should help develop training initiatives to foster these competencies. Linkages between academics and practicing professionals are critical for ensuring the proper education of the public health work force.

Exhibit 13–6 Proposed Action Steps for National Public Health Leadership

A. Organize a national forum of key stakeholders from both the public and private sectors to examine human resource allocation and trends in public health. Potential forum participants in addition to the Public Health Functions Steering Committee members include the American Association of Health Plans, Health Care and Financing Administration, state Medicaid directors, social workers, substance abuse and mental health professionals, nurses, professional organizations, and the business community in general.

B. Develop and implement modules for Leadership Training Institutes that enable public health leaders to better assess their roles in providing public health services in a changing environment.

C. Involve frontline public health practitioners from all types of organizations in the efforts to enumerate, plan for, and educate the public health work force.

Exhibit 13–7 Proposed Action Steps for State and Local Public Health Leaders

---

A. Ensure that work force planning takes place in all appropriate jurisdictions. Allocation of human resources should be determined by state and local governments or on a regional basis when appropriate due to resources, geography, or other factors.
B. Within each jurisdiction encourage the participation of medical care delivery systems and others with public health responsibilities to achieve mutual goals in work force development.
C. Develop a partnership with states to quantify the supply and demand of personnel providing essential public health services at the state, local, and private sector levels.

The fifth prong is to prepare for the increased use of distance learning that will occur in the new century (Exhibit 13–11). The point is not to demean face-to-face learning but to foster other learning options for public health professionals. Distance learning technologies are constantly evolving, and each technology will be especially effective in some applications and ineffective in others. Public health professionals seem to opt for on-site training because of the obvious fact that public health practitioners practice their craft face to face with clients. However, distance learning can be integrated into the overall education system without reducing the ability of practitioners to handle actual encounters with clients.

Exhibit 13–8 Proposed Action Steps Related to Work Force Composition

---

A. Identify a lead agency or organization to provide leadership in continuing efforts to assess the size, composition, and distribution of the work force as related to essential services of public health.
B. Examine methods used by professional organizations such as the American Nurses Association, American Medical Association, American Psychological Association, American Dental Association, and National Environmental Health Association to classify their respective work forces and incorporate where helpful.
C. Develop a standard taxonomy based on the 10 essential public health services to qualitatively characterize the public health work force. This classification scheme must be derived through collaboration and consensus of the entire public health community.
D. Use the SOC System of the work force and data from the Bureau of Labor Statistics and census surveys to track shifts in the staffing mix of personnel among the governmental, private, and voluntary sectors.
E. Identify and take action steps to ensure that the public health work force is ethnically and culturally diverse.
F. Work with the Office of Management and budget to include appropriate public health entries in the SOC System to facilitate identification of public health worksites, such as local health departments and other organizations providing essential public health services.

Exhibit 13–9 Proposed Action Steps for Competency Development

A. Verify that identified competencies are indeed necessary for efficient and effective practice of public health. Validations of these competencies should be provided by a panel of practice-based experts who are in public health organizations, including employers.
B. Identify competencies critical to all public health practitioners and those critical to successful practice in specific organizational settings. The competencies should be viewed as "organizational" competencies, those required for the entire work force deployed within a given public health setting. (Although all public health practitioners should be familiar with the essential services of public health, few, if any, individuals will be equally competent in all areas.) Categorizing competencies should be conducted by a review panel of experts including practitioners and employers from all practice settings.
C. Improve long-range planning. Public health competencies are evolutionary. They are affected by changes in responsibilities and the practice of public health. There must be a formal mechanism to update competencies to reflect changing demands. A mechanism for assuring current and accurate competencies may take the form of an institute, task force, or other entity supported by government, foundations, and/or the academic community. Responsibilities will include monitoring trends in the demand for public health services and interpreting those demands in terms of the skill and knowledge needed to provide the 10 essential services of public health.

Using Education and Collaboration To Heal the Division between Public Health and Medicine

The last few decades have seen the rise of divisiveness between medicine and public health.[21] Many of the physicians chosen to head health departments whose statutes require a physician at the helm had little knowledge of public health. In fact, public health seemed artificially separated from primary care. In many countries, primary care and public health are seen as one. Several years ago, the author traveled to Armenia to teach a group of public health professionals about public health leadership. The experience led him to make two important observations. First, clinical activities supported at a countrywide level define the official public health policy. Primary care is public health. Second, independent public health leadership is generally not possible in a country where the nationalized system of health care is politically controlled. Administrators have the responsibility to maintain the status quo. The 21st century will see renewed collaboration between medicine and public health in the United States. This type of collaboration has been called cross-sectoral.[22]

Four actions are necessary for the relationship between medicine and public health to improve.[23] First, both physicians and public health professionals must be educated about strategies for fostering cross-sectoral collaboration. Second, each group must legitimize the process. Third, physicians and public health professionals must develop tools to promote the collaboration approach. Finally, they must examine barriers to collaboration and program options and create policies to

Exhibit 13–10 Proposed Action Steps for Curriculum Development

A. Ensure that the practice community has a substantial role in the curriculum development process. Examine existing models that link the academic and practice communities as a first step in facilitating practitioner involvement and target efforts and resources in their replication.

B. Determine the current status of "competency" of the work force. Develop and implement a methodology (survey, direct observation, etc.) to assess the current level of proficiency in the practice of the competencies. This research effort will include an evaluation of how the competencies have been acquired (on-the-job training, formal education, mentoring, continuing education, etc.) and the perceived adequacy of these approaches in the context of the communities being served.

C. Develop measurable performance indicators for identified competencies.

D. Survey public health training/education institutions to assess the extent to which competencies are currently being employed to structure the curriculum.

E. Conduct an analysis of the competency statements and make revisions for their most effective use in curriculum development. Education and training specialists should conduct this analysis.

F. Identify gaps between high-priority competencies that are needed and those competencies already present in the work force. The competencies proposed by the Competency-Based Curriculum Workgroup incorporate projections of competencies needed now and in the future (five years hence). After additional review, these projections can serve as a baseline. Identification and prioritization between the actual and the needed profile of competencies may best be accomplished by a panel composed of practice association representatives, academic institutions, and federal agencies.

G. Translate competencies into discrete didactic and field-based learning experiences and activities.

H. Create a matrix of addressed and unaddressed competencies based on public health organizational needs with the results of the instructional provider survey (data collected during the needs assessment activity) by cross-referencing each element in the competency listing.

I. Support a curriculum development process that is sensitive to the needs of local communities in order to be responsive to the local priorities of each agency, state, or local community relating to the essential services of public health.

J. Recommend to the Council for Education in Public Health and other organizations within the accreditation community that competency-based approaches be incorporated into the standards for educational institution accreditation and into the standards for professional certification and/or licensure.

K. Develop criteria for identifying providers of public health training and education that are "models of excellence" and support these providers through grants and other forms of support. Implement the operation of a "clearinghouse" to promote sharing of exemplary teaching approaches among institutions.

support collaboration. All four of these actions have a strong training component. Public health leaders need the skills to carry out collaboration and need to train staff to support collaborative efforts. In other words, they must understand both the culture of medicine and the culture of public health.

Table 13–1 presents goals and strategies (under the headings "Synergy" and "Models") for medicine–public health collaboration. The use of "synergy" is

Exhibit 13–11 Proposed Action Steps for Distance Learning

A. Establish a formal structure to advocate for the integration of distance learning techniques into practice and academic entities involved in public health strategies for training, education, and communication. Actions necessary for this to proceed include:
   - Evaluate previous studies that document distance learning resources among partners.
   - Develop a strategy for participant registration that is compatible across agencies and that is supported by a technology that allows for orders of magnitude expansion and comparability of data.
   - Establish a standard practice and methodology for stakeholder's evaluation of distance learning results.
   - Institute a common practice for program promotion and marketing.
   - Develop a strategy to facilitate sharing resources across organizational lines (e.g., interagency agreements, cooperative agreements, grants, memorandums of understanding).
   - Initiate standards for distance learning technology that permit system integration across agencies.
   - Encourage and support the use of public/private assignments to promote collaboration in training.
   - Share innovative and effective procurement mechanisms for distance learning services (e.g., task order contracts and other procurement mechanisms).
   - Assist in identifying and developing distance learning faculty and subject matter experts and establishing incentives for their support.
   - Provide grant assistance for development of distance learning programs at regional and local levels.
B. Directly link distance learning systems and program development priorities to the information generated by the Workgroups on Workforce Composition and Competency-based Curriculum.
C. Routinely gather input from key partners regarding training needs and technological capabilities.
D. Develop agency expertise in distance learning; participate in relevant organizations such as the United States Distance Learning Association (USDLA) and Government Alliance for Training and Education (GATE).
E. Provide access to information about public health distance learning programs and resources through mechanisms such as FedWorld Training Mall and the Public Health Training Network Website.
F. Organize a mechanism for pooling and accessing resources and expertise on distance learning across all of public health.

intended to indicate that the results of collaboration are greater than would occur if the activities were performed separately.

Training raises important concerns for public health leaders. These leaders need to make a commitment to continuing their own education and to supporting the continued learning of others, including community partners. Training for practitioners needs to be experientially based so that the skills acquired can be put into practice. As regards training, public health leaders must

   - be lifelong learners
   - master emerging information technologies

Table 13–1 Models of Medicine and Public Health Collaboration

	Synergy	*Models*
I	Improving health care by coordinating services for individuals	A. Bring new personnel and services to existing practice sites B. Establish "one-stop" centers C. Coordinate services provided at different sites
II	Improving access to care by establishing frameworks to provide care for the uninsured	A. Establish free clinics B. Establish referral networks C. Enhance clinical staffing at public health facilities D. Shift indigent patients to mainstream medical settings
III	Improving the quality and cost-effectiveness of care by applying a population perspective to medical practice	A. Use population-based information to enhance clinical decision-making B. Use population-based strategies to "funnel" patients to medical care C. Use population-based analytic tools to enhance practice management
IV	Using clinical practice to identify and address community health problems	A. Use clinical encounters to build community-wide databases B. Use clinical opportunities to identify and address underlying causes of health problems C. Collaborate to achieve clinically oriented community health objectives
V	Strengthening health promotion and health protection by mobilizing community campaigns	A. Conduct community health assessments B. Mount health education campaigns C. Advocate health-related laws and regulations D. Engage in communitywide campaigns to achieve health promotion objectives E. Launch "Healthy Communities" initiatives
VI	Shaping the future direction of the health system by collaborating around policy, training, and research	A. Influence health system policy B. Engage in cross-sectoral education and training C. Conduct cross-sectoral research

- share information
- mentor others
- support training initiatives
- train their partners
- orient training toward the future of public health
- make training programs experientially based

TRAINING THROUGH MENTORING

In public health, training can be enhanced by incorporating mentoring as one of the components. The Illinois Public Health Leadership Institute uses mentoring to undergird leadership development in its one-year training program. Four different types of mentors are included in the training (Figure 13–2). First, a mentor advocate—a public health leader with 10 years of experience—is assigned the responsibility of facilitating the training experiences of a team of public health leaders. The mentor advocate helps each team member network with an experienced public health professional, helps team members deal with concerns and questions, and assists in the development of the team's training projects. The mentor advocate is available to the trainees throughout the year.

In order to explore new skills in the work setting, each leadership trainee selects an agency advisor to help solve work-related problems. Whatever the problem, the solution needs to involve the application of leadership skills and the placement of the problem in a public health core functions context. The trainee has the responsibility of giving the agency advisor readings or case studies that explain or demonstrate the conceptual approaches included in the leadership development training. The trainee and advisor can also explore ways to use leadership skills in the public health agency.

The third mentor is the trainee's "buddy," a person who has gone through the leadership development program a year or more ago. The buddy offers the new trainee insights about the leadership training approaches. He or she can provide friendship, can help the trainee interpret the program's readings and case studies, and can strengthen the public health leadership networking activities. The buddy relationship puts the responsibility for the development of these activities clearly in the hands of the buddy and the trainee.

Finally, trainees develop mentoring relationships with their peers. A training team creates opportunities for the team members to interact, and individual members can look to other members for guidance. Peer mentoring clearly enhances the learning experiences of the trainees by enriching their understanding of readings and presentations and allowing them to get more out of experientially based projects.

The Illinois Public Health Leadership Institute, founded in 1992, was the first state leadership institute funded by the Centers for Disease Control and Prevention (CDC). In 1999, it was renamed the Mid-America Regional Public Health Leadership Institute, and it now trains public health leaders from Illinois, Indiana,

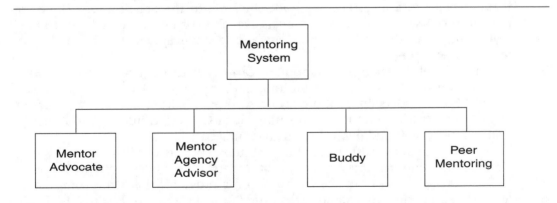

Figure 13–2 Leadership development mentoring system.

Wisconsin, and North Dakota. Public health leaders in 28 states have access to state or regional public health leadership development programs (Figure 13–3). There has been increasing recognition of the importance of the training they provide. Owing to the expansion of leadership development programs, the CDC has encouraged the development of the National Public Health Leadership Development Network Conference to address the common concerns of public health leadership programs.

Public health leaders will be both mentees and mentors at various stages in their careers. In particular, they should consider

- volunteering to mentor a leadership development team
- serving as an agency advisor to public health professionals confronted with local or state public health issues
- increasing networking between graduates of public health leadership programs
- utilizing peer mentoring as a way to spread the use of effective conflict resolution and decision-making strategies
- encouraging the development of state and regional leadership programs

A LEADERSHIP LADDER OF LEARNING

Learning needs to be a lifelong process. Public health leaders live in a constantly changing environment, and the public health agenda is partly unpredictable. As stated above, public health leaders will need different training opportunities at different times in their professional lives, but it is clear that mentoring adds to virtually any learning experience. Figure 13–4 presents a lifelong learning agenda for leaders. As leaders move up the ladder, they begin to focus more on national or even global public health concerns rather than local ones and also to become aware of the abstract aspects of leadership and develop conceptual models to guide their leadership activities.

On the first step of the ladder, where public health professionals initially take on supervisory or other administrative roles, they need to learn how to utilize basic management and leadership tools. They need training in planning, organizing, monitoring, and administering.[24] They also need to learn to distinguish clinical activities from management activities and to learn leadership skills that will help them advance to a more creative leadership role in the organization. There are numerous courses and training materials available for new leader-administrators. The foundation skills are fairly concrete and less conceptual than at the higher levels of leadership.

Entry-level leadership development can occur through involvement with a profession-specific group or a multidisciplinary group. After 3–5 years in an organizational leadership position, leaders will benefit from training at a state or regional public health leadership institute. Such training is intended to integrate leadership concepts and public health governing paradigms.

National public health leadership institutes, such as the CDC-funded Public Health Leadership Institute, are useful for leaders in key state positions. Top-level leaders may also gain from specialized training programs that stress some major leadership functions. For example, the International Center for Health Leadership Development at the University of Illinois at Chicago has developed a series of

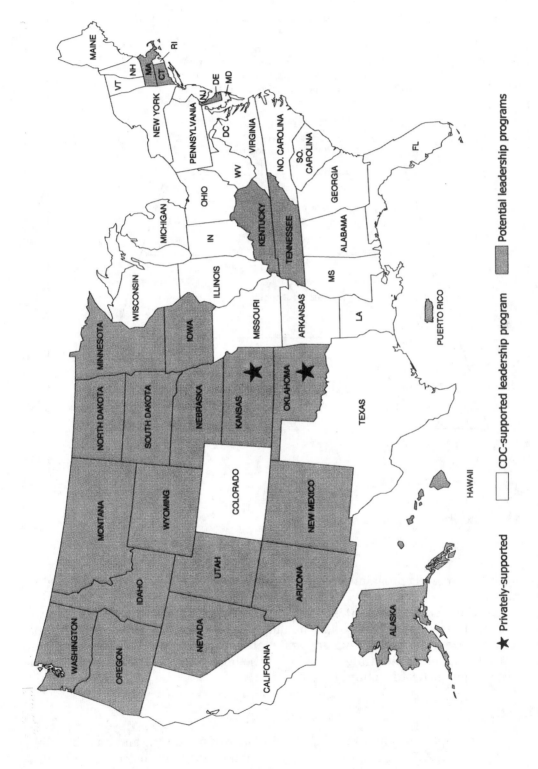

Figure 13–3 Leadership development network.

★ Privately-supported

☐ CDC-supported leadership program

▨ Potential leadership programs

National   Abstract

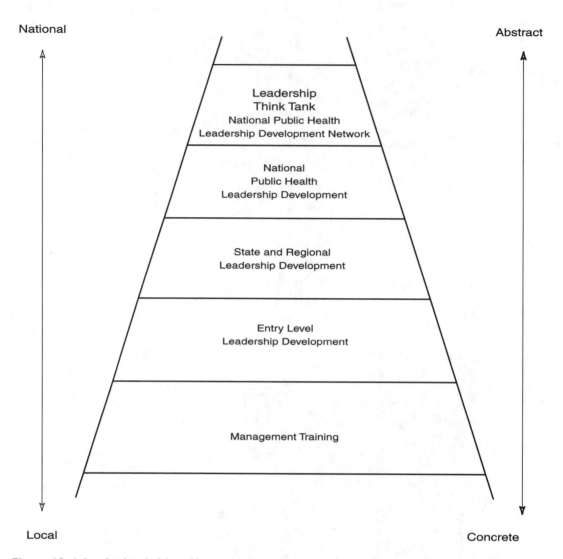

Leadership
Think Tank
National Public Health
Leadership Development Network

National
Public Health
Leadership Development

State and Regional
Leadership Development

Entry Level
Leadership Development

Management Training

Local   Concrete

Figure 13–4 Leadership ladder of learning.

week-long training programs on partnering, coalition building, and policy development.

At the highest step on the ladder, public health leaders can become involved in a think tank in order to explore public health issues with graduates of national leadership development programs and state and local public health leadership institutes. Public health think tanks are in the business of producing policy papers to guide public health action.

SUMMARY

This chapter has emphasized the importance of mentoring and training public health leaders. Mentoring in all its guises enhances leadership development. A combination of mentoring and training facilitates the learning of leadership skills. Therefore, experienced leaders must be willing to mentor novice leaders, who, of course, must be willing to be mentored. In addition, public health leaders who head agencies and health departments must find ways to foster mentoring within their organizations.

Discussion Questions

1. What are the benefits of mentoring for the mentee?
2. What are the benefits for the mentor?
3. What examples of mentoring have you experienced, either as mentee or mentor?
4. How are personal mentoring and team mentoring related?
5. What skills are needed for someone to become a mentor?
6. What strategies would you propose to bring medicine and public health closer together in your community?

Exercise 13–1

MENTORING

Purpose: to explore both sides of a mentoring relationship and to evaluate the experience of being a mentor and a mentee

Key concepts: mentee, mentor

Procedure: As a homework assignment, each student writes two one-page stories, the first about a situation in which the student was mentored, the second about a situation in which the student acted as a mentor. The stories are read to the class and discussed. (If the class is large, it should divide into groups, and each group will listen to and discuss the stories of those in that particular group.)

Case Study 13–A

The Mentoring Experience: What Is a Mentor?

Shirley F. Randolph

The literature defines a mentor in a number of ways . . . none of which fulfills the mission of mentors as envisioned by the Illinois Public Health Leadership Institute. So, those of us who enjoyed the privilege of being in the original group of five mentors developed a definition to fit that vision.

The definition agreed on by the mentors has two parts. Part one covered the mentors' role during the three-day Conference with the initial group of 25 Fellows. The mentors determined their role for the Conference would be one of facilitator and "coach."

Part two of our definition of "mentor" refers to the mentoring role following the Conference. The mentors defined their role for that portion of their year-long responsibility to be one of teacher, counselor, friend and "encourager."

The mentoring experiences that are described herein relate to part one: facilitator and "coach" during the three-day Conference.

The most critical experience . . . not only for me as a mentor but also, I think, for the five fellows assigned to my group . . . was to be part of a small cadre of public health professionals, all of whom are leaders in their agencies, who developed a sharing, caring, and trusting relationship with all members of the group. There was plenty of "give and take" and exchange of viewpoints and information as we moved through the three-day agenda.

My responsibility as a facilitator turned out to be easily fulfilled due to the professional approach taken by each of "my" Fellows and the fact that each had prepared her/himself by reviewing materials in advance of the Conference.

The role of "coach" turned out to be exciting, rewarding, and fun as the Conference progressed. It was a challenge to be "coach" to five bright, well-prepared individuals. It was also a tad "scary" because being a mentor to a group of public health practitioners was a role I had never performed prior to the Conference.

The challenge was to direct attention to new concepts, to encourage the group to examine issues from a different perspective; and to delve into certain aspects of the issues presented in the case studies we dissected. That meant that I, as a mentor, had to stretch my personal limits in order to be an effective coach!

In my attempts to be effective as a coach, I uncovered a truism that constitutes another critical experience . . . mentoring is not a mystery. It goes beyond the sharing of information and guidance from a more experienced person to one with less experience: the traditional mentoring role. Mentoring is the giving of time and thought. It is caring coupled with gentle guidance.

I discovered that being a mentor also requires patience and a willingness to listen carefully. Some of the choice discussions in our group evolved from pertinent issues and personal experiences brought up and shared with the group by the Fellows as opposed to discussions stimulated by the content of the more formal sessions.

One of the unexpected experiences of being a mentor occurred when I realized that maybe one of my most important contributions as a mentor could be just being available when needed. To be someone who could reinforce an idea, or affirm a reaction, or lend credence to a different approach.

I experienced many other, less subtle "happenings" during the first annual conference of the Illinois Public Health Leadership Institute. Such as:

- the harried feeling of being pushed to cover as much ground and to "cram in" as much information as possible in short three days,
- the pressure to excel and to make the initial conference a "showpiece!!"
- the lack of time to relax and socialize more with the entire group of Fellows,
- the excitement that comes with learning something new,

- the mental and physical exhaustion following an intense, 12-hour—or longer—day,
- the joy of sharing time and thoughts with long-time public health colleagues,
- the excitement of making new public health friends,
- the eagerness and anticipation for each new session on the agenda,
- the nostalgia that came with spending time on a university campus,
- the satisfaction of "seeing a plan come together!,"
- the pleasure in knowing that the vision for the Institute was "right-on target" judging from the response of the Fellows,
- The intellectual stimulation that occurs when listening to ideas presented by noted public health leaders; and,
- the annoyance that comes with not doing well playing parlor games!!

That about sums it up! Bottom line: my experiences as a mentor were first rate. Just say yes, if you're asked to serve as a mentor, whether it be for the Illinois Public Health Leadership Institute, or in a more traditional role within your community, or the agency in which you work. You will be richly rewarded!

REFERENCES

1. C.R. Bell, *Managing as Mentors* (San Francisco: Berrett-Koehler, 1996).
2. F. Wickman and T. Sjodin, *Mentoring* (Chicago: Irwin Professional Publishing, 1996).
3. Bell, *Managing as Mentors.*
4. B. Nelson and P. Economy, *Managing for Dummies* (Foster City, CA: IDG Books Worldwide, 1996).
5. T. Peters and N. Austin, *A Passion for Excellence* (New York: Random House, 1985).
6. J. Carruthers, "The Principles and Practices of Mentoring," in *The Return of the Mentor: Strategies for Workplace Learning,* eds. B.J. Caldwell and E.M.A. Carter (London: The Falmer Press, 1993).
7. Carruthers, "The Principles and Practices of Mentoring."
8. Wickman and Sjodin, *Mentoring.*
9. Wickman and Sjodin, *Mentoring.*
10. E. Alleman, "Two Planned Mentoring Programs That Worked," *Mentoring International* 3, no. 1 (1989): 6–12.
11. Alleman, "Two Planned Mentoring Programs That Worked."
12. C. Dahle, "Women's Ways of Mentoring," *Fast Company* 17 (1998): 187–195.
13. W.A. Gray, "Situational Mentoring: Custom Designing Planned Mentoring Programs," *International Journal of Mentoring* 3, no. 1 (1989): 19–28.
14. S.P. Robbins and M. Coulter, *Management,* 6th ed. (Upper Saddle River, NJ: Prentice-Hall, 1999).
15. J.G. Liebler et al., *Management Principles for Health Professionals,* 2d ed. (Gaithersburg, MD: Aspen Publishers, 1992).
16. Wickman and Sjodin, *Mentoring.*
17. Carruthers, "The Principles and Practices of Mentoring."
18. C. Dahle, "Women's Ways of Mentoring."
19. Public Health Service, *Public Health Workforce: An Agenda for the 21st Century* (Washington, DC: U.S. Department of Health and Human Services, 1997).
20. Public Health Service, *Public Health Workforce.*
21. R.D. Lasker, *Medicine and Public Health* (New York: New York Academy of Medicine, 1997).
22. Lasker, *Medicine and Public Health.*
23. Lasker, *Medicine and Public Health.*
24. Robbins and Coulter, *Management.*

Part IV

Leadership, Evaluation, and Research

Chapter 14

Measuring the Leader

Work experience, hardship, opportunity, education, role models, and mentors all go together to craft a leader.

J.A. Conger, *Learning to Lead*

Leadership is multidisciplinary as well as multilayered, and no single measure of leadership exists. Most quantitative evaluation instruments do not have specific public health leadership dimensions and are quite general to begin with. Case studies, interviews, and stories, of course, provide qualitative information. The quantitative and qualitative information that is available can be used to evaluate the development of leadership skills and determine whether leadership development programs lead to changes in behavior.

The purpose of this chapter is not to review all the leadership assessment instruments on the market but rather to describe several instruments currently used in various public health leadership development programs. This chapter will also explore the concept of 360° feedback and consider recent arguments for and against credentialing public health administrators.

A LEADERSHIP COMPETENCIES FRAMEWORK

The late 1990s saw a renewal of interest in training the public health work force, including public health leaders. The issue of leadership training is being addressed by the Public Health Functions Project, which is coordinated by the Assistant Secretary of Health and the Surgeon General.[1] Exhibit 14–1 presents the 10 tasks this project has undertaken. A project subcommittee was appointed to

provide a profile of the current public health work force and make projections regarding the work force of the twenty-first century. The subcommittee should also address training and education issues including curriculum development to ensure a competent work force to perform the essential services of public health now and in the future. Minority representation

345

Exhibit 14–1 Public Health Functions Project

The following tasks will be undertaken as part of the Public Health Functions Project:

1. Develop a taxonomy of the essential services of public health that can be readily understood and widely accepted for use by the public health community.
2. Using the taxonomy developed, assess the public health infrastructure and document the federal, state, and local expenditures on essential services of public health.
3. Propose a mechanism to ensure accountability for outcomes related to the delivery of essential public health services at the state and local levels, in return for greater flexibility in administration of federal grants to support public health.
4. Develop a strategy for communicating to the general public and key policymakers the nature and impact of essential public health services.
5. Document and publish analyses of the health and economic returns on investments in essential public health services.
6. Identify the key categories of public health personnel necessary to carry out the essential services of public health, assess the nation's current capacity and shortfalls, and establish a mechanism for ongoing monitoring of work force strength and capability.
7. Develop and publish a full set of evidence-based guidelines for sound public health practice.
8. Collaborate with the PHS Data Policy Committee to identify the information and data needs for the effective implementation of the essential services of public health and develop a strategy for the interface between the personal services and population-wide systems, ensuring the availability of information necessary to both.
9. Develop a process to ensure the appropriate collaboration of the public health community and adequate inclusion of public health perspectives in the development of national health goals and objectives for the year 2010.
10. Develop a strategy for regular communication among interested parties at the national, state, and local levels on progress related to these activities.

should be analyzed and the programs to increase representation should be evaluated. Distance learning should be explored. The Subcommittee should examine the financing mechanisms for curriculum development and for strengthening the training and education infrastructure.[2(p.v)]

One of the subcommittee's tasks is to look at the feasibility of a competency-based curriculum. In the past, learning objectives were used to evaluate educational attainment. A competency-based system is intended to be more oriented toward outcomes. Both learning objectives and competency-based outcomes can be useful for gauging a student's or trainee's mastery of new skills and abilities. Learning objectives define the key topics of the course or curriculum in a general way, whereas competencies define what a student or trainee is supposed to master over the long run. The critical issue is how to measure progress toward achieving the competencies and objectives.

The project subcommittee reported on six priority areas for a competency-based curriculum: cultural competency, health promotion skills, leadership development, program management, data analysis, and community organization. It identified a number of action steps for acquiring the competencies.

The development of competencies is a complex process. At the 1995 annual meeting of National Public Health Leadership Network (then under a different name), a project was undertaken to develop a series of leadership competencies for use in the creation and evaluation of state and regional public health leadership programs. The task groups formed at the meeting named four core categories for the competency exercise: transformational leadership skills, political competencies, transorganizational skills, and team-building skills. Over the course of 1996, the framework evolved into the version presented in Appendix 14–A.

Transformational leadership skills are needed by public health leaders because leaders are change agents. Leaders need to have a mission and vision and need to motivate and manage change effectively. As for political competencies, leaders need to understand how the political process works, how to negotiate, how to build alliances, and how to market public health and educate the community about public health issues. Since so much public health activity occurs between organizations, public health leaders need transorganizational competencies, including an understanding of organizational dynamics, interorganizational collaboration mechanisms, and social forecasting and marketing. The team-building skills they require include the ability to develop team-oriented structures for purposes of planning and implementing objectives and evaluating progress toward the objectives, the ability to facilitate team development, and the ability to mediate when a conflict occurs.

The framework presented in Appendix 14–A provides a template for learning and for making sense of the multidimensional aspects of public health leadership. No framework should be etched in stone. It must be allowed to evolve. Data need to be collected to determine if the identified competencies can be taught and put into practice.

The main problem with most competency frameworks is that the competencies are not defined with sufficient specificity to permit their measurement. Take, for example, the competency "Identify, articulate and model professional values and ethics," which is obviously very general and difficult to gauge. The solution is to break down each competency into specific components that can be measured. In addition, there must be an applied research strategy to evaluate the leadership competencies routinely and revise them as necessary. None of this is to imply that the leadership competency framework is useless. The process of refining the framework has just begun and will probably take several years to complete. The end result hopefully will be a performance standards system capable of evaluating leadership outcomes.

CREDENTIALING AND ACCREDITATION

The credentialing of public health professionals became a live issue in the 1990s. In 1971, the U.S. Department of Health, Education, and Welfare defined credentialing as "the process by which a nongovernmental agency or association grants recognition to an individual who has met certain predetermined qualifications specified by that agency or association. Such qualifications may include: (a) graduation from an accredited or approved program; (b) acceptable performance on a qualifying examination or series of examinations; and/or (c) completion of a given amount of work experience."[3]

The supporters of credentialing argue that it will increase the credibility of public health professionals in the political arena as well as with the public at large. Professional standards will be developed that will guide public health programs. Some supporters want to tie credentialing to licensure. The critics argue that no credentialing system is possible because of the multidisciplinary background of public health professionals.

Schools of public health point out that they go through an accreditation process overseen by the Council on Education in Public Health. Accreditation would be prima facie evidence that graduating students have the necessary competence to practice public health, and a master's degree in public health from an accredited school of public health should preclude the necessity of further testing. On the other hand, many public health practitioners have not been trained in public health and thus don't have the stamp of approval conferred by graduation from a school of public health. In addition, there is a question whether schools of public health are teaching the skills that practitioners need to have. For example, leadership courses do not exist in some schools of public health.

A report to the U.S. Health Resources and Services Administration defined accreditation as follows: "Accreditation is generally used to refer to the evaluation of academic programs which prepare individuals for professional practice and to determine whether such programs meet predetermined standards. Accreditation may be carried out by public and private agencies or associations."[4(p.9)]

Licensure, credentialing, and accreditation are related, although proponents of credentialing may argue that accreditation is not a guarantee the accredited public health professional has acquired the desired knowledge. Credentialing proponents point out that a process of evaluating professional knowledge helps develop standards for professional performance.

A report prepared for the Association of Schools of Public Health discussed factors that need to be included in any sound credentialing system.[5] First, role delineation that distinguishes between professionals who have different skills and levels of knowledge is a requisite. Because the role of public health administrators would be distinguished from that of other practitioners in the field, the credentialing of public health leaders could occur. Second, the credentialing system must specify the knowledge and skills required to carry out the duties of a credentialed professional and public health leader. Third, the system must determine the education, training, or experience necessary to generate the required competencies. Fourth, a testing procedure or other forms of assessment must be devised to determine when a practitioner has achieved entry-level competency levels as well as more advanced levels of ability and knowledge. Finally, the system must include a process for recertification and require certified practitioners to undergo recertification periodically. Since leadership tools and skills change over time, the recertification process would encourage advanced training.

In the early 1990s, the American Public Health Association looked at the issue of professional credentialing.[6] The committee assigned to the task found very little information in the literature related to credentialing. To further its understanding of the issue, the committee conducted interviews with leaders in the field and with credentialing experts and also surveyed these two groups. The committee found that public health leaders generally did not support the development of a credentialing system. The leaders recognized that a credentialing system would need to be multifaceted and be able to accommodate a number of subspecialties and different education levels. The reaction of the credentialing experts was similar. The committee concluded that, despite the obvious benefits of credentialing, there was no consensus on the form credentialing should take.

One successful credentialing system has been developed by the Society for Public Health Education (SOPHE) for undergraduate health educators.[7] The National Commission for Health Education Credentialing (NCHEC) was organized to carry out the certification of health educators. Since 1988, almost 1,600 individuals have become certified health education specialists. The certification process, which is based on what NCHEC has determined are necessary educational and professional experiences, is voluntary. New criteria were introduced in 1992. A health educator cannot take the examination unless he or she has a college degree from an accredited institution. A candidate also must have a minimum of 25 college semester hours in health education.

At the present time, there are more than 100 sites in the United States where the examination is given twice a year. Those people who pass the certification examination are seen as having met the minimal health education requirements. During the late 1990s, standards for measuring graduate-level health educators were developed. The idea is to have a second certification examination for advanced degree health educators. SOPHE also became concerned with leadership and developed a leadership program for its members.

Questions have been raised about the qualifications of local health officers. The Health Services and Resources Administration gave a three-year grant to the School of Public Health at the University of Illinois at Chicago to develop procedures for credentialing health administrators. It is too early to evaluate the experiment, but the experience of public health leadership programs around the country indicates that public health leaders gain from the leadership development process. What they gain, on the other hand, is difficult to determine in other than a general way.

360° LEADERSHIP ASSESSMENT AND FEEDBACK

We all have perceptions of ourselves that others around us may not share. Leaders are no exception. They may view themselves one way and be viewed by their colleagues in quite a different way. Therefore, the assessment of a leader needs to include a self-evaluation as well as evaluations by colleagues. In other words, it should be a 360° assessment.

The 360° assessment process involves a multi-level evaluation that focuses on whether the leader's style of leadership supports or obstructs achievement of the mission and goals of the organization. In a comprehensive 360° assessment, all key stakeholders have a voice in evaluating the leader and assessing the direction in which the organization is moving.[8]

Requirements of a 360° assessment include the following.[9] First, the leaders of the organization must determine whether sufficient enthusiasm for and commitment to the process exists in the organization and whether they are willing to institute changes based on the results of the assessment. Second, they must collect high-quality assessment data. Finally, they must identify possible responses to the results, such as the development of leadership training programs or formal mentoring programs.

A 360° leadership assessment instrument, the Leadership Practices Inventory (LPI), evaluates leaders based on their performance of best leadership practices.[10] The five practices in the initial LPI, selected on the basis of interviews with senior and midlevel administrators and on leadership case studies, were (1) challenging the process, (2) inspiring a shared vision, (3) enabling others to act, (4) modeling the way, and (5) encouraging the heart.

The second edition of the LPI has 30 leadership practice items, and for each item there are 10 possible responses, from "almost never" to "almost always." (In the first edition, there were only five choices for each item, from "rarely" to "very frequent.") The score for a given practice therefore can range from a low of 6 to a high of 60. One version of the LPI is used for self-evaluation and a second version is used for evaluation by observers (colleagues and stakeholders). The LPI can be used at different times to determine whether the leader has made progress in performing the five leadership practices.

Using the original LPI, data on 43,000 leaders from around the world were collected, and means, standard deviations, and internal reliability measures were computed.[11] Most of the leaders were from the business sector but some were from academia and the public sector. The reliability rates fell between .81 and .91. Enabling others to act was seen by leaders and their observers as the most common practice, followed by challenging the process, modeling the way, encouraging the heart, and, in last place, inspiring a shared vision.

In another study using the LPI, baseline leadership information was collected from 163 public health leaders selected by the Illinois Public Health Leadership Institute as fellows between 1992 an 1997.[12] There may be a self-selection bias built into the study, since fellows are likely to have identified themselves as leaders before embarking on the leadership program and to be committed to leadership development to enhance their skills. Thus far, public health leaders have not specifically been studied. Another study is presently underway to explore changes in LPI scores as a result of training. Comparisons of public health leader self-evaluations and observer evaluations have not been done thus far. Some preliminary data indicate that observers rate their leaders higher than the leaders rate themselves.

Mean scores for business leaders and public health leaders are presented in Table 14–1.[13] The scores for public health leaders are consistently higher, but a confounder is the fact that the sample of business leaders includes academics and human service professionals. The scores for the two groups were not significantly different on the practice "challenging the process," an indicator of orientation to change, nor on the practice "inspiring a shared vision" (both groups scored relatively low). The public health leaders scored significantly higher than the business leaders on the other three practices, all of which are associated with the quality of work-related relationships.

One of the difficulties of using the LPI in studies of leadership is that the main purpose of the instrument is to assess individual leaders through self-evaluation and observer evaluation. The aggregation of LPI data should hide the characteristics of individual leaders, but nonetheless they need to be informed of the fact that their evaluations may be used for research. The instrument also may create biases

Table 14–1 Means and Standard Deviations for Public Health and Business Leaders

Leadership Practice Item	Business Leaders (N=43,889)		Public Health Leaders (N=166)		Significant Difference
	Mean	SD	Mean	SD	
Challenging the process	22.38	4.17	23.4	3.46	None
Inspiring a shared vision	20.48	4.90	21.6	3.98	None
Enabling others to act	20.48	4.37	25.3	2.46	$p \leq .0015$
Modeling the way	22.89	4.16	23.8	3.24	$p \leq .001$
Encouraging the heart	21.89	5.22	23.6	3.59	$p \leq .001$

in the responses since it is tied to a conceptual model that the developers promote. Not every leader supports this model.

In addition, a 360° assessment is expensive and time consuming.[14] Not only must the measurement instruments be bought, but staff need to be trained to interpret the results. Another issue is whether leaders are willing to reveal self-perceived weaknesses to their colleagues and whether subordinates feel comfortable rating their leaders. This issue is of special concern in smaller organizations. If anonymity is not maintained and the observer evaluations are negative, animosity may occur between leaders and their professional colleagues. Finally, there is the question whether the process will make any difference.[15]

Despite these issues, the process can result in important information. If the leadership data are linked to organizational needs, organizational efficiency and effectiveness can be improved. The results need to be communicated to the entire work force, but with a sensitivity for the possible impact on the person who was evaluated. On the whole, the 360° approach offers the individual and the organization information that can improve the services provided by the organization.

QUALITATIVE LEADERSHIP ASSESSMENT

Public health programming is driven by population-based statistics, including mortality and morbidity rates. The problem is that the vitality of public health as an approach and perspective can get lost in the numbers, with the result that public health loses credibility among community residents.[16] As a consequence, public health leaders need to acquire qualitative information to help them evaluate their performance and to publicize public health as a way of enhancing their credibility.

Qualitative information often comes in the form of case studies. The case studies of interest to us here describe public health practitioners in action and present conclusions about what was done right and what could have been done better. As we will use the term, *case* refers to whatever is the subject of a case study (usually a single event or a series of events).

Case studies, for our purposes, can be divided into four classes: (1) specific empirical studies, (2) general empirical studies, (3) specific theoretical studies, and

(4) general theoretical studies. Empirical case studies describe actual cases, whereas theoretical case studies are constructed specifically to illustrate some point. Specific case studies have definable boundaries, and general case studies are examples already available that can be used to demonstrate a perspective.

The cases chosen for research inquiry are typically different from those chosen for training purposes. In this section, we are interested in the latter, especially their potential to clarify the application of leadership principles in the real world of public health practice. Training case studies describe how professionals handle problems and thus can serve as guides to future action. Leaders can develop their own case studies in order to analyze public health community activities and evaluate their own leadership skills.

Public health case studies are used for three main purposes.[17] First, they can be used to offer insights into how a public health agency carries out its activities. Second, they can be used to help public health leaders explore different scenarios as part of a problem-solving process. Exhibit 14–2, for instance, presents a number of public health scenarios helpful for defining outcomes that might occur if a public health agency instituted a certain policy or embarked in a certain direction. Third, case studies can be used to illuminate why events unfolded in a certain way and to explore better ways to handle an emergency situation, for instance.

As regards the last two uses, the role of leadership and the causal consequences of actions need to be interpreted carefully. It is always difficult to tease out the causal factors in a complex set of relationships and happenings. In addition, the events that make up a case rarely repeat themselves in exactly the same way.

Some case studies are merely free-flowing stories about examples of leadership, for instance. These stories nonetheless must have a message intended for a well-defined audience.[18] There are three main types of leadership stories. One is the "Who am I?" story. The second is the "Who are we?" story. The third is a story of the realization of a vision. It is possible to add a fourth category consisting of "What I learned on my summer vacation?" stories. These stories describe what a leader learned from other leaders or from workshops on leadership.

Case study stories have plots intended to elucidate ideas or values. They should be tested before being released to the public to make sure that their messages are clear. One variant of the personal story is the biographical portrait.[19] A portrait of an historical or present-day leader, such as C. Edward Koop, can be employed for the same purposes as a personal story. Another variant is to focus on a leader whose values stand in contrast to those of a typical public health leader, such as a senator from a tobacco state.

An interview can also make up the content of a case study. Questions serve as the mechanism for getting information. For example, the author interviewed more than a 130 public health leaders in four countries in order to explore their understanding of the meaning of public health, their vision of the future, and the changing characteristics of leaders. (Exhibit 14–3 consists of a guide for interviewing public health leaders.)

An interesting variation on the interview is the focus group, in which leaders, for example, might answer questions as a team. A conversation is another variation—a variation explored in Exercise 14–1.

A case study protocol for public health practice narratives was developed for public health practitioners in a leadership development program under the

Exhibit 14–2 Public Health Scenarios Based on Schwartz Categories

Scenario 1: Winners and Losers
A health reform plan passes Congress. The plan presents a system redesign that is state based and involves local health alliances. The health plans incorporate most of the direct service functions of local health departments. Block grant funds that remain are given directly to the health alliances for distribution. This scenario initially positions the local health department as a loser.

Scenario 2: Challenge and Response
The American Public Health Association creates a strong lobbying coalition that includes representatives from all the major public health interest groups and organizations. As Congress reviews changes in the financing of health services, the public health community is able to affect legislation so that CDC and state public health agencies become responsible for collecting all data related to health care, are responsible for oversight of all health programs, become the lead agency for all government-sponsored primary prevention programs, are directly funded for health-related community programs by a block grant, and so on. Public health meets every challenge and wins.

Scenario 3: Evolution
There is a major change in the economy of the state. Several new biotechnology companies move to the state, and many new jobs are created. The state unemployment rate drops to 3 percent. With the increase in employment, the number of people on welfare drops significantly. With new jobs, the teenage pregnancy rate drops, as does the incidence of gang-related violence, since gang members get jobs.

Scenario 4: Revolution
Congress passes a major piece of legislation. The government decides to get out of the public health business. All public health activities are transferred to the private health care system.

Scenario 5: Cycle
Five years after the evolution scenario above takes place, the American economy collapses. A major depression occurs. People lose their jobs. Gang warfare increases. The teenage pregnancy rate expands significantly.

Scenario 6: Infinite Possibilities
A health reform package passes that provides universal coverage.

Scenario 7: The Lone Ranger
Through the efforts of public health professionals and researchers, a cure for AIDS is found, a chemical substance that purifies all water is discovered, and a vaccine that prevents Alzheimer's disease is developed. Because of these breakthroughs, the American public unequivocably supports all public health initiatives.

Scenario 8: My Generation
The early years of the 21st century see a major increase in births in the United States.

The above scenarios can be looked at individually or can be combined to form more complex scenarios.

Exhibit 14–3 Interview Guide for Public Health Leaders

---

1. What are the reasons that you decided on a career in public health?
2. How would you define public health?
3. What is your definition of leadership?
4. What are the necessary leadership practices and skills that a public health leader needs to use?
5. Are these practices and skills different from the practices and skills of business leaders?
6. What elements of public health's organizational system enhance or create barriers to leadership?
7. What is the role of public health in carrying out the core functions of assessment, policy development, and assurance?
8. What is your vision for public health in the 21st century? What are the three most important systems issues for the future and what are the key health issues for the future?
9. How successful is the system in promoting community coalitions to address the health of the community?
10. Are public-private partnerships that address public health concerns possible? What is public health's role in managed care?
11. Does the public understand public health? If not, what can you do to change this situation?
12. Should public health be integrated into the general health sector or should public health be maintained as part of a separate governmental office?
13. What distinguishes a practitioner, a manager, and a leader?
14. Is the mentoring of future leaders important? What type of mentoring program do you recommend?
15. What is the role of politics in public health?

---

assumption that structured case studies provide trainees and other lifelong learners with models of public health practice.[20] Case studies can also be used to explore cutting-edge issues in public health that are in need of resolution. In other words, case studies can be based on completed events or on situations in progress.

Each case has a unique character.[21] For example, even similar cases will differ in historical background, setting, or economic, political, legal, social, or cultural aspects. They also can have a different slant depending on the reason they were written.

Case studies, as stories, have characters, a plot, and a setting. Their purpose is to give insight into leadership styles and practices, personality concerns, power concerns, organizational intrigues, politics in action, media involvement, and so on. They can be effective mentoring tools; the mentor can assign a case study for the mentee to read, and then the two can discuss the issues raised in the case study. A problem-based case study can present a possible vision of the future.

The best case studies are built on real experiences. Whereas ideal cases can be constructed, most people seem to relate better to real-life situations that seem real in their unfolding. That is one of the reasons that every case study in this book is factually based, although names and places have sometimes been changed to protect the actual participants.

Most case studies are written as narratives and have a beginning, middle, and end[22] (Exhibit 14–4). The opening should present the issue that the case is intended

Exhibit 14–4 Case Study Development Protocol

Opening (first few paragraphs)
- Name and title of responsible professional
- Date: month and year (fix the case in time)
- Synopsis of decision required or problem setting or issues presented, keeping in the forefront the core functions of health departments

Case body (no more than 4–5 pages)
- Department/agency history, if pertinent
- Environmental setting, if pertinent
- Political concerns
- Expanded description of the decision or problem situation
- Human interaction facts, etc.
- Human element
- Personality impact
- Public relations factor
- Presence/absence of vision/enthusiasm
- Organizational relationships
- Other case characters or entities
- Program and process
- Financial concerns, where pertinent

Closing (last paragraph or two)
Conclusion of the case
Suggested methods:
- Setting the scene to establish a sense of urgency about the problem or decision
- Setting out a range of decision options

---

to illustrate and describe the setting and key characters. The middle, or the body of the case study, describes the events that make up the case. If this is done properly, then the lesson of the case becomes clear. In some instances, elements of the setting and key characters may be described in more detail than was provided in the opening. Political factors that affected the outcome may be critically examined. Many case studies include all sorts of supplemental documentation to elucidate the circumstances. The closing reviews the issue in light of the events described and analyzes the decisions made by the key characters.[23] It may explore possible options that might have led to an outcome different from the one that actually occurred. (Some case studies are intended to deal with multiple issues and use a slightly different organization to address the issues in a coherent manner.)

Case Study 14–A has the classic organization described here. It deals with the issues of privatization of laboratory services and the lack of involvement by public health laboratory directors in public health policy issues.

Exercise 14–2 provides the opportunity to write a case study. The work of researching and writing the case study, which may take several weeks, is done using teams. The case studies presented in this text can serve as models.

QUANTITATIVE LEADERSHIP ASSESSMENT TECHNIQUES

Leadership assessment comes in more than one variety. Part of the explanation is that the standard leadership assessment instruments grow out of different theories of leadership. Another part of the explanation is that there are at least five levels of leadership and different traits and behaviors that are needed for each level. Most leadership assessment techniques are oriented toward the personal level, but leadership can also be evaluated at the team, agency, community, and professional levels.

Since it is usually the individual who fills out the leadership assessment instrument, most leadership assessment relates to personal traits and behavior, and these traits and behaviors, unsurprisingly, are stressed by psychometricians. One of the best-known personality assessment tools has been adopted by a number of public health leadership programs. The Myers-Briggs Type Indicator (MBTI), based on Jung's theory of psychological types, measures personality along four dimensions.[24] The first is the extroversion (E) and introversion (I) dimension. Where someone falls along this dimension is determined by whether he or she relates more to the external world or more to his or her inner world. The second dimension, defined by the contrast between sensing perceptions (S) and intuitive perceptions (N), measures whether a person focuses on the here and now or on future possibilities and abstract theory and symbols. The next dimension, defined by the contrast between thinking (T) and feeling (F), measures whether a person responds to situations rationally or emotionally. The fourth dimension, defined by the contrast between judgment (J) and perception (P), measures whether the person tends naturally to engage in organizing, planning, and decision making or instead tends to want to keep options open.

The MBTI instrument is quite comprehensive[25] and requires the person being tested to answer numerous forced-choice questions. After completing the questionnaire, the person receives a report on his or her profile. The author, who filled out the questionnaire in order to gain a better understanding of how it is used, was found to be an ENTJ. The report said that the author tends to be decisive and frank, quick to take charge of people and projects, applies logic and analysis, prefers action to contemplation, and often pays more attention to tasks than to the people.

To discover how leaders in the public sector would score, researchers tested and compared five groups of leaders in local, state, and federal government.[26] The first group included 1,394 senior federal government administrators tested from 1983 to 1986. The next three groups, tested in the early 1980s, consisted of managers attending special government institutes at the University of North Carolina. The fifth group consisted of about 100 social service administrators from Nebraska. Figure 14–1 shows how these groups scored on the four dimensions. The point to note is that leaders do not score in a uniform way. Different patterns emerge. Leaders with different styles engage in different leadership practices.

The Leader Behavior Analysis II instrument differs substantially from the MBTI. It presents the person being tested with 20 typical job situations that involve a leader and one or more staff members. After reading each scenario, the person, putting him- or herself in the position of the leader, selects one of four possible actions. The instrument, which can be self-scored, investigates three dimensions. The

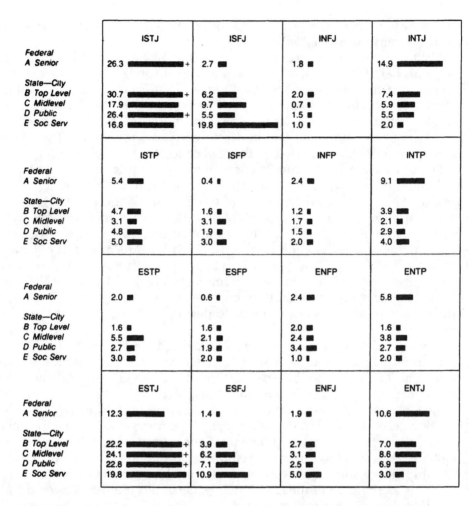

Figure 14–1 Myers-Briggs Type Indicator percentages for managers in federal, state, and local government.

first is flexibility (whether the person tends to try to be directive or be supportive). There are four score categories for this dimension:

- S1: high directive, low supportive behavior
- S2: high directive, high supportive behavior
- S3: high supportive, low directive behavior
- S4: low supportive, low directive behavior

The responses to the pertinent scenarios are used to compute a style flexibility score between 0 and 30. The higher the score, the greater the flexibility.

The second dimension is leadership effectiveness, and the third is diagnosis. Scores for these dimensions are computed in roughly the same way as for the first dimension. There is also a form for others to fill out, which allows for a 360° personal leadership evaluation.

A study of an earlier version of this instrument found that leadership assessment tools help leaders to evaluate their leadership styles and compare their self-perceptions with the perceptions of colleagues.[27] The sample included evaluations of 20,000 leaders from 14 cultures (each evaluation comprised a self-assessment and assessments by others). About 2,000 leaders from industry and education were interviewed, and about 500 in-depth interviews were done. The situational leadership model was supported by the data collected.

There is a Team Leadership Practices Inventory that is basically similar to the LPI developed for leaders and colleagues.[28] The Team LPI is based on the same five leadership practices used in the initial version of the LPI: challenging the process, inspiring a shared vision, enabling others to act, modeling the way, and encouraging the heart. Since the use of teams has increased in most organizations, evaluating how teams function is essential. Each team member fills out the Team LPI, which has 30 items. The scores for each practice are totaled and then averaged. By using the Team LPI, a team can determine its strengths as well as the practices that need improvement. The LPI is highly correlated with the Team LPI. Both instruments are less concerned about leadership style than about the practices of leadership.

There has been growing interest in leadership skills and practices at the organizational level. In 1984, a study of effective organizational leadership was undertaken,[29] and it led to the development of the Leader Behavior Questionnaire (LBQ). The LBQ consists of 50 questions. It is intended to measure focused leadership (listening ability), communication abilities, trust leadership, respectful leadership (how leaders treat others), risk leadership, bottom-line leadership (the belief of leaders that they can make a difference), empowered leadership (sharing power), long-term leadership (visionary leadership), organizational leadership, and cultural leadership (leadership based on the values of the organization). An important underlying assumption of the LBQ is that leadership is multidimensional and that each of its dimensions must be evaluated.

An important assessment-related breakthrough occurred in the mid-1990s. The health care sector became more interested in the measurement of outcomes as a way of evaluating effectiveness.[30] Performance measurement encompasses the measurement of program inputs, intermediate outcomes (process issues), and end outcomes.[31] One goal of performance measurement is to determine whether changes in public health expenditures affect the outputs of public health agencies and the final outcomes for the community.

A new Institute of Medicine report presented a framework for improving the health of community residents. The community health improvement process is shown in Figure 14–2. It encompasses the identification and analysis of health issues, the development and implementation of strategies to resolve the issues, and the monitoring of the implementation process and outcomes. One of the steps is to develop an indicator set that links the implementation of strategies with their outcomes so that the effectiveness of the strategies can be determined, which is the essence of performance measurement. Figure 14–3 presents a performance measurement model consisting of six steps. Despite the existence of this model, public state and local agencies have been slow in adopting the performance measurement approach.[32]

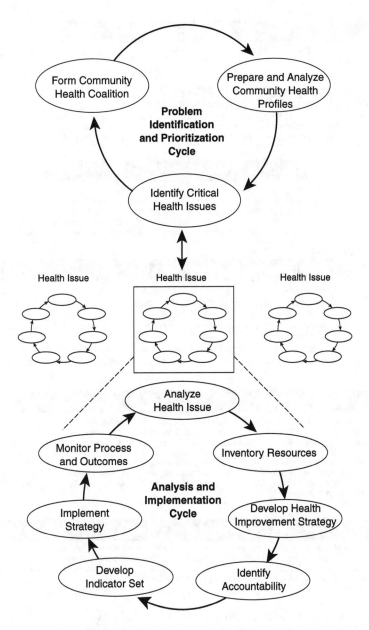

Figure 14–2 The community health improvement process (CHIP).

Performance monitoring is related to evidence-based public health.[33] Evidence-based public health promotes the use of traditional biostatistics measures, epidemiology, healthy communities assessment, and continuous quality improvement methods. Public health agencies and their leaders have not used the tools at hand in an effective manner, nor have they routinely approached their responsibilities from a population-based perspective.

STEP 1

Relate the performance measure to an important national, state, or local priority area.

Maryland has undertaken work related to the national health objective to reduce coronary heart disease deaths to no more than 100 per 100,000 people.

STEP 2

Measure a result that can be achieved in 5 years or less.

Maryland has identified an achievable result that is linked scientifically to the Healthy People 2000 Heart Disease and Stroke priority area: Increase the proportion of people who engage in light to moderate physical activity to at least 30 percent of the population.

STEP 3

Ensure that the result is meaningful to a wide audience of stakeholders.

Target stakeholders are essentially all Marylanders, with an emphasis on school-age children and people at high risk for diseases and medical conditions associated with physical inactivity (for example, persons with hypertension and high cholesterol). Stakeholders include principals, teachers, students, parent-teacher associations, the state education department, state and local health and recreational agencies, public health and medical professionals, and others.

STEP 4

Define the strategy that will be used to reach a result.

The State of Maryland has selected four strategies:
1. Implement a combination of strategies that include consumer education and skills development, health assessment, professional training, and environmental changes.
2. Reinforce risk reduction messages and promote programs and policies in schools, worksites, faith communities, and other settings.
3. Focus on youth and families so that healthy habits are started early and nurtured in the family.
4. Use a health promotion approach tailored to reach diverse ethnic and socioeconomic groups.

STEP 5

Define the accountable entities.

The accountable entities depend upon the strategies selected and the way in which a particular community is organized. For Maryland's Strategy 2, these entities include schools, worksites, and community centers. For example, the Cecil County Public Schools have agreed to be accountable for specific tasks related to Strategy 2 and are working in partnership with the Cecil County Health Department to offer health lifestyle programs to elementary school children. The programs, such as the **Heart Challenge Course**, bring teachers and food service workers together to promote healthy eating habits and physical fitness through educational games, classroom projects, and other activities that appeal to children.

STEP 6

Draft measures that meet statistical requirements of validity and reliability and have an existing source of data.

In consultation with biostaticians and epidemiologists, organizations can draft measures that are statistically sound. One of Maryland's performance measures might be "Increase to 30 percent the proportion of students in each Cecil County elementary school who engage in light to moderate physical activity for 30 minutes or longer every school day by participating in school physical fitness activities."

Figure 14–3 Performance measurement step by step. This example is based on the State of Maryland's *Healthy Maryland 2000* document.

Public health leaders need to develop the competencies to carry out performance monitoring. Currently, they often assign the task of performance monitoring to others. They also need to ensure that performance measurement is accepted by agency staff and that the information gained is used by the staff to improve operations. In fact, performance measures for evaluating the activities of leaders in the performance process need to be developed as well.

SUMMARY

Evaluation plays a multifaceted role in public health. Evaluation techniques are used for uncovering the public health problems that exist in a given community and for assessing the implementation of the programs intended to deal with such problems. They can also be used to assess the level of a leader's skills and abilities.

The chapter began with a description of the leadership competencies framework and listed some of the competencies that public health leaders need to have. It then discussed the question whether a system should be put in place for credentialing public health leaders—a question over which public health leaders are divided.

Quantitative leadership evaluations are problematic at best. One alternative is to do a qualitative evaluation using case studies and other qualitative techniques. No matter what type of evaluation is done, however, the evaluation should include the opinions of both the leader being evaluated and the opinions of colleagues. In short, it should be a 360° evaluation. Furthermore, the evaluation should cover the leader's performance at the agency level and also at the community level.

Discussion Questions

1. What is one of the problems with using competencies as a means of evaluating leadership?
2. What are the pros and cons of credentialing leaders?
3. What are five personal leadership lessons you learned during the last year?
4. What is a 360° assessment?
5. What are some difficulties associated with performing a 360° assessment?
6. What is a qualitative leadership assessment and what are some techniques for performing such an assessment?

Exercise 14–1

CONVERSATIONS WITH LEADERS

Purpose: to learn how peers view public health and what they think about current public health leadership issues

Key concepts: core functions, evaluation of leadership, focus group, interviewing skills, leadership skills

Procedure: It is possible to learn many things from peers. The class should divide into focus groups of 6–8 members. Each group engages in a discussion of leadership using the interview questions in the text as a guide (Exhibit 14–3). The discussion should last at least an hour, although it is not necessary to go through all the questions. The group should allow the discussion to go in any direction it naturally moves. The class can repeat the exercise several times, each time concentrating on a different set of issues.

Exercise 14–2

DEVELOPMENT OF A PUBLIC HEALTH CASE STUDY

Purpose: to develop a public health case study to examine how leaders address public health issues

Key concepts: case study, core functions, essential services, leadership, team learning

Procedure: The class should divide into teams of five to eight members. Each team will be responsible for writing a case study using the Munson protocol (Exhibit 14–4). Much of the work will take place outside of class. Follow these steps: (1) Select a facilitator to monitor each phase of the project. (2) Identify a public health case worthy of being written about. (3) Investigate the case and collect information for writing up the case. (4) Analyze the case from a policy development perspective. (5) Identify leadership issues involved in the case. (6) Write up the case (the study should be 5–10 pages). (7) Give an oral report on the case to the other teams.

Case Study 14–A

Organization of Public Health and Clinical Laboratory Services in a Reformed Health Service Delivery System

INTRODUCTION

In 1993 the U.S. Congress passed comprehensive legislation that would establish universal health care coverage by the year 2000. Congress mandated that each state would develop a strategic plan that would integrate and restructure the public and private health care programs. The commissioner of health, Dr. Strangelove, has designated you, Dr. Vision, to develop a plan to define the role of hospital, commercial, public health, and academic laboratories as part of the state of Innovation's strategy for a reformed health system.

CASE BODY

The result of three decades of heavy clinical laboratory utilization has been the development of a fractured, duplicative, and costly laboratory system in the state of Innovation. The laboratory network in this state fits the general description of the current health system: a patchwork of private and public programs, with goals and objectives as varied as the groups and organizations represented in the system." Clinical laboratories represent a significant component of the rapidly increasing costs of health care. The Health Care Financing Administration estimates that spending on laboratory services comprises 4.5 percent of all national health care expenditures.

Clinical laboratories, like the rest of the health care community, have been significantly affected by the nation's health reform legislation, the Health Services Act of 1993. The primary vehicle for the implementation of the legislation is the new Health Services Commission. The Health Services Act will enable each state to control spending by:

1. shifting the state toward a system of "managed" health care
2. defining a uniform benefit package and developing standards of certified health plans through which the uniform benefits package will be provided
3. setting the maximum rate a certified health plan may charge for the uniform benefit package
4. establishing a maximum health care inflation rate and lowering the rate until it matches the rate of general inflation
5. setting rules for fair competition among certified health plans
6. minimizing malpractice and its costs
7. simplifying the administration of claims, billing, and information
8. promoting the use of cost-effective health care practices and services
9. define the role and function of public health agencies

Dr. Vision realizes that the task ahead of him will be a challenge and very controversial.

1. First, the development of any coalition between laboratory organizations, physicians, pathologists, laboratory managers, hospital and commercial laboratories, and government will be exceedingly difficult to achieve.
   a. There will be opposition to a government agency leading the discussion about the role of laboratories in a reformed system. There will be suspicion, lack of trust, and concern about the regulatory approach that government agencies might mandate.
   b. For the most part there has been little or no historical interaction between individuals/organizations who will be involved in the coalition; therefore, the plan must be carefully developed and staged, ensuring that a process for developing consensus has been established.
   c. The activities of coalition will be monitored closely; therefore, there cannot be any secrecy and must be open to the public, outside review, and scrutiny. There must be a system for dissemination of information, and recommendations to the laboratory and medical community.
   d. There will be strong opposition to the possibility that the plan will lead to the re-engineering and downsizing of commercial and hospital laboratory staff.
   e. The issue of competition between public health laboratories and private sector facilities will be raised as well as the need to consider the privatization of diagnostic services provided by government laboratories. This obviously will be a contentious point since DuVision will have a vested interest in the outcome.
2. The nature of health problems has changed dramatically during the 20th Century; chronic conditions have become predominant as well as new and reemerging infectious diseases.

3. The utilization of managed care plans and capitation to control costs and share the risk with providers has increased dramatically. The march of managed care, new technologies, and alternative treatment settings will prompt a 34 percent decrease in inpatient hospital days over the five years from 1994 to 1999. Ambulatory facilities will eliminate many surgical inpatient days, use of birthing centers will increase, mental health care will be delivered more often in residential settings such as halfway houses, and home care will be the most dramatic and fastest growing segment of the health care industry. These changes will have a significant impact upon diagnostic laboratory testing. Hospital laboratories will undergo significant reduction in routine and inpatient testing, vertical integration will occur, and regional delivery systems will consolidate and centralize laboratory testing. Large national commercial laboratories will capture the vast majority of testing.

4. The role of laboratory medicine will be expanded into promoting health and preventing disease. Home testing will increase, as will the need to promote direct public access to preventive and screening testing. Genetic testing obviously is going to expand. Hospital and commercial laboratories will play a much more active role in the nation's disease surveillance, promoting the need for a statewide electronic network between private clinical laboratories and the public health systems. Other anticipated changes in the future laboratory system include
   • active management of laboratory utilization, elimination of unnecessary testing, and utilization of practice guidelines
   • standardization of lab instrumentation and testing methodology and increasing automation
   • utilization of clinical patient outcome measures of laboratory quality

Proposal Solution

The implementation of health reform makes strategic planning imperative for all components of the health system. Historically there have been few efforts to draw the clinical laboratory community together into cooperative efforts toward long-range planning except in the area of laboratory regulation and the credentialing of laboratory personnel. This initiative has been developed to assist the leadership of the clinical laboratory community in the state of Innovation in assessing the impact of health reform and in developing recommendations for integrating the diverse segments of the existing laboratory system into a more cost-effective and -efficient structure. The process will include creation of a steering committee, to provide recommendations to Dr. Vision for the guidance, direction, and oversight of the initiative. The steering committee may also appoint technical advisory workgroups to study and develop specific recommendations on such issues as the following:

• structure and integration of delivery system
• utilization of clinical laboratories in medical decisions or development of practice parameters
• laboratory regulations
• impact of malpractice tort reform on laboratory utilization

- utilization of new technology in laboratories
- personnel resource training and credentialing
- utilization of out-of-state laboratories
- reimbursement policies
- direct billing
- laboratory information systems—collection, analysis, integration, and dissemination of data
- surveillance of emerging infectious diseases
- point-of-care testing
- home testing
- public access to laboratory testing

The steering committee will consolidate its recommendations into a report to be submitted to the commissioner of health, Dr. Strangelove, for his consideration in establishing public policy.

Dr. Vision must first establish a process to identify and appoint members from the department and community to the steering committee, individuals who are experts in laboratory science, strategic planning, public policy, development of community constituencies, and consensus building and who are representatives of medical specialties.

Next, the steering committee must establish a strategic-planning process, including identification and prioritization of major components and issues. In order to address those issues listed, it is essential that a mechanism be developed to collect and evaluate health-related data to determine the need for diagnostic laboratory services. Finally, it must be determined by the steering committee how it will solicit public input.

REFERENCES

1. Public Health Functions Project, *The Public Health Workforce: An Agenda for the 21st Century* (Washington, DC: HHS/Public Health Service, 1997).
2. Public Health Functions Project, *The Public Health Workforce.*
3. U.S. Department of Health, Education, and Welfare, *Report on Licensure and Related Health Personnel Credentialing* (Washington, DC: U.S. Department of Health, Education, and Welfare, 1971).
4. A.C. Gielen et al., *Health Education in the 21st Century: A White Paper,* report prepared for Health Resources and Services Administration (Washington, DC: Health Resources and Services Administration, 1997).
5. E. Carpenter, *Proposed Credentialing System for Public Health Professionals: What Would It Mean for Schools of Public Health* (Washington, DC: Association of Schools of Public Health, 1990).
6. W.C. Livingood et al., *Perceived Feasibility and Desirability of Public Health Credentialing: Final Report* (Washington, DC: American Public Health Association, 1993).
7. Gielen et al., *Health Education in the 21st Century.*
8. M.R. Edwards and A.J. Ewen, *360° feedback* (New York: ANACOM, 1996).
9. R. Lepsinger and A.D. Lucia, *The Art and Science of 360° Feedback* (San Francisco: Jossey-Bass, 1997).
10. J.M. Kouzes and B.Z. Posner, *Leadership Practices Inventory (LPI): Facilitators Guide,* 2d ed. (San Francisco: Jossey-Bass and Pfeiffer, 1997).
11. J.M. Kouzes and B.Z. Posner, *The Leadership Challenge,* 2d ed (San Francisco: Jossey-Bass, 1995).
12. L. Rowitz and E.J. Jurkowski, "Leadership Practices and Public Health Professionals" (submitted for publication).
13. Rowitz and Jurkowski, "Leadership Practices and Public Health Professionals."
14. Lepsinger and Lucia, *The Art and Science of 360° Feedback.*
15. Lepsinger and Lucia, *The Art and Science of 360° Feedback.*
16. J.M. Kouzes and B.Z. Posner, *Credibility* (San Francisco: Jossey-Bass, 1993).

17. H.C. White, "Cases Are for Identity, for Explanation, or for Control," in *What Is a Case? Exploring the Foundations of Social Inquiry,* eds. C.C. Ragin and H.S. Becker (Cambridge: Cambridge University Press, 1992).
18. N.M. Tichy, *The Leadership Engine* (New York: Harper Business, 1997).
19. G. Wills, *Certain Trumpets* (New York: Simon & Schuster, 1994).
20. J. Munson, *Case Study Development: Guidelines and Protocols with Cases* (Chicago: University of Illinois School of Public Health, Illinois Public Health Leadership Institute, 1994).
21. R.E. Stake, "Case Studies," in *Handbook of Qualitative Research,* eds. N.K. Denzin and Y.S. Lincoln (Thousand Oaks, CA: Sage Publications, 1994).
22. Munson, *Case Study Development.*
23. Munson, *Case Study Development.*
24. M.H. McCaulley, "The Myers-Briggs Type Indicator and Leadership," in *Measures of Leadership,* eds. K.E. Clark and M.B. Clark (West Orange, NJ: Leadership Library of America, 1990).
25. K.C. Briggs and I.B. Myers, *Myers-Briggs Type Indicator Step II Booklet (Form K)* (Palo Alto, CA: Consulting Psychologists Press, 1991).
26. McCaulley, "The Myers-Briggs Type Indicator and Leadership."
27. P. Hersey et al., *Management of Organizational Behavior,* 7th ed. (Upper Saddle River, NJ: Prentice Hall, 1996).
28. J.M. Kouzes and B.Z. Posner, *The Team Leadership Practices Inventory* (San Francisco: Pfeiffer and Co., 1992).
29. W.G. Bennis, "The Four Competencies of Leadership," *Training and Development Journal* 38, no. 8 (1984), 15–18.
30. G.E.A. Dever, *Improving Outcomes in Public Health Practice* (Gaithersburg, MD: Aspen Publishers, 1997).
31. K.E. Newcomer, "Using Performance Measurement To Improve Programs," *New Directions for Evaluation* 75 (1997): 8–13.
32. H.P. Hatry, "Where the Rubber Meets the Road: Performance Measurement for State and Local Public Measurement," *New Directions for Evaluation* 75 (1997): 31–44.
33. Dever, *Improving Outcomes in Public Health Practice.*

Appendix 14–A

Leadership Competency Framework: Public Health Leadership Competencies for State/Regional Programs

I. CORE TRANSFORMATIONAL COMPETENCIES
  A. Sense of Mission
    1. Identify, articulate, and model professional values and ethics
    2. Facilitate mission development
    3. Reassess and adapt mission to vision
  B. Visionary Leadership
    1. Envision the future in terms of alternatives for change
    2. Articulate vision and facilitate implementation
    3. Proactively encourage and support others to share the vision
    4. Accept and incorporate innovative concepts/methods into strategic decision making
  C. Effective Change Agent
    1. Facilitate utilization and application of systems theory
    2. Articulate the difference between transformational and transactional change and competencies to perform them
    3. Develop and utilize feedback mechanisms in relation to appropriate change strategies
    4. Identify, create, and balance critical tension in relation to change dynamics theory
    5. Facilitate utilization and application of change dynamics theory
    6. Facilitate empowerment of others to take action
    7. Enable in others the ability to envision and select critical actions to be taken in a temporal context
    8. Communicate effectively to translate a sense of mission and vision into action
    9. Facilitate and create dialogue
    10. Model active learning and personal mastery
    11. Determine and model when and how to include risk taking in strategic actions
    12. Model integration of cultural sensitivity and competence

II. POLITICAL COMPETENCIES*
  A. Political Processes
    1. Develop, implement, and continually refine mission-driven strategic-planning processes at policy, management, and operational levels
    2. Facilitate and direct organizational strategic-planning efforts, including identification of assets and resources, development of major policy options, and broad strategies for their implementation
    3. Guide, analyze, and interpret to others for action, communications concerning political processes, and variables operating at federal, state, and local levels

---

* We wish to acknowledge the contributions of the University of North Carolina School of Public Health Doctoral Program Leadership Competencies, which were used as a resource to finalize this section.

4. Provide community education and advocacy to achieve national, state, and local year 2000 objectives
5. Identify and analyze the policy issues and alternatives related to given public health problems
6. Given the analysis of policy issues and alternatives related to given public health problems, identify constituencies and fellow advocates for coordinated action
7. Develop and implement collaborative strategies and planning processes, such as coalition and advocacy group development, to facilitate empowerment and involvement of all stakeholders, including a broad and diverse representation of the community
8. Evaluate, select, and implement models (e.g., APEX, PATCH, and Community Models Standards) to guide community political action and other basic capacity-building efforts related to improving the public health system
9. Cooperate and collaborate with efforts to translate community and organizational analyses and plans into specific legislative proposals
10. Guide the community and organization in assisting and supporting legislative deliberation and action on public health issues
11. Translate policy decisions into organizational and community structure, programs, and services

B. Negotiation
1. Guide and mediate in the investigation and resolution of acute public health crises
2. Identify key stakeholders and resources necessary for mediating, negotiating, or collective bargaining with political sectors, political action committees, or stakeholders

C. Ethics and Power
1. Recognize, build, and utilize power-based alliances from a values-based, ethical perspective

D. Marketing and Education
1. Foster development and implementation of media alliances to communicate the public health mission, values, objectives, and priorities to selected audiences/targets, including executive and legislative bodies, community organizations, and stakeholders
2. Utilize media alliances to communicate routinely with the public regarding public health needs, objectives, and accomplishments and to provide critical or crises-related information.

III. TRANSORGANIZATIONAL DYNAMICS

A. Understanding Organizational Dynamics
1. Create and employ assessment tools (public health and social science models) to assess organizational needs, assets, and resources with respect to the mission
2. Define and teach new organizational structures when need is apparent and opportunity arises
3. Encourage system structures utilizing knowledge of organizational development behavior and culture

B. Interorganizational Collaborating Mechanisms
1. Identify and include key players, influentials, and gatekeepers in collaboratve ventures

2. Develop and implement collaborative strategies and planning processes, such as task force and coalition development
3. Facilitate networking and participation of all stakeholders, including broad and diverse representation of private/public and traditional/nontraditional community organizations
4. Facilitate identification of shared mission and creation of common vision
5. Create transorganizational structures utilizing values-based approach and ethical standards
6. Develop a collaborative strategic action plan
7. Facilitate change dynamics and critical tensions within collaborative systems
8. Identify and utilize models and techniques for partnering
9. Evaluate collaborative strategies and mechanisms

C. Social Forecasting and Marketing
1. Identify and interpret emerging trends
2. Create predictions and build scenarios
3. Translate predictions and scenarios to the public
4. Utilize techniques of social marketing (e.g. media communication, health communications, and community relations
5. Provide information analysis and interpretation to community partners and constituents

IV. TEAM-BUILDING COMPETENCIES
A. Develop Team-oriented Structures and Systems To Accomplish Planning, Operation, and Evaluation Objectives
1. Assess the organizational environmental impact on achieving a shared vision
2. Create entrepreneurial spirit within team structures
3. Encourage acceptance and balancing of critical tensions to facilitate change in systems
4. Create administrative policy and team structures regarding customer orientation and continuous quality improvement
5. Foster outcomes-based team activities related to strategic planning and evaluation objectives
6. Facilitate the development of learning teams, which promote organizational learning from a systems perspective

B. Facilitate Development of Teams and Work Groups
1. Set clear goals and expectations
2. Facilitate development of shared mission, vision, and value statements
3. Encourage risk taking
4. Create incentives and reward and celebrate accomplishments
5. Analyze and guide communication skills and processes
6. Facilitate appropriate group processes
7. Facilitate development and utilization of appropriate problem-solving, conflict resolution, and decision-making skills
8. Facilitate empowerment and motivation to accomplish objectives
9. Participate in the development and integration of cultural sensitivity and competence
10. Model servant leadership (i.e., selflessness, integrity, perspective mastery)
11. Develop opportunities and resources for personal mastery and team learning

    12. Create systems, including structures and resources, for appropriate evaluation

C. Serve in Facilitation and Mediation Roles
1. Facilitate problem-centered coaching
2. Clarify team member roles and responsibilities
3. Establish effective work group processes and relationships
4. Utilize negotiation skills to mediate disputes
5. Diagnose and intervene in marginally productive and/or demoralized team situations

D. Serve as an Effective Team Member
1. Model effective group process behavior (i.e., listening, dialoging, negotiating, rewarding, encouraging, motivating)
2. Model effective team leadership traits (i.e., credible, enthusiastic, committed, honest, caring, trustworthy)
3. Develop and refine group process assessment skills
4. Assist others to balance critical tension to facilitate change

Chapter 15

Leadership Evaluation and Research

It requires a very unusual mind to undertake the analysis of the obvious.

Alfred North Whitehead, *Science and the Modern World*

During the 1990s, the public health community realized the importance of developing public health leaders. A national Public Health Leadership Institute was created by a consortium of California universities through a grant from the Centers for Disease Control and Prevention (CDC). The first state public health leadership institute was founded in Illinois in 1992, also with CDC support. There are currently a number of public health regional and state leadership development programs covering 28 states (see Figure 13–3). As leadership programs have proliferated, there has grown a concern about the effectiveness of these programs in training leaders.

Leaders need information for making decisions. Ongoing program evaluation creates an atmosphere in which effective leadership and organizational learning can flourish.[1] Leaders need to show strong support for program evaluation and include evaluation as a part of the mission and vision of their agency. They also need to be involved in the evaluation process and work with other agency professionals to ensure the process is successful. The organization will not achieve excellence without opportunities for continual learning provided by training and leadership development programs.

In 1999, the CDC reported on the deliberations of the CDC Evaluation Working Group regarding effective program evaluation.[2] The working group developed a framework for program evaluation in public health (Figure 15–1). The top part of Exhibit 15–1 lists the steps in the evaluation process, from engaging stakeholders in the process to ensuring the lessons learned are applied. The bottom part of the exhibit lists the four major standards of program evaluation: utility, feasibility, propriety, and accuracy.

The term *program* has a broad meaning.[3] Indeed, the CDC Evaluation Working Group listed 12 different program categories: direct service interventions,

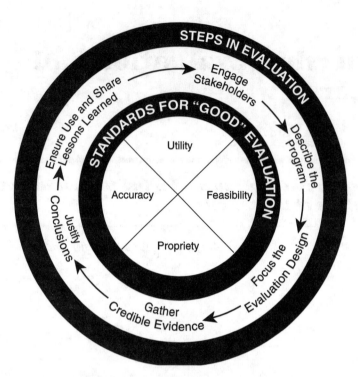

Figure 15–1 CDC program evaluation framework.

community mobilization efforts, research initiatives, surveillance systems, policy development activities, outbreak investigations, laboratory diagnostics, communication campaigns, infrastructure building projects, training and education services, administrative systems, and other programs. In this chapter, the focus is on the evaluation of leadership development programs.

EVALUATION OF TRAINING PROGRAMS

A training program must have a reason for being. If a training program is developed but no one registers for it, it obviously does not address a need. That is why the first step in the training process is to determine whether the proposed training program is required. The program planners should investigate the needs of the target population using focus groups, surveys, and interviews. The planners themselves will also have an agenda that should be built into the needs assessment. If the purpose of the assessment is to determine the need for training in governance, then the assessment must include questions about governance.

In a study done on board of health members' understanding of public health, it was found that the members believed their most important role was in the area of policy development.[4] They believed they were least effective in the area of assessment. In addition, board members thought that they were not given appropriate training for their board activities and that the principles of governance

Exhibit 15–1 Narrative Steps and Standards of the CDC Evaluation Framework

Engage stakeholders
  Those involved, those affected, primary intended users
Describe the program
  Need, expected effects, activities, resources, stage, context, logic model
Focus the evaluation design
  Purpose, users, uses, questions, methods, agreements
Gather credible evidence
  Indicators, sources, quality, quantity, logistics
Justify conclusions
  Standards, analysis/synthesis, interpretation, judgment, recommendations
Ensure use and share lessons learned
  Design, preparation, feedback, follow-up, dissemination
Utility
  Serve the information needs of intended users
Feasibility
  Be realistic, prudent, diplomatic, and frugal
Propriety
  Behave legally, ethically, and with due regard for the welfare of those involved and those affected
Accuracy
  Reveal and convey technically accurate information

were not clear. They were also concerned about the lack of funds for the running of the board, the lack of information about public health in general, and the lack of awareness of political priorities and statutory regulations. All of these findings can be translated into training objectives.

Once the training topics are determined, the program's objectives are set and the program is developed.[5] Among the things that need to be determined are procedures for the selection of participants, the times and places of the training, the best speakers for each topic, and methods for evaluating the program's outcomes.

The third step is to offer the training program itself. Measurements need to be done before or at the start of the training program and also at its conclusion in order to determine changes that occurred. Session and speaker evaluations also need to be done in order to assess the quality of the program. It is beneficial to tie the program evaluation to changes reported by the trainees. Research can be done on

- the association between program elements and leadership change
- lessons learned from the training course (see Exercise 15–1)
- leadership competencies measurable and unmeasurable
- differences between new leaders and more established ones
- differences between trainees and colleagues who have not been trained

- differences between continuing education approaches and academic approaches
- 360° measures at the start and the conclusion of the training program

If trainees do not take new information and skills back to their agencies, the training course loses much of its effectiveness. One way to spread the benefits of training is for training graduates, using what they learned, to develop a training workshop for colleagues who were unable to attend the training.

The last step in the training process involves following the trainees over time to determine what parts of the program work in practice. By taking the same measurements as were taken during the training, the planners can determine the changes that occurred over time and pinpoint areas in which skills deteriorated. The information gained can be used to develop follow-up programs and make the current program more effective in the future. A few public health leadership institutes have created annual update courses for graduates of their programs.

Evaluation itself can be divided into four components. First, the trainees' reactions to the program need to be assessed. There may be differences between reactions to in-house programs and reactions to programs outside the organization.

Second, the learning that occurred has to be evaluated. The hoped-for results of training include the acquiring of new skills and new knowledge.

Third, behavior changes due to the training need to be identified. The ultimate goal of all training programs is to alter the behavior of the trainees in ways that improve their effectiveness on the job. The expected behavior changes do not always occur, sometimes because leaders go to the training course with a personal agenda or believe that they already know everything about leadership that they need to. In addition, trainees who are primarily managers sometimes do not understand the difference between managing and leading. Finally, trainees often face community or organizational barriers to putting their new skills into action.

Fourth, the long-term effects of the training need to be studied. One leader who attended a state-based leadership program showed very little change of behavior at the end of the program but reported that he eventually used the skills learned two years later to improve the agency environment. This example shows the difficulty of evaluating results in a training program. Follow-up is clearly important, as is measuring behavior change in a control group that has not been through training.

The above model has been criticized for not going far enough. Performance evaluation needs to extend into the community.[6] In addition, the work environment must be analyzed to determine whether changes in behavior will be possible. It is important to keep in mind that behavior change is affected not only by the training but also by such factors as attitude and the reaction of others to proposed changes.[7]

EVALUATION OF LEADERSHIP DEVELOPMENT PROGRAMS

The Center for Creative Leadership undertook a study of leadership programs for school superintendents in Florida.[8] The study focused on the outcomes of training, the influence of the curriculum on the outcomes, and influence of other factors on the outcomes. Three general outcomes were discovered to have occurred. First, leaders became committed to continuous learning and believed that they had acquired continuous learning strategies and skills. Second, they acquired personal leadership skills and underwent personal changes. Third, they were able to perform their jobs more effectively.

With regard to factors affecting the outcomes, the trainees were influenced by their contact with facilitators, who appear to have taken a mentoring role. These facilitators helped the trainees to conceptualize their experientially based learning projects. The trainees also kept a journal during training, which helped document their learning experiences and contributed to the development of their leadership abilities.

The outcomes of training differ for different individuals.[9] Some leaders have much experience and use the new training to fine-tune their skills. Others struggle with self-control and self-esteem issues and have trouble maintaining flexibility. These leaders often do not benefit from leadership programs. A third group of leaders thrive in leadership programs and make substantial progress in developing their skills. For example, they often learn the importance of sharing power and how to create a better balance in their lives. Exercise 15–1 explores the expectations that students had starting the leadership program and the extent to which their expectations were met.

At the end of this chapter two program evaluation case studies are presented. The first, Case Study 15–A, describes the process of developing an evaluation program for the South Central Public Health Leadership Institute. One of the themes is that funding concerns can have an impact on training programs. The project team recognized the importance of evaluation and the complexity of the leadership development process, and they explored the possibility of using observers to monitor the training process. However, they decided that the leadership trainees would not accept this technique, and so they adopted a 360° self-evaluation and observer feedback procedure in which confidentiality was protected.

Case Study 15–B describes the planning activities that occurred in developing a program evaluation strategy for the national Public Health Leadership Institute. The institute was interested in discovering the effective of the leadership program over an eight-year period (1991–1999). The retrospective evaluation explored what alumni were doing, what skills have been used, and what skills can be attributed to the training experience. Results from this evaluation are not presently available.

SUMMARY

This chapter looked at the issue of evaluation of training programs, specifically leadership development programs. A number of research questions were raised for future leadership investigations. The case studies that follow concern program evaluation at a regional and a national public health leadership institute. They document the complexity of leadership development and the concerns of trainers regarding how to assess leadership training and make it more effective.

Discussion Questions

1. Why is leadership program evaluation important?
2. What is one difficulty in evaluating leadership programs?

2. How do leadership development programs differ from other training or educational programs?
3. What leadership issues do you think should be the focus of research?
4. Would are some benefits to be gained by keeping a leadership journal?

Exercise 15–1

GREAT EXPECTATIONS

Purpose: to investigate the relationship between personal expectations and training experiences

Key concepts: evaluation, leadership development, leadership expectations, lessons learned

Procedure: In exercise 1, each student wrote down five expectations he or she had regarding the course. Each student should now review those expectations, indicate to what degree each was met, and whether he or she learned things that were not anticipated. The class should then divide into groups of 5–10 members and discuss the expectations and their fulfillment or lack of fulfillment.

Case Study 15–A

Be Careful What You Ask For, You May Get It

Sheila W. Chauvin and Ann Anderson

Issue: How does one assess effective leadership and leadership development among public health professionals? *Time Period:* May 1997—October 1999. *Professionals involved:* Alata Angst, project director; Ben Thare, program coordinator; Helen Bach, evaluation consultant.

Alata sat at her desk feeling rather good about the progress of the new leadership development program. This first year had been really stressful, as is often the case with any new program. Alata had worried quite a bit about how the program would be perceived in the region, as participants were being drawn from practicing and experienced supervisors, managers, and leaders in the public health sector. She had just returned from the project team meeting for the South Central Public Health Leadership Institute (SCPHLI), and from all indications the first year had been successful indeed. A good thing, as everyone had worked so hard. Participants in the first cohort had completed feedback forms at the end of each multiday session

---

This case study was developed based on the experiences of the South Central Public Health Leadership Institute, Tulane University School of Public Health and Tropical Medicine, and the development of an objectives- and performance-based 360° feedback process.

throughout the year, and their comments revealed high levels of satisfaction with most of the program offerings and activities. Of course, as always there were a few negative and pessimistic comments, and there were indeed areas for improvement and expansion that the project team agreed they would need to target in the future. However, for the most part everyone thought that the first year of development and implementation was a success. Ben Thare, the project coordinator, had raised an interesting issue during the meeting: is it sufficient to gauge the effectiveness of the institute based simply on participants' satisfaction with the sessions? Shouldn't the team base its judgments on the extent to which participants actually demonstrate new and enhanced leadership skills in everyday practice? That's the true test, isn't it? As he said, satisfaction and the "friendly factor" were not necessarily going to get people to participate in the second year.

Ben's comments were working their way to the surface as Alata sat contemplating the future of the SCPHLI. Ben's right. How do we really know if the institute is making a difference? Certainly this was going to be an issue, probably sooner than she or Ben or even the participants might realize. While they had funding for the institute now, Alata knew that she would need additional extramural funding to continue and enhance the institute in the future, especially if they were going to add more states to the group of participatory states. A visual reminder lay on her desk in the form of a request for proposals from the Centers for Disease Control and Prevention (CDC). If the team was going to seek funding for the institute from the CDC, surely they would need a stronger evaluation plan than just session feedback forms asking participants to comment on what they liked and disliked. Ben was right. Even if she wasn't seeking additional funding, sooner or later officials in the various state agencies were going to want evidence that sending their public health leaders to multiday retreats and seminars was worth their investments of time, effort, and dollars. Sooner or later, state agency directors were going to expect visible evidence back "in the trenches."

But what could they do? What kind of evidence would they need? This was clearly out of Alata's comfort zone. Public health administration and microbiology were areas in which she could hold her own, even excel, but measuring the effectiveness of educational programs was clearly not part of her expertise. Certainly Alata had statistical support available in the school, but statisticians didn't know much about evaluating educational programs or things like leadership development, change facilitation, communication, conflict resolution, coalition building, coaching and mentoring skills, and so on. Now Alata was concerned! Who could help? Maybe the institute wasn't as successful as she had thought originally. Maybe it was just fluff, as had been suggested by a few of the negative and pessimistic comments that she was now reflecting on once again. As Alata continued to think about how the team could really know whether the institute was making a difference in participants' leadership development and practices, she got up and started to walk down the hall toward Ben's office. She thought, Ben should be back from the team meeting by now. He raised the question about effectiveness and evaluation, so maybe he has some ideas as to how to proceed? Yes, that's it, ask Ben.

ONE WEEK LATER

Alata and Ben walked into the office of Helen Bach. They were meeting with Helen to discuss how they might examine the extent to which the SCPHLI participants develop and use key leadership concepts and skills in everyday practice. Luckily, Ben had met Helen earlier in the year at a conference, during which he learned about Helen's background in leadership development and change process and her expertise in instrument development and program evaluation. Lucky that Ben met her in the first place and doubly fortunate that she had the background that seemed ideally suited to meet their project needs. Alata knew about Helen and the medical education research office that she directed in the School of Medicine, but she hadn't realized that the unit might be a potential resource. In any case, they were glad the connection was made. With the CDC proposal deadlines looming near, they would not have had much time to search for an evaluation consultant, much less one with a leadership development background. As they waited in the reception area to meet with Helen, Alata and Ben reviewed the program goals and expectations that they planned to share with Helen.

AFTER THE MEETING

As Alata and Ben left Helen's office, they were feeling both drained and overwhelmed. They had no idea that evaluating the effectiveness of the leadership institute could be so complex. Going into the meeting, both Alata and Ben thought they could just administer some type of test or survey and have some of the staff or faculty in the biostatistics department "crunch the numbers" and give them the results. What Helen had suggested was more of a performance-based assessment. Direct observation by several trained assessors over several occasions would be an ideal approach, she had told them, but the associated costs and time constraints were formidable. In addition, potential difficulties and political and interpersonal considerations were at the top of the list for decision making. For example, who would assess, how would assessors be trained and monitored, who would own the data, and how would the data be used for programming decisions and for helping individuals improve their leadership abilities? These were some of the questions raised and scenarios discussed.

Ultimately, the results of any assessments must be used for decision making and continuous improvement. Certainly, if the participant's direct supervisors were the ones doing the assessments, there might be little potential for collaborative reflection and professional development to occur, at least at first. For example, individuals might tend to view the assessments as yet another formal job evaluation rather than an opportunity to learn and develop new abilities. On the other hand, if peers were trained to do the observations, how would their assessor responsibilities affect day-to-day work relationships? Should the peer assessors be individuals who work with participants on a regular basis or should they be brought in from some other office, agency, or region to conduct "snapshot" observations and assessment reports? In what context should the assessments be explained and occur? And then there were all the instrument development, validity, and reliability issues that Helen raised for them to consider. How were they going to accomplish this? Alata and Ben had no idea what they had asked for. What they had was a task of elephantine proportions.

Alata and Ben felt like they should run—not walk—out of Helen's office. This was way too much work and complexity for their program. Participants would never agree to be observed and rated on behaviors, and after their discussion paper-and-pencil tests did not seem much better than session feedback forms. But they felt a ray of hope when Helen suggested that they limit the scope of work and take things one step at a time. Obviously she had noted the look of being overwhelmed on Ben and Alata's faces. She said, "Folks, this is an evolutionary process, not a revolution." Phew! Alata and Ben stayed in their seats and leaned forward with interest. Helen went on to describe several other options for their evaluation goals. She mentioned self-assessment and peer-assessment methods and told them about techniques that were currently being described as 360° feedback processes. Helen also discussed concepts such as self-efficacy and organizational context and explored the notion of assessment performance levels at the beginning of the institute and then again at the end (i.e., pre- and postassessments). By the end of the meeting, they had an action plan in place and a renewed sense of confidence about the tasks that lay ahead. As they left Helen's office, they thought about the last thing she said to them: "If you're going to eat an elephant, do so one bite at a time. Let's approach this as a team."

Over the next several months, Helen worked with Alata and Ben to review the goals and objectives of the SCPHLI to identify key leadership traits that were being addressed by the program. As she explained, it would be impossible to measure everything, so they should concentrate on the specifics of the program. They also began to work on a process that included pre- and postassessments and self- and peer-assessment components. Once again, ideal approaches were identified first, but then, once they figured out what their resources were, they settled for less than the ideal.

In the end, the SCPHLI had an observation-based questionnaire that included multiple descriptions of leadership behaviors grounded in the program goals and objectives. Participants completed a self-assessment form at the beginning and at the end of the institute. They identified five individuals in their work environment with whom they work regularly and who agreed to complete a confidential peer-assessment form of the questionnaire, again before and after participation in the institute. A process was developed by which all data were submitted directly to Helen's office and voluntary and confidential assurances were established. Preassessment profiles and postassessment profiles were completed by the staff in Helen's office and mailed directly to each participant, with options for confidential and individualized consultation. Only group or cohort assessment data were available to the project team, and no individually identifiable data were shared. In essence, they were able to achieve many of the 360° feedback features and minimize the political and interpersonal threats that are often associated with on-the-job performance assessments.

OCTOBER 1999

Alata sat at her desk feeling rather good about the progress of the SCPHLI. She had just returned from the project team meeting. As another cohort containing participants from four states completed the institute, Ben shared in the meeting evidence that suggested another successful year indeed. A good thing, as everyone had worked so hard—not this year, but for the past several years. Alata thought about the first year that they implemented a pilot version of the self-assessment questionnaire and the anxiety it had raised among the participants and the large number of individuals who initially expressed their apprehension about peers completing a similar form. She remembered watching Ben manage the group discussions about the participants' concerns pertaining to confidentiality of assessment data. She thought, just hearing the word *evaluation* does tend to make the hair on the back of your neck stand on end. Now, two years later, most, if not all, participants embrace the pre- and postassessments for the 360° feedback process. At first individuals thought about evaluation as being done "to them" now it seems evaluation is being done "with them." She looked out the window and chuckled to herself: guess we do need to be careful about what we ask for—we just might get it!

Case Study 15–B

Development of the CDC/UC Public Health Leadership Institute Retrospective Evaluation Questionnaire

Carol Spain Woltring, Wendy Constantine, and Liz Schwarte

THE CDC/UC PUBLIC HEALTH LEADERSHIP INSTITUTE

Launched in 1991, the CDC/UC Public Health Leadership Institute (PHLI) is funded by the Centers for Disease Control and Prevention (CDC) through a cooperative agreement with the UCLA School of Public Health. It is managed jointly and in partnership with the Public Health Institute. CDC established the PHLI in response to the landmark 1988 IOM Report *The Future of Public Health*, which called for strong public health leadership. Since its inception, the institute has graduated 444 senior public health leaders from across the country from local, state, and federal public health agencies, academia, the health systems, and national organizations.

The institute's mission is to strengthen America's public health system by enhancing the capacity of senior public health officials to address the challenges facing public health. The goals of the institute are to develop scholars' abilities to create and implement, with their organizations and communities, a shared vision for the public's health; the skills to mobilize the organizational and community resources and capacity necessary to address public health challenges and achieve the national health objectives; and a national network that fosters lifelong learning and shapes the future of public health.

Now, more than ever, the field of public health needs the individuals who direct our public health and health organizations to be not only good managers but also good leaders. We need leaders who know themselves and have a clear sense of priority and purpose, leaders who can courageously lead change in their organizations and promote community building, and leaders who can communicate their message.

Each year, the institute selects approximately 60 health officials and health leaders to be scholars in a year-long program that includes teleconferences, readings, electronic seminars, an intensive on-site week, and completion of a leadership initiative. The institute fosters close and substantive interaction with colleagues, university faculty, and other experts on leadership and public health. In recent years, the PHLI curriculum has focused on the following core curriculum areas: Personal Growth for Leadership Excellence, Leading Organizational Change, and Community Building and Collaborative Leadership for Health Promotion. A variety of communication skills are also emphasized. The program and curriculum have evolved in response to the learning that occurs with each new cohort. For example, learning teams and Web-based communication were introduced, and the orientation program at the APHA annual meeting grew in scope. The selection of teleconferences has grown over the years. Finally, the scholar community has also been developed to include nongovernmental health leaders as well.

In 1993, in response to our goal to develop a national network, PHLI alumni formed the Public Health Leadership Society (PHLS). The society has over 200 paid alumni members. It provides an opportunity for alumni to continue their learning experiences and leadership development; maintain professional and personal relations; and contribute to innovative thinking about public health issues, often in collaboration with other national public health organizations. The society has played a significant and synergistic role in extending the institute's impact.

WHY EVALUATE THIS LEADERSHIP DEVELOPMENT PROGRAM?

We hear from our alumni and others that a great deal of personal development and learning has occurred among the institute scholars as well as their organizations and communities. Their networks have expanded, and the field of public health as a whole has benefited from the enhanced leadership skills of PHLI alumni. As we began planning for the ninth and final year of the PHLI cooperative agreement, it became imperative to evaluate the impact of the institute on our alumni and those around them. We know that the institute is highly respected within the field and that our alumni are in positions of leadership in their organizations and professional organizations. We also know from the scholar leadership initiative stories, some of which have been published, and from process and short-term impact evaluations that the institute has succeeded in enhancing scholars' professional lives, in some instances quite profoundly. Alumni have related many stories at alumni gatherings about the institute's impact on their ability to act courageously, influence their organizations, and impact the field of public health and their communities.

Our evaluation *mission* is to demonstrate our belief that PHLI has made a difference and to deepen our own knowledge and that of our funding agency (CDC) and the public health and leadership development fields about the impact of PHLI. Our overall *objectives* are to (1) evaluate (for the field, key stakeholders, the funder [CDC], and "sister" organizations [the state and regional leadership institutes]) the impact of the PHLI national leadership training program on the participants, their organizations, their communities, and the field of public health, and (2) evaluate the PHLI model and solicit views about what a future PHLI should look like.

EARLY EVALUATION PLANNING

In the spring of 1999, we began development of an evaluation framework. Our goal was to have collected most of our new data by early November 1999 and to produce the final report by the early spring of 2000. Although we knew a lack of resources would be a problem (our cooperative agreement does not include funds for a retrospective evaluation), we were determined to conduct a comprehensive evaluation of the program's impact from 1991 to 1999. Our staff took on the added responsibility of conceiving and overseeing a large complex evaluation project. We secured resources, a consultant, and some in-kind support from our own organization, the Public Health Institute. We began by discussing our ideas with colleagues at the Public Health Institute and Professor Deborah Glik at the UCLA School of Public Health. Dr. Glik served as evaluator for years 4–7 (1994–1997) of the institute and was the author of a report comparing two years of the institute on a variety of leadership competency scales. In addition, we spoke to our alumni, faculty, and steering committee members as well as colleagues at the Public Health Practice Program Office at CDC. We also sought the input of colleagues from outside of PHLI. These discussions culminated in a series of outlines and a timeline (July 1999–January 2000) that proved essential to guiding our work.

We struggled with the question of what we should measure, given the complexity of the program effects, program evolution, long-term and short-term impacts on the program, and problems of attribution (our scholars and alumni have been impacted by other experiences). We decided on a multipronged approach consisting of (1) a retrospective alumni evaluation questionnaire; (2) lessons learned from staff, management, and faculty; (3) observations of individuals who did not participate in PHLI but are knowledgeable and respected leaders who could comment on the impact of PHLI on the field of public health; and (4) an analysis of PHLI's impact on other organizations, institutions, and leadership development programs.

Our first task (which we are reporting on here) has been the planning, design, and implementation of a retrospective evaluation questionnaire. The questionnaire assesses the investment and impact of PHLI on its goals and the degree to which our graduates' leadership skills at the personal, organizational, community, network, and continuous learning levels could be attributed to PHLI.

STRATEGIC PLANNING FOR A RETROSPECTIVE EVALUATION

It quickly became clear that we needed an expert survey designer—someone who could craft meaningful, concise questions. We hired a consultant with over 25 years of experience in survey design and a background in health research and the design and delivery of training programs for professionals.

The first step was to thoroughly orient the consultant to our program and evaluation goals and begin the transfer of institutional knowledge and intuition to the development of a succinct survey tool. Her challenges were to obtain within a short period of time an overview of our mission and curriculum as well as goals for the retrospective evaluation and to design and test a survey instrument. We have learned a lot about working collaboratively with an evaluation consultant and utilizing her expertise optimally. For example, our evaluation consultant contributed greatly to the conceptual underpinning of the evaluation approach by conducting a thorough search and analysis of the literature (see below).

EVALUATION QUESTIONNAIRE DESIGN

The Literature Review

The next step undertaken was to review the current literature on training evaluation in general and leadership training evaluation in particular and on the analysis of professional networks. Searching the Web led to the identification of highly relevant literature. Resources that proved particularly useful were *Evaluating the Effectiveness of Training Programs*[10] and several publications of the Center for Creative Leadership, of Greensboro, North Carolina.[11,12]

A particular challenge to us was the development of items to tap the development of networks among PHLI alumni. Much of the literature on the analysis of networks concerns statistical procedures for conceptualizing and estimating the development of complex social networks. The Web search identified research conducted by Haythornthwaite on the development of networks among distance learners.[13] Dr. Haythornthwaite was contacted by e-mail, and she forwarded to our consultant the survey items used to collect her network growth data. This was a particularly valuable resource for the development of items for our evaluation questionnaires.

Of all of the literature we reviewed, the most important to our evaluation was *Evaluating Training Programs: The Four Levels.*[14] Here was outlined the need to not only assess the transfer of skill or knowledge to the job but also measure the results of this change on the organization's performance. This conceptual framework served to clarify our goals of assessing the impact of PHLI on the job skills of the alumni and on the performance of the organizations for which they work, on their community, and on the field of public health.

For several weeks, our team enjoyed a lively exchange of relevant publications and articles and stimulating discussions about the information that we were after and the best approaches to get us there. We believe that our utilization of theoretical perspectives and practical resources from the literature substantially added to the quality of our evaluation design.

Creating the Questionnaire

Planning the Design

Our challenges in drafting the questionnaire lay in integrating training evaluation theory from the literature with PHLI's need for data. We also sought to utilize, where appropriate, items from two previously conducted year-end evaluations. The items for the prior evaluations had been designed to assess scholar learning in a number of key curriculum areas, and the reliability of the scales used had been assessed. These items consequently could serve as excellent starting points for several sections of the new evaluation questionnaire. Creating a structured, detailed outline of the questionnaire components prior to question drafting was a critical step in meeting the challenge of integrating these diverse resources.

Drafting the Items

Using previously asked items in original and revised form and new items drafted using accepted principles of survey design, all domains identified on the outline (personal, organizational community, network, and support of continuous learning) were covered by either an item or a scale comprising a subset of items.

The resulting questionnaire included measures of the impact of PHLI training on the respondents' personal leadership style as well as on their organizations and committees. Other questions concerned the respondents' support of continuous learning (including providing training opportunities for themselves, for others within their own organizations, and for others in the public health profession). Finally, questions were included on the impact of their PHLI training on the development of their professional networks.

In addition to the areas described above, the questionnaire included demographic questions regarding the respondents' gender, age, number of years in public health, and job changes. These questions will be useful in the data analysis to examine whether particular subgroups of alumni benefited more than others from their exposure to PHLI. Finally, the questionnaire included a few items on new materials and other resources that the alumni had found particularly useful since attending PHLI.

Pilot-Testing the Questionnaire

We conducted a formal pretest of the questionnaire and draft cover letter with five of our alumni. The purpose of the pilot was to test the clarity of the questions, gain input on the format, and assess the time needed to complete the entire survey and the particular sections. Two different types of question formats were tested by these respondents for the set of items measuring the impact of the PHLI training on the leaders' organizations. We provided a short "pretest debriefing form" on which alumni recorded comments. At the completion of pretest data collection, a comprehensive pretest report was reviewed by our team.

One of our goals was to construct a survey instrument that could be completed in 20–25 minutes. We knew from experience and the literature that we would not get a good response rate if the questionnaire were too long. The pretest required an average of 36 minutes administration time—16 minutes over our 20-minute goal. The questionnaire was subsequently shortened by eliminating items that were burdensome or not absolutely essential to our research needs, reducing the number of responses requested in certain open-ended questions, and clarifying the wording. In addition to shortening the instrument, substantially revised after the pretest, we decided to conduct a small pilot test to ensure that we had met our goal in reducing the administration time and clarifying the questions.

Throughout the instrument development process, it was challenging to balance the breadth and depth of our substantive interests with the need to produce a concise survey instrument. We successfully met this challenge, with some pain, as certain potentially useful items were deleted.

IMPLEMENTING THE EVALUATION

Fielding the Survey

Data collection will require approximately two months. We will use the total design method advocated by Dillman[15] for obtaining an excellent response rate. All alumni will be mailed a reminder postcard one week after the initial survey mailing. Over a two-month period, the entire survey package will be mailed out again twice to those who didn't respond to the original mailing. Our goal is to achieve a 70 percent rate of response.

It is challenging to balance the need for multiple respondent contacts (to obtain a good response rate) with sensitivity to the many requests on these leaders' time. We attempted to meet this by printing an attractive questionnaire booklet, clearly formatting the items, and including few open-ended questions.

Data Analysis

The data will be entered in several batches as completed questionnaires are received. Data analysis will begin prior to the close of data collection. An immediate next step will be to formally specify an analysis plan, including table designs.

A Reflection on Study Limitations

There are a number of potential limitations to the approach we chose for our eight-year retrospective evaluation. First, some of the alumni had completed the program as long as eight years ago. Their memory of the PHLI experience as well as its impact on their leadership and on their organizations is therefore subject to *recall bias*, that is bias due to imperfect recall of past events.[16] We minimized this by beginning the questionnaire with specific questions regarding their PHLI training, including the years they were enrolled, their engagement in specific program components, and their employment and professional role at that time and now. These initial items served as *memory aides,* stimulating the alumni to better recall their PHLI experience.

A second limitation is that all of the data are self-reported by the alumni themselves. Because of this, there is danger of response bias, that is, a lack of objectivity in reporting their own learning and accomplishments. We believe, however, that for the purposes of this evaluation, the alumni themselves would have the best insight as to the usefulness of the PHLI experience to their own work, organizations, and communities.

Ideally, one would supplement the insights of the alumni with data collected from supervisors, peers, and others regarding their assessment of the PHLI alumni's leadership before and after training (as in a 360° evaluation) as well as data consisting of indirect measures of improvements in organizational performance. It was not possible to include such measures for this evaluation, both because of a lack of resources and because of the significant passage of time since many of the alumni's PHLI experience. While we believed it was possible to stimulate alumni to recall their PHLI year and to report the resulting impact on their work, there would be no way to obtain parallel retrospective reports from others about the training's impact. Additionally, it would be difficult to obtain indirect measures of leadership effectiveness in public health.

In conducting evaluations, it is optimal to compare the performance of a group receiving an intervention with a control group that has not received the intervention or has received a different intervention. For obvious reasons, we were not able to use a control group to which to compare the leadership and accomplishments of the PHLI graduates.

Finally, because PHLI itself conducted this evaluation, there was concern that alumni would feel constrained to report positive impacts. We dealt with this potential source of bias in two ways. First, alumni were asked in the cover letter to give honest feedback to PHLI to assist in future planning, an important value to this group. Secondly, alumni were assured that their answers would be confidential. All completed questionnaires were mailed back to our evaluation consultant to underscore the complete confidentiality of their responses. When PHLI receives the data, there will be no way to associate a response with a given alumnus.

LESSONS LEARNED

- A true partnership with our evaluation consultant has been critical to our effort. Our consultant's experience in survey design led to the efficient construction, testing, and polishing of a relevant, highly structured, professional survey instrument. As the stakeholders for the evaluation, however, it was critical that we worked together closely with our consultant to ensure a full understanding of our program needs, inclusion of relevant evaluation domains, and use of appropriate vocabulary.
- Starting with a theoretically based conceptual framework is critical for designing a tightly focused, meaningful questionnaire. Such a conceptual framework also

helps in deciding which items are not essential when pretesting reveals that some items must be deleted to keep within time constraints.

- We found the Internet a valuable resource for quickly identifying and obtaining needed resources during the literature review phase.
- Careful planning for the instrument development, testing, proofreading, and printing were critical components of the process. Although more time would have been optimal, our survey design process lasted two and a half months.
- Testing the evaluation instrument with "real" participants is a critical component of the survey design process. Including alternate formats in the pretest instrument is an excellent way of deciding optimal question structure.

CONCLUDING COMMENTS

We believe our retrospective evaluation questionnaire will yield useful data for our program and to the profession. At the time of this writing, our survey instrument is on its way to 444 alumni. Our next tasks (beyond those discussed above related to analysis planning) are to

- develop stakeholder interview tools and conduct interviews
- summarize information gained from previous evaluations and other existing sources of information about the institute's influence
- develop a detailed outline and dissemination strategy for the final report
- write and disseminate the final report

We anticipate our findings to be available by July 2000 on our Website, www.cfhl.org.

REFERENCES

1. S.T. Gray, *Leadership Is: Evaluation with Power* (Washington, DC: Independent Sector, 1995).
2. Centers for Disease Control and Prevention, "Framework for Program Evaluation in Public Health," *MMWR* 48 (1999): RR11.
3. Centers for Disease Control and Prevention, "Framework for Program Evaluation in Public Health."
4. E. Jurkowski et al., "The Core Functions and the Role of Governance within the Public Health Arena: A Perspective from Board of Health Members (submitted for publication).
5. D.L. Kirkpatrick, *Evaluating Training Programs: The Four Levels*, 2d ed. (San Francisco: Berrett-Koehler, 1998).
6. J. Hale, "Evaluation: It's Time To Go Beyond Levels 1, 2, 3, and 4," in *The 1999 ASTD Training and Performance Yearbook*, eds. J.A. Woods and J.W. Cortada (New York: McGraw-Hill, 1999).
7. M.L. Lanigan, "New Theory and Measures for Training Evaluation," in *The 1999 ASTD Training and Performance Yearbook*, eds. J.A. Woods and J.W. Cortada (New York: McGraw-Hill, 1999).
8. C.D. McCauley and M.W. Hughes-James, *An Evaluation of the Outcomes of a Leadership Development Program* (Greensboro, NC: Center for Creative Leadership, 1994).
9. McCauley and Hughes-James, *An Evaluation of the Outcomes of a Leadership Development Program.*
10. P. Boverie et al., "Evaluating the Effectiveness of Training Programs," *Developing Human Resources*, 1994 annual ed. (San Diego, CA: Pfeiffer & Co., 1994).
11. McCauley and Hughes-James, *An Evaluation of the Outcomes of a Leadership Development Program.*
12. D.P. Young and N.M. Dixon, *Helping Leaders Take Effective Action: A Program Evaluation* (Greensboro, NC: Center for Creative Leadership, 1996).
13. C. Haythornthwaite, "A Social Network Study of the Growth of Community among Distance Learners," *Information Research* 4, no. 1 (1998).
14. Kirkpatrick, *Evaluating Training Programs: The Four Levels*, 2d ed.

15. D. Dillman, *Mail and Telephone Surveys: The Total Design Method* (New York: Wiley, 1978).
16. S. Sudman and N. Bradburn, *Response Effects in Surveys: A Review and Synthesis* (Chicago: Aldine Publishing Co., 1974).

Part V

The Future

Chapter 16

Leadership for the 21st Century

*"Everyone overrates the significance of his own era. .
. . Things change."*

Robert Stone, *Damascus Gate*

The purpose to this book is to explore public health leadership in depth and suggest ways in which leadership knowledge can be translated into practice, especially in the coming years. American society is changing, and old leadership approaches are no longer working. Change will not stop with the new millennium, neither in society in general, nor in the area of public health. Therefore, public health leaders have to be trained to work in an environment of constant change.

American social life does not seem to be governed by natural laws.[1] Because different eras bring forth different social circumstances, different types of leaders are needed at different times. It is clear that leaders will guide social developments whatever the social climate is.

Many organizational practices now in use are out-of-date. Drucker identified seven organizational assumptions that no longer hold true.[2] He also identified seven realities of contemporary management. The seven realities entail that no cookie-cutter approach to the development of organizations is feasible. People cannot be managed all in the same way. Everybody is different. Each organization has multilevel activities and services, and no one service drives the organization. New technologies, such as communication via the Internet, are constantly being created. Complexity rules. In addition, the command and control approaches of the past will no longer be acceptable. Finally, global concerns will drive the organizations of the future.

LEADERSHIP CHALLENGES IN THE 21st CENTURY

Public health leaders face 13 critical challenges at the beginning of the 21st century (Exhibit 16–1). First, there is the managed care revolution. Official public health agencies have often viewed managed care as a threat. The threat is greatest

Exhibit 16–1 Today's Public Health Challenges

- Growth of managed care
- Privatization
- Welfare reform
- Emphasis on accountability and performance
- Steering versus rowing
- Invisibility of public health
- Government and health department reorganization
- Explosion of information technology
- Emergence of new and re-emergence of old diseases
- Changing demographics
- Enhanced role of prevention
- Growing number of uninsured
- Shifting public expectations

for those local public health agencies that primarily provide direct services to their communities. Agencies not in the direct service business view managed care as a way to increase access to health care for people with health care needs. These agencies are also more likely to hold the position that public health needs to get back to its traditional focus on prevention.

Closely tied to the issue of managed care is the issue of privatization. Public health leaders need to explore the possibility of spinning off programs to the private sector, especially as the coming era is likely to be one of shrinking resources.

The welfare revolution of the 1990s is also affecting public health. People are moving off welfare into jobs, but many low-paying jobs do not come with health insurance. Thus, states are coping with the redefinition of eligibility for Medicaid coverage. Public health agencies may decide to expand their direct service programs to treat former welfare recipients, in which case they will have an obligation to ensure their programs are accountable. Outcome-based performance measurement will become required. Public health agencies have been good at documenting process but not so good at documenting both short- and long-term outcomes.

Public health leaders need to be more proactive and not follow the crowd. They need, in other words, to steer the course of public health program change rather than be among the rowers. They have the leadership skills to move public health organizations forward and they need to apply them to this task.

Public health agencies and their best practices have often remained hidden from the public. In the author's study of public health leaders, the great majority of the leaders interviewed recognized that the public is not aware of what public health agencies do. Public health leaders must continue to engage in health communication and social marketing activities.

During the 1990s, a number of states reorganized their public health agencies or even abolished them. As a result, public health programs have been transferred to other state agencies or absorbed into an umbrella human services agency. The reorganization, in some instances, has been done without pertinent evaluation data or a method of approach. Millions of dollars have been spent on experiments that may not work. To help them succeed, public health leaders have an obligation to promote public health as creatively and comprehensively as they can, whether using traditional or new means, such as the Internet.

It is not possible to accurately predict the emergence of new diseases and the re-emergence of old diseases locally, nationally, or globally. One worry is that some disease-causing microorganisms are becoming drug resistant. Public health needs to stress organizational flexibility to allow agencies to respond quickly to new emergencies. Some states utilize rapid response team models to address emergencies. Public health leaders need to be at the table when community disaster plans and bioterrorism plans are written.

Another challenge is presented by the continuing cultural and ethnic diversification of the American population. Public health leaders will have to monitor demographic changes as well as the health status of each of a wide variety of subpopulations. The performance of community health assessments will become ever more critical as the 21st century progresses.

Public health must focus on prevention activities. Prevention has always been a large part of the public health mandate. At the same time, public health leaders must address the needs of the continually increasing number of people who are uninsured.

Finally, public health leaders must respond to the concerns of the public. The public has a tendency to change its expectations on a regular basis, but it is impossible to predict what the public's new expectations will be.

To the list of challenges in Exhibit 16–1 should be added a 14th challenge: public health leaders have an obligation to develop a set of ethical standards pertaining to public health and to use these standards for guiding the public health process. The standards will concern issues as diverse as the privacy of records to end-of-life decisions.

PUBLIC HEALTH DURING THE THIRD WAVE

In Chapter 4, the third-wave theory was discussed.[3] Exhibit 16–2 lists 12 third-wave public health issues. The third wave began with the transition from industrial forms of organization (which are characteristic of the second wave) to information-based forms of organization. The last two decades of the 20th century have seen major changes in technology and the emergence of knowledge as an important commodity.

Table 16–1 compares certain elements of the second wave with corresponding elements of the third wave. Some of the changes have already occurred. For example, many alternative family approaches were already common in the 1990s, the use of educational vouchers to allow parents to select public or private schools for their children is under discussion, and some parents educate their children at home utilizing computers and educational software.

On the other hand, the large-organization model still prevails, and mergers are making big organizations bigger. It is true that there has been an increase in small specialty organizations, but this has been going on for a long time. Also, national struggles have continued to plague the world, and whether democracy will finally triumph as the one viable political system is open to question. In fact, the meaning and direction of our democratic society has come under increasing scrutiny. Trade unions have lost their strength, and many professionals are redefining the

Exhibit 16–2 Public Health in the Third Wave

---

1. Expanded models of public health
2. Team-based problem solving
3. Community health coalitions based on partnership
4. Privatization of assurance activities
5. Decentralization of responsibilities across the community
6. Communitywide governance
7. Value generation
8. A new political structure
9. Third-wave leadership
10. Integration between individuals' needs and the community's needs
11. Complete community empowerment
12. Universal access to a multitude of services to improve quality of life

---

workplace. Thus, the year 2000 finds American society still tied to the second wave, although clear examples of third-wave realities are disrupting society.

Exhibit 16–3 lists 10 products that reflect the transition between the second wave and the third wave. Many of the products will have an impact on public health whether or not the third-wave theory is valid. For instance, public health leaders will require more information to do their jobs well. The human genome project will change our understanding of how diseases work and will lead to new techniques for helping people. Innovation will be the order of the day. Strategies for running organizations will be based on the leadership model rather than the management model. The old ways and the old methods will have to be modified.

Public health leaders and their human services colleagues will have to make public health a community-based activity through partnering with community leaders and community residents generally. Citizens of the 21st century will have to assume responsibility for improving their personal health and fitness. If it

---

Table 16–1 The Second and Third Waves Compared

Second-Wave Civilization	Third-Wave Civilization
Nuclear family	Alternate families
Mass education	Individual education
Giant corporations	Small specialty organizations
Centralized nation-state	New democracy
Mass trade unions	Demassification
Hand work	Mind work

Exhibit 16–3 Products of the Third Wave

1. Information and innovation
2. Management strategies
3. Culture and pop culture
4. Advanced technology
5. Software
6. Education
7. Training
8. Medical care through the private sector
9. Financial services
10. Military protection

appears that technology is advanced now, wait 20 years. Think of the changes that have occurred in the last two decades. Desktop computers became as powerful as the massive computers of the past. The Internet grew from nothing into a whole new means of communicating, transferring information, and doing business.

The American educational system will have to change. The educational process will be different for each individual. The challenge will be to determine how to use our educational tools to meet the needs and wants of people committed to lifelong learning. The expansion of distance-learning programs will be part of the answer. Training opportunities, include mentoring opportunities, will need to grow if public health professionals are to keep up with the changes in their field.

The medical care sector is already changing. Managed care is only one approach. One major trend will be the creation of integrated systems of care. Another will be the development of public-private partnerships. New financial services will also evolve. Finally, national and international military protection will require the continued development and production of more advanced weapon systems.

During the third wave, leaders who integrate their leadership skills and their management skills will be the ones who are most successful. In short, leadership and management will become united.

Following are 10 key leadership issues for the information age:

1. Leaders will need strategies oriented toward growth rather than retrenchment. They will also have to engage in strategic thinking rather than merely tactical thinking.
2. Customer- and community-focused activities will become more prominent.
3. More and more knowledge sources will appear. For example, the Internet will expand the professional horizons of public health practitioners.
4. The information age is also the age of teams, coalitions, and partnerships. Networking will be the preferred method of operation.
5. Public agencies will discover that they cannot serve all segments of the population. The service sector will need to be shared by both public and

private entities. An integrated health care system will evolve, with public health agencies as lead partners. Each partner in the integrated system will serve specific client sectors.

6. Accounting systems will become more relevant to public health activities. Public health agencies will need to budget on the basis of core functions, organizational practices, and/or essential services rather than traditional public health service activities.

7. All partners in an enterprise will need to be empowered. Empowerment must be balanced against control.

8. Shared values will change. Leaders will have to review shared values regularly since changes in values have an impact on the program effectiveness of public health agencies.

9. Leaders must honor the best practices and the most effective individuals.

10. Leaders must work to transform a second-wave organization into a third-wave one.

Leaders need guidance in how to motivate and manage change to facilitate the transformation to the third wave or the modification of the present system.[4] So will leadership commitment to the transformation. Figure 16–1 presents a model of transformation for health care organizations. One critical task to address before starting a transformation is to make certain that a real need for change exists. If change is inevitable, then the leaders need to restructure teams and coalitions so as to bring about the change with as little difficulty as possible.

A successful transformation requires that all the steps shown in Figure 16–1 be followed. Leaders will need to adopt strategic planning, total quality process, re-engineering, and reinvention methods, among others, to expedite the change process. The next stage involves the commitment of all players to the idea of change and the philosophical underpinnings of the management strategies selected to help bring about the change. Next, the leaders need to encourage creativity in the work force and promote innovation. These factors will change not only the way people work but also the way public health organizations look.

It is not necessary to accept the third-wave theory. Much more important is to accept the changes that are occurring in our society as we enter the 21st century. This is clearly a time of major change in which leaders from all segments of our society will need to address the issues that are causing the change and arising out of the change. Public health leaders will need to answer the call for a new form of public health that is based on the following principles:

- Public health must clarify its mission, its vision, and its parameters and sell its vision to the public.
- Public health must become proactive rather than reactive.
- In a mostly private health system, public health must become the voice of the public. Public health should not be privatized.
- Public health must remain the provider of last resort (although *last* means *last*).
- Boards of health must be strengthened.
- A federal presence in public health must continue.
- Prevention must be stressed and marketed.
- Environmental health and occupational health must be treated as public health partners.

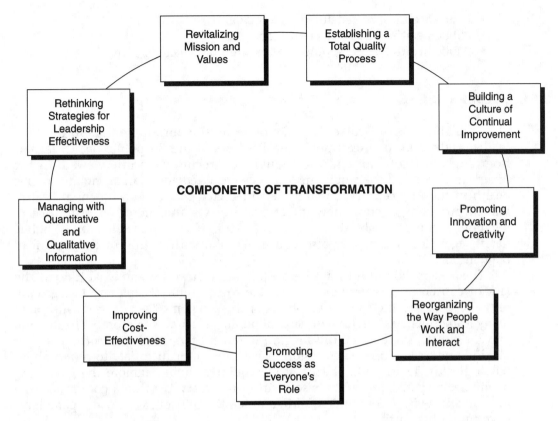

COMPONENTS OF TRANSFORMATION

Figure 16–1 Components of transformation.

- State laboratories need to be involved in setting up the public health agenda.
- Assessment activities must be strengthened through the use of modern technology and applied epidemiologic methods.
- Public health professionals must become policy makers.
- Leadership development must not only be stressed but also be financially supported.
- Stronger links need to be forged between academics and practitioners. The links need to incorporate the core academic fields of public health and the core functions of public health.
- The multidisciplinary nature of public health must be strengthened at the same time that a unified perspective on public health must be promoted among public health's constituencies.
- State-level public health agencies must remain largely independent.
- The partnership between state-level health agencies and local health agencies must be strengthened.
- Public health agencies must think globally but act locally.
- Public health agencies must teach the public about public health.
- Coalitions, including public-private partnerships, must be built.

- Assurance must be redefined on a regular basis.
- Public health must sell its best practices.
- Public health leaders should run for and hold elected office.

THE LEADERS SPEAK

Case Study 2–A discussed a study done by the author from 1996 to 1998. In the study, 100 American public health leaders and 30 public health leaders from England, Scotland, and the Republic of Ireland were interviewed. In the American portion of the study, the leaders were asked about an agenda for public health in the 21st century. Some leaders predicted that certain potential health-related problems, such as new infectious diseases and increased resistance of microorganisms to antibiotics, might erupt and affect the overall tasks of public health agencies. Some were also concerned about the aging of the American population.

The leaders did not fully agree on what public health is and what it does. The lack of consensus was probably partly due to the multidisciplinary background of the leaders and the specific emphasis of the programs they oversaw. Although many leaders believed that the mission of public health was to promote health and prevent disease, some found this mission statement too simplistic. Without a clear mission and a well-formulated vision, it becomes difficult to talk to others about public health. Thus, public health leaders jointly should explore the governing public health paradigms and revise them as necessary, develop a consensus on a mission and a vision for public health, and sell the mission, vision, and paradigms to community constituents.

During the last few decades of the 20th century, public health leaders have tended to respond to health crises rather than plan public health agendas likely to prevent crises. The goal for the 21st century is for public health leaders to take charge of their destiny and devise action plans directed toward improving the health of community residents. Proactive approaches should be the order of the day and the century.

Public health leaders will continue to act as the voice of the public in matters of health. Since public health agencies perform oversight activities, complete privatization of public health will not occur, and public health agencies will need to be integrated into the health care system. Since the development of a national health system in the United States remains a remote possibility, oversight by public health leaders is critical.

Boards of health and local and state departments of health should act as partners rather than adversaries. Board members are community gatekeepers and have an obligation to promote the community's priorities. Because of the importance of their role, board members need training in how to do their job. If boards become strengthened, the whole infrastructure of public health will become strengthened as well. It would help if board members network with other board members, with all boards of health in the state (if a board of health structure exists), and with the public health practitioners at the local and state levels. Public health leaders are aware of the lack of connection between the federal health agencies, the state health department (or, in some states, the human services agency), and local public health agencies. It is important to create strong links between these three levels of government, and public health leaders, among others, will have to take the initiative in forging these links. A federal presence is critical if policy is to be formulated for the nation.

Public health leaders need to push a primary prevention agenda. In many places, although prevention constitutes a major portion of the public health agenda, the public health leaders do little to promote the agenda. Public health agencies and their leaders need to address primary prevention in a strategic manner and come up with approaches for improving the health of the public through the prevention of disease.[5] Prevention includes actions that reduce susceptibility or exposure to health threats (primary prevention), detect and treat disease in early stages (secondary prevention), and alleviate the effect of disease and injury (tertiary prevention).[6]

During the late 20th century, local public health agencies concentrated their efforts on secondary and tertiary prevention programs. A shift to primary prevention initiatives, in which people become responsible for their own health, is needed.

Public health encompasses occupational health and safety as well as environmental health. Unfortunately, these disciplines tend to be neglected by public health leaders with a strong personal services orientation. Environmental health and occupational health specialists need to be given the same standing as other public health professionals. Also meriting a seat at the table are state and local laboratory directors, many of whom have been trained in a number of areas, including public health science. The professional diversity that characterizes public health is not a weakness but one of its strengths.

The public health leaders interviewed by the author recognized the importance of the community assessment process and argued that assessment techniques need to be improved. One recommendation was to train public health partners in the basics of epidemiologic methods in order to combine community assessment and epidemiology. Without question, public health leaders must acquire good computer skills and become acquainted with new information technologies as they emerge. Sharing epidemiologic and other types of data with public health leaders across the country will become the norm.

Public health leaders will need to become more versed in policy development. As experts, these leaders can influence elected officials and thereby promote the public health agenda at the local, state, and federal levels. In addition, public health agencies, like other human services organizations, need money to operate and carry out their mandate. Financial support is critical, and public health leaders will need to seek funding from multiple sources. State funding will cover only part of a health department budget, and so public health leaders will need to act as entrepreneurs in getting outside funding.

Public health leaders need to share ideas with their academic partners. Faculty members are often excluded from the strategic-planning process, yet they bring to the table a knowledge of health-related sciences, an understanding of the core disciplines of public health, and a knowledge of emerging health problems—all of which can be extremely important for addressing the problems that public health leaders face.

As noted, public health professionals come from many different disciplines, and although the diversity in educational background is an important strength, public health leaders must create a unified perspective to present to the public.

To put it one way, while speaking with many voices to each other, public health leaders must speak with a common voice when dealing with community partners.

The public health leaders interviewed were intrigued, to varying degrees, with three models for the future of public health: a situation in which independent public health agencies exist, an integrated system in which public health is one of the players, and an integrated system in which public health is the organizer of the system. Although some of the leaders liked each of the three models, they generally believed that it is necessary to maintain an independent public health presence in the community. Maintaining independent agencies will be critical if the United States does not develop a national health service.

There is a caution here. Public health leaders in other countries pointed out that public health often gets lost in a national health system. In England, the public health leaders found much of their time was spent purchasing services for their districts. American public health leaders were concerned about the possibility that the state health department would get absorbed into a state human services superagency. They believed that the state health department should be maintained as a separate entity within state government.

Public health agencies at different governmental levels must act as partners and cease to be antagonistic. Public health leadership programs are a means of creating partnerships between state and local agencies because the trainees come from all levels of government. Local public health leaders should communicate with state leaders and understand their concerns, and they should also be aware of the current activities of the World Health Organization and, where necessary, incorporate international health concerns into their planning efforts. Local leaders also need to communicate to the proper authorities information about local health issues that may eventually have a national or international impact.

Despite the efforts to promote public health, the public still does not understand the nature of the field. Without the support of the public, public health leaders will have difficulty planning for the future. The solution is for public health leaders to develop a multi-pronged approach to both health communication and social marketing. They also need to get out into the community, forge partnerships in the public and private sectors, and educate their partners about public health.

It is through assurance activities that creative intervention strategies will be tested and evaluated. Yet assurance itself will have to be redefined regularly, as new techniques are developed and tested. Assurance in the year 2000 will be different from assurance in the year 2010.

Finally, the public health leaders interviewed by the author emphasized the importance of selling public health's best practices and not being shy about it. If public health leaders do not market themselves well, the public health field as a whole suffers.

SUMMARY

This chapter reviewed the main challenges facing public health leaders as the new century—the new millennium—begins. All of these challenges have been discussed in greater detail in various places throughout the book. The strategies that public health leaders will need to use in order to meet these challenges are both numerous and diverse in kind. Among the most important, at least if public health leaders are themselves to be believed, is to return to public health's traditional focus on primary prevention. Another is to work at educating the public about public health, for it is clear there is general ignorance about what public health practitioners do. By pushing a prevention agenda and publicizing public health successes, along with the other strategies listed, public health leaders will go a long way toward ensuring that public health has the future that it deserves and that the public deserves it to have.

Discussion Questions

1. What current public health challenges do you see as most needing the attention of public health leaders?
2. What strategies might public health leaders use to meet some or all of these challenges?
3. What are some new characteristics of public health predicted to occur in the so-called third wave?
4. Why is there a lack of consensus on what public health is, even among public health practitioners?
5. How can public health leaders promote a prevention agenda?
6. How can public health leaders support the creation of an integrated health care system?
7. Will government public health agencies exist in 2050? Why or why not?

REFERENCES

1. P.F. Drucker, "Management's New Paradigms," *Forbes,* October 5, 1998, 152–156.
2. Drucker, "Management's New Paradigms."
3. A. Toffler, *The Third Wave* (New York: Morrow, 1980).
4. J. Kotter, *Leading Change* (Boston: Harvard Business School Press, 1996).
5. B.J. Turnock, *Public Health: What It Is and How It Works* (Gaithersburg, MD: Aspen Publishers, 1997).
6. Turnock, *Public Health.*

Table of Sources

CHAPTER 1

Table 1–1. *Source*: from *On Becoming a Leader* by Warren Bennis. Copyright © 1989, 1994 by Warren Bennis, Inc. Reprinted with permission of Perseus Books Publishers, a member of Perseus Books, L.L.C.

CHAPTER 2

Figure 2–1. *Source*: Reproduced by permission. *From Leadership Dilemmas—Grid Solutions* copyright © 1991 by Robert R. Blake and the Estate of Jane S. Mouton, Austin, Texas. Gulf Publishing Company, Houston, Texas, 800–231–6275. All rights reserved.

Figure 2–2. *Source*: Diagram - "The Four Leadership Styles"- from *Leadership and the One Minute Manager* by Kenneth Blanchard, Ph.D., Patricia Zigarmi, ED.D. and Drea Zigarmi, ED.D. Copyright © 1985 by Blanchard Management Corp. Reprinted by permission of HarperCollins Publishers, Inc.

Figure 2–3. *Source*: Reprinted by permission of *Harvard Business Review*. From "How To Choose a Leadership Pattern" by R. Tannenbaum and W.H. Schmidt, May-June/1973. Copyright © 1973 by the President and Fellows of Harvard College; all rights reserved.

Table 2–1. *Source*: Reprinted with permission from P. Hersey, K.H. Blanchard and D. Johnson, *Management of Organizational Behavior*, p. 368, © 1996, Prentice-Hall, Inc.

Table 2–2. *Source*: Reprinted with the permission of The Free Press, a Division of Simon & Schuster, Inc. from *Bass & Stogdill's Handbook of Leadership: Theory*,

Research, and Management Applications, Third Edition by Bernard M. Bass. Copyright © 1974, 1981, 1990 by The Free Press.

Table 2–3. *Source*: Reprinted with permission from J.M. Kouzes and B.Z. Posner, *The Leadership Challenge*, p. 21, © 1995, Jossey-Bass Inc., Publishers.

Case Study 2–A. *Source* Reprinted from L. Rowitz, Inner World to the Future: Leaders' Perspective on the Future, *Journal of Public Health Management & Practice*, Vol. 3, No. 4, pp. 68–71, © 1997, Aspen Publishers, Inc.

CHAPTER 4

Figure 4–1. *Source*: from Rogers and Dearing, Agency-Setting Research: Where Has It Been? Where Is It Going? in *Communication Yearbook*, Vol. 11, J.A. Anderson, ed., p. 5, © 1988 by Sage Publications, Inc. Reprinted by permission of Sage Publications, Inc.

Figure 4–2. *Source*: Reprinted with permission from R.S. Wellins, W.C. Byham, and J.M. Wilson, *Empowered Teams*, p. 23, © 1991, Jossey-Bass Inc., Publishers.

Figure 4–3. *Source*: Reprinted with permission from P. Hersey, K.H. Blanchard and D.E. Johnson, *Management of Organizational Behavior, 7th Edition*, p. 368, © 1996, Prentice-Hall, Inc.

Figure 4–4. *Source*: Reprinted from J.G. Liebler and C.R. McConnell, *Management Principles for Health Professionals, 3rd Edition*, p. 65, © 1999, Aspen Publishers, Inc.

Figure 4–5. *Source*: Reprinted with permission from B. Nanus, *Visionary Leadership*, p. 13, © 1992, Jossey-Bass Inc., Publishers.

Exhibit 4–1. *Source*: With permission, from the *Annual Review of Public Health*, Volume 18, © 1997, by Annual Reviews http://www.AnnualReviews.org.

Exhibit 4–2. *Source*: Ten Principles of Empowering People from *10 Steps to Empowerment* by Diane Tracey. Copyright © 1990 by Diane Tracey. Reprinted by permission of HarperCollins Publishers, Inc.

Exhibit 4–3. *Source*: Reprinted with permission, *Developing Effective Coalitions: An Eight Step Guide*, © 1994, Contra Costa County Health Services Department Prevention Programs.

Exhibit 4–4. *Source*: Reprinted from Public Health Practice Program Office, *Principles of Community Engagement*, 1997, Agency for Toxic Substances and Disease Registry, the Centers for Disease Control and Prevention.

Exhibit 4–2–A. *Source*: Reprinted with permission from C. Mallory, *Team Building*, pp. 17–18, © 1991, National Press Publications.

CHAPTER 5

Figure 5–1. *Source*: Reprinted with permission from Institute of Medicine, *The Future of Public Health*, p. 43, © 1988, National Academy Press.

Table 5–1. *Source*: Adapted from W.W. Vyal, *Public Health Infrastructure and Organizational Practice Definitions*, 1991, Public Health Practice Program Office, the Centers for Disease Control and Prevention.

Figure 5–4. *Source*: Reprinted from E.L. Baker, et al., Health Reform and the Health of the Public, *Journal of the American Medical Association*, Vol. 272, No. 18, pp. 1278–1282, 1994, American Medical Association.

Table 5–2. *Source*: Adapted from J. Harrell and E. Baker, *The Essential Services of Public Health*, 1997, American Public Health Association.

Exhibit 5–1. *Source*: Adapted from J. Harrell and E. Baker, *The Essential Services of Public Health*, 1997, American Public Health Association.

CHAPTER 6

Figure 6–1. *Source*: Reprinted from *Assessment Protocol for Excellence in Public Health*, 1991, the Centers for Disease Control and Prevention, National Association of City and County Health Officials.

Table 6–1. *Source*: Reprinted from *PATCH: Planned Approach to Community Health*, 1994, the Centers for Disease Control and Prevention.

Figure 6–2. *Source*: Reprinted from *PATCH: Planned Approach to Community Health*, 1994, the Centers for Disease Control and Prevention.

CHAPTER 8

Exhibit 8–1. *Source*: Reprinted from Illinois Administrative Code, Title 55, Sec. 600, 1993, State of Illinois.

Appendix 8–A. *Source*: Reprinted from *Public Health Improvement Plan: A Progress Report*, 1993, Washington State Department of Health, Olympia, WA.

CHAPTER 9

Figure 9–1. *Source*: Reprinted with permission from J.E. Hulett Jr., A Symbolic Interactionist Model of Human Communication Part 1, *AV Communication Review*, Vol. 14, No. 1, p. 14, © 1966, AECT.

Figure 9–2. *Source*: Reprinted with permission from J.E. Hulett Jr., A Symbolic Interactionist Model of Human Communication Part 1, *AV Communication Review*, Vol. 14, No. 1, p. 18, © 1966, AECT.

Exhibit 9–1. *Source*: Reprinted from J.G. Liebler and C.R. McConnell, *Management Principles for Health Professionals, 3rd Edition*, pp. 235–236, © 1999, Aspen Publishers, Inc.

Table 9–2. *Source*: L. Wallack and L. Dorfman, Media Advocacy: A Strategy for Advancing Policy and Promoting Health, *Health Education Quarterly*, Vol. 23, No. 3, pp. 293–317, copyright © 1996 by Sage Publications, Inc. Reprinted by permission of Sage Publications, Inc.

Exhibit 9–2. *Source*: Reprinted from V. Covello and F. Allen, *Seven Cardinal Rules of Rush Communication*, 1988, Office of Policy Analysis, U.S. Environmental Protection Agency.

Table 9–3. *Source*: Reprinted with permission from G.T. Fairhurst and R.A. Starr, *The Art of Framing*, p. 101, © 1996, Jossey-Bass Inc., Publishers.

Table 9–4. *Source*: *Dialogue*, L. Ellinor and G. Gerard, eds., Copyright © 1998, John Wiley & Sons. Reprinted by permission of John Wiley & Sons, Inc.

Figure 9–3. *Source*: Reprinted from L. Potts and L. Rowitz, Social Marketing/Health Communication: Leadership Opportunities for the 1990s, *Journal of Public Health Management & Practice*, Vol. 2, No. 4, p. 75, © 1996, Aspen Publishers, Inc.

Figure 9–4. *Source*: Reprinted with permission of The Free Press, a Division of Simon & Schuster, from *Social Marketing* by Philip Kotler and Eduardo L. Roberto. Copyright © 1989 by The Free Press.

Case Study 9–C. *Source*: Reprinted from *Marketing Social Change*, pp. 45–46, 1995, the Centers for Disease Control and Prevention.

CHAPTER 10

Figure 10–1. *Source*: Reprinted with permission from J.E. Rohrer, *Planning for Community-Oriented Health Systems*, © 1996, American Public Health Association.

Table 10–1. *Source*: Adapted with permission from J.M. Bryson, *Strategic Planning for Public and Nonprofit Organizations (Revised Edition)*, © 1995, Jossey-Bass Inc., Publishers.

Exhibit 10–1. *Source*: Reprinted from *Out of the Crisis* by W. Edwards Deming. Copyright 1986 by the W. Edwards Deming Institute.

Exhibit 10–2. *Source*: From *The Five Pillars of TQM* by Bill Creech, copyright © 1994 by W.L. Creech. Used by permission of Dutton, a division of Penguin Putnam Inc.

Figure 10–2. *Source*: From *The Five Pillars of TQM* by Bill Creech, copyright © 1994 by W.L. Creech. Used by permission of Dutton, a division of Penguin Putnam Inc.

Figure 10–3. *Source*: Reprinted with permission from M. Brassard, *The Memory Jogger*, © 1989, Goal and QPC.

Exhibit 10–3. *Source*: Page 58 from *The Reengineering Revolution* by Michael Hammer. Copyright © 1995 by Hammer and Company. Reprinted with permission of HarperCollins Publishers, Inc.

Exhibit 10–4. *Source*: Reprinted with permission from D.K. Carr and H.J. Johansson, *Best Practices in Reengineering*, pp. 209–210, © 1995, McGraw Hill, Inc.

Figure 10–4. *Source*: Reprinted from *The Reengineering Handbook*. Copyright © 1994 Raymond L. Manganelli, et al. Reprinted by permission of AMACOM, a division of American Management Association International, New York, NY. All rights reserved. http://www.amanet.org.

Exhibit 10–5. *Source*: Data from D. Osborne and T. Gaebler, *Reinventing Government*, © 1992, Addison-Wesley; The National Commission on the State and Local Public Service, *Hard Truths/Tough Choices*, © 1993, Nelson A. Rockefeller Institute of Government; F.J. Thompson, ed., *Revitalizing State and Local Public Service*, © 1993, Jossey-Bass Inc., Publishers; *Healthy People*, Publ. No. 79–55071, 1979, U.S. Department of Health and Human Services; and Agencies of Excellence Committee, *Blueprint for a Healthy Community*, 1994, National Association of City and County Health Officials, the Centers for Disease Control and Prevention.

Exhibit 10–6. *Source*: Reprinted from A. Gore, *The Report of the National Performance Review*, 1993, Government Printing Office.

Exhibit 10–7. *Source*: Reprinted from National Performance Review, *Putting Customers First: Standards for Servicing the American People*, 1994, Government Printing Office.

Table 10–2. *Source*: from *Banishing Bureaucracy* by David Osborne and Peter Plastrik. Copyright © 1997 by David Osborne and Peter Plastrik. Reprinted by permission of Perseus Books Publishers, a member of Perseus Books, L.L.C.

CHAPTER 11

Figure 11–1. *Source*: *Management* by Robbins/Coulter, © 1999. Reprinted by permission of Prentice-Hall, Inc., Upper Saddle River, NJ.

Exhibit 11–1. *Source*: Data from J.G. Liebler, R.E. Devine and J. Rothman, *Management Principles for Health Professionals*, 2nd Edition, © 1992, Aspen Publishers, Inc. and S.P. Robbins and M. Coulter, *Management, 6th Edition*, © 1999, Prentice-Hall, Inc.

Figure 11–2. *Source*: Reprinted with permission from W. Hendricks, *How to Manage Conflict*, p. 33, National Press Publications, 1–800–255–4436.

Exhibit 11–2. *Source*: Reprinted with permission from M.K. Shoenfield and R.M. Shoenfield, *The McGraw-Hill 36 Hour Negotiation Course*, p. 10, © 1990.

Exercise 11–2. *Source*: Adapted from E. Jurkowski and B. Neuberger, *Negotiation Skills for Community Re. Source Planning*, 1995, the Centers for Disease Control and Prevention, Illinois Public Health Leadership Institute.

CHAPTER 12

Figure 12–1. *Source*: Reprinted from Statistical Abstract of the U.S., 1997 Mid-Projection Series, Bureau of the Census.

Exhibit 12–1. *Source*: Reprinted with the permission of Alpha Books, an imprint of Macmillan USA, a division of Pearson Education, from *The Complete Idiot's Guide to Leadership*, by Andrew Dubrin. Copyright © 1998.

Figure 12–2. *Source*: Reprinted with permission of the publisher. From *Cultural Diversity in Organizations*, copyright © 1993 by T. Cox, Jr., Berrett-Koehler Publishers, Inc., San Francisco, CA. All rights reserved. 1–800–929–2929.

Exhibit 12–2. *Source*: Reprinted with permission of the publisher. From *Cultural Diversity in Organizations*, copyright © 1993 by T. Cox, Jr., Berrett-Koehler Publishers, Inc., San Francisco, CA. All rights reserved. 1–800–929–2929.

Figure 12–3. *Source*: Reprinted with permission of the publisher. From *Developing Competency To Manage Diversity*, copyright © 1997 by T. Cox, Jr. and R.L. Beale, Berrett-Koehler Publishers, Inc., San Francisco, CA. All rights reserved. 1–800–929–2929.

Figure 12–5. *Source*: Adapted with permission from *Minority Managerial Programs*, © 1997, American Association of Health Plans.

Exhibit 12–3. *Source*: Reprinted from President's Initiative on Race, *Health Care RX: Access for All*, 1998, Health Re. *Sources* and Services Administration, U.S. Department of Health and Human Services.

Exhibit 12–1–A. *Source*: Reprinted from T. Wolff and G. Kaye, eds., *From the Ground Up: A Workbook on Coalition Building and Community Development*, pp. 54–55, 69, © 1995, AHEC/Community Partners, by permission of the editors.

CHAPTER 13

Exhibit 13–1. *Source*: Reprinted with permission from J. Curruthers, The Principle and Practices of Mentoring, in *The Return of the Mentor: Strategies for Workplace Learning*, B.J. Caldwell and E.M.A. Carter, eds., p. 20, © 1993, The Falmer Press, Taylor & Francis, Inc.

Exhibit 13–2. *Source*: Reprinted with permission from F. Wickman and T. Sjodin, *Mentoring*, p. 70, © 1996, The McGraw-Hill Companies.

Exhibit 13–3. *Source*: Reprinted with permission from Criteria for the Selection of Mentors, University of Illinois School of Public Health, Illinois Public Health Leadership Institute.

Exhibit 13–4. *Source*: Reprinted with permission from F. Wickman and T. Sjodin, *Mentoring*, p. 70, © 1996, The McGraw-Hill Companies.

Figure 13–1. *Source*: from E.M. Anderson and A.L. Shannon, Toward a Conceptualization of Mentoring, *Journal of Teacher Education*, pp. 38–42, copyright © 1988 by American Association of Colleges for Teacher Education. Reprinted by permission of Sage Publications, Inc.

Exhibit 13–5. *Source*: Reprinted with permission from B.R. Sandler, Women as Mentors: Myths and Commandments, *Chronicle of Higher Education*, © 1993

Exhibit 13–6. *Source*: Reprinted from Public Health Service, *Public Health Workforce: An Agenda for the 21st Century*, p. 11–12, 1997, U.S. Department of Health and Human Services.

Exhibit 13–7. *Source*: Reprinted from Public Health Service, *Public Health Workforce: An Agenda for the 21st Century*, p. 12, 1997, U.S. Department of Health and Human Services.

Exhibit 13–8. *Source*: Reprinted from Public Health Service, *Public Health Workforce: An Agenda for the 21st Century*, p. 12, 1997, U.S. Department of Health and Human Services.

Exhibit 13–9. *Source*: Reprinted from Public Health Service, *Public Health Workforce: An Agenda for the 21st Century*, p. 13, 1997, U.S. Department of Health and Human Services.

Exhibit 13–10. *Source*: Reprinted from Public Health Service, *Public Health Workforce: An Agenda for the 21st Century*, p. 14–15, 1997, U.S. Department of Health and Human Services.

Exhibit 13–11. *Source*: Reprinted from Public Health Service, *Public Health Workforce: An Agenda for the 21st Century*, p. 16, 1997, U.S. Department of Health and Human Services.

Table 13–1. *Source*: Reprinted, with permission from The New York Academy of Medicine, from *Medicine & Public Health: The Power of Collaboration* by Roz D. Lasker and The Committee on Medicine and Public Health (Chicago: Health Administration Press, 1997).

Figure 13–2. *Source*: Adapted from S.F. Randolph, *Mentoring and the Illinois Public Health Leadership Institute*, 1993, University of Illinois School of Public Health, Illinois Public Health Leadership Institute.

Figure 13–3. *Source*: Reprinted from Public Health Practice Program Office, 1999, the Centers for Disease Control and Prevention.

CHAPTER 14

Exhibit 14–1. *Source*: Reprinted from Public Health Service, *Public Health Workforce: An Agenda for the 21st Century*, 1997, U.S. Department of Health and Human Services.

Exhibit 14–2. *Source*: Adapted from *The Art of the Long View* by Peter Schwartz. Copyright © 1991 by Peter Schwartz. Used by permission of Doubleday, a division of Random House, Inc.

Exhibit 14–4. *Source*: Reprinted with permission from J. Munson, *Case Study Development: Guidelines and Protocols with Cases*, © 1994, University of Illinois School of Public Health, Illinois Public Health Leadership Institute.

Figure 14–1. *Source*: Reprinted with permission from M.H. McCaulley, The Myers-Briggs Type Indicator and Leadership, in *Measures of Leadership*, K.E. Clark and M.B. Clark, eds., p. 389, © 1990, Leadership Library of America, Center for Creative Leadership.

Figure 14–2. *Source*: Reprinted with permission from *Improving Health in the Community: A Role for Performance Monitoring*, p. 6. Copyright 1997 by the National Academy of Sciences. Courtesy of the National Academy Press, Washington, D.C.

Figure 14–3. *Source*: Reprinted from *Improving the Nation's Health with Performance Measurement, Prevention Report*, Vol. 12, No. 1, p. 3, 1997, Office of Disease Prevention and Health Services, U.S. Department of Health and Human Services.

Appendix 14–A. *Source*: Reprinted from K.S. Wright, et al., *Competency Development in Public Health Leadership*, 2000, American Journal of Public Health, in press.

CHAPTER 15

Figure 15–1. *Source*: Reprinted from Framework for Program Evaluation in Public Health, *Morbidity and Mortality Weekly Report*, Vol. 48, 1999, the Centers for Disease Control and Prevention.

Exhibit 15–1. *Source*: Reprinted from Framework for Program Evaluation in Public Health, *Morbidity and Mortality Weekly Report*, Vol. 48, 1999, the Centers for Disease Control and Prevention.

CHAPTER 16

Exhibit 16–1. *Source*: Personal communication with P. Lenihan 1998.

Exhibit 16–3. *Source*: from "Products of the Third Wave" - from *The Third Wave* by Alvin Toffler, Copyright © 1980 by Alvin Toffler. Reprinted by permission of HarperColllins Publishers, Inc.

Figure 16–1. *Source*: Reprinted with permission from E. Murszalek-Gaucher and R.J. Coffey, *Transforming Healthcare Organizations*, p. 57, © 1990, Jossey-Bass Inc., Publishers.

Index